SEVEN DAY LOAN

THE ADMINISTRATION
OF AESTHETICS

CULTURAL ✢ POLITICS

A series from the Social Text Collective

Aimed at a broad interdisciplinary audience, these volumes seek to intervene in debates about the political direction of current theory and practice by combining contemporary analysis with a more traditional sense of historical and socioeconomic evaluation.

THE ADMINISTRATION OF AESTHETICS

Censorship, Political Criticism, and the Public Sphere

Edited by Richard Burt
(for the Social Text Collective)

Cultural Politics, Volume 7

University of Minnesota Press
Minneapolis
London

Copyright 1994 by the Regents of the University of Minnesota

Chapter 5, "*Ulysses* on Trial: Some Supplementary Reading," appeared in *Criticism* 33 (Summer 1991); used with permission of Wayne State University Press. Chapter 7, "Freud and the Scene of Censorship," is from *Writing through Repression: Literature Censorship Psychoanalysis,* Johns Hopkins University Press, 1994; used with permission of the publisher. Parts of chapter 10, "The Contrast Hurts: Censoring the Ladies Liberty in Performance," appeared in *Discourse* 9 (Spring/Summer 1987) in "Subliminal Libraries: Showing Lady Liberty and Documenting Death"; used with permission of Indiana University Press. An earlier version of chapter 12, "Reading the Rushdie Affair: 'Islam,' Cultural Politics, Form," appeared in *Social Text* 29 (1992); reprinted by permission. "Fracas at Frisbee U." appeared in the *Village Voice* October 9, 1990; reprinted by permission of the author and the *Village Voice.* "PC at Hampshire College" appeared in the *Wall Street Journal* January 4, 1991; reprinted with permission of the *Wall Street Journal.*

Published by the University of Minnesota Press
2037 University Avenue Southeast, Minneapolis, MN 55455-3092
Printed in the United States of America on acid-free paper

Library of Congress Cataloging-in-Publication Data

The Administration of aesthetics : censorship, political criticism, and the public sphere / edited by Richard Burt (for the Social Text Collective).
    p.   cm. — (Cultural politics ; v. 7)
    Includes bibliographical references and index.
    ISBN 0-8166-2365-1 (hard : alk. paper)
    ISBN 0-8166-2367-8 (pbk. : alk. paper)
    1. Censorship.   2. Criticism—Political aspects.   I. Burt, Richard, 1954-   .   II. Social Text Collective.   III. Series: Cultural politics (Minneapolis, Minn.) ; v. 7.
    Z657.A245   1994
    323.44—dc20   94-3881

The University of Minnesota is an
equal-opportunity educator and employer.

*For Christine Kravits
in extreme appreciation of her
advanced aesthetic*

Contents

Part III.
The New Censorship and Postmodernity

Acknowledgments

This collection emerged out of two special sessions I put together for the Modern Language Association in 1990 and 1991 and discussions with Andrew Ross and George Yúdice (who proposed that it be published through the *Social Text* Collective). I am deeply indebted to John Michael Archer for having solicited several essays in this volume and for his generous, hard work in helping to put it together. David Norbrook, Amy Kaplan, and Jeffrey Wallen provided valuable suggestions about organization. My thanks as well to the copy editor, Lynn Marasco. I would especially like to express my gratitude to Christine Kravits (aka TinaK) for her support and help with this project. I owe her more than words can say.

Introduction: The "New" Censorship
Richard Burt

Many intellectuals have been disturbed by what some have termed the "new" censorship of aesthetics in the 1980s and early 1990s, a phenomenon that has been widely interpreted as the fulfillment of the radically conservative Reagan/Bush agenda.[1] Cultural critics have viewed the intense, prolonged assault on high and low modes of aesthetic production, circulation, and consumption beginning in the 1980s in the context of the prosecution elsewhere of a right-wing agenda. Attacks on publicly funded exhibitions of artists like Robert Mapplethorpe and Andres Serrano, on MTV videos, on rap music by 2-Live Crew and Ice-T, and on television advertisements as well as the FBI's seizure of works and equipment of photographers like Jock Sturges on the grounds that they are child pornographers— these events in the cultural realm are set against the fallout from political events: the 1989 Supreme Court ruling that flag burning is protected by the First Amendment; the Gulf War; and the regulation of sexuality, particularly the erosion of female reproductive rights and the refusal to legalize gay and lesbian rights.[2] Along similar lines, cultural critics have regarded the privatization of public space and public institutions under Presidents Reagan and Bush as a form of censorship: critics fear, for example, that the recent legal narrowing of what counts as "fair use" of words and images by the public has made commodification into an instrument of censorship. Broad social criticism through the "appropriation" or parody of images is prevented by the impossibility of reproducing privately owned appropriated or parodied images; corporate sponsors of public museums sponsor only "safe" art, effectively censoring controversial or confrontational art that might hurt sales of the sponsor's products; bookstore chains are concentrated in the hands of a few large corporations, which can censor small publishers by refusing to order their books, even when they sell.[3]

With a Democratic administration now in power in the United States, some critics might breathe a sigh of relief, believing that the culture wars have been lost by the right and that we have now returned to a more enlightened, liberal administration of aesthetics. The contributors to this volume would not want to discount any gains made by a new president, and their essays do not dissent from left analyses of the new censorship (given the prominence of the debate over funding for the National Endowment for the Arts [NEA] and the Public Broadcasting Service [PBS] and the attack on the "cultural elite" in the 1992 presidential campaign, it is hard to see how one *could* dissent).[4] They suggest, however, that it would be mistaken to think that the problem of censorship has disappeared (or that it could).[5] For a salient consequence of the new-censorship debates is that the meaning of censorship has itself been interrogated and contested: while some critics have tried to keep in place a narrow modern definition (censorship as state power) in order to avoid confusing it with other, perhaps less brutal kinds of constraints (say, market censorship), others have argued that in the postmodern present, censorship has been displaced by less visible kinds of domination and control and that the word should be either redefined more broadly or abandoned.[6] Indeed, from one perspective, Bill Clinton's self-advertised competence as a "consensus builder" paradoxically marks him as a participant in the chief mode of censorship in the United States, namely, the manufacture of consent.[7]

The essays included in this book are united in their desire to call attention to some crucial difficulties with using censorship, old or new, as a tool of cultural criticism. Opposing censorship is generally assumed to be a straightforward matter. In responding to the radical right, recent art, criticism, theater, and museum exhibitions have tended to assume that censorship clearly divides right and left: the right is for it, the left is against it; the right acts as an agent of censorship, the left is its victim; the right is for "safe" or ornamental art without sexual content, the left accepts confrontational public art with graphic sexual images; the right is for artistic decency, the left is for artistic diversity.[8]

Yet in practice, opposing recent instances of censorship has proven to be more complicated and more contradictory than many cultural critics, artists, art gallery owners, book publishers, and civil liberties lawyers assume. Critics of the new censorship tend to assume that censorship operates ahistorically: all censors and all artists are basically the same.[9] (The new censorship is new only in the limited sense that it marks the return of an old practice once thought to have been vanquished by more enlightened, tolerant, intelligent, progressive members of modern society.) Even when they are reading censorship cases within a historical narrative, cultural critics rely on ahistorical oppositions between unchanging agents and forces: criticism and censorship fight out a battle for social change over public space, setting public art against privatization, corporate sponsorship, and commodification. By defining opposing political camps in the moralistic terms of those who are for censorship and those who are against it, critics unify both camps and make them monolithic: the censors are demonic philistines, the censored ipso facto are clever, noble, and good.

Yet many recent events do not resolve themselves easily into neat conceptual oppositions and identities. What counts as censorship is not always clear. Indeed, it is hard to see how one could call many contemporary cases censorship without either seriously distorting the traditional understanding of the term or redefining it to include so many practices—ranging from institutional regulation of free expression, market censorship, cutbacks in government funding for controversial art, boycotts, lawsuits, and marginalization and exclusion of artists based on their gender or race to "political correctness" in the university and the media—that the term is overwhelmed, even trivialized, its usefulness as a tool of cultural criticism called into question. If one argues, for example, that an opponent or reformer of the NEA who claims he or she is not trying to censor in fact really does want to censor and is dissembling or disavowing his or her true intentions, one implicitly discounts the rather significant difference between going to the gulag for saying something subversive and not getting an NEA grant because one's work is said to lack artistic merit.[10] Moreover, not all cases of the new censorship are easily aligned: Jeff Koons's recent Heaven exhibition, with his kitschy sculptures and "pornographic" paintings of himself and his then wife Ilona Staller, porn star and Italian parliamentarian, differs from exhibitions of photographs by Robert Mapplethorpe or Andres Serrano, which in turn differ from the performances of the self-proclaimed "post post-porn modernist" Annie Sprinkle.[11] To be sure, one could try to discriminate between cases of real censorship and censorship that is merely staged, as when a Madonna video is censored by MTV and consequently sells extremely well (access denied in one place multiplies access elsewhere). Similarly, one could discriminate between victims of censorship in terms of their centrality or marginality (and hence inclusion or exclusion) in relation to centers of cultural and political power. One might argue, for example, that Madonna benefited from being censored whereas NEA artists have not, the latter being further from the center of the culture industry.[12] Yet how would one account for NEA artists who profit from the controversy over their works, as have Andres Serrano and Jock Sturges, whose prices have risen astronomically in the wake of the attention they received? How different are they from Madonna? And given that the call for censorship is always publicly dramatized, can one so easily differentiate real from staged censorship? Similarly, if one wants to argue that censorship must be redefined to mean marginalization, what kind of regulation or exclusion might not count as censorship?[13] Is exclusion the same thing as stopping production or blocking access? How would censorship differ from ideological subjection?

Opposing censorship, whether it is broadly or narrowly defined, is similarly problematic. Is it possible for avowedly political critics to oppose censorship without contradicting their arguments and aesthetic or critical practices? While many artists and critics have argued that art, knowledge, and sexuality are political, often criticizing modern liberal institutions and values as modes of domination, and while many have attacked specifically modernist assumptions about aesthetics and subjectivity such as self-expression, genius, originality, and individual creativity, they invoke precisely these assumptions when they defend freedom of artistic expression from censorship or attempt to legitimate "moral rights" for artists.[14] Similarly, in defending controversial artists who have been awarded or refused NEA grants, artists and critics maintain that the work funded is art, not pornography or child pornography: they oppose artistic merit to mere politics and patronage.[15] And while artists defend the critical practice of appropriation of words and images in the name of fair use, they appeal to copyright law and literary property to prosecute right-wing appropriations of erotic or avowedly political art as mutilations and distortions.[16]

Perhaps even more crucially, opposing censorship *tout court* is difficult because of the complexity of the present political landscape. Any clear division between a progressive anticensorship politics and a procensorship neoconservative or reactionary politics is muddied by the fact that those on the left and the right occupy the same discursive terrain: both sides adopt the same rhetoric; both sides say they are against censorship and for diversity; each side accuses the other of trying to exercise censorship. It is difficult to sort out true claims and charges from false, since who "really" has at heart the values on which a progressive politics is generally assumed to depend (diversity, healthy debate, and so on) and who can best defend them will always be contested.

The essays in *The Administration of Aesthetics* intervene in discussions of censorship new and old by shifting the focus of critical inquiry from the present discourse of diversity in which they have been framed (a discourse in which diversity counters repressive controls of discourse) to what I would call a discourse of legitimation (in which the diversity of a given discursive field will always be limited by the delegitimation, either conscious or unconscious, of particular discourses). In making this shift, this volume aims to open up the possibility of substantive political realignments among those who are disenchanted with both the stereotypical right-wing criticisms of political critics and aesthetics and the stereotypical left-wing defenses of political criticism and aesthetics. The point is not simply that the word *censorship* is often misused in current discussions; more crucially, it is that censorship never operated in the modern terms in which it is generally thought to have operated—as negative, repressive exercises of power such as destroying materials, blocking access to them, limiting their distribution and circulation, and assigning penalties for collecting and consuming forbidden materials. By adopting the word *administration* to embrace the essays, I want to call attention to the way they disturb the assumptions—widely shared by the cultural left and the cultural right—that there are stable oppositions between criticism and censorship, between centralized, dominant groups and marginalized, subordinate groups. By *administration* I mean the locus of different, dispersed kinds of regulation.[17] Focusing on a range of historical eras from early modern to postmodern and covering cases of print and visual media in Europe and the United States, the essays in this volume make problematic the traditional understanding of the terms *censorship, criticism,* and *public sphere* and the conceptual and historiographical identities and oppositions on which a traditional understanding of these terms depends. This volume prompts one to wonder whether regulating aesthetic production (state censorship) and regulating aesthetic consumption (criticism) can be opposed, how radically prepublication censorship differs from postpublication censure.[18]

In this introduction, I wish to articulate how the essays in this volume intervene in current discussions of censorship, making explicit the contributors' broadly shared assumptions about the practices of censorship and criticism and the institution of the public sphere, and to clarify new points of view and possibilities for contemporary cultural criticism. I will begin by elaborating the shared assumptions about censorship, criticism, and public sphere in turn. In varied but complementary ways, the essays extend and complicate the idea that censorship involves a negative exercise of power. First, censorship operates negatively in more than one way, not unidirectionally along a binary axis of the repressed and the free but, more crucially, by delimiting what can be legitimately debated. As Pierre Bourdieu argues, discourse is divided not only between the realms of orthodoxy and heterodoxy, but also between the realms of the disputed (which includes both orthodox and heterodox discourses) and the undisputed.[19] Heterodox discourses are opposed not only to orthodox discourses, but to doxa (what is taken for granted and hence beyond dispute) as well.

Thus, for Bourdieu, there are two distinct kinds of censorship, a manifest censorship and a deeper, "secondary" or structural censorship that it masks:

> The manifest censorship imposed by orthodox discourse, the official way of speaking and thinking about the world, conceals another, more radical censorship: the overt opposition between "right" opinion and "left" or "wrong" opinion, which delimits the universe of possible discourse, be it legitimate or illegitimate, euphemistic or blasphemous,

masks in its turn the fundamental opposition between the universe of things that can be stated, and hence thought, and the universe of that which is taken for granted.[20]

What Bourdieu terms a "secondary censorship" complicates a standard view of censorship as that which marks the opposition between heterodox and orthodox discourses, since this secondary or structural censorship cannot be dispensed with:

> Censorship [as] the structure of the field itself ... governs expression, and not [only] some legal proceeding which has been specially adapted to designate and repress the transgression of a linguistic code. This structural censorship is exercised through the medium of the sanctions of the field ..., imposed on all producers of symbolic goods, including the authorized spokesperson ... and it condemns the occupants of dominated positions either to silence or to shocking outspokenness.[21]

Censorship may be seen, then, not only in terms of repressed and free discourses but also in terms of the receivable and the unreceivable—what cannot be heard or spoken without risk of being delegitimated as beyond the pale of discourse, doxa.

Regarding censorship in this manner introduces a further complication of the traditional negative view of censorship, for there is a dynamic dialectic in the struggle between heterodoxy and orthodoxy: heterodox discourses are simply discourses that would circulate freely were it not for censorship of the traditional sort. In Bourdieu's terms, the important political struggle will necessarily be over what can circulate within the realm of the debatable, not over a particular debate:

> The subordinate classes have an interest in pushing back the limits of *doxa* and exposing the arbitrariness of the taken for granted; the dominant classes have an interest in defending the integrity of *doxa* or, short of this, of establishing in its place the necessarily imperfect substitute, *orthodoxy.*[22]

Heterodoxy works both to expand the realm of the debatable and to shrink the orthodoxy, delegitimate it as completely as possible; heterodoxy will engage in delegitimating tactics in the process of legitimating itself.

Furthermore, the essays in this volume view censorship as a positive exercise of power, not just an institutional practice that delegitimates discourses by blocking access to them. Censorship not only legitimates discourses by allowing them to circulate, but is itself part of a performance, a simulation in which censorship can function as a trope to be put on show. Even burning books is not the simple, negative exercise of power it at first appears to be: public book burnings are less about blocking access to forbidden books than they are about staging an opposition between corrupting and puri- fying forces and agencies (represented synecdochically by the books and by their destruction).

As one of the contributors, Jiřina Šmejkalová-Strickland, puts it, getting rid of the censor does not get rid of the problem of censor- ship.[23] An end to censorship across the board is never an option. Cen- sorship regulates who is in and who is out of the critical conversa- tion. Opposition to censorship serves not to guarantee a diversity free of censorship, but to regulate membership in the critical com- munity by appealing to the notion of diversity as a criterion of inclusion and exclusion. Calling someone a censor is a means of excluding that person from dialogue. Thus, diversity (or free speech) cannot rightly be completely opposed to censorship, since diversity will always be regulated (exclusions are necessarily built in). Whatever or whoever threatens this diversity will be dele- gitimated (Jesse Helms et al.). To be sure, delegitimation does not amount to censorship as it is traditionally understood, since it in- volves distortions and displacements rather than outright destruc- tion. But it is not wholly distinct, either. As a negative exercise of power, delegitimation cannot be radically differentiated from more direct means of control such as stopping production of forbidden materials or blocking access to them.

In complicating the modern understanding of censorship as a repressive, self-identical practice, this collection of essays has neces- sarily also complicated a central assumption about criticism, namely, that it is opposed to censorship, providing an antidote to the evils of censorship by allowing for rational debate about diverse points of view. Viewed historically, the institution of criticism is usually regarded as part of what Jürgen Habermas has termed the modern public sphere, a discursive sphere he says emerged in the eighteenth century after the demise of state censorship.[24] Underlying this histo- riography is a series of interlocking conceptual and historiographical oppositions between criticism (or art) and censorship; state censor-

ship externally imposed and self-censorship; public access and privatization (corporate commodification versus fair use); a repressive
early modern state censorship and an enlightened modern public
sphere (which emerged with the institution of fine arts and literary
criticism).[25] The essays here suggest, however, that criticism is not
radically opposed to censorship; rather, these practices are on a continuum. Critical dialogue is often regarded as the solution to conflicts. But who would be allowed into it? On what basis? How would
a dialogue be regulated? How do you tell authentic or critical dialogue from its co-opted, simulated, or dissembled forms?

Along similar lines, this collection questions Habermas's notion
that the public sphere is a space of discursive circulation opposed to
censorship, thereby allowing ideally for undistorted communication. The public sphere constitutes a censored and censoring space,
the contributors maintain, not a critical space opposed to state censorship. The present proliferation of boycotts from the left and the
right within the public sphere does not mark a decline in a postmodern phase (with would-be censors emerging in relation to a
fragmenting identity politics), but extends earlier ways in which the
public sphere regulated, excluded, and censored discourses. Moreover, in the public sphere, communication cannot be reduced to a
direct line between the producing subject and the produced object
at one end, and the consuming subject and the consumed object at
the other. The produced object, for example, is transfigured by its
circulation and consumption in the public sphere: literacy limitations and modes of reproduction and consumption (mass versus
individual) mean that the produced object will be altered (some
might say distorted) in transmission and reception. This transfiguration of the object complicates recent attempts to control reception,
attempts that grant artists the right not to have their work mutilated
or distorted after they sell it.[26] Whether transfiguration itself is a
form of artistic appropriation or whether the reporting of the
debate on political correctness by the press is accurate or distorted
will necessarily be determined by the negotiations and regulations
of particular interpretive (legal and art world) communities.

It remains now to clarify the force of this volume as an intervention in contemporary cultural criticism that recasts discussions of
both the new and old censorship by locating them in a discourse of
legitimation rather than a discourse of diversity. Some readers might

question the wisdom of shifting the terms of critical discussion and disturbing otherwise stable binary oppositions between censorship and criticism, between the public sphere and its corporate privatization. What kind of an intervention is this? If it avoids the kinds of stereotypical criticisms and defenses of political criticism, exactly what kinds of alignments can it free up? What precisely are the gains? And what about the risks? Isn't one gutting a critique of censorship if one gives up a stable definition of it (and, consequently, of stable definitions of opposing terms such as *freedom, liberty, memory,* and so on)? Isn't it better to keep the old terms and oppositions, even if there are serious problems with using them, out of political necessity? Shouldn't the opposition between censorship and criticism be shored up rather than dismantled, so that political opposition can thereby be strengthened?

The essays in this volume interrogate the meanings of the terms *censorship* and *political criticism* to allow for a more ambivalent relation to both the left and the right, not to arrive at a more truly progressive position. By resisting the temptation to side unequivocally with either a liberal, modern tradition or a postmodern, antihumanist critique of that tradition, the authors aim to avoid the predictable, moralistic simplifications that arise from the sense that conceptual and political oppositions and identities are secure. In my view, succumbing to the pressure to strengthen the oppositions and identities that apparently enable a supposedly progressive critical practice would only return us to the problems we have seen arise in abstract debates pitting those who favor censorship against those who oppose it. The desire to maintain critical "opposition" to censorship arises largely from a misrecognition of the politics that fulfilling such a desire would most directly serve. The opposition between right-wing censors and left-wing critics merely differentiates a critic who is legitimate from one who is not; it determines what does and does not count as legitimate criticism.[27]

Given the stake so many critics now have in identity politics and multiculturalism as remedies to censorship, it is worth amplifying this point.[28] In attempting to give subordinate groups greater freedom, identity politics has regularly reproduced the problem of censorship. The activist group Queer Nation led attempts to stop the filming and, when that failed, the exhibition of the movie *Basic Instinct,* attempts that some called censorship and others called a protest. Similarly, the Simon Wiesenthal Center's call for a boycott of Ice Cube's *Death Certificate* on grounds that it was anti- Semitic and anti-Korean met with criticism that the boycott was a form of cen- sorship. Two controversial cases about Nazi propaganda and revi- sionist histories of the Holocaust raised similar questions. Robert Faurisson, a historian who claims that the Holocaust never occurred, was convicted in France in 1991 of disputing crimes "beyond dis- pute." Is it censorship to convict Faurisson of disputing crimes be- cause they cannot now be legally disputed? When Brandeis Univer- sity bought the rights to *Der ewige Jude* (The eternal Jew), a Nazi propaganda film made in 1942, to prevent it from circulating on video, it generated a similar censorship controversy.[29]

And consider an even more telling case involving identity politics, the administration (in the usual sense) of cultural diversity in higher education, a topic that has been largely unmentioned in the debate about "political correctness." Administrative practices constitute the most obviously political way of remedying perceived forms of insti- tutionalized injustices such as racism, sexism, and homophobia. Yet the administration of diversity can be disturbingly contradictory. The present demands for "diversity" assume that those who repre- sent it have stable identities. Those hired in a particular field are ex- pected to stay in that field. The administration of an abstract "diver- sity" may thus ultimately suppress many kinds of local diversities.[30]

By situating analysis of censorship, criticism, and the public sphere within a discourse of legitimation, I hope to achieve two ends: first, to legitimate a historicist mode of critical and ideological analysis centered on institutions; and second, to delegitimate certain ways of discussing issues that are misleading and that involve simplified crit- ical and administrative solutions to perceived forms of repression, carried out in the name of a so-called progressive politics. Broadly speaking, the essays in this collection more or less explicitly rethink the terms in which modern and postmodern forms of power are presently distinguished. Distinctions between modernity and post- modernity have rested in large part on distinctions between modes of domination; censorship as it has traditionally been understood has been a key way of differentiating both between early modern and modern modes of domination and between modern and post- modern forms of domination (the latter being externally imposed and the former internally assimilated through commodification rather than through political power).[31] In calling into question the modern conceptual definitions of censorship and its opposing terms, this collection calls into question the definition of *modernity* and its opposing terms, *early modern* and *postmodern*, as well.[32]

The essays are arranged along historiographical lines in three groups—early modern, modern, and postmodern—in order to examine uncritically held, sometimes ahistorical assumptions about modern forms of censorship by juxtaposing modern with early modern and postmodern forms of censorship. This collection interrogates, then, the notion that there were revolutionary breaks (say, in the English Revolution or in the Velvet Revolution of Czechoslovakia) marking where the past ended and where the present started, that we can oppose "us" who stand against censorship to "them" who stand for it.

The first group of essays, "Criticism, Censorship, and the Early Modern Public Sphere," contests the notion that the early modern and the modern can be contrasted in terms of an opposition between censorship and an uncensored public sphere.[33] In "*Areopagitica*, Censorship, and the Early Modern Public Sphere," David Norbrook shows that Habermas's public sphere is an early modern rather than a modern formation. Similarly, in "Power and Literature: The Terms of the Exchange 1624-42," Christian Jouhaud draws on Bourdieu to show that the aesthetic and the public sphere emerged earlier. Norbrook and Jouhaud offer not just a redating of the public sphere, but also a dialectical reconsideration of the complex relation between censorship and criticism. Donald Hedrick further counters an ahistorical view of censorship, moving from Shakespeare's flower imagery to Bowdler's expurgations of it in his *Family Shakespeare* edition to Mapplethorpe's uncensorable photographs of flowers. In "Jean-Jacques Rousseau: Policing the Aesthetic from the Left," Dennis Porter calls attention to the historical amnesia about left censorship within the French Revolution. Challenging the traditional narrative of modernity in which the Enlightenment prepared the ground for a revolution that put an end to censorship, Porter locates continuities between the political culture of the Enlightenment and the political cultures of totalitarian states of this century, in which complete visibility was a political ideal.

Part II, "Censorship and Modernity," addresses questions about modernity and subjectivity in relation to literary and artistic modernism. Though literary modernism was until recently celebrated for landmarks of decensorship (*Ulysses, Lolita, Lady Chatterley's Lover*), modernism is now in disrepute, its liberating value marred for many cultural critics by sexism and affiliations with fascism and imperialism. The essays in this section call into question both of these views. Brook Thomas in "*Ulysses* on Trial: Some Supplementary Reading" and Stuart Culver in "Whistler v. Ruskin: The Courts, the Public, and Modern Art" suggest that it is not at all clear that one could ever move beyond the strategies and critical oppositions used to legitimate modernist texts or modern art. Michael Levine's "Freud and the Scene of Censorship" is a critique of the way a modern humanist-centered subject who resists censorship or a posthumanist one who internalizes it dominates present discussions of censorship.

Part III, "The New Censorship and Postmodernity," addresses questions of censorship in the postmodern present, focusing on access, circulation, reproduction, and reception. Jiřina Šmejkalová-Strickland, Timothy Murray, and I attend to censorship as a performance. In "Censoring Canons: Transitions and Prospects of Literary Institutions in Czechoslovakia," Šmejkalová draws on Judith Butler's notion of performance to contrast censorship and canon formation in Czechoslovakia before and after the revolution of 1989. Šmejkalová's local analyses show that the contrast is hardly as simple as is generally assumed. In " 'Degenerate "Art"': Public Aesthetics and the Simulation of Censorship in Postliberal Los Angeles and Berlin," I question present equations of modernism and fascism by examining a recent international exhibition that simulated a Nazi exhibition entitled Degenerate "Art" that attacked modern art; in attempting to criticize the Nazi exhibition, the Los Angeles County Museum of Art inadvertently reproduced many of the Nazis' censorious techniques. Timothy Murray examines the celebration of one of censorship's opposite numbers, namely, liberty. In "The Contrast Hurts: Censoring the Ladies Liberty in Performance," he juxtaposes the NEA's denial of funding to four avant-garde performance artists and the 1986 celebration of the Statue of Liberty. Murray notes the ironies attendant on the regulation of this "command performance": while no one was excluded, no one was excepted from watching it, either.

Rob Wilson and Aamir Mufti look at censorship and criticism in terms of global circulation and reception. In "Cyborg America: Policing the Social Sublime in *Robocop* and *Robocop 2*," Wilson inverts the usual focus of censorship as repression, examining instead why a particular kind of repression or policing has proven to be so well accepted in recent movies produced in the United States. In "Reading the Rushdie Affair: 'Islam,' Cultural Politics, Form," Mufti too focuses on reception, considering the ways in which Rushdie's *Satanic Verses* was transfigured in an Islamic public sphere, a sphere defined by the relatively low literacy of Islamic audiences and the modes of circulation (press reports, film, and so on) and consumption (mass audiences as opposed to the individual reception a novel traditionally assumes). The Islamic public sphere in this sense is a modern space of contestation.

The volume concludes with an essay that addresses censorship in the context of recent debates over academic freedom. In "Political Correctness: The Revenge of the Liberals," Jeffrey Wallen argues that the academic community supports its claim to be an arena of free and open debate only by denying freedom and openness to some through an assault on the principles of liberalism. The media attention to political correctness, too easily characterized as a right-wing backlash, also marks the revenge of the liberals.

In addressing censorship in such a topical manner, Wallen's essay implicitly raises questions about the volume, which, broadly speaking, makes sense of the topical by placing it in a historical context. Whereas the right sees political correctness as part of a larger problem of cultural elitism, the left sees it as an instance of the conservatives' need for a new official enemy after the end of the cold war. Right-wing attacks on NEA funding of minority, gay, and lesbian artists are no coincidence. However much more sympathetic one may be to the left's view, it is worth pointing out that both the left and the right make sense of political correctness by retrospectively reading it synecdochically as part of a larger cultural trend. In assuming a divide between the topical and the historical, both sides construct a false temporality of conflicts: a local, ephemeral conflict is thought to be succeeded by a larger, more enduring one; that is, the local conflict becomes insignificant, merely topical, the moment it is absorbed and displaced into a broader conflict.

In calling into question the term *censorship*, this volume intends to advance our understanding of the local and global persistence of censorship as something more than its endless topicality. In keeping topical and historical perspectives on censorship in play, the essays

open up a more complex relation between local and historical conflicts and make possible the writing of a less sequential narrative by
constructing a dynamic rather than a divide between the topical and
the historical. We may read the topical as a local readjustment to, the
repercussions of, a still-happening event: the topical and the historical are always both in play at any given moment; they are not
sequential. The *Nachträglichkeit* (deferred action) relation between
topicality and historicality may be likened to an earthquake: it is
often difficult to tell whether a given tremor anticipates the "big
one" or is an aftershock. The present breakdown of consensus over
the meaning of censorship is not limited to the fact that left and
right have now apparently changed places, that the left is now for
speech codes and political correctness while the right defends free
speech. Rather, the breakdown makes manifest that the libertarian
or absolutist position on free speech has always been a mirage:
standing against censorship, whether it is practiced by the left or by
the right, depends on a list of censors so heterogeneous that the
term *censorship* becomes meaningless.[34] Instead of attempting to
shore up a position that was never really defensible in the first
place, the essays in this volume take the politics of the breakdown
as their focus, opening up new questions about the relations
between conflict and consensus, between censorship and criticism,
in the administration of aesthetics.[35]

NOTES

Parts of this introduction were presented to the Modern Language Association in special
sessions that I also chaired: "Historicizing the New Censorship" (1990) and "Policing the
Aesthetic: Political Criticism and the Public Sphere" (1991). I would like to thank John
Michael Archer, Janet Benton, Amy Kaplan, Christine Kravits, Jeff Wallen, and George
Yúdice for their valuable comments on an earlier draft of this introduction.

1. The phrase "the new censorship" first appeared on the cover of *Art in America* in
November 1989. For analyses of censorship of the fine arts as a radical right phenomenon,
see Carole S. Vance, "The War on Culture," *Art in America* 77, no. 9 (September 1989):
39-45; Carole S. Vance, "Reagan's Revenge: Restructuring the NEA," *Art in America* 78, no.
11 (November 1990): 49-55; Mary Ann Staniszewski, "Photo Opportunities," *Art and Auction* 11, no. 11 (November 1989): 20-22; and Andrew Ross, "The Fine Art of Regulation," in
The Phantom Public Sphere, ed. Bruce Robbins (Minneapolis: University of Minnesota
Press, 1993), 257-68. A number of journals and magazines have recently devoted special
issues to censorship. See in particular the special issue on censorship *PMLA* 108, no. 1 (January 1994); "The Body in Question," *Aperture* 121 (Fall 1990); Censorship I, ed. Barbara
Hoffman and Robert Storr, *Art Journal* 50, no. 3 (Fall 1991); Censorship II, ed. Barbara

Hoffman and Robert Storr, *Art Journal* 50, no. 4 (Winter 1991); "Banned," *New Statesman and Society,* April 19, 1991; "Kultura Kontrol," *Lusitaniana* 1, no. 3 (Fall 1990); and "Censoring the Media," *Felix* 1, no. 1 (Spring 1991). For a specific account of sexuality and censorship, see Ian Hunter et al., eds., *On Pornography: Literature, Sexuality, and Obscenity Law* (New York: St. Martin's, 1992). For a broad historical overview, see Paul Hyland and Neil Sammels, eds., *Writing and Censorship in Britain* (London: Routledge, 1992), and Judith Huggins Balfe, ed., *Paying the Piper: Causes and Consequences of Art Patronage* (Urbana and Chicago: University of Illinois Press, 1993). For many of the documents central to the "culture wars," see Richard Bolton, ed., *Culture Wars: Documents from the Recent Controversies in the Arts* (New York: New Press, 1992), and Paul Berman, ed., *Debating P.C.: The Controversy Over Political Correctness on College Campuses* (New York: Bantam, 1992). For narratives of many recent cases, see Stephen C. Dubin, *Arresting Images: Impolitic Art and Uncivil Actions* (New York: Routledge, 1992), and Edward de Grazia, *Girls Lean Back Everywhere: The Law of Obscenity and the Assault on Genius* (New York: Random House, 1992).

2. In addition to Bolton, *Culture Wars,* and Dubin, *Arresting Images,* see John R. MacArthur, *Second Front: Censorship and Propaganda in the Gulf War* (New York: Hill and Wang, 1992); Lisa Jones, "The Signifying Monkees: 2-Live Crew's Nasty-Boy Rap on Trial in South Florida," *Village Voice* 35, no. 45 (November 6, 1990): 43–47; and Carole S. Vance, "Photography, Pornography, and Sexual Politics," *Aperture* 121 (Fall 1990): 52–65.

3. See Martha Buskirk, "Commodification as Censor: Copyrights and Fair Use," *October* 60 (Spring 1992): 82–103, and Herbert Schiller, *Culture Inc.: The Corporate Takeover of Public Expression* (Oxford: Oxford University Press, 1989).

4. The 1992 presidential campaigns intensified the issue of arts censorship. *Tongues Untied* (aired on the "P.O.V." public television series) was dropped by a number of affiliates and a documentary critical of Cardinal John O'Connor entitled *Stop the Church* was dropped entirely. Footage from *Tongues Untied* was used in a Pat Buchanan campaign advertisement and ended up forcing then NEA chair John Frohnmayer to resign. In June 1992, Vice President Dan Quayle attacked the "cultural elite"; see Andrew Rosenthal, "Quayle Attacks a 'Cultural Elite' in Speech Invoking Moral Values," *New York Times,* June 10, 1992, A1. At the Republican convention, Pat Buchanan ended his speech by calling on Americans to "take back your culture, take back your country." Later in 1992, an NEA peer panel's recommendation that an exhibition entitled Corporal Politics receive funding was overruled by acting chair Anne-Imelda Radice; on this case, see Barbara Janowitz and Ed DuRante, "NEA Vetoes Unleash Protests, Walkouts," *American Theater* 9, no. 4 (July/August 1992): 47–49. PBS also came under fire in Congress for having a "liberal" bias; see "PBS Tilts Toward Conservatives, Not the Left," *Extra!* 5, no. 6 (June 4, 1992): 15. And in *Rust v. Sullivan* (argued before the Supreme Court in 1992) the Bush administration used the gag ruling on abortion as a justification for content regulation of the arts.

5. This mistake is made by Elizabeth Hess in "Indecent Exposure," *Village Voice* 38, no. 2 (January 12, 1993): 83–84. For other optimistic assessments of Bill Clinton, see Robert Cimbalest, "Clinton and the Arts: He Never Stops Learning," *Art News* 92, no. 1 (January 1993): 122–25, and Maurice Bergman in cooperation with Ronald Felman, "The Future of the NEA," *Art Forum* 31, no. 5 (January 1993): 72–73. On Clinton's stated position, see Jack Rosenberger, "Clinton's Culture Plank," *Art in America* 80, no. 7 (July 1992): 27.

6. For a traditional definition of censorship, see Annabel Patterson, "Censorship," in *The Encyclopedia of Literature and Criticism,* ed. Matthew Coyle et al. (London: Routledge, 1990), 901–14. For arguments in favor of a narrow definition of censorship, see John Leo,

"The Words of the Culture War," *U.S. News and World Report*, October 28, 1991, 31, and Kathleen M. Sullivan, "The First Amendment Wars," *New Republic*, September 28, 1992, 39. For arguments in favor of a broad definition, see Sue Curry Jansen, *Censorship: The Knot That Binds Power and Knowledge* (Oxford: Oxford University Press, 1988); Robert Atkins, "A Censorship Time Line," *Art Journal* 50, no. 3 (Fall 1991): 33; Allan Parichini, "Speakeasy," *New Art Examiner* 20, no. 4 (December 1992): 10-11; and Carol Jacobsen, "Redefining Censorship: A Feminist View," *Art Journal* 50, no. 4 (Winter 1991): 44-53. Andrew Ross maintains that the term *censorship* should be abandoned in discussions of contemporary contests over culture. See his essay "The Fine Art of Regulation," 257.

7. Edward S. Herman and Noam Chomsky, *Manufacturing Consent: The Political Economy of the Mass Media* (New York: Pantheon, 1989). A more skeptical critic might argue that Clinton is not much of a friend of political artists. To show that he was not an agent of special interests and "bean counters," Clinton made a controversial criticism of rapper Sister Souljah during the 1992 campaign. See Gwen Ifill, "Clinton, in Need of a Lift, Plays Racial Card," *New York Times*, June 16, 1992, A12, A9, and Gwen Ifill, "Clinton Won't Back Down in Tiff with Jackson over a Rap Singer," *New York Times*, June 20, 1992, A1, A9. The right will continue to make the arts an issue; see, for example, Roger Kimball's negative review of the 1992 meeting of the Modern Language Association, "Heterotextuality and Other Literary Matters," *Wall Street Journal*, December 31, 1992, A12. Moreover, the Justice Department is seeking to uphold *Rust v. Sullivan*. I am inclined to take this more skeptical position. I want to make it clear, however, that my skepticism is rooted in my sense that what counts as censorship will always be contested, not in a belief that an authentic Democratic liberalism (or cultural diversity) would be an antidote to censorship.

8. For examples of this kind of opposition, see chapter 9 in this volume.

9. Cultural critics tend to distinguish principled opponents of censorship (who resign from the NEA or who refuse an NEA grant in protest of the NEA's refusal to fund particular artists) from complicit collaborators, demanding consistency from "waffling" bureaucrats like former NEA chair John Frohnmayer and museum curators like Christina Orr-Cahal (who refused to show Mapplethorpe at the Corcoran in 1989) and Elisabeth Broun (who attempted to block Sol le Witt's contribution to the Smithsonian exhibition on Eadweard Muybridge). (See Michael Kimmelman, "Peeping into Peepholes and Finding Politics," *New York Times*, July 21, 1991, E1, E29.) Yet one might ask whether refusing an NEA grant is the right thing to do. Might it not be better to sign a pledge, take the money, and then do whatever one wants with it?

10. Similarly, critics, artists, and museum and gallery exhibitions have drawn exaggerated, distorted parallels between Hitler's "kultur kampf" and present-day right-wing opponents of the arts. See Patrick Buchanan, "In the New Kultur Kampf, the First Battles Are Being Fought," *Richmond Times Dispatch*, June 19, 1989, and Howardena Pindell, "Breaking the Silence," *New Art Examiner* 18, no. 2 (October 1990): 22-23.

11. For useful discussions of these and other cases, see Amy Adler, "Postmodern Art and the Obscenity Law," *Yale Law Journal* 99 (1990): 1359-79, and de Grazia, *Girls Lean Back*. See also "The Obscene Body," *Drama Review* 33, no. 1 (Fall 1989); the interviews with Annie Sprinkle and Karen Finley in *Angry Women*, ed. Andrea Juno and V. Vale (San Francisco: Research Publications, 1991); and Lauren Berlant's forthcoming *Live Sex Acts*.

12. On Madonna's proximity to her "censors," see Ernest Larsen, "In the Realm of the Censors," *Transition* 53 (1991): 105-15.

13. Howardena Pindell speaks of de facto censorship of artists of color in "Breaking the

Silence." See also Carol Jacobsen, "Redefining Censorship," 51; the October 1990 cover of *New Art Examiner* (a reproduction of their poster: "Relax Senator Helms, the Art World *Is* Your Kind of Place!"); and C.Carr, "Guerrilla Girls: Combat in the Art Zone," *Mirabella*, July 1992, 32-35.

14. Martha Buskirk, "Moral Rights: First Step or False Start?" *Art in America* 79, no. 7 (November 1991): 37-45.

15. See, for example, Carole S. Vance, "Misunderstanding Obscenity," *Art in America* 78, no. 5 (May 1990): 49-52.

16. On Jeff Koons, see *Jeff Koons* (San Francisco: San Francisco Museum of Art, 1992), especially Brian Wallis, "We Don't Need Another Hero: Aspects of the Critical Reception of the Work of Jeff Koons," 27-33, and Martha Buskirk, "Commodification as Censor: Copyrights and Fair Use," *October* 60 (Spring 1992): 82-103.

17. I take the term *administration* from Theodor Adorno not to endorse his positions but to suggest that the 1930s debates over expressionism and socialist realism have not been transcended by postmodern political criticism. See Theodor Adorno, "Against Administered Art," in *Aesthetic Theory*, trans. C. Lenhardt (New York and London: Routledge & Kegan Paul, 1984), 355, and the essays "The Culture Industry Reconsidered" and "Culture and Administration," in J. M. Bernstein, ed., *The Culture Industry: Selected Essays on Mass Culture* (London and New York: Routledge, 1991), 85-92 and 93-114.

18. Jürgen Habermas, *The Structural Transformation of the Public Sphere: An Inquiry into a Category of Bourgeois Society*, trans. Thomas Burger (Cambridge, Mass.: MIT Press, 1989). See also the essays in Craig Calhoun, ed., *Habermas and the Public Sphere* (Cambridge, Mass.: MIT Press, 1992). On literary criticism and the public sphere, see Peter Uwe Hohendahl, *The Institution of Criticism* (Ithaca, N.Y.: Cornell University Press, 1982), and Terry Eagleton, *The Function of Criticism: From the Spectator to Post-Structuralism* (London: Verso, 1984). For a critique of the way Habermas and his followers oppose literary criticism to censorship, see Richard Burt, *Licensed by Authority: Ben Jonson and the Discourses of Censorship* (Ithaca, N.Y.: Cornell University Press, 1993), 26-77.

19. Pierre Bourdieu, "Censorship and the Imposition of Form," in *Language and Symbolic Power*, trans. Gino Raymond and Matthew Adamson, ed. John B. Thompson (Cambridge, Mass.: Harvard University Press, 1991), 137-59. On the inevitability of displacement and distortion in censoring and uncensoring, see Richard Burt, "(Un)Censoring in Detail: Thomas Middleton, Fetishism, and the Regulation of Dramatic Discourse," forthcoming in *Thomas Middleton and Early Modern Textual Culture: A Companion Volume*, ed. Gary Taylor et al. (Oxford: Oxford University Press, 1994), and Burt, "Baroque Down: The Trauma of Censorship in Psychoanalysis and Queer Film Revisions of Shakespeare and Marlowe," in *Shakespeare in the New Europe*, ed. Michael Hattaway et al. (Sheffield: Sheffield University Press, 1994).

20. Pierre Bourdieu, *Outline of a Theory of Practice*, trans. Richard Nice (Cambridge: Cambridge University Press, 1977), 169-70.

21. Bourdieu, "Censorship," 138.

22. Bourdieu, *Outline*, 169 (Bourdieu's emphasis).

23. Jiřina Šmejkalová-Strickland, in this volume (chapter 8).

24. See Habermas, *Structural Transformation*.

25. For recent work on the "public sphere," see chapter 1 in this volume; W. J. T. Mitchell, ed., *Art and the Public Sphere* (Chicago: University of Chicago Press, 1992); Joan Landes, *Women and the Public Sphere in the Age of the French Revolution* (Ithaca, N.Y.: Cornell University Press, 1988); and Robbins, ed., *Phantom Public Sphere.*

26. See chapter 12 in this volume.

27. Politicizing the aesthetic, often thought to be an antidote to neoconservative and liberal attempts to falsely divide politics and aesthetics, is equally implicated in censorship. It is now a commonplace that art and criticism are political, that there are no built-in consequences. For the left, however, some of the consequences are now regressive. Consider the following example: because art is political, conservatives like Bruce Fein argue, it ought to be regulated.

28. For a powerful defense of identity politics, see George Yúdice, "For a Practical Aesthetic," *Social Text* 25/26 (1990): 129–45, and "We Are *Not* the World," *Social Text* 31/32 (1992): 202-17. For an equally powerful critique, see Joan Scott, "Multiculturalism and the Politics of Identity," *October* 61 (Summer 1992): 12-18. For a discussion of the way that multiculturalism has played itself out in the public sphere, see Charles Taylor, *Multiculturalism and "the Politics of Recognition"* (Princeton, N.J.: Princeton University Press, 1992).

29. See also Lauren Berlant and Elizabeth Freeman, "Queer Nationality," *Boundary 2* 19, no. 1 (Spring 1992): 149–80, and Mari J. Matsuda et al., *Words That Wound: Critical Race Theory, Assaultive Speech, and the First Amendment* (Boulder, Colo.: Westview, 1993). For the cited examples of the ways in which the left has split over issues of censorship, see Kathy Holub, "Ballistic Instinct," *Premiere*, August 1991, 80–84, 104; "Censors on the Street," *Time*, May 13, 1991, 70; Laurent Greilsamer, "Holocaust Historian Awaits Judgement of Paris," *Guardian Weekly*, May 12, 1991, 12; Laurent Greilsamer, "Pour 'Contestation de crimes contre l'humanité' M. Robert Faurisson est condamné a 100 000 francs d'amende avec susis," *Le Monde*, April 20, 1991, 11; Rebecca Lieb, "Nazi Hate Movies Continue to Ignite Fierce Passions," *New York Times*, August 4, 1991, 16; Chuck Philips, "Wiesenthal Center Denounces Ice Cube's Album," *Los Angeles Times*, November 2, 1991, F3; and John Pareles, "Should Ice Cube's Voice Be Chilled?" *New York Times*, December 8, 1991, H30.

30. My account of university administration is largely a paraphrase of Jeffrey Wallen's brilliant unpublished essay "Academic Freedom and Diversity: Congruence or Conflict?"

31. See especially Francis Barker, *The Tremulous Private Body: Essays on Subjection* (New York: Methuen, 1984).

32. In arranging the essays in these terms, I mean to disturb rigid differentiations between early modern, modern, and postmodern rather than cement walls between them. Indeed, some of the essays in the postmodern section discuss postmodern cases and some discuss modern cases. I want to call attention to the porous state of each of these terms in order to head off any attempt to historicize differences in the formation of what Bourdieu terms the "literary field," contextualizing different kinds of censorship or performances across time. The problem with this kind of contextualization is that it inevitably reinscribes a unified discursive space beyond regulation or censorship. I argue this point more closely in *Licensed by Authority*, 22-25.

33. On the importance of early modern censorship to an understanding of postmodern censorship, see chapter 1 in this volume and Burt, *Licensed by Authority*, 150-68. See also Stanley Fish, "There's No Such Thing as Free Speech, and It's a Good Thing Too," in Berman, *Debating P.C.*

34. See Sullivan, "First Amendment Wars"; Allan Parichini, "Speakeasy," *New Art Examiner* 20, no. 4 (December 1992): 10–11; *Artistic Freedom under Attack*, 1991 Report by People for the American Way; and Nat Hentoff, *Free Speech for Me—But Not For Thee: How the Left and Right Censor Each Other* (New York: HarperCollins, 1992).

35. For more on the politics of the breakdown, see my essay "Baroque Down."

Part I

Criticism, Censorship, and the Early Modern Public Sphere

Areopagitica, Censorship, and the Early Modern Public Sphere

David Norbrook

Milton's *Areopagitica* is buried under the weight of its own celebrity: it has turned into a quarry of fine and somewhat empty phrases, legitimizing the belief that in modern liberal societies a near-universal freedom of speech has been attained. Recently, however, there has been a sharp reaction. The liberal cult of *Areopagitica* is criticized as mystifyingly idealist, positing a complete autonomy of the discursive subject in abstraction from material constraints on discourse. Recent work on *Areopagitica* has been strongly influenced by Michel Foucault's insistence that universal moral principles are always effects of power. Foucault takes a sharply revisionist line on the traditional values of a progressive politics. "One makes war to win, not because it is just": in this "Nietzschean" analysis, there can be no question of progress toward social justice, merely a random succession of forms of violence, each of which will legitimize itself in moralistic terms.[1] It is not surprising that Foucault should adopt a mordantly critical view of the belief in progress toward freedom of expression. If the ideal of a completely uncensored, unconstrained discourse is an illusion, then the emergence of the liberal campaigns against censorship can be seen as an ideological strategy to reinforce the idea of a pure, private, autonomous subject. As Foucault provocatively puts it, individual authorship emerged only when authors were subject to punishment. Censorship created the liberty that then protested against it: no mutilation, no Milton.[2] And in fact Milton supported some forms of censorship.[3] Despite the claims of autonomy, it is argued, what were really at issue were the demands of an

3

increasingly individualistic, capitalist economic system. *Areopagitica* can be read as a founding moment of this discourse, with its recurrent parallels between ideas and merchandise and its vigorous defense of the rights of the author against external intervention.[4]

These revisionist readings of *Areopagitica*, however, have some serious limitations. The Foucauldians' iconoclasm, salutary as it can be, has often been manifested in a very one-sided way.[5] In reacting against the liberal model (which, however, is often caricatured), recent critics have come up with a rigidly deterministic model of the links between knowledge and power. The transition from the Stuart monarchy to the republic is seen not as the product of popular political agency but as determined from above by a state whose powers appear more massive and irresistible than those of the Hegelian *Geist*.[6] The phenomenon of political opposition is rendered a priori impossible by the dependence of knowledge on power. Foucauldian theory has thus fallen in with a very differently motivated form of revisionism, with the claim by certain political historians that prerevolutionary England was a world of patronage and clientage in which critical political thought was virtually unknown. Censorship, then, was not a serious problem because there was no serious pressure to transgress the limits of traditional thought; and in any case, censorship restrictions were far less draconian than Milton claimed in *Areopagitica*.[7] Milton's pamphlet thus emerges as the product of a personal grievance rather than part of a common political agency.

There is, I believe, a certain irony in the readings of *Areopagitica* that have resulted: *Areopagitica* itself challenges the very kinds of split between public and private, between power and knowledge, that are currently ascribed to it.[8] This is not to say that Milton is a Foucauldian *avant la lettre*. But perhaps, as Donald Guss has suggested, there is a certain validity in the anachronism of seeing him as a Habermasian *avant la lettre*.[9] For Habermas has tried to develop a theory of the links between knowledge and power that would avoid the reductiveness of Foucauldian discourse, offering a model of power as cooperative as well as merely agonistic, criticizing the instrumental rationality of one mode of Enlightenment thought while still locating spaces for critical and reflective thought that is capable of some degree of autonomy. It is not my purpose here to offer a defense of Habermas's theories in general, which raise many problems; the status of his putative "ideal speech situation" has been much questioned. It is worth recalling, however, that the concept originated in a historical survey that specifically connected an ideal of unconstrained communication with concrete material and political contexts. I shall try to show that Habermas's model of the "bourgeois public sphere" opens up a more adequate historical contextualization of *Areopagitica* and that one reason for this is a certain interplay between Habermas's theories and Renaissance rhetorical and political theory.

It must be said at once that *The Structural Transformation of the Public Sphere* is not as it stands a reliable historical guide; it needs a great deal of qualification and supplementation with more recent work. On the other hand, its publication had a theoretical as well as a historical impact. Habermas attempts to qualify the extremely dark picture of Enlightenment rationality presented by Adorno and Horkheimer in *Dialectic of Enlightenment*, tracing the emergence of a communicative rationality alongside a more narrowly instrumental rationality. His sense of the political issues at stake was sharpened by disquiet at the political ambience of another important critique of the Enlightenment, Heidegger's *Letter on Humanism*, which also appeared in 1947, and adroitly located the blame for the century's misfortunes on the "humanism" of the Enlightenment rather than on the Nazi reaction against its principles. Habermas was disturbed far earlier than poststructuralist theorists by the politics of the enormously influential *Letter*, by the way in which Heidegger had "stepped on stage after the War, like a phoenix from the ashes" in a "felicitously de-Nazified" form.[10] *Structural Transformation* ends with an account of the commodification of twentieth-century discourse not so different from his predecessors', but it does attempt to provide a more nuanced narrative of the process.

In doing so, the book can be accused of giving an idealized history of the early modern bourgeoisie, who are presented as establishing a space for critical inquiry that would be unconstrained by traditional power interests, a mediating area between civil society and state.[11] While Habermas certainly notes the underlying economic constraints on the public sphere, his highly rationalistic portrait of the bourgeoisie fails to acknowledge the strong religious motivations behind the emergence of the public sphere in England. As a result, he oversimplifies its origins, dating them to the years 1694-1695 on the basis of three criteria: parliamentary government, the collapse of licensing for the press, and the formation of the Bank of England. The first two of these conditions, however, had been temporarily fulfilled fifty years earlier, in the period of the English Revolution—a historical phenomenon of which Habermas makes no mention. Whatever its underlying economic determinants, the ideological motivation of these developments had been to a considerable degree religious rather than secular. Jonathan Scott has pointed out that the seventeenth century was "a century of disaster for European protestantism, which was reduced in its course to the fringes of the continent, and from 50 per cent to under 20 per cent of its total area."[12] The powerful pressure for parliamentary control of public affairs and for public discussion was fueled in the first instance by the fear that the English monarchy could not be trusted to resist that process, but was on the contrary likely to be complicit in it. Those fears could on occasion outweigh traditional anxieties about "popularity." Milton's vindication of the freedom of the press needs in the first instance to be seen in the jumpily defensive context of this European ideological struggle, rather than of a serenely confident, "liberal humanist" belief in inevitable progress. By the end of the century there had been a certain secularization that allowed Habermas to emphasize economic factors in the fully emergent public sphere. It may be questioned, however, whether that secularization ever entirely superseded the more directly religious motivations for the maintenance of a public sphere.

Despite these limitations, Habermas's public-sphere model does have the merit of making connections between areas that have often remained in different institutional compartments—the development of Parliament, political theory, literary history, and the study of the mass media. Such a global approach brings out phenomena that have been underplayed in revisionist historiography. The reaction against "grand narratives," though often presented as a modest refusal of authoritarian totalizing, may in fact prove obfuscatory, condemning such discrete analyses to remain isolated and atomized; only some more global approach that is responsive to political agency can make sense of their interrelations. If one takes a synchronic cross section through England in its unparliamentary moments, one ends up with something like the paradigm of the revisionists and some new historicists, a pre-Enlightenment world of bodily submission. If, however, like some recent historians one takes a close look at periods of parliamentary crisis, there emerges a very different picture of a society in conflict, in which agents are consciously collaborating to contest a loss of popular control of key decisions. There was a significant expansion in the political public sphere, especially from the 1620s onward, an emergent civil society whose means of communication—reports of parliamentary debates, newsletters, satires, and so on—circulated horizontally, cutting across the vertical power structures emanating from the court. The electorate significantly expanded, and elections became increasingly ideologically charged.[13] This process culminated in the political opening of the 1640s. By 1649 the journalist Daniel Border could write that in the reign of Queen Elizabeth, men were

> rather guided by the tradition of their Fathers, than by acting principles in reason and knowledge: But to the contrary in these our dayes, the meanest sort of people are not only able to write &c. but to argue and discourse on matters of highest concernment; and thereupon to desire, that such things which are most remarkable, may be truly committed to writing, and made publique.[14]

Recent research bears out Habermas's analysis of growing pressure for a political public sphere—what a contemporary described as a "*publick* and *communicative spirit*."[15] The steady revaluation of the traditional low estimate of "public opinion" can be traced in Milton's striking claim that "opinion ... is but knowledge in the making" (554).

While permitting a global perspective, Habermas's model does avoid a simple teleology: it can be adapted to account for the massively uneven development of the public sphere in the seventeenth century and beyond. It is not the case that after 1640, or after 1695, there suddenly was a securely established public sphere. On the contrary, there was a continuing political struggle to open up or to restrict its emergence. The newspaper press of the 1640s was gradually checked first by the republic and then by Cromwell before being dealt a coup de grâce by Charles II. The electorate expanded steadily up to the 1640s, underwent restrictions under Cromwell, and went through innumerable fluctuations down to the Whig ascendancy and beyond. Triennial Parliaments were gained and then lost. As Habermas declares at the end of his book, the contest for a fully articulate public sphere is still continuing as we face what he terms a neofeudal era of media barons; and the British Charter 88 movement is currently campaigning for the fulfillment of some demands first made by the Levellers 340 years ago.

Habermas's model potentially permits a more nuanced narrative of modernity and the public sphere than those readings that find a sudden transmutation around the middle of the seventeenth century. And while it unduly downplays religious factors, it does open up secular elements in the development of the public sphere—and in Milton's discourse in *Areopagitica*—that deserve fuller attention. Habermas pointed the way toward complicating the stereotyped notions of Renaissance individualism and bourgeois humanism that are still found in many current narratives of early modern subjectivity.[16] There is a significant ambiguity in the term *bourgeois* or *Bürger*: it can be variously translated as "bourgeois," an economic category concerned with the private negotiations of civil society, or as "citizen," a political category opening to the public sphere. Habermas draws attention to our need for a history of the citizen as well as of the bourgeois.

Certain sections of the bourgeoisie in the early modern period were intensely engaged with public issues. One reason was that they sought legitimation in an emulation of the classical political world. That history was already being written by 1962; significantly, two of its most prominent pioneers were exiles from Nazi Germany, Hans Baron and Hannah Arendt. Both took a somewhat more favorable view of humanism than their compatriot Martin Heidegger. Arendt strongly disagreed with the critique of agency and the will in Heidegger's *Letter on Humanism*,[17] but this did not make her a conventional liberal humanist: she was concerned also to contest the privatizing tendencies of modern liberalism, and she shared something of Heidegger's desire to turn to the ancient Greeks as a critique of modern trends, though with a significantly different political inflection. In his public sphere book, Habermas drew strongly on Arendt's *The Human Condition*, which appeared in 1958. Arendt there strongly contested the separation between public and private, the "flight from the whole outer world," that had characterized much liberal thought. She went back to the classical polis, in which individual fulfillment was to be found not in the private but in the public sphere, in playing an active role in civic life. The word *priva-*

tus retained its etymological sense of privation, of something lacking. Arendt urged a reconstruction of the classical valorization of the public life, which she later located in such unexpectedly collocated institutions as the early revolutionary soviet and the early American town meeting. For Arendt, one of the crucial features of the specifically political life was the fusion of speech and action. She points out that Aristotle defined man as a being capable of speech, and that the Latin translation as *animal rationale* elided the centrality of speech for the Greek polis. Discourse, then, was not a private realm cut off from power but precisely a means of engagement with the public world. The word *rhetor* effectively meant "politician."[18] The criteria of rationality in the polis were not narrowly instrumental or cognitive; public life demanded a practical reason or prudence (*phronesis*), linking word and concept, power and knowledge in a quest for intersubjective agreement. Habermas drew on Arendt's analysis of classical political thought in formulating his own concept of praxis and of communicative as opposed to instrumental rationality.[19]

Arendt and Habermas anticipated a vein of scholarship that became more and more important in the 1970s and 1980s, tracing the complex effects of the revival of the values of the classical polis in early modern civic humanism.[20] The rise of the Roman empire and then of the church had marked a radical shift in relations between public and private. In the medieval world, with rule in the hands of a personal lord, public and private realms became inextricably mingled. The polis came under the hegemony of a super-*oikos*, the household of the emperor or monarch, and citizens became subjects, forced to revere their king as a father rather than debating with him as an equal. At the same time, a matter of much concern to Milton, the state and church vied with each other for monopolies of religious life, with "the Popes of *Rome* engrossing [note the economic term] what they pleas'd of Politicall rule into their owne hands" (501) and public revenues being siphoned into an unaccountable religious bureaucracy. That is one reason why, for Milton, "popery" is not to be tolerated: it "extirpats all ... civill supremacies" (565). But it is not just the state but the people who are thus disempowered; the people are now trying "to reassume the ill deputed care of their Religion into their own hands again" (554). In the secular sphere, too, the civic humanists of the Renaissance challenged that medieval blurring of public-private boundaries. Habermas gives a useful account of the ways in which the word *common,* in the medieval period connoting a social lowliness that was effectively the opposite of the public world of the court, became revalued into a positive sense of the public and universal.[21] It was from the attempt to reclaim the public domain, the res publica, from private monopolies of power that *republican* as a noun emerged in the mid-seventeenth century. And *Areopagitica* can more fruitfully be seen against the background of Renaissance republicanism than of a later liberalism.

With the assault on private monopolies of power there went a comparable critique of monopolies of discourse, a call for universality of communication. This call for open communication was most vigorously made in the circle of the German émigré Samuel Hartlib, who welcomed the parliamentary reforms of the 1640s as an opportunity for establishing international communications in news and in theological and scientific knowledge.[22] The Hartlibians can be seen as exemplifying a shift toward instrumental rationality, calling for plain and simple communication and therefore somewhat suspicious of classical rhetoric. For some contemporaries, in fact, far from embodying a modern notion of language and truth, Milton was problematic precisely because he was not modern enough. Though Hartlib commissioned *Of Education* from Milton, some of his circle regarded it as somewhat too high-flown; and one of Hartlib's German correspondents complained that *Areopagitica* was "rather too satyrical throughout . . . and because of his all too highflown style in many places quite obscure." Nevertheless, he hoped that the tract would be translated into German and given "good circulation in other lands where such tyranny reigns."[23]

It is in fact hard to make clear-cut distinctions in this period between a "modern" rationality, the classical discourse of civic *phronesis,* and the apocalyptic Protestant belief in progressive revelation. The Hartlibians shared with civic humanists the belief that rational inquiry depended on collective endeavor: to translate, not very satisfactorily, into Habermasian terms, instrumental rationality could best develop in a climate of communicative rationality. As John Hall, a great admirer of *Areopagitica,* wrote to Hartlib in 1647, the reform of learning could not depend on "the sparkles of a few private men"; echoing Milton's critique of a "fugitive and cloister'd virtue," Hall wrote that they must be "forc't from that solitude where in they

Handwritten note at top of page: real fugitives - cloisters & fugitives - lis of monasteries but also virtue in-the-world...

wold be imersed."[24] Another member of the circle, Sir Cheney Culpeper, who was also interested in Milton's prose writings, attacked scholars who were "suffered to liue a monkishe life to the prejudice of the publike." Culpeper saw Hartlib's proposal to estabish an "Office of Address" with a "Bureau of Communication" as part of a wider, apocalyptic process of bringing down monopolies: after the "monopoly of Power which the King claimes" there would fall "the monopoly of trade," "the monopoly of Equity ... the monopoly of matters of conscience & scripture ... all these & many more wee shall haue in chace & what one hownde misses another will happen in the sente of & thus will Babilon tumble, tumble, tumble."[25] This process formed part of a "democraticall growinge spirite" whose final outcome could not yet be foreseen.[26] Such assaults on monopolies did indeed open up a greater space for private interests;[27] yet it is reductive to see the assault on monopolies of discourse simply as a rationale for laissez-faire capitalism. Culpeper's vision of an ongoing democratic revolution implied the importance of public as well as private spaces. As Pocock has demonstrated, there was a continual tension between the demands of commerce and those of virtue in republican theory; similar tensions can be found in the language of *Areopagitica.*[28]

If such proposals for a "modern" transformation of communications often adopted an apocalyptic idiom, they also drew on the idiom of classical republicanism. The more innovatively minded recognized that a revival of classical rhetoric and public discourse had to adjust to changed political and technological resources; the printing press made possible new modes of public rhetorical debate. The insistence on common participation in public affairs legitimized the expansion of the press, and newsbooks' titles often aligned them with classical forms of public speech: the courtly *Mercurius Aulicus* versus the parliamentarian *Mercurius Civicus.* This was the only period of English history when a newspaper entitled *Observations Historical, Political, and Philosophical, upon Aristotles First Booke of Political Government* would have been considered marketable.[29] *Areopagitica* was an important factor in turning at least one young republican, John Hall, toward the newspaper medium, and Milton encouraged another journalist, Marchamont Nedham, to return to the parliamentarian cause. Nedham commented of his newspaper that "J entitle it [Mercurius] Politicus, because the present

Gou[er]nm[ent] is verà πολιτέια [*politeia*] as it is opposed to the despotick forme."[30] Nedham was not only the first great English journalist but also a significant theorist of republicanism. Milton has frequently been disparaged for associating with this vulgar popularizer, a charge that sits uneasily with concomitant attacks on his elitism.[31]

Areopagitica formed part of that common project of reclaiming public space: the tract, Milton insisted, was "not the disburdning of a particular fancie" but was voicing a "common grievance," the "generall murmur" (539). Here and elsewhere, Milton used the word *public* and its compounds about twice as much as *private*; books, he proclaimed, were "the living labours of publick men" (493). Francis Barker claims that the Order of Parliament that Milton commends in *Areopagitica* provided for "the protection of copyright vested, for the first time, in the author";[32] but while such a reading fits in with the thesis that Milton privatized literary production, there is no evidence that Milton or the Order he mentions effected such a transfer. In fact, the system by which copyright rested with the publisher rather than the author did not prevent authors from having a say in the content and revision of their works,[33] and Milton certainly took such an interest; but in the 1640s he was as much concerned with the collective as with the private aspect of literary production. He had witnessed in Italy the contrast between the restrictive system of aristocratic patronage and the more open press of the Venetian republic.[34] If the latter system allowed the author more autonomy, it was nonetheless associated with an ethos of public spirit, and it was that ethos that the Hartlib circle were concerned to instill in England. John Hall repeatedly proclaimed his determination to be "subservient to the Commonwealth of letters";[35] it was in that spirit that Milton turned away from his private literary studies to his prose writings.

What Milton objects to about prepublication licensing is precisely that it claws back what ought to be a public space for a particular interest, that of the presbyterian "at home in his privat chair" (540). Similarly, the Leveller William Walwyn urged Parliament to oppose licensing because "It is not to be supposed that You who have so long spent Your time in recovering the common liberties of *England*, should in conclusion turne the common into particular."[36] Milton insists that writing ought to be a collaborative process—a writer "likely consults and conferrs with his judicious friends" (532). This process is one reason why good texts are seldom fixed and finished: a writer who is "copious of fancie" will want to keep revising (532). Intellectuals should "joyn, and unite into one generall and brotherly search after Truth" (554) and welcome anyone willing to "bring his helpfull hand to the slow-moving Reformation which we labour under" (565). Here it is presumably the slowness of progress that makes the reformation seem a labor, though there is perhaps a buried reference to the birth of new ideas; here and elsewhere writing is seen as work, an "act" (532). Milton declares that *Areopagitica* itself has been part of this collaborative process: he is voicing complaints that he had heard in Italy and was shocked to find being uttered "so generally" in England when he returned. He was "loaded ... with entreaties and perswasions" to write his treatise (539). The worst effect of licensing is that it turns the intellectual community into egotists who are "over timorous" (556, 558) and fear "the shaking of every leaf" (539). Milton conjures up this effect in his brilliant vignette of Italian title pages: "Sometimes 5 *Imprimaturs* are seen together dialogue-wise in the Piatza of one Title page, complementing and ducking each to other with their shav'n reverences" (504). Milton conflates the public space of the title page with that of the Italian cities where the defeat of the republican communality of the Roman forum and later of the piazza are registered in the common complicity in servility of the groveling instruments of the hierarchy, acting "dialogue-wise" because the genuine dialogue of republican culture has been reduced to empty stage dialogue. Elsewhere Milton compares the imprimatur to the papal prison, the "castle St. *Angelo*" (537). Milton warns that such values have been transferred to England in his reference to licenses being obtained from "the West end of *Pauls*" (504). St. Paul's was a crucial site for the emergent public sphere in England: the district around the churchyard was a center for printers and booksellers, while the interior of the church had functioned as a kind of forum where news was exchanged, and the sermons at Paul's Cross had sometimes been politically controversial. Laud had expelled the strollers from the church to a neoclassical portico where political gossip would be overshadowed by regal statues, and had muzzled the sermons: these moves, in conjunction with ecclesiastical, "patriarchal" (533) control over licensing, seemed to threaten to reduce English spaces likewise to such deferential theatricality. The presbyterians would reintroduce a climate of fear, making people "afraid of every conventicle" (541, cf. 547).

Milton dramatizes the reverse process, of writing with a "ventrous edge" (534), a "fearlesse and communicative candor" (2:226), by defying the licensers in publishing without an imprimatur or printer's name and by the boldness of his approach to Parliament. He emphasizes that, like Isocrates and Dion Prusaeus, he is in "a private condition" (486), but he does so in order to bring out the contrast with his desire to "advance the publick good." He dramatizes the process by which he overcomes his initial "feare" of public discourse and claims an equal right to members of Parliament themselves to discuss public issues. His aim is to animate "private persons" with a new respect for Parliament in its receptiveness to "publick advice" (488); its openness contrasts with the "cabin[et] Counsellours" who tried to confine decision making within a narrow and exclusive space. Parliament is becoming more responsive to the demands of its people, opening up a public sphere that "obeyes the voice of reason from what quarter soever it be heard speaking" (490). Milton emphasizes that the most enlightened states accept advice from overseas as well as from their own nation; figures like Comenius had been drawn to England from the Continent because of Parliament's apparent enthusiasm for reform, and later in *Areopagitica* Milton lays new emphasis on this internationalism (552). Just as the House of Commons comes to see itself as representing a general rather than a particular interest, so Milton's private voice becomes common. In an escalating communicative interchange, Parliament was beginning to print its proceedings, while as Milton had admiringly noted, it was more and more open to petitions even from "the meanest artizans and labourers, at other times also women" (I, 926). In praising "the magnanimity of a triennial Parlament" (488) Milton explicitly links a general moral virtue with a specific political form: Parliament had gained control over its regularity of summoning from the king and was hence more open to the public's demands. Conversely, the people's creativity had been facilitated by the material conditions created by Parliament. The role of Parliament throughout the tract deserves attention: as the central nexus between communication and power in a society without a court (the king goes conspicuously unmentioned), it is best able to govern when it is most responsive to communicative processes diffused throughout society. In a complex dialectic, Milton says that it is impossible that "ye [Parliament]" should "first make your selves, that made us so, lesse the lovers, lesse the founders of our true liberty" (559).[37] The people's intellectual achievements are "the issue of your owne vertu propagated in us" (559): Parliament instills a *virtù* in the people that is at once moral and Machiavellian.

The jaw-breaking title of *Areopagitica* makes more sense when the licensing controversy is set in this wider context of reclaiming public space. "Things concerned with the Areopagus": the reader's attention is directed away from legal minutiae and toward the constitution of ancient Athens. That concern can be seen as an instance of Milton's elitist pedantry: Sue Curry Jansen has given the name "Areopagite" to the self-satisfied literary intellectual.[38] But what is at issue in Milton's Greek allusions is something a lot more politically sensitive than scoring points in cultural literacy: for his first readers, an admittedly limited audience of humanists, his allusions had a high political charge. The title and allusions effectively make the text an early manifesto of English republicanism.

To understand the potential explosiveness of Milton's allusions to the rhetoric of the Greek polis, we need to try to forget the encrustations of later liberal cults of Athenian democracy and remember just how raw and new an enthusiasm for Athens would have been at this time. Most political discourse centered on conflicting versions of a time-hallowed "ancient constitution"; it is hard today to recall how provocative Milton was being in attacking the ancient English feudal constitution as "the barbarick pride of a *Hunnish* and *Norwegian* statelines" (489). In *Areopagitica* the English monarchy dwindles to a dead voice from the tomb of Henry VII (567), just as the figure of the king is conspicuously absent from Milton's reworking of the story of Solomon's temple (555). Instead, Milton, like James Harrington, turns to the classical polis as embodying an ancient prudence superior to the degenerate political forms of feudalism. One reason for condemning licensing is that it is a modern invention, not part of the ancient "prudence" (522) that republicans wished to emulate, and hence unworthy of the "prudent spirit" of Parliament (490). The demand for unlicensed printing proves to be a transitional demand: to embody fully the principles behind that demand, to reform "the rule of life both economicall and politicall" (550), would involve a radical restructuring of the English state, a "generall reforming" (566). The reception of *Areopagitica* indicates that it fueled demands for changes going far beyond the immediate issue of licensing.[39]

Areopagitica is a prime illustration of Thomas Hobbes's fear that a cult of Greek and Roman liberty was beginning to emerge in England.[40] Having translated Thucydides' history as a warning against democracy, Hobbes attacked the great orator Pericles, the hero of Athenian democracy, on the ground that "the tongue of man is a trumpet of warre, and sedition."[41] The Athenian ethos is conveyed not only in the title but also in the quotation from Euripides' *The Suppliant Women* on the title page.[42] The full connotations of the speech act involved in this citation cannot be explored here, but it can be pointed out that the passage Milton cited was itself metacommunicative, discussing the differing speech acts characteristic of different political forms. A herald arrives from the kingdom of Thebes and asks, "What man is master in this land?" Theseus replies that he has got off to a bad start in asking for a master: the city is free and not ruled by one person, and the poor have an equal share. The herald responds to this challenge by forgetting all about the message he came to deliver and shifting to the political implications of the medium, the forms of discourse characteristic of a democracy. Athens is controlled by the mob, who are incapable of judging arguments properly and are therefore swayed this way and that by rhetoricians. If poor men work hard they will have no time to learn about public affairs.

This exchange was heavily freighted with political implications in its original context. Edith Hall writes that Greek drama was militantly ideological, displaying "breathtaking anachronism" in projecting the values of Athenian democracy onto the distant eras it portrayed. The tragedies helped to portray a "discourse of Barbarism," constructing an image of the other of Athenian democracy. The Athenian polis was seen as "the highest rung on the ladder of human evolution," and monarchical states were presented as primitive and barbaric. In Athenian tragedy Thebes sometimes functioned as Athens's other, a barbarian residue; but this antithesis often functioned as a submerged allusion to the more immediate rivalry with Sparta, whose more aristocratic regime was attacked by democrats but covertly favored by conservatives.[43] The Theban herald adopts the stock arguments of pro-Spartan, antidemocratic thinkers—arguments that were also of course adopted by conservative Athenians like Plato, whose sympathies went toward Sparta. In 1644 such arguments were currently being marshaled against the parliamentarians by the royalists who similarly pilloried their enemies as uncouth barbarians favoring mob rule. Milton attacked those who saw "the common people" as "a giddy, vitious and ungrounded people" (536). The Athenian discourse of barbarism made a particularly powerful riposte to such arguments, and Milton quotes on his title page from Theseus's reply to the herald, in which he denounces absolute rule and praises democracy where the poor and the rich must be subject to the same, written laws. He gives a historical analysis of democracy, seeing it as part of a progress from primitive absolutism toward a written constitution. And it is in this context that Theseus offers the defense of free speech that Milton places on his title page. Milton's version is:

> This is true Liberty when free born men
> Having to advise the public may speak free,
> Which he who can, and will, deserv's high praise,
> Who neither can nor will, may hold his peace;
> What can be juster in a State then this?

This exchange is not just about freedom of speech as some separable political issue: it can be read as a straightforward opposition, not just between monarchy and republicanism, but between monarchy and democracy. This fact was registered in Renaissance editions, one of which glossed Theseus's speech as a "praise of democracy."[44]

At a time when Parliament's cause was still officially monarchist and the republican M.P. Henry Marten had been expelled for questioning that stance, Milton's allusion was cautious; it was nonetheless pointed, turning his own title page from an authoritarian piazza to an embodiment of a classical forum. His "Frontispice" was "dangerous" (524).[45] His more particular concern, freedom of expression and publication, itself raised more general political issues; as has been seen, the exchange between Theseus and the herald implies that moral values need to be considered in relation to specific political structures and their characteristic speech acts. Blair Worden has questioned whether the seventeenth century had any universalizing concept of freedom of publication as a right, rather than a privilege handed down from above.[46] But Greek discourse offered a number of terms for such a right with implications broad enough to be easily extended to the new medium of print. As I. F. Stone has pointed out, the right to speak out boldly on any issue was effectively identical with the civic identity of the free Athenian, and there were at least four different words for freedom of speech, of which perhaps the strongest was *parrhesia*.[47] This is a favorite word in Euripides: as Jocasta says in the *Phoenissae*, "this is slavery, not to speak one's thoughts."[48] The word occurs twice in the *Electra*, the play with which Milton in "Captain or Colonel" imagined charming the royalists. Its fortunes had declined with the decline of Greek democracy: the more conservative Romans had often translated *parrhesia* as *licentia* or *contumacia*. Such pejorative associations tended to cling to the word: the Elizabethan rhetorician Henry Peacham warns that "rude boldnesse" must be tempered by "humble submission."[49] The edition of Euripides owned by Milton reflected that negative attitude toward Athenian democratic values; its commentary on the Theseus-herald exchange declared that grave authors like Xenophon and Aristotle had condemned such *parrhesia* or *licentia plebis*.[50] Milton, by contrast, celebrates such boldness, and *Areopagitica* urges its readers to translate the values of the polis into the England of the 1640s. The pamphlet's subtitle draws attention to the changes made possible by shifts in medium: though presented as a "speech," it is of course so only in a formal, generic sense; yet Milton also reminds us that English traditions deny the ordinary citizen access to the nation's assembly, a right that any Athenian freeman enjoyed. In one sense Milton then appeals over Parliament's head to a wider public sphere; in another sense he also foregrounds his exclusion from a Parliament that represented its people only in a very indirect sense. Before long, the Levellers were to press for more direct forms of representation. Milton was to quote twice from this same speech in his defense of the regicide, the *First Defence of the English People*.[51]

The *Areopagitica* title page, however, bears a contradictory message. Milton modifies Euripides to stress that participation in politics is a matter of free choice and that not all will choose to participate.[52] And his title evokes the Areopagus, a residual element of aristocratic power that was ousted in a democratic revolution. Milton compared himself to Isocrates, who had called for the Areopagus to be restored to its old authority. Such anomalies have led some critics to read the title ironically, while Annabel Patterson suggests that they

point to a hermeneutics of ambiguity and indeterminacy.[53] Indeterminacy, however, is not quite the term; we are left in no doubt
about the wickedness of the royalists, let alone of the Catholics, and
those who were on the receiving end of the policies Milton was to
support in Ireland will not have found them very indeterminate. It
is within a particular framework of a reformed Protestant constitution that Milton does admit openness. Like Machiavelli, Milton believes that an element of disunity may be beneficial rather than
destructive for an expanding commonwealth. In an oxymoron that
would have seemed even more staggering then than it does now, he
praises God for shaking kingdoms with "healthfull commotions to a
generall reforming" (566).[54] And among those commotions Milton
implicitly includes tensions between democratic and aristocratic elements. In choosing democratic Athens rather than conservative
Rome as his model, and then emphasizing one of the Athenians'
more conservative institutions, Milton sets up a complex counterbalancing of political forces. In 1644 the aristocratic element was represented by the House of Lords, and throughout the tract Milton insis-
tently uses the coordinate form "Lords and Commons" as part of a
larger rhetorical pattern of doublets, building up a picture of unity
in controlled variety. His insistence on the House's role, while doubt-
less partly designed to reassure anxious readers, was not necessarily
as conservative in implication as it may seem: some leading members of the independent party were to be found in the Lords, formulating an aristocratic variety of republicanism.[55] Milton's urging
that the state be magnanimous, that it offer "liberall and frequent
audience" to the sects (567), appeals to a semiaristocratic sense of
condescension. After the revolution, however, it was the elected
Council of State that came to seem the obvious equivalent of the
Areopagus, and Milton's friend Marchamont Nedham and many
other republicans made the analogy.[56] Down to 1660, Milton was to
hold to the general principle of counterbalancing a full democracy
with a contrary element.

It was not necessarily that Milton always feared popular radical-
ism: he feared that some or most of the people were not radical
enough, that they would be swayed by an easy sympathy for the
rituals of monarchy. By the end of the 1640s he was lamenting that
the British lacked experience in republican culture. His variety of
republicanism was vanguardist: the radical elite would gradually

wean the people off their devotion to traditional forms. And it was also militant: rhetoric is consistently associated with preparation for battle. The tract was published at a time when the war had gone very badly and the presbyterians were calling for a settlement that would probably leave in place a state church and suppress the sects. Since the presbyterians seemed to be strengthening their power in Parliament, renewal of the licensing laws was likely to mean a consolidation of their hold on power, and possibly the dissemination of royalist propaganda (570). In the first instance, the protests against licensing at this time had the highly particular aim of trying to counter the moves to suppress the sects and negotiate with the king from a position of relative military weakness. Milton throws his weight behind those who were campaigning for the formation of the New Model Army. The Areopagus was named after the god of war. The revolution was to involve virtually continuous military campaigning, first at home and then abroad, for the defense and then the expansion of the republic; Milton supported these campaigns, and he had given military education a prominent place in *Of Education*. His powerful evocation of the military as well as intellectual activities of a city under siege recalls the extraordinary collective agency when elaborate defenses were built up by London's citizens—including oysterwomen who marched to work under an emblem of the goddess of war.[57] The vivid reference to royalist newssheets circulating with the ink still wet is a reminder to Parliament that wartime conditions need vigilance. Milton evokes Livy's story of the heroic struggles of the young Roman republic, with the royalists cast in the role of the barbaric Carthaginians (557). Given the polemical thrust behind his attack on presbyterian licensing, Milton's later role as a licenser was less radically inconsistent than it may seem, though it undoubtedly did represent a retreat.[58] Like many republicans, he thought that a historic opportunity had been provided for the foundation of a republic in 1649: if the chance was lost it might not recur; he therefore countenanced the suppression of tracts and newspapers agitating for its overthrow. He does, however, seem to have considered the republic to be at least partly fulfilling the ideals of *Areopagitica*, and continued to appeal to the pamphlet in supporting the licensing of works considered heretical.[59]

The martial language of *Areopagitica* has been seen by some re-

cent commentators as exposing a more general link between Enlightenment values and violent repression, between the will to
knowledge and the will to power: in *Areopagitica*, that connection
is the more apparent because Enlightenment rationality has not yet
fully disguised its own violence.[60] Such a reading would square with
Foucault's only extensive engagement with seventeenth-century
England, a lecture in which he presented a radically antihumanist
discourse as emerging from the pressure of political crisis. Writers
like Coke and Lilburne, Foucault claims, threw out illusions like justice and truth and saw history as a "state of war between two hostile
races," which they wanted to bring to a final millennial act of revenge.[61] It requires considerable distortion, however, to turn Lilburne into a Nietzschean *avant la lettre*: his justification of godly
warfare did not derive from an epistemological relativism. And
however strongly Milton may have insisted that prophets had to be
armed, what is remarkable in the context is the force of his argument against militaristic values, against allowing the practical means
of revolution to destroy the ends. The images of the defensive city
under siege are counterposed to celebrations of open, receptive bodies (e.g., 537, 547, 548). In the terms of Pericles' funeral oration, Milton
presents London as a new Athens, able to nourish the arts even in
times of war, and derides the "muselesse and unbookish" Spartans
whose "surlinesse" minded "nought but the feats of Warre" (496).
And yet the urgency of the war effort remains vivid in his language,
conjuring up almost surreal images:

> The shop of warre hath not there more anvils and hammers waking, to
> fashion out the plates and instruments of armed Justice in defence of
> beleaguer'd Truth, then there be pens and heads there, sitting by their
> studious lamps, musing, searching, revolving new notions and idea's.
> (554)

Here manual and intellectual labor are working in harmony rather
than opposition, but the force of the figurative language, where the
mechanical instruments whether of making arms or of writing take
over from the men doing the work, gives an unusual twist to this
analogy. Milton's famous emendation of "wayfaring Christian" to
"warfaring Christian" (515) indicates his desire to startle his readers
with striking juxtapositions. Perhaps the most startling for contemporary readers would have been this: "The Temple of *Janus* with

his two *controversal* faces might now not unsignificantly be set open" (561). While the closing of Janus's gates signified for royalists the unity and peace of Stuart rule, Milton finds such closed unity stifling and endorses the opening of the gates: the wars of truth are not a final goal but are better than the frozen January of a tyrannical peace (545). Unity is still to be sought, but it lies in the future rather than the present; in the meantime, discourse must indeed be Janus-faced.

Milton works through the tension between aristocratic and populist elements, and between war and peace, in the turbulent style and structure of his tract. His frequently noted commercial figures, which compare truths to commodities, serve to deflate a traditional elitism that sets mental against manual labor; yet his equally assertive foregrounding of literary culture works against a purely utilitarian model of democratic discourse: in this prose poetry with its constant interplay of vernacular and Latinate diction, commerce and virtue are set in a complex tension.[62] In lavishing on the traditionally despised medium of the pamphlet the imagistic and allusive resources normally thought appropriate to court poetry or masques, the pamphlet embodies a challenge to fit readers to redirect their cultural energies to the struggle for liberty. The text is a public manifesto of a republican rhetoric and poetics as well as a republican politics, revealing the nation's quest for liberty "by the very sound of this which I shall utter" (487). Milton consciously reworks the poetics of royalist poets for whom unity was the central virtue of monarchies and disunity the vice of republics; like Machiavelli, Milton turns such arguments against the royalists, celebrating the greater dynamism of disunity while insisting that mechanisms can be found to save it from becoming anarchy. Milton inaugurates a long tradition of contrasting English rhetorical openness with French neoclassical formality when he writes that "*Julius Agricola* ... preferr'd the naturall wits of Britain, before the labour'd studies of the French" (552).[63] Milton revises conventional valuations of the body politic figure to find an image for the difficult unity he aims at in the state, a unity very different from the sterile conformity urged in the traditional monarchist figure of the body politic: a flushed countenance is a sign not of sickness but of resourceful adaptation to change (557). Milton uses the term *sublimest* to describe such mental processes; and in pushing figures beyond the conventional

limits of representation he may well have been thinking of Longi-
nus's treatise on the sublime, which his admirer John Hall was soon
to translate. The constantly shifting, sublime body of the text images
the reconstituted body of a reformed state. Truth, for Milton, needs a
body in order to speak, and yet that body resists full representation,
and to represent it fully is already to bind it by tuning truth's voice
according to the time (563).[64] Milton sets his visionary sight against
the deluded sight of everyday perception:

> We boast our light; but if we look not wisely on the Sun it self, it smites
> us into darknes.... The light which we have gain'd, was giv'n us, not to
> be ever staring on, but by it to discover onward things more remote
> from our knowledge. (550)

Milton thus anticipates the dialectic of outer and inner lights that he
was to work out more fully in *Paradise Lost*. The ultimate guarantor
of the validity of Milton's text would then be the degree to which it
inspired a continual revaluation of the reformative process that it
inaugurates.[65]

Milton's tract proposes, then, a quest for truth that is more rhetorical than simply logical: truth exceeds "the pace of method and discours" (521), and as many critics have pointed out, Milton enacts this
process of excess in his virtuoso linguistic displays. This does not
mean that his text is infinitely open-ended, or that rhetoric completely subverts rationality: the tract's apocalyptic discourse is firmly
committed to the erroneousness of Catholic doctrine and to the ultimate revelation of Protestant truth. Its openness remains confined to
a relatively narrow spectrum of advanced Protestant opinion, at a
particular moment when new revelations are in progress. Nevertheless, Milton's rhetorical strategy highlights the points of tension
between knowledge and power, between truth and its institutional
and linguistic embodiments. His presentation of the active citizens of
London as "reading, trying all things, assenting to the force of reason
and convincement" (554) conveys this tension between Truth as
absolute and Truth as process. Milton's position is not at this point
simply antinomianism, with personal truth transcending any institutional embodiment: he accepts the need for a state church and insists
that progress in the quest for truth has been made possible by the
"State prudence" of Parliament (570, cf. 490, 557). Milton's display of
rhetorical *copia* at once celebrates and exemplifies the "flowry crop

of knowledge and new light sprung up and yet springing daily in this City" (558). The truth emerges in dialogue, not simply in individual inspiration; some forms of power can make knowledge possible, and Parliament's pursuit of liberty is the "immediat cause" of the elevation of men's spirits (559). There is thus a convergence between the timeless truths of Christianity and the time-bound prudence of the classical polis. There remains, however, a strong tension: the evil of licensing is precisely that it encourages a "temporizing and extemporizing" attitude (531), a subordination of long-term inquiry to short-term interests, of knowledge to power. Authorized books, writes Milton after Bacon, *are but the language of the times* (534). In his analysis of the corruption of knowledge under empire and papacy, a more open and communicative rationality becomes subordinated to a narrowly instrumental rationality. *Areopagitica* conveys the intellectual and political ferment that emerges when those millennial processes begin to be reversed.

Far from merely calling for a retreat into the privacy of negative liberty, then, *Areopagitica* at once glorifies and embodies a revival of public spirit. And yet the civic humanist reclaiming of public space certainly did imply a redefinition of the private, and it remains to consider some of the implications of that redefinition. Though Habermas has hardly been true to his principle of dialogue with relation to feminism, his analysis does draw attention to problems of significance to feminist critique.[66] In the classical polis, women were normally denied access to the public sphere and confined to the household.[67] Insofar as the public sphere marked a return to the polis, it can be argued, it narrowed the scope for female agency. When Milton declared that "the whole breed of men" came forth from the household, he was translating Bucer's less explicitly gendered *cives* (II, 476). Just as the tragedians of the Athenian polis looked back with horror to an older order where women were allowed to corrupt the realm, so Milton was fiercely hostile to the influence of Charles's queen. Habermas points out that the emergent public sphere was a male preserve and that there are signs that some women resisted it for that reason.[68] In *Areopagitica* there is a strong emphasis on the "manhood" (487) or brotherhood (554-55) of reformers, recalling Carole Pateman's analysis of the seventeenth-century social contract as inherently fraternal and hence excluding women.[69] There is an unease about female agency on the figurative level: licensing is a Juno who tries to suppress the birth of Hercules, image of republican *virtù* (505).

And yet there was room for tension in Milton's attitude to gender roles. The private world of the household was after all a condition for public endeavor: Milton speaks of "the houshold estate, out of which must flourish forth the vigor and spirit of all publick enterprizes" (II, 247). Moreover, Habermas points out that the revival of the classical public-private split was asymmetrical, that the private sphere was not simply demoted but invested with a new affective significance as a sphere of intimate communication that would provide a base for the male's entry into the public sphere. As marriage took on this new ideological role it became involved in contradictions: as agent of society and emancipation from society, a site of patriarchal authority and of human closeness, liberation for the male and constraint for the female.[70] Those contradictions are of course obtrusive in Milton's divorce tracts. For Milton, speaking is just as crucial to the private as to the public sphere; he seeks "an intimate and speaking help...a fit conversing soul" as opposed to "a mute and spiritles mate" (II, 251). The *oikos* becomes a miniature polis. Puritans tended to give a strongly ideological character to the household as a kind of alternative public sphere, a counterweight to the corrupt institutions of church and state. And yet Milton insists that the head of the household should have a prepolitical, God-given authority and presents marital conversation as a relief, "delightfull intermissions" (II, 597). The woman's role is at once to provide dialogue and to listen to a monologue; she must become a vehicle for agency without herself achieving it. This is a textbook example of what Habermas describes as systematically distorted communication.

There is, then, a considerable irony in the fact that *Areopagitica*, that great paean to undistorted communication in the public sphere, should have arisen out of a crisis of communication in the private sphere. Nevertheless, there are unevennesses in Milton's impicit and explicit positions. The figurative strategies of *Areopagitica* point at the inadequacy of existing modes of representation, both linguistic and political, and it is striking that in his climactic image of the national body as sublime, that body shifts gender in midsentence (558). Milton recognized the crucial effects of new technology: the invention of the printing press opened up public access in a way

that potentially cut across not only class but also gender. Three of
Milton's poems of the 1640s emphasize the public role of women,
and two—or at least one—commemorate women who were involved in the public sphere.[71] Women were taking an increasing
interest in public affairs, to the extent of putting new pressure on
traditional voting rights. Although most parliamentarians regarded
the prospect of votes for women with horror, this position was not
universally adopted: John Selden, who is highly praised in *Are-*
opagitica, strongly insisted on women's fitness for high office.[72] Milton himself did not go so far, but he did praise Parliament for accepting petitions by women, a phenomenon that occasioned much
controversy; and in arguing against restrictions on prophecy he was
opening the way for the female writers and prophets who were to
become such a controversial feature of the 1640s and 1650s. Milton
made a remarkable identification with such figures when he included another quotation from Euripides on the title page of *Tetrachor-*
don, the tract immediately following *Areopagitica*:

> If you put new ideas before the eyes of fools
> They'll think you foolish and worthless into the bargain;
> And if you are thought superior to those who have
> Some reputation for learning, you will become hated.[73]

The speaker here is Medea, who denounces those who criticize her
for bringing up her children with unorthodox ideas.

Milton sets up in his readers at the very least a double take: Euripides was after all reputed to be particularly hostile to women, and
Medea is certainly no model heroine; yet her eloquence in defense
of her rights does exemplify the kind of boldness of speech Milton
is celebrating. He expected the title page to shock complacent readers, as we know from the sonnet he subsequently wrote in which
he envisaged a reader picking up the book and puzzling over the
title. The irony of the sonnet is that the strategy fails: the ignorant
readers, who are presumed to be presbyterians, stumble over the
harshly unnaturalized Greek word. Milton's communicative strategy
in his pamphlets is a complex one: he addresses an audience sympathetic to the classical polis over the heads of more conventional figures. On one level, this is certainly an elitist strategy, deliberately
evading more direct communication. Yet its social gesture is complex: the sixteenth-century scholars Milton admired had argued that

Greek was closer to the structure of English than Latin, more easily adaptable to the common understanding: evoking the Greek language and Greek political structures had a doubly populist aspect.[74] Milton defies conventional communicative structures that he regards as repressive in order to galvanize his readers into imagining new structures. I have tried to suggest that the text is not infinitely open, that it does have some very specific—and not entirely liberal—strategies to propose. Yet by engaging as strongly as it does in the materiality of discourse, by a politically self-conscious form of reflexivity, it points beyond its immediate contexts rather than merely tuning its voice "according to the time."

NOTES

This essay owes a particular debt to I. F. Stone, who at a Folger Institute seminar on seventeenth-century political thought raised the need to bring Greek ideas to bear on English discourse and also demonstrated that perhaps the public sphere has not entirely diminished to academic "interpretive communities." I am also grateful to Richard Burt, Edith Hall, Lorna Hutson, Peter Lindenbaum, and Diane Purkiss for discussion of specific issues, and to William Kolbrener for showing me the draft of a forthcoming article.

Citations from Milton's prose are from *The Complete Prose Works of John Milton*, ed. Don M. Wolfe et al., 8 vols. (New Haven, Conn.: Yale University Press, 1953-82). Citations from *Areopagitica*, which appears in vol. 2, give the page number only; citations from other texts give volume and page number.

1. For Foucault's claim, in a debate with Noam Chomsky, that there could be "no objection" (except from a bankrupt and sentimental humanism) to a proletarian revolution involving "a violent, dictatorial, and even bloody power," see Fons Elders, *Reflexive Waters: The Basic Concerns of Mankind* (London: Souvenir, 1977), 182. This exchange dates from Foucault's Maoist phase and cannot be taken as a final guide to his political agendas; the contrast with Chomsky's libertarian socialism, however, is interesting.

2. See, for example, Abbe Blum, "The Author's Authority: *Areopagitica* and the Labour of Licencing," in *Re-Membering Milton: Essays on the Texts and Traditions*, ed. Mary Nyquist and Margaret W. Ferguson (London and New York: Methuen, 1987), 74-96 (82).

3. This point is, however, often made by recent critics with an air of novelty, as if it had been covered up by a liberal humanist conspiracy; in fact it has been extensively commented on from David Masson's great nineteenth-century *Life* down to the Yale edition, as Michael Wilding points out in an important reading: "Milton's *Areopagitica*: Liberty for the Sects," *Prose Studies* 9 (1986): 7-38 (38 n.63). The dismissive term "liberal humanist" elides political complexities in the text's reception: the term hardly applies either to some of the communist sympathizers who extolled *Areopagitica* on its anniversary in 1944 or to George Orwell, who strongly criticized their willingness to suppress the facts about Spanish anarchism. See George Orwell, "The Prevention of Literature," in *Collected Essays, Journalism and Letters of George Orwell*, ed. Sonia Orwell and Ian Angus, 4 vols. (London: Secker and Warburg, 1968), 4:59 ff., and George Orwell and Reginald Reynolds,

eds., *British Pamphleteers, vol. 1: From the Sixteenth Century to the French Revolution* (London: Wingate, 1948), 68-69.

4. The most extreme postmodern reading draws on the work of the French *nouveaux philosophes* to demonstrate that in Milton's prose "the Third Reich speaks *avant la lettre*" and that "terrifying modern institutions" like "liquidation centres or gulags . . . rest on principles which are at least broached in texts like *Areopagitica*": Herman Rapaport, *Milton and the Postmodern* (Lincoln and London: University of Nebraska Press, 1983), 168 ff.

5. For a proposal to connect Foucault's analysis of the early modern period with that of historians of political thought such as J. G. A. Pocock, see Graham Burchell, "Peculiar Interests: Civil Society and Governing 'The System of Natural Liberty,'" in *The Foucault Effect: Studies in Governmentality*, ed. Graham Burchell, Colin Gordon, and Peter Miller (London: Harvester Wheatsheaf, 1991), 119-50. As Burchell notes (123), Pocock offers a history of citizens, Foucault a history of subjects.

6. Francis Barker, *The Tremulous Private Body: Essays in Subjection* (London and New York: Methuen, 1984), sees *Areopagitica* as "the text of a new power," its values the "*effect* of a powerful new dominion" (48, emphasis added).

7. For revisionist accounts, see Sheila Lambert, "Richard Montagu, Arminianism and Censorship," *Past and Present*, no. 124 (1989): 36-68, and "The Printers and the Government, 1604-1637," in *Aspects of Printing from 1600*, ed. Robin Myers and Michael Harris (Oxford: Oxford Polytechnic Press, 1987), 1-29. See also Blair Worden, "Literature and Censorship in Early Modern England," in *Too Mighty to Be Free: Censorship and the Press in Britain and the Netherlands*, ed. A. C. Duke and C. A. Tamse (Zutphen: De Walburg Pers, 1988), 45-62. I am grateful to Professor D. F. McKenzie for giving me copies of his unpublished Lyell lectures, which question conventional accounts of censorship and publication in the period. Both Lambert and McKenzie emphasize the role of the market as being at least as important as politics in limiting the circulation of books; but as theorists of "market censorship" have reminded us, markets are not necessarily unpolitical; and they would not have been regarded as such in the seventeenth century.

8. This is one reason why several readings have sought the text's unconscious meanings, which can more easily be made to yield the "liberal humanist" position it is expected to hold. For a critique of such readings, see William Kolbrener, "'Plainly Partial': The Liberal *Areopagitica*," *ELH* 60 (1993): 57-78.

9. Donald L. Guss, "Enlightenment as Process: Milton and Habermas," *PMLA* 106 (1991): 1156-69.

10. Peter Dews, ed., *Habermas: Autonomy and Solidarity: Interviews with Jürgen Habermas* (London: Verso, 1986), 159.

11. Neil Saccamano, "The Consolations of Ambivalence: Habermas and the Public Sphere," *Modern Language Notes* 106 (1991): 685-98, suggests links between the limitations of Habermas's historical analyses and the more general theory of the ideal speech situation. On the other hand, Foucauldian discourse can be accused of mechanistic rigidity in writing the possibility of critical discursive spaces out of history: in a revealingly static and reductive metaphor, Barker describes civil society as the "recto" of the state's "public verso" (Barker, *Tremulous Private Body*, 48).

12. Jonathan Scott, *Algernon Sidney and the Restoration Crisis, 1677-1683* (Cambridge: Cambridge University Press, 1992), 8. Scott's book provides some valuable contexts for Milton.

13. For an introduction to recent work in this area, see Richard Cust and Ann Hughes,

eds., *Conflict in Early Stuart England: Studies in Religion and Politics 1603-1642* (London and New York: Longman, 1989).

14. *The Perfect Weekly Account,* January 17-24, 1649, 357-58; quoted by Anthony Cotton, "London Newsbooks in the Civil War: Their Political Attitudes and Sources of Information," D.Phil. dissertation, Oxford, 1971, 327.

15. Thomas Fuller, *Ephemeris Parliamentaria* (London, 1654), Preface. I owe this reference to Joad Raymond.

16. On Habermas's debt to Renaissance humanism, see Victoria Kahn, "Habermas, Machiavelli, and the Humanist Critique of Ideology," *PMLA* 105 (1990): 464-76.

17. Elisabeth Young-Bruehl, *Hannah Arendt: For Love of the World* (New Haven, Conn., and London: Yale University Press, 1982), 362 ff.; for Heidegger's chilly response to Arendt's *The Human Condition,* see 307.

18. Hannah Arendt, *The Human Condition* (Chicago: University of Chicago Press, 1958), 27, 26 n.9.

19. There is no space here to explore the considerable differences between Arendt's and Habermas's concepts of practical reason; see Jürgen Habermas, "Hannah Arendt: On the Concept of Power," in *Philosophico-Political Profiles,* trans. Frederick G. Lawrence (London: Heinemann, 1983), 171-87, and Daniel Lubman, "On Habermas on Arendt on Power," *Philosophy and Social Criticism* 1 (1979): 79-98. Kahn, "Habermas, Machiavelli," makes a comparison between Machiavelli and Habermas somewhat comparable to Luban's between Arendt and Habermas: in each case, Habermas's ideal of consensus is seen as politically as well as philosophically limited.

20. The seminal work in this area is of course J. G. A. Pocock, *The Machiavellian Moment: Florentine Humanism and the Atlantic Republican Tradition* (Princeton, N.J.: Princeton University Press, 1975); see also Gisela Bock, Quentin Skinner, and Maurizio Viroli, eds., *Machiavelli and Republicanism* (Cambridge: Cambridge University Press, 1991).

21. Jürgen Habermas, *The Structural Transformation of the Public Sphere: An Inquiry into a Category of Bourgeois Society,* trans. Thomas Burger with Frederick Lawrence (Cambridge, Mass.: MIT Press, 1989), 5.

22. See the magisterial account by Charles Webster, *The Great Instauration: Science, Medicine and Reform 1626-1660* (London: Duckworth, 1975).

23. Leo Miller, "A German Critique of Milton's *Areopagitica* in 1647," *Notes and Queries* 234 (1989): 29-30 ("fast all zu satyrisch, auch wegen seines all zu affectaten styli an veilen orten ohne ursach gar obscur"). *Areopagitica* is not named in the letter, but Miller suggests that it is the only plausible candidate; it is just possible, however, that the reference could be to one of the divorce tracts. I am grateful to Dr. Timothy Raylor for providing me with a copy of this letter. Dr. Raylor has pointed out that Milton's relations with Hartlib were closer than has sometimes been suggested: see his "Milton and Hartlib," forthcoming in *Renaissance Studies.* Milton's *First Defence* was widely circulated, and censored, in Germany.

24. Sheffield University Library, Hartlib Papers 9/10/2A, 9/10/1A-B, letter to Hartlib March 29, 1647. The Hartlib Papers are quoted from transcripts prepared by the Hartlib Papers Project, University of Sheffield, by permission of the project directors and the university librarian. Contractions here and elsewhere have been silently expanded.

25. Letters to Hartlib, January 28, 1645, 13/70A; March 4, 1646, 13/136A.

26. Letter to Hartlib, March 11, 1646, 13/140A.

27. See J. A. W. Gunn, *Politics and the Public Interest in the Seventeenth Century* (London: Routledge & Kegan Paul, and Toronto: University of Toronto Press, 1969).

28. On Milton's ambiguous attitudes to commerce, see Wilding, "Milton's *Areopagitica*," 25, and Christopher Kendrick, *Milton: A Study in Ideology and Form* (New York and London: Methuen, 1986), 41 ff. and passim, and on their interaction with his conceptions of authorship, see Sandra Sherman, "Printing the Mind: The Economics of Authorship in *Areopagitica*," *ELH* 60 (1993): 323-47.

29. The news was carried in the latter pages of each issue, and the controversial political commentary was clearly the main object of interest. The author, John Streater, an ex-soldier who printed Harrington's *Oceana*, shows a strong awareness of the links made in the Greek polis between language and political action. Freedom of speech ensures the dominance of public over private interests: just as "the whole is before the parts" so "the publick should be before the private" (no. 9, June 13-20, 1654, 66). Though there is no evidence that Streater had read Milton, he certainly represents the kind of artisanal audience with a passionate interest in recreating the Greek polis that Milton was trying at once to reach and to create; criticisms of Milton's elitism risk patronizing the radical political culture of the day.

30. *The Life Records of John Milton*, ed. J. Milton French, 5 vols. (New Brunswick, N.J.: Rutgers University Press, 1950), 2311.

31. Thus in a sharply revisionist essay Abbe Blum asserts that Nedham was really a closet royalist and that Milton was complicit with him in exchange for Nedham's showering Milton with praise; unfortunately, she relies on dated sources and assumptions for her account of Nedham: Blum, "Author's Authority," 91-92, 96, and contrast Cotton, "London Newsbooks" chapter 9, and Joad Raymond, ed., *Making the News: An Anthology of the Newsbooks of Revolutionary England 1641-1660* (Moreton-in-Marsh, Gloucestershire: Windrush, 1993), chapter 8.

32. Barker, *Tremulous Private Body*, 49; Blum, "Author's Authority," 93 n.11, questions whether Milton argues for authorial copyright. Ambiguity arises from Milton's phrasing: he endorses that part of the 1643 ordinance that "preserves justly every mans Copy to himselfe" (491). The ordinance itself, however, definitely reaffirms traditional arrangements. I am indebted to Professor D. F. McKenzie for discussion of this point.

33. Lyman Ray Patterson, *Copyright in Historical Perspective* (Nashville, Tenn.: Vanderbilt University Press, 1968), 65 ff.

34. Peter Lindenbaum, "John Milton and the Republican Mode of Literary Production," *Yearbook of English Studies* 21 (1991): 121-36.

35. Hall to Hartlib, February 8, 1647(?), 60/14/20A.

36. Cited in *Complete Prose Works*, 2:86.

37. Cf. Milton's declaration in a subsequent tract, *Tetrachordon*, that more works would be forthcoming as "my public debt to your public labours" (2:579).

38. Sue Curry Jansen, *Censorship: The Knot That Binds Power and Knowledge* (New York and Oxford: Oxford University Press, 1988), 71 ff.

39. It has often been claimed that *Areopagitica* had very little contemporary influence: see, for example, Nigel Smith, "*Areopagitica*: Voicing Contexts, 1643-5," in *Politics, Poetics, and Hermeneutics in Milton's Prose*, ed. David Loewenstein and James Grantham Turner (Cambridge: Cambridge University Press, 1990), 103-22 (118). Though the point cannot be argued here, I believe that for a significant minority it had a considerable influence. For example, Noah Biggs's tract *Mataeotechnia Medicinae Praxeos* (London, 1651) draws heavily on some of the most celebrated passages in *Areopagitica* to call for the reform of

medicine. On Biggs and his possible links with the Boyle and Hartlib circles, see Webster, *Great Instauration*, 191, 263-64.

40. *Behemoth; or, The Long Parliament*, ed. Ferdinand Tönnies (London: Simpkin, Marshall, 1889), 3.

41. Thomas Hobbes, *De Cive: The English Version*, ed. Howard Warrender (Oxford: Clarendon, 1983), 88. In his antiepiscopal tracts Milton twice refers to Pericles, "a powerfull and eloquent man in a Democratie, [who] had no more at any time then a Temporary, and elective sway, which was in the will of the people when to abrogate" (1:640; on the funeral oration, see 1:701).

42. For discussion, see Annabel Patterson, *Censorship and Interpretation: The Conditions of Writing and Reading in Early Modern England* (Madison: University of Wisconsin Press, 1984), 115-16. While I agree with some of Blum's reservations about Patterson's analysis, her own reading of the title page as demonstrating Milton's narrowly individualistic self-aggrandizement fails to take any account of the Euripides quotation that makes up the largest single component.

43. Edith Hall, *Inventing the Barbarian: Greek Self-definition through Tragedy* (Oxford: Clarendon, 1989), 190 ff. On Thebes as the other of Athens, see Froma I. Zeitlin, "Thebes: Theater of Self and Society," in *Greek Tragedy and Political Theory*, ed. J. Peter Euben (Berkeley, Los Angeles, and London: University of California Press, 1986), 101-41, especially 116 ff.

44. *Euripidis tragoediae*, ed. Gulielmus Xylandrus (Basel, 1558), 424: "Democratiae uituperatio." Theseus's retort has the marginal comment "Tyrannidis uituperatio, & laus Democratiae."

45. Cf. *An Apology for Smectymnuus*, 1:876, where Milton attacks his antagonist's title pages for preempting open discussion.

46. Worden, "Literature and Political Censorship," 45-47.

47. I. F. Stone, *The Trial of Socrates* (New York: Little, Brown, 1988), 215-24; Stone notes the link with *Areopagitica* on 224.

48. Euripides, *Phoenissae*, l. 392. *Parrhesia* also occurs in five other surviving plays by Euripides. It does not occur at all in Thucydides; Isocrates, Milton's model for *Areopagitica*, used it twenty-four times.

49. Diane Parkin-Speer, "Freedom of Speech in Sixteenth Century English Rhetorics," *Sixteenth Century Journal* 12 (1981): 65-72 (67-68).

50. *Euripidis tragoediae: cum Latina Gulielmi Canteri interpretatione*, ed. Paulus Stephanus, 2 vols. (Geneva, 1602; Bodleian Don. d. 27-28), 2:116 (notes on *Supplices*; there are successive runs of pagination). Such topics as *parrhesia* were cross-referenced: a note on the word in the *Ion*, 672, refers the reader to the debate between Theseus and the herald. *Parrhesia* was translated as *libertas loquendi* or *dicendi*. On Milton's close reading and annotation of his copy, see Maurice Kelley and Samuel D. Atkins, "Milton's Annotations of Euripides," *Journal of English and Germanic Philology* 60 (1961): 680-87.

51. Milton quoted twice from the scene in his *First Defence of the English People* (4.1:440, 455). The exchange is also cited by another republican, Peter English, in *The Survey of Policy* (London, 1654), 57. On the Areopagus and Euripides in regicidal contexts, see also *Complete Prose Works* 3:205, 589.

52. David Davies and Paul Dowling, "'Shrewd Bookes, with Dangerous Frontispices': *Areopagitica*'s Motto," *Milton Quarterly* 20 (1986): 33-37; but see John K. Hale, "*Areopagitica*'s Euripidean Motto," *Milton Quarterly* 25 (1991): 25-27.

53. Joseph Anthony Wittreich, "Milton's *Areopagitica*: Its Isocratic and Ironic Contexts,"

Milton Studies 4 (1972): 101-15 (for a different ironic reading, from the school of Allan Bloom, see Paul M. Dowling, "*Areopagitica* and *Areopagiticus* The Significance of the Isocratic Precedent," *Milton Studies* 21 [1985]: 49-69); Patterson, *Censorship and Interpretation*, 111-19.

54. Cf. David Loewenstein, *Milton and the Drama of History: Historical Vision, Iconoclasm, and the Literary Imagination* (Cambridge: Cambridge University Press, 1990), 49 ff.

55. J. S. A. Adamson, "The Baronial Context of the English Civil War," *Transactions of the Royal Historical Society* 40 (1990): 93-120.

56. On the Areopagus as the aristocratic element in government, see Marchamont Nedham, *The Case of the Commonwealth of England, Stated*, ed. Philip A. Knachel (Charlottesville: University of Virginia Press, 1969), 105, and Algernon Sidney, *Discourses Concerning Government*, 3rd edition (London, 1751), 133.

57. Valerie Pearl, *London and the Outbreak of the Puritan Revolution: City Government and National Politics, 1625-43* (Oxford: Oxford University Press, 1961), 262-65.

58. Blum, "Author's Authority," 74, explains the inconsistency in terms of "Milton's desire both to repudiate and embrace a discourse of power associated with a principle of authorial autonomy"; rather than trying to locate such a uniform unconscious "desire" in Milton, I would see him as being far more uneasy about a presbyterian-dominated regime than about a republic established by the independents.

59. Leo Miller, "New Milton Texts and Data from the Aitzema Mission, 1652," *Notes and Queries* 235 (1990): 279-81. Though the republic's censorship regulations were particularly draconian, as in other periods the application of the regulations was inconsistent: see Michael John Seymour, "Pro-Government Propaganda in Interregnum England 1649-1660," unpublished Ph.D. thesis, Cambridge, 1977, 410-16.

60. Francis Barker, "In the Wars of Truth: Violence, True Knowledge and Power in Milton and Hobbes," in *Literature and the English Civil War*, ed. Thomas Healy and Jonathan Sawday (Cambridge: Cambridge University Press, 1990), 147-69.

61. Michel Foucault, "War in the Filigree of Peace: Course Summary," trans. Ian Mcleod, *Oxford Literary Review* 4 (1980): 15-19; cf. Francis Barker, "In the Wars of Truth: Violence, True Knowledge and Power in Milton and Hobbes," in Healy and Sawday, *Literature and the English Civil War*, 91-109.

62. Tom Paulin compares the "city of refuge" passage to Whitman: *Minotaur: Poetry and the Nation State* (London and Boston: Faber & Faber, 1992), 30-31.

63. On the politics of the Longinian tradition, see Michael Meehan, *Liberty and Poetics in Eighteenth-Century England* (London: Croom Helm, 1986).

64. On sublimity, cf. Smith, "Voicing Contexts," 109-10, and David Norbrook, "Marvell's 'Horatian Ode' and the Politics of Genre," in Healy and Sawday, *Literature and the English Civil War*, 147-69 (155-56).

65. Stanley Fish, "Driving from the Letter: Truth and Indeterminacy in Milton's *Areopagitica*," in Nyquist and Ferguson, *Re-Membering Milton*, 234-54, gives an excellent account of the ways in which the text summons its readers to continual self-criticism. While Fish recognizes, contra Barker, that Milton's individualism has political implications (253-54), he underestimates the extent to which Milton sees material institutions as potentially enabling, rather than simply resisting, change. He thus inscribes in the text the dualism he makes in his analysis of the modern academy, with the "literary" processes of reading cut off from the "political" world outside the academy (48-52).

66. For a nuanced critique, see Nancy Fraser, *Unruly Practices: Power, Discourse and*

Gender in Contemporary Social Theory (Minneapolis: University of Minnesota Press, 1989), 113-43.

67. This generalization, made by Arendt and accepted by Habermas, 52, is increasingly coming under challenge; one area in which women did have a public identity was in certain religious rituals, forming an interesting parallel with seventeenth-century women's quest for a voice through prophecy. (I owe this point to Margaret Williamson.)

68. Habermas, *Structural Transformation*, 33. Streater, *Observations*, no. 5 (May 2-9, 1654), 36, attacks dainty ladies who are unwilling to undertake household work.

69. See Carole Pateman, *The Sexual Contract* (Oxford: Polity, 1988).

70. Habermas, *Structural Transformation*, 43 ff.

71. Sonnets IX, XIV (to the wife of the printer and book collector George Thomason), and possibly X (to Lady Margaret Ley). See Anna K. Nardo, *Milton's Sonnets and the Ideal Community* (Lincoln and London: University of Nebraska Press, 1979), 43 ff.; Nardo accepts E. A. J. Honigmann's suggestion that the Ley sonnet was written to preface her edition of her father's writings. For a fascinating study of the possibilities offered by print culture for female agency—at least for those in the anomalous legal position of widows—see Maureen Bell, "Hannah Allen and the Development of a Puritan Publishing Business, 1646-51," *Publishing History* 26 (1989): 5-66.

72. Selden's *Ianus Anglorum* provides the epigraph for Charlotte Carmichael Stopes, *British Freewomen: Their Historical Privileges*, 3rd edition (London: Swan Sonnenschein, 1907).

73. Euripides, *Medea*, ll. 298-301, trans. Rex Warner, in *The Complete Greek Tragedies: Euripides 1*, ed. David Grene and Richard Lattimore (Chicago and London: University of Chicago Press, 1955), 69.

74. *The Three Orations of Demosthenes*, trans. Thomas Wilson (London, 1570), sigs. *ir ff. See also J. B. Trapp, "The Conformity of Greek and the Vernacular," in *Classical Influences on European Culture, A.D. 500-1500*, ed. R. R. Bolgar (Cambridge: Cambridge University Press, 1971), 239-44.

Power and Literature: The Terms of the Exchange 1624-42

Christian Jouhaud

This essay is about the relations between power and literature in France in the years of Richelieu's ministry (1624-42). Against soothing visions of literature—maintained sometimes by literary history itself—which tend to sanctify literary talent in claiming that good writers always have a vocation for liberty and that only the mediocre ones place their pens at the service of power, I would like to show, on the contrary, how the new values of literary purism, from which the profession of writer (*écrivain*) began to define itself, were produced in the context of dependence on political power. This notion of dependence demands a service rendered, which gives us pause. What does it mean to write in the logic of power? How do power and literature mutually profit when their energies overlap?

In 1985 Alain Viala's *Naissance de l'écrivain* appeared with the subtitle *Sociologie de la littérature à l'âge classique.*[1] Viala studied in this book the birth of the title of writer as a social qualification. He tried to show how, at a precise moment in French literary production (between 1630 and 1680), a social personage began to find himself defined by a specific activity of writing, which henceforward constituted his status, "whether as a mode of subsistence ... or as a mode of title."[2] The notion of *field* borrowed from the sociology of Pierre Bourdieu served as a base on which to construct the demonstration.[3] For Bourdieu the *literary field* is the space "in which one discusses what it means to be a writer"[4]—that is, a particular social space, endowed with a certain autonomy, contained within larger social spaces, which constitutes an adequate scale for analyzing literary production, relations between writers, and the relations of literature with other types of symbolic and economic activities. From the point of view of a social history of literature, the concept of field allows one to go beyond two unsatisfying traditions: the one that draws a direct connection between the social background of authors and the meaning of works, and the one that tries to dislodge a projection of global society in the works by resorting explicitly or implicitly to the concept of *reflection*[5] (not to mention certain historicizing attempts that have taken literature as documentary source, an amorphous echo of something else, while forgetting the—precisely literary—specificity of this source). To reason in terms of field amounts, on the contrary, to accenting the multiple and complex mediations between the space of the writers and the space of the works (between professional itineraries and aesthetic choices, between the plot of careers and the elaboration of works).

For Viala, what is known as the classical age is the moment when the first literary field is formed. This eruption of a new social space is the fruit of a powerful process of autonomization. "New forces" assert themselves through the struggle for literary purism. But, after having conquered an initial autonomy marked by the birth of new institutions, by the appearance of new forms of recognition, and by the transformation of audiences and of sociabilities, this moment is fettered by political power, which confiscates it (the uncompleted process again becoming active, however, after this momentary halt). Elsewhere, I endeavored to criticize this conclusion, even as I underlined its important methodological breakthrough.[6] Starting from the analysis of a practice of writing that Viala noted for its "omnipresence" ("duplicity"),[7] I tried to make evident the determining weight of political models on literature at the moment when the constitution of the field was beginning—a social and institutional weight but a weight on the practices of writing as well. From there I ventured to define the birth of the new social space particular to literature as a political rationalization of the surrounding space, the *cultural field*. Autonomy was acquired in the context of an increased dependence on power; this dependence could no longer pass for a "confiscation" but became the initial condition of the construction of autonomy, a constituent element of the first literary field.

Along with Viala, I accorded a great importance to the Fronde

(1648-53) as a catalyst of the process under way. I defended else-where the idea that the crumbled power of the party leaders during the Fronde did not correspond to some sort of feudal reaction, but, on the contrary, marked during a period of state crisis the success of absolutism as a model of domination.[8] In this perspective, it seemed necessary to proceed to the question of the relations between litera-ture and power at the time of Richelieu, that is, at the moment when this model of domination asserts itself and literary purism develops as a value.

The starting hypothesis is thus that the virulence of political mod-els in literature asserts itself during Richelieu's ministry, considered as a specific moment in the political history of the French ancien régime. I wished to establish an empirical approach in order to pose the problem of the relations between literature and power. I let myself be carried by the dynamic and the particularities of two con-figurations of events: the quarrel of the *Cid* and the crisis of 1630-31. The literary quarrel, which is a moment of exacerbated tensions, seemed to me for that reason to reveal an inventory of fixtures: practices, remarks, positions suddenly aired in public. The political crisis of 1630-31, the "great storm," as it is called in the title of a well-known article by Georges Pages,[9] is a moment of choice between two politics and, at the same time, a turning point in the career of Cardinal Richelieu, who eliminates the devout party, the great force of opposition to his politics and his power. To start from two events whose own dynamic goes well beyond the question of relations between literature and power allowed me to avoid considering liter-ature and power as two already constituted domains when my aim was to ponder the construction of these two notions. It spared me as well from having to think from the start in terms of dependence or domination and allowed me to establish the notion of *exchange*.

Furthermore, the context of events called forth the names of writ-ers, from which little by little the dominant figures of the relation emerged: Guez de Balzac, Pierre Corneille, Jean Chapelain, and a few others. Around them—Chapelain, in particular—the acts of the exchange are the subject of a second part. The reconstruction of Chapelain's career and the study of his rise to power served to build a coherent series of acts of exchange marked by concentration and intensity. From this series and to conclude, I extracted three modes of exchange that are significant but not exclusive: collaboration, mobilization, and availability for service.

Two Figures of the Exchange

The Quarrel of the Cid

Corneille's play *Le Cid* was first performed at the Theater of the Marais in Paris in the first week of January 1637, and from the first performances its success was resounding.[10] This success meant instant distinction and gratification for the young writer (he was thirty-one years old at the time). The play was performed three times at the Louvre and twice at the Hôtel de Richelieu. Corneille was accorded an annuity, and, as of January 27, his father received letters of ennoblement.[11] In addition, Corneille decided to publish *Le Cid* very quickly, thereby forcing the actors of the Marais to give up their exclusive profit from the play. *Le Cid* was published, with unheard-of haste, at the end of March. One consequence was a rapid diffusion of the text in the provinces.[12]

This triumph soon encountered shadows, and in April several attacks on the *Cid* appeared.[13] Corneille responded, and what is known as the quarrel of the *Cid*—a violent pamphlet war of several months' duration—began. Power, in the person of Cardinal Richelieu, took a close interest in the matter. He intervened in two ways. During the spring of 1637, he encouraged the Académie française (officially created in 1635) to take an interest in this affair, and at the beginning of October, he ordered the various protagonists to halt their battle of the pen (and they obeyed).[14]

The academy studied the debate and settled it with a judgment made public in December. As the editor of Pellisson's *Histoire de l'Académie française* remarked, it was a way to launch the academy.[15] What occasion could be more striking for the academy to establish itself publicly as an agency of legitimation and consecration, to install and demonstrate its authority, and, at the same time, to silence the objections of the Parlement of Paris, which refused to register the academy's letters of creation? The parlement feared that the new institution would encroach on its power of censorship, which was already a cause of heated dispute with the Sorbonne (the Faculty of Theology). By addressing the issue of the *Cid*, the academy demonstrated both its specific character as a literary assembly and its ambition to dominate the territory over which it had just been installed. On June 13, the academy announced that it was going to examine the *Cid*; on July 9, the parlement finally registered the letters patent of January 1635 that established the academy.

Just as much as the theatrical rules and the propriety of the play—against which G. de Scudéry (1601-67) directed the attack that launched the quarrel[16]—the theme of the confrontation is Corneille's management of his success. In addition to the éclat of the first performances and the haste in publishing the play was the scandal provoked at about the same time by the appearance of a piece of verse by Corneille (entitled *L'Excuse a Ariste*) that seemed like a manifesto of self-glorification and disdain of other writers:

> My work without support rises to the Theater
> Each is free there to blame or idolize it,
> There, without my friends professing their sentiments
> I sometimes snatch too much applause,
> There, content with the success that merit brings
> By illustrious advice I dazzle no one,
> I satisfy at once both populace and courtiers,
> And my verses in all situations are my only partisans;
> By their beauty alone my pen is esteemed:
> It is to myself alone that I owe all my Fame,
> And I think nevertheless I have no rival
> Whom I should offend if I treated him as my equal.[17]

Why were such verses, apart from the thundering pride they express, perceived as a dangerous provocation? Where did the danger lie? The verses emphasize, on the one hand, distance from the friendly and professional solidarities of literary men and, on the other, direct contact between author and public as the sole legitimate foundation of success, thereby implying that success may be based on the secret of a technique (of an art) cultivated in solitude.

Such propositions manifested a rupture with professional practices and with a theoretical approach that had finally appeared to triumph in the preceding years. Corneille himself had not long before expressed the importance of the confraternity of authors, opening an edition of his play *La Veuve* (1634) with twenty-six prefatory pieces by friends and colleagues.[18] Many among them, beginning

with Scudéry, would be his adversaries in the quarrel. The traditional practice of mobilizing other authors at the start of a work spoke
of the importance of the judgment of peers, of belonging to a body
with common interests. The Corneille of the *Excuse a Ariste* turned
his back on all of this in the name of his own success.

The rupture illuminates the real stakes of the debate over the
respect of theatrical rules. It is not a matter of knowing, as has been
said, whether or not the *Cid* respects the rules, but of verifying that
at the time when theorists were attempting to provide a basis in reason, through rules, for theatrical success, Corneille was defending
another idea of success. For the triumph of the rules was also the triumph of a group of theorists and practitioners who based a professional solidarity, a group identity, on knowing and respecting these
rules. By asserting his independence and claiming his success as
secret and as alchemy, Corneille delivered a forceful blow that his
adversaries and former friends denounced as the intention to establish a tyranny. Scudéry wrote at the end of his *Observations sur le
Cid*: "I was obliged to point out to the author of the *Cid* that he
should content himself with the honor of being a citizen of so fine a
republic without imagining inappropriately that he may become
tyrant of it."[19] His tyranny established itself through the seduction of
theatergoers by the novelty and by the secret of pleasing.[20]

Secrecy or publicity of reason, solitary power to seduce or codifi-
cation of the conditions of success through group solidarity (a solidarity that, obviously, does not exclude hierarchies)—one cannot
help being struck by the political tone of this debate. We must not
yield too quickly, however, to analogies. Let us remain on the terrain
where the fight began. The protagonists bear, each in his own fashion, the evidence of a relation between a writing and a professional
behavior. We shall follow this trail by plunging into the melee.

What is known as the quarrel of the *Cid* is a group of thirty-seven
texts, all very different from one another in size, editorial presentation, and tone.[21] Some are really small books, others simply loose
sheets. Fifteen of them are hostile to Corneille, fourteen are favorable toward him, and the others maintain a balance. These figures
show that the author of the *Cid*, contrary to so many assertions, is
not the poor, innocent victim of a cabal: he wages a combat that he
provoked and did not flee.

These texts, which are often complex, form what I have called

elsewhere a "polemic meshing of gears."[22] One publication brings on
a response, which itself gives rise to another. From one to another
the tone rises, the polemic violence grows stronger, a dynamic displaces the debate. Thus, from an academic quarrel one ends up questioning the persons involved. One unmasks the adversary even as
one conceals the position from which one speaks, unless, on the
contrary, one brandishes it, the better to prove the legitimacy of the
attacks. This dynamic says a good deal about the values that traverse
the social world of writers. At the start, the values proper to literature as a specific activity are put forward. By the end, the ordinary
values of seventeenth-century urban society seem, on the contrary,
to have brutally invested (or reinvested) the social space of the literary: birth, wealth, career apart from literature (offices, for example),
integration with aristocratic clienteles. There are many examples
that could demonstrate this argument; I mention only the one that
seems to me the most striking. One of the adversaries of Corneille,
Jean Mairet (1604-86),[23] was very violently attacked in *L'avertisse-*
ment au Besançonnais Mairet. The attack focused on Mairet's origins—his geographic origins (Franche-Comté is a land of the Empire,
which allows one to call Mairet a German) and especially his social
origins ("you are of no better household than his [Corneille's] valet
de chambre"). The only riposte in the *Apologie pour Monsieur*
Mairet would be to publish a long paternal and maternal genealogy
intended to prove the honorability of his birth.[24]

This polemic, which at the start has the theater as its object, can
itself be analyzed as a sort of theatricalized spectacle on the public
stage in which questions of the theater are treated. One notices then
the effects of the staging of violence (Corneille menaced by beat-
ings), the recollections of the diffusion of these lampoons (a peddler
declares, "It is these scoundrel poets . . . who fight by picking at each
other with their beaks like fishwives: it is already a week now that
we have spread their insults").[25] One notices, above all, a contradiction. In front of the readers—so many real or potential spectators of
the theater—an action is performed (the battle of the writers). The
progress of this action results in the revelation of a certain number
of traits of the social world of writers: their disloyal professional
practices, their social origins, the values for which they are fighting,
their appetites, and so forth. All of this is exposed, indiscriminately,
to the public eye at the very moment when writers are debating

whether the public has the right and the ability to legitimate a literary work by its approbation or rejection. This debate rests first of all on the idea of a classification or ordering of the public, of a discrimination between the public suitable for legitimating and the "populace," who must be distanced from the theaters or silenced. Now, the quarrel plays before the clients of peddlers and calls for their arbitration:

> Messieurs les poètes . . . under the pretext of defending yourselves, you yourselves have broadcast your infamy and each of you reproaches himself for what is the most unbecoming to your condition: I could not have imagined that our poets, wishing to pass for gentlemen, would heap each other with insults like the porters of the Grève with fisticuffs.[26]

As actors in the quarrel the poets thus identified themselves with the portion of the public whose access to the power of legitimation they tried to deny. One could read there a sign of their inability to have themselves recognized as an agency of legitimation, and, in a parallel way, their inability to establish the legitimacy of judgment of that part of the public they recognized as suited for legitimation. Still, the critics, who were generally both theorists and practitioners forged with the theatrical rules an instrument destined to establish, or at least to stabilize, the criteria of legitimacy. The restoration of Aristotle's rules, or what one presented as such (it matters little here), that is to say, the respect for verisimilitude (*vraisemblance*), for decorum (*bienséance*), and for the famous "unities" (of time, place, and action), ought to permit one, despite the promiscuity of the shared spectacle, to divide the public into three groups. The learned (*les doctes*) are initiated by their knowledge of the rules into the secrets of representation. The cultivated folk (*honnêtes gens*) are capable of being moved by the correct effects of the regulated theater even though they do not always perceive its reasons. The populace is incapable of understanding, feeling, or being touched; tragedy makes them laugh.[27]

In the eyes of their heralds, theatrical rules would thus have the virtue of creating social differentiations within the public. Without them, everything would be confused, from the best tragedy to the buffooneries of showmen. Thanks to them, a solid barrier can be erected between the second and third groups. Thanks to them, masks fall: those who are refractory or impermeable are abandoned to an irreversible process of popularization. The others may be taught; this is, for example, the goal that La Mesnardière, a man very close to Richelieu, proposes in his *Poétique*, which appeared in 1639.[28] Behind these debates on the public two stakes emerge: on the one hand, the recognition, for a public of "cultivated folk," of the capability to judge and, thereby, to consecrate a work; on the other hand, the strengthening of the writers' central role through the diffusion of a teaching, of a doctrine, that gives access to this right to judge and that amounts to the defense of their interests as a specific professional group.

The quarrel of the *Cid* reveals at once the elegance of this fine edifice and the contradictions that undermine it. Among these contradictions, three in particular reveal the extent to which the literary field was at that time a barely sketched out space, open to energies that have come from elsewhere:[29] (1) The triumph of rules in the theater, established at the beginning of the 1630s, seemed to consolidate the solidarity and social identity of writers, but it took only a Corneille, engaged through the brilliance of his success in a personal strategy, to claim to be a partisan of the rules and *at the same time* to turn away from the solidarities of a milieu, for the beautiful republic to seem at the mercy of a forceful blow that his adversaries could repulse with only the rules as weapons—rules once more invested with stakes that far exceeded them. (2) The dynamic of the confrontation betrays what it needed to hide: the values that construct literature as a specific activity can barely stand up to values that are more brutal, more efficient in categorizing people, and more comprehensive. (3) The academy alone really profited from the quarrel. The polemic battle had the effect of an appeal on the debates held in prior years.[30] Those debates resurfaced in this new framework. By settling the quarrel, the academy, stimulated and controlled by Richelieu, would also thus cut off these long-standing debates; its power would be retroactive. The academy rose to this power through the values of the writers' social world, but, once power gave it the authority to consecrate and to define literary purity, the academy confiscated those values and would practice only the solidarity of a strictly controlled body.

The "Great Storm" (1630-31)

Georges de Scudéry (1607-67), the most prolix of Corneille's adversaries in the quarrel, had solicited the intervention of the man who held the role of pontiff of belles lettres in his provincial retreat, Jean-Louis Guez de Balzac (1597-1654).[31] The latter had replied very politely but sided rather with Corneille ("it is a little more impressive to have satisfied a whole kingdom than to have written a well-ordered play").[32] He recalled that he, too, had been at the center of a six-year (1624-30) literary quarrel that erupted after the publication of his *Lettres*. This work had meant success for him but also violent attacks, sometimes formulated in terms similar to those used against Corneille. They had reproached Balzac too of claiming by his very success a "usurped sovereignty."[33] Support from Balzac, perhaps unexpected, was not an unmixed advantage for Corneille: Balzac's literary authority was immense (in part, moreover, because of his withdrawal and the rarity of his interventions), but he had experienced a political disgrace, which since 1631 had effectively confined him to his seigneurie of Balzac, near Angoulême.

In 1631 Richelieu had gained the upper hand after the very grave political crisis of November 10 and 11, 1630, known as "the day of the dupes" (because his adversaries at one point believed they had triumphed and obtained his dismissal, before changing their expectations), in which his power had seemed to vacillate.[34] He had finally succeeded in eliminating the opposition movement known as the "devout party" and had pushed into exile the queen mother, Marie de Médicis, who protected this party.[35] This reversal of the situation, whether real or apparent (perhaps Richelieu had never been threatened), was a magisterial political coup, as de Pontis, a former officer of the king's guards, described it in his *Mémoires*:

> At the point when one already regarded Cardinal de Richelieu as a man entirely beaten down by the party of those who hated him and with no hope of ever being able to rise again, he fooled in a second all his enemies, and by one of the shrewdest political coups ever seen, he trampled those who triumphed over him.[36]

Also in 1631, Balzac published *Le Prince*. Everything suggests that he cared a great deal about this text, from the announcements that preceded it to the attention given to the appearance of the very beautiful first edition.[37] The book celebrates at great length and from page to page Louis XIII and his politics, which are systematically praised, including the aspects that displeased the devout party. Still, it was very quickly apparent that the book displeased Richelieu. The text of *Le Prince* is followed by two epistles to the first minister, the first dated August 4, 1630, and the second March 3, 1631. Balzac announces in these epistles the appearance of a second volume and a third, the manuscript of which, he claims, was already addressed to the cardinal, inasmuch as it deals with the minister's specific role. Neither of these volumes was ever published, either because Richelieu prevented their publication, or, more probably, because Balzac, disgusted by the welcome given his first volume, abandoned the idea.[38] *Le Prince* met, however, with a rather favorable public reception, as evidenced by numerous editions and references to it by many authors. But power gave it a hostile reception, while it was precisely the approbation and support of power that Balzac was seeking. He failed in his effort to convert his literary success into political success.

The second epistle to Richelieu gives an important place to the crisis of November 1630 (eleven out of thirty-three pages). Balzac especially evokes the most critical moment. He absolves Richelieu of the accusations made against him and to this end insists on the minister's disarray faced with the queen mother's furies:

> If you have the misfortune of not being agreeable to a Princess, at least you do not have to reproach yourself for being unfaithful to her.... The request she made of the king to remove you from his affairs was not so much a result of her indignation against you as it was the first blow of the conspiracy that had been formed against France and that they had presented to her under the guise of devotion so that she believed herself worthy in ruining you.... I imagine that you are not content with this fortune, your possession of which does not please everyone.... having worked for such a long time and so completely toward the perfect Union of Their Majesties, I do not doubt that it causes you real displeasure to see your labors ruined and your work destroyed.[39]

Tallemant des Reaux, whom one must use with caution and consider as a good rumormonger, says that Richelieu called Balzac a "giddy person."[40] Basically, Balzac had presented on a public stage, which his literary authority made vast, a version of events that displeased the cardinal. He emphasized, in a manner that he believed suitable for justifying it, the weakness of power subject to the hazards of relations between a mother and her son. Moreover, to do this he adopted a position of enunciation that made him seem to share the best-kept secrets, as if he lived in a sort of intimacy with the cardinal. Finally, these remarks appeared to be out of sync with the dynamic of the action: what could be said, barely, at the end of 1630 was no longer appropriate in the spring of 1631, when Richelieu had finally prevailed, his enemies were routed, and he sought in every way to make a show of his strength to discourage any oppositional propensities.

Maybe Balzac really was a thoughtless person, for he had been warned by Richelieu himself, seven years before, in a letter finally added to his collected letters. We must cite the essential passage in this letter:

> The ideas behind your letters are strong and as far removed from ordinary imaginations as they are conformable to the common sense of those who have superior judgment. The diction is pure, the words as carefully chosen as possible so as to have nothing affected about them, the sense clear and distinct, and the sentences harmonious and well rounded. This feeling is all the more frank since in approving everything that comes from you in your letters, I did not conceal from you [the fact] that I found dissatisfaction with what you included about others, fearing that the freedom of your words might suggest that there was the same freedom in their temperament and manners, and might cause those who knew them more by name than by conversation to form a judgment of them other than the one you yourself would have intended.[41]

Let us take seriously the two aspects of this judgment: criticism and praise. The liberty of the letter writer's words shocks the cardinal when he speaks of others, that is to say, to the powerful persons that Balzac chose as correspondents (among them, Richelieu, when he was already a cardinal but not yet first minister). What would be acceptable in a private conversation is no longer acceptable when there is a risk of uncontrolled divulgence. Balzac's main adversaries had emphasized the impropriety and danger—indeed, the obscenity—of his statements (*énoncés*),[42] but Richelieu objected to a form of enunciation (*énonciation*). The publication of a collection of letters (most of them real but reworked) has the effect of displacing remarks apparently made in a private sphere into a public space. As a form the letter carries with it a sense of realness, which takes effect at the moment when it is diffused as a literary production (and even as literary prowess). From that moment there is great risk that a contradiction will appear between the two public faces of the important persons concerned: between the private face, which the letter makes public, and the face that their social position or political function requires them to wear in public. It is possible, to be sure, that no contradiction would appear, but the risk of its cropping up depends on the writer; he has, in this particular form of enunciation, the power to bring forth the contradiction and to make it subversive.

At the same time, by his stylistic praises, Richelieu accepts and recognizes the letter as a literary form. He does not subscribe to those criticisms that denounced the letter as false eloquence and the source of immoral descriptions of the ego.[43] His stylistic arguments are clear: fertility of the *inventio* (strong conception and surprise), precision of the *dispositio*, force of the *elocutio*, to return to the classifications of ancient rhetoric. The reference to purity of diction underscores the theatrical dimension of the letters: they are definitely related to eloquence, that is to say, according to Furetière's *Dictionnaire*, to "the art of saying well ... things appropriate for persuading."

Hidden behind these compliments, behind this acknowledgment of the letter as a practice of eloquence, are important stakes. The term *diction* underscores the fact that the letter form creates a framework that transforms the written into an oratorical action (fictional but benefiting from the real effect evoked earlier). From the start, Balzac's *Lettres* were defined as an exercise in eloquence, as a new form of eloquence that built its persuasive effect on the theatricalization of a relation, the description of which was entrusted to an indirect account (with the same narrative status as narratives in a play). In addition, the *collection* of letters multiplies the situations of communication and the modes of interaction between correspondents, juxtaposing in this way forms of eloquence with recipients.[44] All of this calls into question again the canons of the art of oratory, whose rules were constructed upon a classification of discourse, based on the reality of a limited number of oratorical actions and corresponding to a similarly limited number of circumstances and places for public speech: harangues made in front of the great in councils or assemblies, pleadings in a court, sermons in church.

Balzac's eloquence, if crowned with success and transformed into a model, would thus have a *delocalizing* effect on the criteria by which eloquence is appreciated. In other words, it would prove by its effectiveness that one can do without the legitimate circumstances of oratorical action and still be persuasive (whether these circumstances are real or produced in writing matters little: it is the allegiance to received criteria that counts), and that one can divert the energy from these circumstances toward literary purism.[45] Still more important: the art of persuasion, which depends on seduction, thus finds itself separated from the ends that justify one's recourse to it, such as public service, edification, the interest of the state, and so forth. Taking the place of all of this is a theater, the representation destined for all of the relation of one soul (the one who writes) to another (the one who receives the letter), an eloquence that is founded on an illusion[46] and that, moreover, asserts itself as a new model of faultless eloquence.

If the perfection of eloquence may be produced outside the places of oratory action, then these places lose their power and their right to recognition and consecration, as much over the new forms as, consequently, over the forms that integrated themselves with their logic (panegyrics, memorials, etc.). This process is a displacement not simply of places or circumstances but of authority: the "public" of readers and specialists who define good taste[47] is substituted for the public of peers in which the values and solidarities of those bodies that practice oratory action are embodied. This displacement of authority toward the values of a literary purism under construction also has a political dimension. As the prefacer of Balzac's *Lettres* writes: "We are no longer [living] in that time when one publicly blamed the government of the State and when orators held lieutenants-general of the armies to account and ... in consequence there is no longer a possibility of this sort of eloquence."[48]

We see a link of "sympathy," in the old sense of the word,[49] being built here between the expansionism of literary purism and the expansionism of a power caught up in the management of *corps* (bodies) and institutions inherited from the past. This dispute over the authority of corporate solidarities made the terrain of public eloquence available to the only public speech free of corporative constraints, not that of the king, Louis XIII, a stammerer, but that speech of which the second prefacer of the *Lettres* boasts when he evokes that other eloquence, which is lively and animated both in voice and in action, that makes you reign sovereignly in the assemblies; it is certain, Monseigneur, that this incomparable quality makes you more powerful there than does the authority that the king has entrusted to you: the tone of your voice alone has an occult property to charm all who listen to you.[50]

Can one guess well enough to whom these praises are addressed?

Like a player who immediately risks his winnings, Balzac with *Le Prince* risks in the political arena the literary gains of the *Lettres*. But he does not heed the warning of 1624: in his second epistle he applies to Richelieu the imprudent writing that the latter had reproached him for using with regard to "others." In Balzac's eyes, the *unveiling* of the crisis of 1630-31 could have for his readers an accrediting effect on the whole of the treatise: he who is thus capable of penetrating the ultimate secrets of the great clearly demonstrates that he has a vocation for dissertating on the actions of the king and on the government of the state. Richelieu's reading was completely different. Instead of perceiving the pertinence, he detected the impertinence and danger of the book.

The rejection of *Le Prince* had consequences for the career of the author, who we know dreamed of political office and who would have accepted a bishopric, but it also cost him a good deal of his credibility, since the condemnation came from a virtuoso in politics. One could go further and put forth the hypothesis that Balzac committed another error in appreciation. The *Lettres'* delocalizing of eloquence held great interest in the eyes of power, but this interest should not have led the author to take politics as a subject. By producing a displacement that served the action of power, he acted, willy-nilly, as a political agent in the territory of literature; he was integrated with a logic of political action. In posing as a political author, he abandoned this logic and this function in order to enter, without offering the necessary pledges, into the sanctuary where the reasons that explain the interest of a politics of literature for power (whose ends are not literary but political—which is itself a political secret) are kept.

One may test this hypothesis with the example of an author, Jean Chapelain, who made choices opposite from those of Balzac. In 1633, he writes for Richelieu a *Jugement sur l'Histoire des guerres de Flandres* of Cardinal Bentivoglio.[51] Criticizing the bias of the Italian cardinal in his account of the revolt of the United Provinces against Spain (1577-1609), he opposes a French model of overstepping religious confrontations through the arbitration of the state (for its own greater benefit) to the Spanish model of a sterile and bloody confrontation with Protestantism, which is dangerous even for the Catholic religion. On the one side, the reason of the French state, on the other, the "indiscreet zeal" of the Spaniards. This latter expression attracts attention because it was often used by Richelieu and his propagandists to describe the devout party (defeated in November 1630).[52] If one follows this trail, one notices that Chapelain systematically employs expressions and, especially, styles of reasoning that parallel the positions and analyses of Richelieu and his entourage. Now, this text is not a political work but a critic's reflection on the art of writing history. By transposing segments of political thought borrowed from Richelieu, he implicitly refers to the moment when they definitively prevailed in the politics of the state, without saying anything else about this crisis, and he inscribes his writing in a logic of political service.

It is striking to see that this opposition in the way of referring to the "great storm" of 1630-31 is encountered again, in a much more obvious but essentially identical form, in the polemic that opposes Matthieu de Morgues, the most ferocious pamphleteer against Richelieu, exiled to the Netherlands in 1631 with Marie de Médicis, and Scipion Dupleix, the first minister's favorite historian. The latter published in 1635 his very official *Histoire du regne de Louis le Juste*, which the former criticized very violently in the months that followed.[53] Dupleix divided his account of the crisis of November 1630 into two chapters. By the logic of this account, the central moment, the "day of the dupes," ought to be situated right at the juncture of the two chapters. In fact, it is completely passed over, the division making this omission plausible (one passes from the *causes*, which are set forth in one chapter, to the *effects* in the chapter that follows). De Morgues, on the contrary, dwells at length on this one moment.

Ten years later, after Richelieu's death, Dupleix restates his position on this affair in a renewal of the polemic against de Morgues. This time he evokes at length the entire crisis. He inventories in detail the reasons of each of the protagonists, analyzes the why and wherefore of words spoken and deeds carried out. He concludes that Richelieu's reasons were on the side of *la raison (politique)*, for they alone were capable of explaining the reasons of others. He pragmatically reproduces against his own adversary, herald of the party that the cardinal conquered, the conqueror's line of reasoning. The reasons of the victorious political action thus become the reasons of the writing of the history of this victory. Political reason is thus used here as an active model of rhetorical action.

The "great storm" of 1630–31 is at the center of the career and action of the all-powerful minister. It is also a discriminating moment in the construction, the definition, the establishment, in the logic of power, of writing as a specific form of service. By the accounts they give of it, some betray themselves: others, by their good usage, display in action their political sense.

The Acts of the Exchange

Jean Chapelain (1595–1674): The Race to Leadership

Why Chapelain? One used to learn in school, in the *Satires* of Boileau, that he was the ridiculous author of a monstrous epic poem of thirty thousand lines. We know also that he played an important role at the beginning of Louis XIV's personal reign in the organization of the state's patronage of letters. In reality, he had a long time before, in the course of what one might call a first career, already appeared to win the race to leadership in the literary field. It is this career that I would now like to try to reconstruct. We have already caught a glimpse of how well Chapelain, with his *Jugement sur l'Histoire des guerres de Flandres*, knew how to demonstrate his political sense without ever taking politics as his subject. Let us follow this trail in order to analyze his literary penetration.

Jean Chapelain was born into a well-established family of notaries in Paris.[54] He received a very solid education, first with a tutor, then in the colleges of the University of Paris, where he benefited from the teaching of two great humanists and followed the usual path that proceeded from rhetoric to philosophy. He then undertook the study of medicine, which he interrupted in 1614.[55] In the course of these studies, he seems to have shown a great interest in and a great aptitude for both ancient (Latin and Greek) and modern (Italian and Spanish) languages. All of this led him to the start of a "normal" career for someone of his social rank and education: thanks to the recommendation of two bishops, to whom his teachers introduced him, he entered as a domestic into the aristocratic family of Sebastien le Hardy, marquis de La Trousse, who would soon become *grand prévôt* of France.[56] There he took charge of all of the children's education. This occupation led him to follow the court in its travels and to make valuable acquaintances.[57] He would live in this household until the death of the marquis in 1632 and would thereafter maintain very close ties with his former pupils. The marquis had procured for him the otherwise modest office of archer of the *prévôté*, which he resold in 1633. His long stay in the domestic service of the *grand prévôt* thus allowed him to prepare a rather spectacular social ascent.[58]

It is in his functions as tutor that he made his beginnings in literature. He translated for his pupils *Le gueux ou la vie de Guzman d'Alfarache*, which he published in 1619 (at the age of twenty-four). Four years later, a very attractive opportunity presented itself. The great Italian poet Marino ("the cavalier Marin"), who had lived in France since 1615, wished to publish his epic poem *Adonis*, dedicated to King Louis XIII, with a preface in French. He turned to Malherbe, who did not wish to perform the function of prefacer, but it appears that he recommended the young Chapelain, Italianizing and very learned. Marino, then at the height of his career, was an important personage in the salon of the marquise de Rambouillet (herself of Italian ancestry). His *Adonis* finally appeared in 1623 with a very theoretical preface by Chapelain, who tried to present there the poetic rules in usage in Italian literature.[59] This French preface, sustained by the Italian poet's celebrity, called attention to its author and procured him a brusque renown, more especially as Marino died two years later without having published anything else.

In 1627, Chapelain was received into the aristocratic circle of the Hôtel de Rambouillet, which Marino had frequented. He too would become one of the principal guests, even if his beginnings there, effected under the protection of Robert Arnauld d'Andilly, were rather awkward.[60] We must dwell a moment on the importance of the marquise de Rambouillet's salon.[61] A salon—and this was the most prestigious—is a place of worldly pleasures but also a place where one reads (out loud), where one discusses, where one makes judgments and groupings that extend beyond it. The marquise withdrew at a very young age from the court and from courtly ostentation, but her salon maintained close ties to the court. Princes of the blood attended; the debates held there found their way even to the king's chambers. To enter the salon had a distinguishing value, even for the highest aristocracy (in the construction of this value, Italianism plays a role, as does the principle of the free "election" of members). This capital of distinction allows one to combine the strictest social closure with an openness to a small number of participants of modest birth who are considered to have great talent. Through these meetings, the salon becomes the locus of good usage, as Vaugelas defined it: "It is the way of speaking of the most sane part of the court, *conformably with* the most sane part of the authors of the time." Vaugelas's "conformably" finds there a concrete meaning.[62]

At about the same time, Chapelain began to correspond with Guez de Balzac and to participate in the meetings of a small group of literary men who gathered at the home of the royal secretary Valentin Conrart and who would become the nucleus of the Académie française. Despite a fairly short list of publications, Chapelain began to appear as a key figure of the literary life and of the circles in which the question of literature was debated. But his rise was far from complete. The years 1632 and 1633 were crucial for him. He succeeded at that time in another form of breakthrough.

In a letter of September 25, 1632, he writes to Balzac that "fortune has come to tempt me,"[63] alluding to the proposal that had just been made to him to leave as secretary of the embassy in Rome with the comte de Noailles. One also finds in his correspondence a tremendously interesting letter addressed to Charles Leclerc de Tremblay, the brother of Père Joseph, Richelieu's main collaborator (the gray eminence). In this letter, Chapelain beseeches Tremblay's intervention to help him obtain the Roman post and assures him in advance of his gratitude.[64] Seven months later everything seemed to be set; Chapelain was ready to leave. But he then learned very disturbing news: Francois de Noailles decided that he would not be entitled to the title of secretary of the embassy, that he should be in charge of his domestic affairs as intendant, and that his entire correspondence would be subject to the ambassador's review. So it was that the prestigious post (the same one that Cardinal d'Ossat had held at the start of his prestigious career) turned into a banal charge of ambassador's domestic, which brought Chapelain back to his beginnings. He would not hear of this.

From then on, a single question presents itself to him: how to get out of this affair? Two dangers haunt him. To refuse the post on the eve of departure could seem to be an insult to Noailles, who is well heeded at the court and the brother of a bishop, and to be a sort of insult as well to Leclerc de Tremblay, the younger brother of the all-powerful Père Joseph. As a good strategist, Chapelain will get out of this position of weakness by an offensive. Since the beginning of the year 1633 he has been working on an *Ode à Richelieu*; it is not yet finished, but he sends Richelieu a rough draft, while humbly soliciting his corrections. At the same time, he forwards to Richelieu a first version of his judgment on *L'Histoire des guerres de Flandres* and asks him to forbid his trip to Rome: it is a sort of poker play based upon an offer of service, the sincerity of which his productions come to prove in action.[65]

One week later, Boisrobert, a close adviser to Richelieu for everything that concerns literature and those who write it, informs Chapelain that his reflections on Bentivoglio's book were well received, with one reservation: the cardinal objected to the passage in which he emphasized the importance of the duty of judgment for the historian, considering, for his part, that the historian does not have to judge, but to deliver a simple narration of the facts. Through the intermediary Boisrobert, Chapelain answers and maintains his position in favor of judgment, setting it forth at length, which represents a new act of audacity.

This response should be examined closely. Without judgment, he says, history would be incapable of fulfilling its function, which is to be useful. The historian's judgment substitutes for the reader's lack of judgment (of reasoning) and thus creates a space of credibility. But this implies that the historian has a very precise profile: he must be a right-thinking man, strengthened by an exact reading of the Ancients, informed "by reliable and unreproached memoirs," dispassionate. Those who do not have these qualities not only are incapable of expressing a judgment, but could not even aspire to the writing of history. He well understands why Richelieu is hostile to this right to judgment: "through the just apprehension that the historian will make dangerous use of it." But, he adds, without judgment the situation would be much more dangerous since "each man would be his own historian" or "would reason in his own right on the past and on the future." The key to the question lies thus in the quality of the service of the one who judges, the same service that he is in the process of proposing to the cardinal.[66]

On May 1, 1633, in a letter to Boisrobert, Chapelain announces that he amended his ode following Richelieu's indications,[67] and a few days after his letter concerning judgment, he sends him a revised version of his text on *L'Histoire des guerres de Flandres*. The changes seem minor; we must, however, take them seriously. In the first place, he no longer explicitly defends the need to judge. Then, the very sense of the word *judgment* undergoes an interesting slippage. In the first version, it is a question of a piece of writing with a specific rhetorical status, by which the historian promotes himself to the rank of judge (in this regard he deplored, as a defect of Bentivoglio's work, its small number of judgments). In the second version, the rhetorical specificity disappears; judgment becomes simply a way of presenting things, of constructing the account: the notion is thus superimposed on that of partiality (for which Bentivoglio had been reproached). Chapelain seems to resist the cardinal; he argues against him very sensibly and in the very name of power, but, in practice, without appearing to touch it, he deletes that which caused his new master to react, as if he wished to illustrate the profession of fidelity formulated in his letter:

> Although outwardly I can only call myself a man of Monseigneur since he gave me permission to do so and you made his consent public, it is, nevertheless, true that I have been devoted to him from the time he was called to the leadership of our affairs ... I find strength in my weakness and believe myself able to undertake anything in his name.[68]

On August 5, 1633, Chapelain would finally have the privilege of being received by Richelieu. This encounter left him speechless[69] but not penniless, since starting from that day he received a bonus of a thousand livres a year, which was converted to an annuity the following year.

The year 1633 was definitely a lucky one for Chapelain. Very shortly after his entry into the first minister's service, the duc de Longueville summoned him and offered him patronage for his *Pucelle*, under way since 1625. The duke was a descendent of Dunois, one of Joan of Arc's companions, and he hoped that his ancestor would be well treated in the epic poem that some people were already calling a new *Iliad*. To achieve this he would gladly spend two thousand livres on an annual pension, punctually paid to the new Homer. This is, in any case, Chapelain's version of the story. One may add to it a few supplemental remarks: In the first place, this recognition through history and epic was of great interest to the duc de Longueville, who was fighting at that time to achieve the status of prince of the blood. In the second place, it is very possible that Chapelain had initiated urgent measures on several sides at once, in order to extract himself honorably from the Roman muddle.[70] Finally, his double engagement would permit him to play the intermediary between Richelieu and Longueville. Since they were more or less on good terms, there would be no conflict of loyalties. While awaiting the appearance of *La Pucelle*, its author did not remain inactive in the service of the Longuevilles. He regularly wrote poems about family events (births, cures, deaths), composed devices, and maintained a regular correspondence with the duke, particularly when the latter was with the army, which was frequently the case after 1635. He kept him informed of what was being said, and done, in Richelieu's entourage and at the Hôtel de Rambouillet. He kept an eye on what was written about his martial actions, and he wrote or controlled the articles that appeared in the *Gazette*.

During all these years, Chapelain also maintained a regular correspondence with Guez de Balzac. In general they wrote each other weekly (from 1632 to 1654); Chapelain's letters have survived for the years 1632 to 1640.[71] One discovers there that the two men performed multiple services for each other. These consist first of all in numerous bits of information: Chapelain tells Balzac of Parisian literary life and at the same time transmits military and political news. He sends him books and other objects and oversees the relations of the hermit of the Charente with his Parisian publishers: he corrects manuscripts and proofs, diffuses texts that are still unpublished and watches the reactions they elicit, particularly at the Hôtel de Rambouillet.[72] He also serves as a mediator to ease conflicts and quiet sensibilities.[73] In short, he acts as Balzac's representative to the world of the book trade, to the places of legitimation, and to other writers. Chapelain is not Balzac's only Parisian contact, but he is the best placed to fill all these roles at once. One may even say that, to a large extent, he controlled the path that led to the writer retired in his province, all the more so since the latter announced that he would write no more letters.[74] Those who wished to reach him had to pass by way of Chapelain, who thus filtered the access to one of the places of literary consecration, or at least of recognition. Moreover, in this correspondence classifications are also adjusted through a series of exchanges of judgments, which develop and then congeal after several round trips: it is there that the critical values of literature and those of spontaneous social classifications intersect.[75]

These exchanges seem a bit unbalanced, in Balzac's favor. In March 1639, however, an affair that at first seems trifling, but whose stakes are revealed little by little, comes to balance this impression. A conflict broke out at the Hôtel de Rambouillet concerning the *Suppositi* of Ariosto. The poet Voiture (1597-1648), soon joined by the marquise's daughter, Julie d'Angennes, declared the play tedious and otherwise without interest. Chapelain, on the contrary, defended it. The first stake is doctrinal: Voiture condemns the Italian theater, appreciates the Spanish, relaunching a debate on the theatrical rules that was thought to be closed, especially in this high place of Italianism. From another perspective, the Hôtel de Rambouillet is for Chapelain an essential place from which spreads a preeminence conquered little by little over the social world of literary men. He would run a great risk in being worsted opposite the poet protected by Gaston d'Orleans (the king's brother). Consequently, we see him take this affair very seriously. He mentions it in at least ten letters and insists that Balzac be consulted. Balzac responds rather quickly and sends a whole *Dissertation critique* on Ariosto. One finds within it these lines:

> It will be the wise and learned Monsieur Chapelain who will tell it to you [i.e., the right advice], and I do not know why, being in Paris and only two steps away from the oracle, you wished to consult an old bag in a village.... Our incomparable friend will bring you to the castle-keep, will lead you through all the nooks and crannies, will enlighten you on the details and particularities of all things. He knows what I do not, and what the majority of doctors do not know well.[76]

This intervention closes the debate.

In sum, one will say then that Chapelain represents for Balzac a link maintained with the *center* of literary space, a way of continuing to act there, the hope of a return. This return will never take place, but Balzac, from a distance, remains strong enough to carry the victory for the one he supports in a literary combat. Chapelain performs important services for Balzac, even as he encourages him not to quit his retirement, which he paints for him in the colors of virtue.[77] Chapelain does everything to help Balzac maintain his authority and even to strengthen it, but it is in his interest that it continues to be exercised from retirement.

The court, the Hôtel de Rambouillet, the Arnauld family, Richelieu, Boisrobert, Longueville, the academy from the moment of its creation, Balzac: this enumeration of points of influence or support reveals the social surface of Chapelain. In adding to the list the learned circle of the brothers Dupuy, with which he maintains very good relations, one may draw a sort of star with eight points:

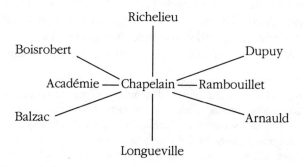

This schema shows how Chapelain benefits from an exceptional point of view over the places where one treats of literature, and it also reveals an extraordinary capacity for circulation from one to another. This ability to circulate and, thus, to comprehend each of the places in its particularity is the keystone of his success, of his fight for leadership in the literary field. Moreover, this circulation from one point to another constitutes the space it crosses as literary space (each of the points having, from another point of view, an implantation and its own sphere of influence and sociopolitical action). By his effective perambulations, the established author "makes literary" the spaces crossed and, thereby, unified. He creates a space for the literary. The struggle for leadership thus appears not only as a symptom of a literary field that is in the process of being constituted (a symptom of its very weak autonomy), but also and especially as an essential element in the construction of this field.

In a very remarkable letter addressed to Balzac on August 28, 1639, Chapelain himself implicitly evokes the importance of this ability to circulate for one who wishes to understand the complexity of the social space in which literature is discussed. He starts from the example of the marquise de Sablé's incomprehension of the writer Gilles Ménage (1613-92): she took him for an "extravagant man" because, Chapelain says, "they have a different style of reasoning." Since the marquise could not consider herself extravagant, she could not help but reproach for this defect a man so different from her, incapable as she was of pondering his difference. It was not, however, just a question of style: Ménage is "steeped in doctrine," expresses himself "in a style that is consistent with his sort of knowledge," and has a manner "completely different from [that of] the court," the only one that the marquise knows how to appreciate and interpret. Chapelain goes on to discuss a subject of great astonishment for his correspondent: the duc de La Rochefoucauld has never heard of Peiresc (1580-1637), an unequaled scholar, scientist, and pupil of Galileo:

> The study of this lord had nothing in common with that of the deceased who was a true and solid scientist who regarded readings of Mr. de La Rochefoucauld as amusements rather than as useful occupations worthy of a serious man. Each seeks and is willingly acquainted with his peers. Perhaps, by the same reason, the late Mr. de Peiresc likewise knew Mr. de La Rochefoucauld only for his birth and for that which history has bequeathed to us of the memorable actions of those of his household.[78]

On the one hand, two representations of the aristocracy, a salon marquise, a great military seigneur, and on the other, a young writer and a great scholar. All have a point in common: their enclosure in a language and in a position, however powerful it may be. The man who analyzes this fixity very obviously can only do so from his own position of mobility. Three comparisons come to mind here. The first is with Scipion Dupleix, who claimed that Richelieu had won in the crisis of 1630 because, alone among the protagonists, he had known how to reconstruct the logic of his adversaries' reasons. The second is with the *Lettres de Balzac*, which produced within the unified space of a book a series of accounts with separate linguistic (*langagières*) conventions (although all on the side of "fine style"). The third, less precise, is with the figure of the "respectable libertine," who, "playing the game of acceptable opinions...may confront them with the order of his own experience."[79]

With Ménage, Chapelain would remember the sound doctrine; with Peiresc (and, later on, with Gassendi), he would appreciate scientific discussions; with the marquise de Sablé, he would be a courtier and speak of poetry; with La Rochefoucauld, he would evoke the martial exploits of Joan of Arc (he had, moreover, had recourse to "military counselors" in order to praise them). This mobility, continuously assumed through the course of his career, reminds us that leadership is not a status that is conquered and then preserved, but a race that never quite reaches the finish; the slightest error slows it, and any fall threatens to end it. Chapelain's glorious success remains all the more fragile since the list of his publications prior to *La Pucelle* consists only of works written for special occasions (which are numerous, by the way) and theoretical writings. His influence depends first of all on his place in the institutions and circles of literary life and also on his connection to political power. The complexity of these networks strengthens his capacity to move among them, but it also multiplies the points from which threats may arise. The quarrel of the *Cid* thus shows itself, in practice, to be a moment of great danger.

Chapelain, however, begins the year 1637 in serenity. Seeing the quarrel burgeoning, he writes Balzac:

> I hope...[in] the year to come...to set myself up as a friendly arbitrator of differences between cultivated folk who make a profession of belles-lettres and those who do not completely resemble them; but let this hope remain secret between us, please, so that I do not need a mediator for myself and so that I always maintain my credit in this matter.[80]

He announces in these lines a sort of plan of action in three points: his willingness to intervene, in a posture that he is fond of, that of a friendly intermediary; his concern to preserve through secrecy his freedom of action; his intention, in acting, to increase his capital (to maintain his credit, which amounts to the same thing). But, as the weeks pass, the tension rises. In June, the academy decides, in response to Scudéry's appeal and on Richelieu's orders, to resolve the quarrel; it extorts (through Boisrobert) the indispensable consent of Corneille and names Chapelain judge. He sets to work. By the end of July he is extremely anxious. Richelieu did not like the first version of his text and curtly informed him that he found it too gentle toward Corneille.[81] At the same time, Balzac's letter to Scudéry, in which the author of the *Lettres* sides with Corneille, begins to circulate. On July 31, Chapelain writes to Boisrobert asking him to *beg* the cardinal

> to consider that I cannot have excused the *Cid* to such an extent in the course of the judgment I make of it, that I ruin it greatly in showing, both in this same course of judgment and by my conclusions, that it lacks the main things that are required for a dramatic poem to be good.

And he adds:

> But if His Eminence judges that the grounds I had chosen as best were not legitimate, assure him that I have no attachment to my opinions and that I remain in the submission and deference that any man of good sense must have for the sentiments of an intelligence so much higher than his own, and I shall follow them and conform to them entirely.[82]

But, on August 7, he writes to Balzac: "I am astonished that you believe that we can decide in favor of *L'Observateur du Cid* (Scudéry) after you wrote such a fine vindication for it and showed, in some sort, that you have taken this play under your protection."[83] On August 22, he is not far from panic:

> What troubles me and with a good deal of cause is to have to offend both the court and the city, the great and the small, one and the other of the contesting parties, and, in a word, everyone, in offending even myself over a subject that should not be treated by us; . . . there is nothing as odious and that a gentleman ought to avoid more than to reprove publicly a work approved by everyone because of its author's reputation or the success of his play: for the least that one may expect from it is to see oneself greeted by lampooners, satires, and curses, and to entertain the company.[84]

One finds expressed here the violence of the suddenly felt political demand ("to offend even myself"), the fear, in displeasing everyone, of drawing upon oneself the aggressiveness of both parties, to be neutralized as a pole of arbitration and beaten down by the combined forces of the adversaries. The most immediate threat: to find oneself the target of public libels and, especially, "to entertain the company." If the cardinal is not satisfied with his text, he will lose a part of the cardinal's confidence, and the cardinal will not be satisfied either with the academy, whose authority he wished to launch, and neither will the academy be satisfied with the one who benefits in its ranks from such a strong position and whom it named as its representative and judge. And so forth. What will a man who has lost the confidence of Richelieu be worth in the eyes of Longueville? His value will certainly diminish. And the Hôtel de Rambouillet, in the forefront of styles, will follow this drop in value, even as it aggravates it. And Balzac? And the others? The structure of the conquest of leadership, thoughtfully constructed, may rapidly collapse, struck by the contagion of losses, for the power Chapelain has in one place depends on that which he has acquired in another.

But beginning with autumn, the tone changes. The dangers that were so pressing a few weeks before seem to have disappeared. In December, the *Sentiments de l'Académie française sur la tragicomédie du Cid* is ready. Soon Chapelain will not hide the satisfaction he draws from it. He freely refers to it in his correspondence and endeavors to make it known that he is, indeed, its author.[85] From his point of view, the story ends well.

Three Modes of Exchange between Power and Literature

To collaborate:

Richelieu followed the drafting of the *Sentiments* very closely. Chapelain wrote an initial version that displeased him. A committee of members of the academy was charged with reworking this text; the result did not please him either. The cardinal then summoned Chapelain and two members of the committee of revision and demanded a new effort, entrusted to the academician Sirmond. It was another failure. They then came back to Chapelain, who had to set to work again on his first version in order to transform it. The definitive text was indeed produced from this last effort, after a final series of corrections, written in the margins of the manuscript from Richelieu's dictation.[86] Today we possess two versions of the text: the version published in January 1638 and Chapelain's manuscript, which contains numerous corrections. The latter has the title *Les sentiments de l'Académie française touchant les observations faites sur la tragi-comédie du Cid,* whereas the printed text is entitled *Sentiments de l'Académie française sur la tragicomédie du Cid.* The change is not insignificant: it reveals a little more ambition.

A comparison of the initial version (which is distinguishable on the manuscript before the corrections) with the corrected manuscript and with the printed text shows numerous differences. Since we know that the supercilious demands of Richelieu presided over the work of revision (set its direction, imparted a logic to it, and sanctioned it), we may consider that by minutely comparing these versions, we shall bring to light the very mark of power.

In the first version, the author (supposedly collective) places himself in the position of a judge, but a judge of a civil suit in which two parties are contesting and in which justice may not identify itself absolutely with one side alone. With this stated, the author turns toward one and then the other of the parties, who are both considered with the same benevolence. The adversaries of the *Cid* are asked to endure its defects with forbearance, its unconditional defenders to admit that Aristotle has more authority than they, and, especially, that there exist two sorts of pleasure, "one perfect, which is produced by perfect things, the other imperfect, which is engendered by the novelty of things rather than by their beauty." The theater has as its aim and raison d'être perfect pleasure alone. Votaries of pleasure at any price risk "resembling the populace which runs after marvels but considers unworthy of its curiosity that which is best ordered in the works of nature or of art, and which, satisfied with its ignorance, gets angry when one tries to disabuse it."[87]

The posture of judge-arbiter is a fiction, a staging of the speech, for, in reality, the scales are clearly tipped to one side. This scenography of an equitable judgment is endowed, as is every fiction, with its own efficacy. It makes the two "parties" into two respectable groups defending antagonistic positions with an equal legitimacy: it presents the quarrel as a public debate over a literary matter. But behind this staging, Chapelain is defending a position, expressed by the distinction between the two pleasures. Imperfect pleasure, qualified as popular, finds itself on the side of illegitimacy, whereas perfect pleasure draws its perfection from its conformity to reason, which nothing expresses better than the theatrical rules and their inventor, Aristotle. In this way, perfect pleasure finds itself transported to the side of utility, a notion that is presented in the fiction of the two parties as antagonistic to that of pleasure and that is thus identified with the camp of the adversaries of the *Cid* (since the demand for pleasure was the basis for constructing the camp of Corneille's supporters).

In the final version of the *Sentiments*, the posture of enunciation has changed: it is no longer a question of trial, parties, or arbitration. Nor is it any longer a question of debate. The appearance between the protagonists of a third actor, the "people," reorients the flow of the argument. The question of the reception of the *Cid*, of its effects on the spectators, will henceforth find itself at the forefront. It is no longer a question of arbitrating a public debate, but of explaining to the spectators why they liked the play. "Their mind, flattered by a few agreeable parts, has become readily flattering of all the rest." How so?

> Violent passions well expressed often produce in those who view them some part of the effect that they have on those who are really feeling them. They deprive everyone of his freedom of spirit, with the result that some delight in seeing represented the errors that others delight in committing. It is these powerful emotions that have elicited this great approval from the spectators of the *Cid* and that must also serve to excuse it.

To *excuse*: here is the key word. It is a matter of excusing the *Cid* for its success, which in no way legitimates the position of those who defend it. The spectators were victims of too sweet an illusion (victims of their pleasure). One must appeal then to their reason. The academy does not ask of them "that they speak out publicly against themselves; it is enough that they condemn themselves in private and that they surrender in secret to their own reason; this same reason will say to them what we are saying, as soon as it is able to resume its former liberty." From the fiction of a judgment one passes, thus, to an address to each reader, identified with each of the play's spectators. The intimate disavowal of an initial enthusiasm—a disavowal demanded of these readers—will remain secret, for the academy, it is precisely stated, does not ask for public recognition. But we know that, much to the contrary, there is no other stake in the business of producing this text than to cause the new institution to be publicly recognized as an agency of legitimation, its authority extending, thanks to the operation produced by this text, to the secrecy of private reasoning, opposed to the continued illusion of public confrontation. The "effect of writing" (*effet d'écrit-*

ure) poses the text as a direct rival of the effects of the *Cid*, but in a different sphere. As for the distinction between the two pleasures, it has completely disappeared.

Spontaneously, we would have a tendency to think that the second version, revised by Chapelain after the carping interventions of Richelieu, is further removed from the real opinions of its author because of these very interventions. Nothing is less certain. If one admits that the balance between the camps, ostensibly emphasized in the first version, had no other purpose than its own staging (since, in the end, it concealed a decision against the supporters of the *Cid*), one may then say that this decision is more clearly and more radically expressed in the second version, and one may then consider that the intervention of power permitted Chapelain to put forth his own analysis more clearly. We must ask, however, as counterproof, if renouncing the scenography of equitable judgment between two parties entailed a loss for Chapelain. We know in what a state of fear—so well expressed in his letters—he prepared this work. The scenography of the arbitration may be viewed in this framework as a way of keeping at a distance the conjugated aggressiveness of the protagonists of the quarrel, the danger of which he had analyzed.

Richelieu, through his demands for modifications, forced the academy and, thus, Chapelain to write unguardedly, to risk a sort of forceful blow in the polemicotheoretical space of the literary—in short, to be imposing. Richelieu pushed Chapelain, in that way, very close to the danger of neutralization, but he protected him from it at the same time, first of all by giving the order to halt the polemics.

Chapelain and the academy in the end profited from their submission to the demands of power, without experiencing the assaults of "lampooners and satires." This case shows how, in the context of dependence, a sort of association between power and literature, profitable to both parties, is built. It remains to say that Chapelain demonstrated on this occasion and, again, at a crucial moment the importance of his doctrinal competence. The *Sentiments* remains in this respect an impressive text, and it is this competence that enabled him to prevail over his colleagues when they were once ordered to take over from him.[88]

To mobilize:

It is the best known, or the least poorly known, aspect of Richelieu's relation to literature and especially to the theater. Writers find themselves clearly implicated in a service relationship that meets the needs of political power. The latter issues an order and the writers write. Theatrical pieces were thus staged in the context of court celebrations. The titles of six pieces commissioned by Richelieu between 1634 and 1642 are often mentioned: *La comédie des Tuileries, La grande pastorale, L'aveugle de Smyrne, Roxane, Mirame, Europe.* The first three are collective works, the last three were written by Desmarets de Saint-Sorlin.[89] In the first case, the association of several authors allowed them to proceed very quickly in order to deliver the commissioned piece on time. As for Desmarets, he was begged to abandon *Clovis,* his great epic poem, and to write continuously for the theater works that would be kept ready for an upcoming court festival. These feasts were given for carnival or some other event worthy of being celebrated (the wedding of one of the cardinal's nieces, for example). They integrated perfectly with a tradition of aristocratic expenditure, which with Richelieu doubled with a concern for governmental ostentation, especially after the beginning of the "open war" in 1635. They then assumed the dimension of a proclamation of confidence. The more their ostentation sparkled, spread by the printed word and ambassadors' reports, the better did power seem to be demonstrated. This demonstration for the use of the chancelleries was seconded by a demonstration of Richelieu's freedom of action, for the use, this time, of the court. This should not be forgotten when one evokes the themes and writing of these plays: the "taste" of Richelieu is scarcely the issue; what counts, especially, is the ability to make the best use of such demonstrations, first of all by mixing them harmoniously with the other festive sequences.[90]

The festival of January 14, 1641, in which *Mirame* was performed to inaugurate the Theater of the Palais Cardinal, has given rise to a very fine analysis by Timothy Murray.[91] *Mirame* formed only one part of the spectacle. The performance was followed by a light meal and a ball on the same site. The arrangement of these sites is important. The new theater was a house "à l'italienne" with a strict separation between the stage and the spectators. The latter were distributed among the galleries, whereas the king, the queen, and the cardinal were perched on a platform at the site of the parquet. Several consequences follow. The spectators in the galleries, duly armed with invitations, have been seated "each according to his condition": ladies, lords, ambassadors, foreigners, prelates, officers of justice, the military.[92] They find themselves seated in such a way that they are not facing the stage. Only the cardinal's group enjoys the privilege of a view. It occupies, moreover, a central position in the house, at the crossing point of the gazes of the spectators in the galleries. From this point of view, the spectators are all in the same uncomfortable position with respect to the stage, whatever their situation in the courtly hierarchy, and are precisely in a position of *spectators* with regard to the great actors of monarchical power: their gaze constructs power as a spectacle and themselves as actors playing the role of spectators in this spectacle and, thus, accepting the stigma of separation from the main scene of the action.

Staged in a logic of munificence, *Mirame* is a play with spectacular machinery, which, although it ostensibly proclaims its respect for the unity of time, hardly respects the new canons of the dramatic art defended, for example, by the academy (Desmarets was himself part of the commission that worked for a while on the *Sentiments*). Digressions and dramatic surprises abound. There was almost nothing that could satisfy "the mind of those who are competent to judge," writes the abbé de Marolles in his *Mémoires,* as if to conclude. But everything passes as if, *there,* that has no importance.

The theatrical performance is the moment when the order produced in the house by the distribution of seats seems to congeal. At the moment of the ball, the spectators divide into two groups, those who dance, raised upon a stage ("the princes, the princesses, the lords, and the ladies"), and those who watch the dancing, while remaining in their position of spectators ("all the rest of the assembly"). The *Gazette,* which reports this new division of roles, devoted more than a quarter of the editorial space of its seventh number for the year 1641 to recounting the festival of January 14. Less than half of this article refers to *Mirame,* mentioning in one sentence the "delicate thoughts" and the force of the reasonings but at much greater length the stage effects and the decor. The account passes without a break from the play to the rest of the festival ("the clouds of a lowered canvas entirely hid the theater; then thirty-one pages came in carrying a collation"). It is definitely a question in this official account of a single spectacle, in which the juxtaposition of sequences gives the impression to the spectators of having been "enchanted through the eyes and the ears."[93]

In the exchange between literature and power, the *mobilization* (here theatrical, because in the 1630s the theater carried all) is a simple process. This simplicity should not obscure other forms of the exchange. It is especially important not to confuse the series. In the court festival, the theater plays a role not much different from that of the ballet, for example (at least in its most recent evolution). In return, the theater as a specific form, autonomous and self-sufficient, is open to other forms of interpretation and uses. We must also distinguish between Richelieu, producer of the court spectacle, and Richelieu, viewer and reader of theater, in solitude or in the intimacy of the small group of faithful friends.

To make available:

At the beginning of his account of the quarrel of the *Cid*, Pellisson declares: "All those who felt they had some talent did not fail to work for the theater: it was the way to approach the great and to be favored by the first minister who, of all the entertainments of the court, savored this one almost exclusively."[94] He pinpoints thus the extraordinary growth of the dramatic art in the field of literary productions. The literary form offers "opportunities" to an enterprising spirit. This craze was accompanied by an unprecedented effort at theorization, often published in the prefaces to plays or the forewords.[95] Several of the protagonists in the quarrel signed similar theoretical passages: Scudéry did, and also Mairet and Corneille. And, as one may expect, Chapelain. Before the *Sentiments* and after the preface of the *Adonis* he wrote two fundamental texts that apparently remained unpublished at the time. One, entitled by its twentieth-century editors *Lettre sur la règle des vingt-quatre heures* and dated November 29, 1630, presents itself as a response to a letter of Antoine Godeau (1605-1672). Everything allows one to suppose that it circulated rather widely in manuscript form in the concerned circles. The other, also in manuscript, was written for Richelieu shortly afterward; it is entitled *Discours de la poésie représentative*.

The first sentence of this treatise reads: "Representative poetry, as well as narrative, has the imitation of human actions as its object, verisimilitude as its necessary condition, and marvel as its perfection."[96] Here at the start are presented the three cardinal elements of Chapelain's poetics: imitation, verisimilitude, marvel. One may recognize there three concepts drawn from Aristotle. But that is only of secondary importance. What really matters is to mark what purpose they serve for Chapelain. The imitation must be so perfect "that no difference appears between the matter imitated and the one who imitates ... for the main effect of the latter is to propose to the mind, in order to purge it of its unruly passions, objects as true and present." This purgation of the passions is accomplished through identification or through vaccination. Let us remember simply the postulation of a powerful effect of theater upon the spectator and the association of the idea of utility with that of imitation. A political reading presents itself here, as practiced by Chapelain himself in the *Sentiments*:

> Bad examples are contagious even for theaters; sham representations cause but too many genuine crimes, and there is a great risk in amusing the people with pleasures that may produce public sorrows: we must be very watchful that neither their eyes nor their ears become accustomed to actions of which they should know nothing.[97]

The second concept, verisimilitude: it is the universal key to imitation (there is no imitation without verisimilitude). The theatrical rules were decreed only so that it would be respected, and also understood and thus reproduced. It is a simulation of the truth, better suited than the truth to arouse belief (indeed, the truth is sometimes horrible, unbearable, *unlikely* [*invraisemblable*]). Verisimilitude may be of two sorts: ordinary ("these are the things that ordinarily happen to people according to their circumstances, their ages, their manners, and their passions") or extraordinary ("all the accidents that happen unexpectedly and that one calls fate, provided that they are produced *by a series of things that happen ordinarily*").[98] It is verisimilitude that permits the theatrical *illusion*: that permits one to produce it by giving the spectator the impression that the thing represented and its scenic representation are superimposed with nothing left over, that permits one to think it, to reproduce it, and thus to make foreseeable (and thereby controllable) the effects of the representation.

Marvel: the force of the theatrical effect comes from the pleasure it procures for the spectator. Verisimilitude is a necessary condition for the delivery of pleasure, but it is not a sufficient one. The true art of the dramatic author is to extract the marvelous from the probable (*vraisemblable*): the delectable surprise ought to arise from that which seems to dismiss any possibility of surprise. "Since the difficulty of it is extreme, it is also that which so often makes the results unsuccessful; it is that which causes so many people who despair of succeeding in it to make use in the construction of their works of this false marvelousness that produces things that are not likely and that one may call monstrous." The marvelous (as opposed to the monstrous, which demeans both writers and spectators) springs from a series of rational linkages that conform to the logic of the spectators' habits (and, as a consequence, to that of the characters constructed with reference to the spectators' expectations) and that conform to the logic of the represented actions. This marvelousness emerges from the respect of a whole set of constraints that are woven to a point of dizziness and followed to the point of obsession. It is for this reason that the "invention" of a play (its intrigue) is considered the delicate moment in its writing; the versification is only a secondary operation.

Imitation, verisimilitude, marvel: these three notions trace the contours of a coherent and self-sufficient theoretical ensemble. They engender each other, forming a closed space in which any theatrical action will be contained and considered. It was convenient here to remain in dialogue with Chapelain, but he is in no way an isolated theorist. The most radical and most complete formulation, with a few exceptions, will be proposed by the book of the abbé d'Aubignac, *La pratique du théâtre*, published in 1657 but formulated from 1640 at Richelieu's demand.[99] In all of this theoretical elaboration, there is one common and central point: oriented entirely toward the spectator, it subordinates the production of the work to a reflection upon its reception, *it is constructed from a logic of effects.* Thus, is it speaking, consciously or not, of anything other than the theater? Can it bring answers to questions posed elsewhere, publicly or secretly? Among these "elsewheres" that are in resonance with theatrical theory, does politics hold a special place, or is it even the locus of the resonance? One could respond to these questions by a whole series of analogies that are more or less hastily constructed;[100] I would simply like to describe the contours of an *availability*.

Let us reread the *Lettre sur la règle des vingt-quatre heures*. Chapelain recapitulates there the goals and conditions of theatrical illusion: it is

> better to surprise the spectator's imagination and lead him without obstacle to the belief that one wishes him to take in that which is represented to him ... to make what is pretended like the truth itself, and to make the same impression on the mind of those present, through the expression, as the thing expressed would have made on those who had witnessed the genuine success ... to remove from those watching any occasion to reflect on what they see and to doubt its reality.

This program describes theatrical representation as an act of persuasion with two principal characteristics: the spectators are passive (one must surprise them, lead them, etc.), and the act of persuasion does not depend on that of which one wishes to persuade (it finds itself totally removed from the question of truth, of morality, of the legitimacy of that in which one wishes to inspire belief). What is said about belief, in the context of a poetics of the theater, connects very well with the beginnings of a theoretical reflection that takes action as its object—a reflection, for example, on political persuasion through the intermediary of the printed word (lampoons, broadsheets) or of imagery.[101] In both cases, it is to an art of effects, to a technique, and to a postulated reception (and, thus, to an analysis of the conditions of the reception) that the charge of persuading is entrusted. In this perspective, theatrical action, just like political action, builds its effectiveness on the association of a secret, in which the *reasons* of the action are constructed, and of a spectacle in which the action is publicly represented.

The joining of the two domains, as if by a mirror image, may be pursued. One takes to dreaming when one discovers in the *Fragments politiques et maximes d'Etat* of Cardinal Richelieu the story of a murderous anger of Alexander that is also the plot of the *Roxane* of Desmarets de Saint-Sorlin, or when one bears in mind that Chapelain's phrase "better to surprise the spectator's imagination and lead him without obstacle to the belief that one wishes him to take in that which is represented to him" figures in a text dated November 29, 1630, barely two weeks after the day of the dupes, Richelieu's great coup de théâtre. The "marvel," this delectable surprise, which ought to follow from an implacable respect for verisimilitude, may be read both as an inoffensive gloss on Aristotle and as an expansion of the theory of the coup d'état of the man of power,[102] unless it is a question, on the contrary, of a concept offered—made available— to political theorists of the "coup d'état." In that perspective, one can consider that the theatrical theory is provisionally substituted for a political theory that shies away from or at least lags behind the action. Moreover, in a time of theatricalized politics, when any status must be proven by the capacity of the one who holds it to assume it publicly at the court and elsewhere, the theater offers a sort of worst-case test. It is the place of the greatest difference between the thing represented and the representation, between that which is shown (ancient histories, distant places, extraordinary situations) and the means of showing it (words that conjure images and stage effects) and, at the same time, the place of the greatest proximity, since the aim is to tend toward the exact superimposing of the represented and its representation, in order to "remove from those watching any occasion to reflect on what they see and to doubt its reality." The action of representation, which succeeds in giving the illusion of the *presence* of the thing represented, whereas all the other forms of representation (including the symbolic) rest on the postulate of the *absence* of the thing represented as a very condition of the representation, is endowed with an exceptional force.[103] The evidence of the presence of the thing represented realizes the ideal of perfect eloquence, as starting from a rational and reproducible action.

For this theater, when it is tragic, takes politics as its object.[104] It displays a political drama in representing this drama through an action that "replays" it. This action offers itself as an exercise of speculation for the man of power who knows the secrets of the representation (verisimilitude, marvel, and their political counterparts). For the one who monopolizes political representation (reserved for power in the absolutist system), the theatrical action tells, once again, how to weave and to unravel a represented action through a rational action of representation. For the others the theatrical representation produces its effect of usefulness and pleasure *but remains opaque.* Thanks to verisimilitude, the learned may reproduce (or understand the reproduction of) the effects of illusion. But this does not mean that they enter into the secrets of politics, even when politics is the object of the theater. It is enough that they respect (or understand) through the verisimilitude the strict logic of the actions; the actions then develop according to their own dynamic and go beyond them. Indeed, the political theater (whose reasons are theatrical) is not separable from a politics of the theater (whose reasons are political). Legitimate theatrical production integrates itself with a political design to which the producers of theatrical writing do not hold all the keys. Power will tend to consider, contrary to the learned, that the border within the public is not between the *honnêtes gens* and the populace but between, on the one hand, the learned in poetics *and* in politics, and, on the other, the mass of the spectators, whom the passive sharing of the spectacle popularizes and makes suitable for receiving, indiscriminately, the effects of the representation.

This would be the pleasure of the man of power at the theater: to contemplate the represented action as finding its ultimate meaning only in the gaze that he casts upon it (the only gaze that is truly informed) and to contemplate it, nevertheless, as completely successful through the simple observation of the effectiveness of its effects upon the passive spectator that, *for once,* he is also. In a single glance, he would discern thus the secret intention, the motives of the action, its results, without mediation, delay, or remainder. This instantaneousness could pass for the dream of power about itself. Corneille, who triumphed with the *Cid* and lost the battle of the quarrel of the *Cid* for having reproduced, on a lesser scale, the errors of Balzac, returns with *Horace* in 1640 after three years of silence. The dedicatory epistle offered to Richelieu (and accepted by him), if it recalls in veiled terms his pretensions in the quarrel, shows above all that he knows henceforward what the theater means for the cardinal. A new version of the secret of the art of pleasing that he claimed to possess?[105] Why not take seriously, if he has discovered the secret of the power that dreams, the sentence that today unfailingly makes an audience smile when it is recited before them: "The service we are rendering to the State is not a small one, since contributing to your amusements, we are contributing to maintaining a health that is so precious and so necessary to it."[106]

"If I have some talent of which I may boast, it is politics, of which, apart from the disposition I may have for it from birth, the ancient Greeks and Latins and the modern Italians and Spanish taught me the reasoning and application."[107] It is Chapelain who writes these lines. A central figure of literary life since the beginning of the 1630s, a fighter for purism, he avows his feeling and his taste for politics: we have been able to measure that we must take these remarks seriously. And what is most political about him is his ability not to confuse literature and politics, to act politically in the specific sphere he helped to construct. Indeed, this distance maintained between the two domains through a political rationality favors the creation of a space peculiar to literature that is autonomous from the constraints as well as the solidarities of a wider cultural field.[108]

If there is autonomy, it is not with respect to power. The quarrel of the *Cid* shows well enough the fragility and the contradictions of the literary field. Its values, slowly elaborated by writers who seek to establish the criteria of legitimate success, shatter at the first shock: the success of an author is transformed into a threatening *coup de force*, whereas the interests and social roots that one expected theory to keep at a distance turn into a farce the spectacle of the theorists' confrontation. And power decides: it instigates, it suspends, it commands, it exploits, it protects. It is not a small matter to manage to establish the force of consecration of a new and totally artificial institution. Autonomy, without which there would be no literary field, is constructed very much in the context of dependence. It does not establish itself at the expense of political power, which, on the contrary, sustains it. It is forged through separation, through a decanting of the cultural field, through the reexamination of values and former solidarities.

From this point one may speak of a logic of service. Balzac fails at it; Chapelain succeeds. As for Corneille, he probably passes from the errors of Balzac to the lucidity of Chapelain. But in the meantime, literary production is transformed: the promises of Balzac's *Lettres* seem to be realized in the theater. Desmarets de Saint-Sorlin abandons *Clovis* for the theater, and Chapelain's *La Pucelle* constantly gives way to more urgent tasks. The operation of the delocalization of eloquence achieved by Balzac strangely overlapped with certain objectives of power, whose own energy could in other respects serve as a model for obtaining rhetorical victories. This face of the exchange introduces the imprecise silhouette of a solidarity between power and literature. If a political rationality allows one to construct the social space traversed by established authors as a literary space, and allows them to carry off theoretical victories, in return, literary theory and the practices of the theater aestheticize political action. They give to the brutality of its effects, to the reality of its violence, to the disorder of its constraints the coherence of a narrative that, arisen from a tabula rasa (or from a web of artificially built constraints, which amounts to the same thing), proceeds toward a fulfillment. Literature contributes thus, finally, to the autonomization of politics, disconnected from its ultimate goals, by producing it as art.[109]

Translated by Mary-Ann Quinn

NOTES

A shortened version of this essay was presented at the Shelby Cullom Davis Center Seminar, Princeton University, April 1990.

1. Alain Viala, *Naissance de l'écrivain. Sociologie de la littérature à l'âge classique* (Paris: Minuit, 1985).

2. Alain Viala, "Du caractère d'écrivain à l'âge classique," *Textuel* 22 (Winter 1989): 49-57.

3. Pierre Bourdieu, *La distinction, critique sociale du jugement* (Paris: Minuit, 1979); *Questions de sociologie* (Paris: Minuit, 1980); "Champ intellectuel et projet créateur," *Temps modernes* 246 (November 1966): 865-906.

4. As a gloss to this aphorism, pronounced by Bourdieu during a radio broadcast: "Irreducible to a simple aggregate of isolated agents, to an additive whole of elements that are simply juxtaposed, *the intellectual field*, in the manner of a magnetic field, constitutes a system of lines of force: that is to say that the agents or systems of agents that belong to it may be described as so many forces that in positioning themselves, opposing and compounding themselves, confer on it its specific structure at a given moment in time. In return, each of them is defined by its belonging to this field" ("Champ intellectuel," 865).

5. See, for example, Lucien Goldmann, *Le dieu caché. Etude sur la vision tragique dans les Pensées de Pascal et dans le théâtre de Racine* (Paris: Gallimard, 1959).

6. Christian Jouhaud, "Histoire et histoire littéraire: Naissance de l'écrivain," *Annales ESC,* July-August 1988, 849-66.

7. On duplicity as a practice of writing, see Viala, *Naissance de l'écrivain*; passim and 297; Jouhaud, "Histoire et histoire littéraire."

8. Christian Jouhaud, *Mazarinades: La Fronde des Mots* (Paris: Aubier, 1985); "La Fronde en mouvement: le développement de la crise politique entre 1648 et 1652," *XVIe Siècle* 145 (1984): 305-22 (in collaboration with Robert Descimon); "De Paris à Bordeaux: Pour qui court le peuple pendant la Fronde (1652)?" *Mouvements populaires et conscience sociale XVIe-XIXe siècles,* Acts of the colloquium, Paris, May 24-26, 1984, collected and presented by Jean Nicolas (Paris: Maloine, 1985), 31-42 (in collaboration with R. Descimon); "Politiques de princes: Les Condé (1630-1652)," *L'Etat et les aristocraties, XIIe-XVIIe siècle, France, Angleterre, Ecosse,* Acts of the roundtable organized by the CNRS, Maison française of Oxford, September 26-27, 1986, texts assembled and presented by Philippe Contamine (Paris: Presses de l'Ecole normale supérieure, 1989), 335-55; "Retour aux mazarinades: 'Opinion publique,' action politique et production pamphlétaire pen-

dant la Fronde," *La Fronde en questions*, Acts of the 18th colloquium of the CMR 17 (Marseille-Cassis, January 28-31, 1988), R. Duchene and P. Ronzeaud, ed. (Aix-en-Provence: Publications de l'Université de Provence, 1989), 297-307.

9. Georges Pages, "Autour du 'Grand Orage,' Richelieu et Marillac, deux politiques," *Revue historique* 179 (1937): 63-97.

10. Testimonials to the success of the *Cid* are reproduced in Georges Mongredien, *Recueil des textes et documents du XVIIe siècle relatifs à Corneille* (Paris: CNRS, 1972).

11. Chronology and bibliography in Corneille, *Oeuvres complètes*, texts established, presented, and annotated by Georges Couton, vol. 1 (Paris: Gallimard [La Pléiade], 1980). Attributing nobility to the father amounted to gaining a degree of nobility for the son.

12. Mongredien, *Recueil*. For example, on April 8, 1637, Fortin de La Hoguette announces in a letter that he whiles away the time in his garrison at Blaye by performing the *Cid* with his friends.

13. Armand Gaste, *La Querelle du Cid. Pièces et pamphlets publiés d'après les originaux* (Paris: 1899). The first pieces against Corneille were *L'autheur du vray Cid espagnol à son traducteur francoys* and the *Observations sur le Cid*; the first response by Corneille was *Lettre apologétique du Sr Corneille, contenant sa reponse aux observations faictes par le S. Scuderi sur le Cid*, followed by *La voix publique à Monsieur de Scudéry sur les Observations du Cid*.

14. *Lettre de M. l'abbé de Boisrobert à M. Mairet*, Gaste, *La Querelle*, 352-54 ("You will read the rest of my letter as an order that I send you at the command of his Eminence").

15. Paul Pellisson, *Relation contenant l'histoire de l'Académie française* (1653), in Pellisson and d'Olivet, *Histoire de l'Académie française*, with an introduction, explanations, and notes by C. L. Livet, 2 vols. (Paris: 1858), v.

16. *Observations sur le Cid*, in Gaste, *La Querelle*, 71-111.

17. Corneille, *Oeuvres complètes*.

18. Ibid., 204-15.

19. Gaste, *La Querelle*, 111. On this question of the tyranny of Corneille, see the thesis of Helene Merlin, *Le public au XVIIe siècle: Entre corps mystique et personne fictive* (Paris: EHESS, 1990), 384-525.

20. On this famous secret, see Guez de Balzac, *Lettre de Monsieur de Balzac à Monsieur de Scudéry*, in Gaste, *La Querelle*, 452-56, and Corneille in a letter to Boisrobert of December 23, 1637, *Oeuvres Complètes*, 806.

21. Gaste, *La Querelle*, had the merit to reconstitute and publish the whole of the dossier without establishing a hierarchy among these texts, which are so different from one another.

22. Jouhaud, *Mazarinades*, especially 213-22.

23. Gaston Bizos, *Etude sur la vie et les oeuvres de Jean de Mairet* (Paris: 1877). Mairet wrote twelve theatrical pieces between 1620 and 1637, but the quarrel of the *Cid*, in which he was violently implicated, seems to have turned him away from literature. One cannot help but remark, at least, the concordance of dates: after the quarrel, he no longer wrote (he died in 1686).

24. Gaste, *La Querelle*, 328-47.

25. *La victoire du sieur Corneille, Scudéry et Claveret. Avec une remontrance par laquelle on les prie amiablement de n'exposer ainsi leur renommée à la risée publique*, ibid., 198-201.

26. Ibid., 200-201.

27. *Résponse de Monsieur de Scudéry à Monsieur de Balzac*, ibid., 457-63; G. de Scud-

éry, L'apologie du théâtre (Paris: Augustin Courbé, 1639); Jules de La Mesnardière, *La poétique* (Paris: 1639); Jean-Francois Sarasin, *Discours de la tragédie ou remarques sur l'Amour tyrannique de Monsieur de Scudéry* (Paris: 1639); Desmarets de Saint-Sorlin, *Les visionnaires* (1637), Argument, in *Théâtre du XVIIe siècle* vol. 2, texts selected, established, presented, and annotated by Jacques Scherer and Jacques Truchet (Paris: Gallimard [La Pleiade], 1986), 404-92.

28. La Mesnardière, *La poétique*, and Scudéry, *L'apologie du théâtre*, 96.

29. I do not evoke here a contradiction I discussed in "Histoire et histoire littéraire" (857-61), a contradiction between a psychophysiology of perception based upon a theory of the imagination and of images valid for all human beings, and a theory of reception, which reasons in terms of exclusion and of groupings. This contradiction is particularly acute in La Mesnardière: in his *Poétique*, he defends the model of a socially differentiated reception, while he denies the possiblility of this differentiation in his *Raisonnements sur la nature des esprits qui servent aux sentiments* (Paris: Jean Camusat, 1638). It is true that it is as a medical doctor that he wrote this second work.

30. See Giovanni Dotoli, "L'année théâtrale clef, 1630-1631," in *Littérature et société en France au XVIIe siècle* (Fasano and Paris: Schena and Nizet, 1987), 167-83.

31. There is no reliable general study on Balzac, which is strange and regrettable; from the point of view of a history of ideas, see F. E. Sutcliffe, *Guez de Balzac et son temps. Littérature et politique* (Paris: Colin, 1959). One must still consult Eusebe Castaigne, "Recherches sur la maison ou naquit Jean-Louis Guez de Balzac, sur la date de sa naissance, sur celle de sa mort, et sur ses différents legs aux établissements publics," *Bulletin de la Société archéologique et historique de la Charente*, 1846, 17-76.

32. Gaste, *La Querelle*, 452-65. Scudéry did not hesitate to publish this response, which, in itself and despite the polite disavowal of his step, put him in the position of an authorized interlocutor of the great and touchy Balzac. He joined to Balzac's letter a refutation that allowed him to have the last word (see n. 27).

33. *Discours d'Aristarque à Nicandre sur les jugements des esprits de ce temps. Et sur les fautes de Phylarque* (1628), 6.

34. Georges Mongredien, *La Journée des Dupes. 10 november 1630* (Paris: Gallimard, 1961); Pierre de Vaissiere, *Un grand procès sous Richelieu. L'affaire du Maréchal de Marillac (1630-1632)* (Paris: Perrin, 1924); G. Pages, "Autour du 'Grand Orage'"; Christian Jouhaud, *La main de Richelieu ou le pouvoir cardinal* (Paris: Gallimard, 1991).

35. There are numerous pamphlets on the exile of Marie de Médicis. See L. Delavaud, *Quelques collaborateurs de Richelieu* (Paris: 1915); D. A. Bayley, "Les pamphlets de M. de Morgues (1582-1670)," *Revue française d'histoire du livre* 18 (1978): 41-86; and "Les pamphlets des associés polemistes de M. de Morgues," ibid. 27 (1980): 41-86.

36. *Mémoires de Monsieur de Pontis qui a servi dans les armées cinquante-six ans, sous les rois Henri IV, Louis XIII et Louis XIV*, prefaced and annotated by Robert Laulan (Paris: Mercure de France, 1986), 171.

37. On *The Prince*, see Etienne Thuau, *Raison d'Etat et pensée politique à l'epoque de Richelieu* (Paris: Armand Colin, 1966), 252-63 (Balzac appears there among the "statist" authors, which shows the limits of an analysis founded on the history of ideas alone); P. Watier, "Guez de Balzac. Le Prince. A Reevaluation," *Journal of the Wartburg and Courtauld Institute* 20 (1957): 215-47 (*The Prince* in the lineage of "mirrors of the prince"); and Gaston Guillaumie, "Quelques variantes du *Prince* de Guez de Balzac," *Mélanges Laumonier* (Paris: 1935, Slatkine: 1972), 377-86.

38. It seems that the core of *Aristippe ou de la cour*, published in 1658 after Balzac's

death, must have been volume 3 of *The Prince*, devoted to the minister; but this text was profoundly revised; one finds there numerous, more or less transparent, allusions to Richelieu and the Pere Joseph. See Christian Jouhaud and Hélène Merlin, "Aristippe ou les équivoques de la publication," *Ordre et contestation au temps des classiques*, vol. 2 (Paris and Seattle: Tübingen, 1992), 155-78.

39. *Epitre à Richelieu* follows the text of *The Prince*, with its own pagination; the account of the day of the dupes is on pp. 39-50. Taken as a whole, the account seems in addition to show a Louis XIII indecisive in the face of his mother. Now, contrary to the legends, it was absolutely necessary for Richelieu that the king appear strong and determined.

40. Tallemant des Reaux, *Historiettes* vol. 2, text established and annotated by Antoine Adam (Paris: Gallimard [La Pleiade], 1970), 42-56.

41. Reproduced in all editions of the *Lettres*, edition used: J.-L. Guez de Balzac, *Oeuvres* vol. 1, ed. Bibas and Butler (Paris: Droz, 1933), 415.

42. For example, *Lettres de Phyllarque à Ariste*, Oeuvres Complètes, Letter XIII: "If he is daring enough to entertain the cardinals with his debauchery, his sciatica, and his gravel, one may easily believe that he is lacking only [a case of] smallpox to draw from it an opportunity to write letters to the pope"!

43. Ibid., Letter XXIV. Balzac's style is attacked as "cacozèle," or a jumble of styles (which places him on the side of the "monstrous"). According to the criteria selected in the classification of Jean-Pierre Camus, *Conférences académiques sur le différend des belles lettres de Narcisse et de Phyllarque, par le sieur de Musac* (Paris: Joseph Cottereau, 1630), particularly 286, Richelieu belongs incontestably among the pro-Balzac group.

44. The juxtaposition of "scenes" proposed by the letters creates a sort of uneasiness concerning the stability of the language: it is transformed with the context of the communication and loses its transparency and its solidity, which makes it coincide with a certain libertine posture (circulation from one linguistic form to the other, with the deeper self excepted). This was, moreover, almost claimed by Balzac in the letter to Hydaspe (Letter XXXVI of the first edition, 1624).

45. Camus, *Conférences académiques*, 127, gives the floor to an adversary of Balzac who defends the oratory specificity of eloquence.

46. As Silhon writes, concerning Balzac, in the *Recueil de lettres* of Nicolas Faret (1627), 133: "A knowledge that relates to the action as to its end has reached its full and greatest perfection when it is able easily, powerfully, and infallibly to produce the effect that it has proposed for itself" (Balzac is in the order of eloquence since he produces effects of pleasure and delight).

47. Moreover, one need only refer to the Letters patent of establishment of the Académie française: "After having performed so many memorable exploits, We had nothing more [to do] than to add the things that are agreeable to those that are necessary, and ornament to utility,... We could begin in no better way than by the most noble of all the Arts which is Eloquence." Reproduced in Marc Fumaroli, "Le Cardinal de Richelieu fondateur de l'Académie française," *Richelieu et le monde de l'esprit*, (Paris: Imprimerie Nationale, 1985), 217-35.

48. It is generally considered that this preface, signed by the Sieur de La Motte Aigron and placed in reality at the end of the first edition (under the pretext of its tardy arrival at the printers), is from the pen of Balzac himself.

49. Cf. Furetière, *Dictionnaire*, "seemliness or conformity of natural qualities, humors,

or temperament, which leads two things to love each other, seek each other, and live in peace together."

50. Preface of Silhon added to the sixth edition (1627), 10.

51. Published in Jean Chapelain, *Opuscules critiques*, ed. Alfred Hunter (Paris: Droz, 1936), 133-52. The book of Bentivoglio: *Della guerra di Fiandra*, part, 1 (Cologne: 1632).

52. For example, Gabriel Hanotaux, *Maximes d'Etat et fragments politiques du Cardinal de Richelieu*, Paris 1880, *Discours prononcé par Richelieu le 3 février 1627 devant une délégation du parlement de Paris reçue par le roi*, concerning the devout [party]: "The excess and the ignorance of their zeal make them sometimes fall into passions that are all the more dangerous since their frenzy makes them see them as holy."

53. S. Dupleix, *Histoire de Louis le Juste XIIIe du nom, Roy de France et de Navarre*, 1635. M. de Morgues, *Lumières pour l'histoire de France pour faire voir les calomnies, flatteries et autres defauts de Scipion Dupleix*. S. Dupleix, *La response a Saint-Germain: ou les lumières de Matthieu de morgues dit Saint-Germain pour l'histoire, esteintes par Messire Scipion Dupleix, conseiller du Roy en ses conseils d'Estat et prive, et Historiographe de France*, 1645.

54. He is the grandson, son, and nephew of notaries. Chapelain is the object of a study that is old but excellent: Georges Collas, *Un poète protecteur des lettres au XVIIe siècle. Jean Chapelain, 1595-1674. Etude historique et littéraire d'après des documents inédits* (Paris: 1912, Slatkine: 1970). One may also consult Antonin Fabre, "La jeunesse de Chapelain," *Le correspondant* 147 (1897): 526-49. Orest Ranum devoted to Chapelain— especially to his "second career"—an important chapter of his book *Artisans of Glory. Writers and Historical Thought in Seventeenth Century France* (Chapel Hill: University of North Carolina Press, 1980).

55. The two humanists, both of whom were later at the Collège du Roi, are Frederic Morel and Nicolas Bourbon (who will belong to the academy). Chapelain completed his course of philosophy at the college de Lisieux; it has been written that he abandoned his study of medicine because of financial difficulties at the time of his father's death, but it is in no way certain that the latter was dead in 1614, and one knows, on the contrary, that his notary's practice was flourishing.

56. The office of *grand prévôt* is an office of the king's household; this officer of the sword (assisted by *maîtres des requêtes*) judges misdemeanors committed in the royal residence and within ten leagues surrounding it and certain affairs of the officers of the king's household.

57. One sees him sign, thus, as a witness to the marriage of the daughter of the marquis de La Trousse, in the company of Charles Leclerc de Tremblay, brother of the Père Joseph (Collas, *Un poète protecteur*, 77).

58. Ibid. The purchase of the charge of royal secretary could be linked to the proposed diplomatic career in Rome.

59. Published in Chapelain, *Opuscules critiques*, 70-111.

60. According to Tallemant, *Historiettes*, vol. 1, 567-76: "Mme. de Rambouillet told me that he had an outfit like one used to wear ten years ago; it was made of dove-colored satin, lined with green plush velvet [*panne*], and trimmed with dove and green lace, *à oeil de perdrix*" (567). After his successful integration at the Hôtel de Rambouillet, Chatelain will no longer need to put on his Sunday best; his black suit will in no way diminish him; he will become an agent rather than an object of judgments. One knows almost nothing of his relations with the Arnaulds, except that they seem to be long standing and very solid.

61. Charles L. Livet, *Précieux et précieuses. Caractères et moeurs littéraires du XVIIe siè-*

cle, 2 vols. (Paris: 1860); Carolyn C. Lougee, *Le Paradis des Femmes. Women, Salons, and Social Stratification in Seventeenth-Century France* (Princeton University Press: 1976); Joan DeJean, "The Salons, 'Preciosity,' and the Sphere of Women's Influence," *A New History of French Literature* (Cambridge, Mass.: Harvard University Press, 1989), 297–303.

62. Claude Favre de Vaugelas, *Remarques sur la langue française*, facsimile of the original edition (1647) presented by Jeanne Streicher (Paris: Droz, 1934); Jacques Revel, "Les usages de la civilité," *Histoire de la vie privée*, under the direction of Philippe Aries and Georges Duby, vol. 3, *De la Renaissance aux Lumières*, under the direction of Roger Chartier (Paris: Seuil, 1986), 169–209, on the Hôtel de Rambouillet, 194–95.

63. *Lettres de Jean Chapelain de l'Académie française*, 2 vols., published by Philippe Tamizey de Larroque, Collection des documents inédits sur l'Histoire de France, 2nd series (Paris: Imprimerie Nationale, 1880) vol. 1, September 1632-December 1640. Henceforth cited as Chapelain, correspondence, with the number of the letter. Letter to Balzac of September 25, 1632: letter II.

64. Chapelain, correspondence, letter IX.

65. Ibid., letters XVI, XVII, and XVIII. On François le Metel abbé de Boisrobert (1592-1662), one may still read Emile Magne, *Le plaisant abbé de Boisrobert fondateur de l'Académie française* (Paris: 1909).

66. He gives thanks also to "the high and admirable clarity in the things [that are] the most muddled" which belongs to the cardinal, implying that the "good memoirs" for writing history ought to come from him; in this too he rejoins Scipion Dupleix, who did not see things any differently (cf. Christian Jouhaud, "Le pouvoir du cardinal de Richelieu et ses premiers historiens," colloquium on Medieval and Early Modern Romance Literature, Dartmouth, 1988, forthcoming).

67. Chapelain, correspondence, letter XVIII: "I hope to show Mgr. within six days the places that I corrected and the approach I took in order to follow his initial intention; after that, if he approves it, one may print the piece and satisfy the world who earnestly demands it upon the reputation that Monseigneur gave it through the case that everyone knows he made of it." In fact, the *Ode à Richelieu* was hailed as the work of one of the best poets of his time.

68. Ibid.

69. Ibid., 41 n. 3: "I stood there as if tongue-tied and lost memory of that which I should have said to him, in order to enjoy the excellence of the things he said to me.... his voice seemed sweeter to me than the most harmonious things I have ever heard."

70. A muddle that proved to be the same for the poet François Mainard, who takes his place; see Charles Drouhet, *Le poète François Mainard (1583?-1646)* (Paris: 1909), 191-232. Mainard's case is interesting, since it would furnish a contrasting example of an author who multiplies the bad choices in the conduct of his career.

71. We know that there is a lacuna in Chapelain's correspondence for the years 1640 to 1659 (Balzac died in 1654).

72. Starting from a central place, such as the Hôtel de Rambouillet or the study of the brothers Dupuy at the Hôtel de Thou, the circle widens. For example, Chapelain, correspondence, letter CCCVI, concerning the *Lettre de consolation* written by Balzac upon the death of the cardinal of La Valette: it is at first read twice at the Hôtel de Rambouillet, then "I shall hand it over to the discretion of some of our faithful who will show it in the places where they are familiar and before the most clever of their acquaintances, above all I shall place it in the hands of Monsieur d'Ablancourt so that he has the joy of it and so that he may give it to the study of the M[essieu]rs Du Puy."

73. Chapelain, correspondence, 106, 721.

74. Balzac found himself in some sense a prisoner of his letter-writing success. Everyone claims letters from him, and each of these letters has the status of a work: he may not then write and launch them lightly. At the same time, this solemn proclamation to write no more letters allows him to honor specially (often on the recommendation of Chapelain) the one who forms an exception to the rule.

75. Very fine example in Chapelain, correspondence, letters CCCXXI and CCCXXVIII, also CCLXII, CCLXXXVII and letter cited 422 n. 1.

76. Ibid., 407 n. 3.

77. In a very great number of letters (in particular pages 43, 44, 68, 92, 290, 389); let us note also the indifference expressed by Chapelain in an intervention in order that Balzac might obtain a brevet of *conseiller d'Etat.*

78. Chapelain, correspondence, letter CCCXXX.

79. Claude Reichler, *L'âge libertin* (Paris: Minuit, 1987), 29.

80. Chapelain, correspondence, letter XCLIX. The letters concerning the quarrel of the *Cid:* XCLIII, CIII, CVIII, CIX, CXI, CXII, CXIII, CXV, CXX, CXXI, CXXIX, CXXX, CXXXI, CXXXVII, CXLIV, CXLVIII, CXLIX, CLVII, CLVIII.

81. Pellisson, *Relation*; Georges Collas, "Richelieu et le Cid," *Revue de France,* February 1, 1929, 472-97 and "Richelieu et le Cid," *Revue d'Histoire littéraire de la France,* 1936, 568-72 (refutes Louis Batiffol, *Richelieu et Corneille, la légende de la persécution de l'auteur du Cid* [Paris: 1936]); Antoine Adam, "A travers la Querelle du Cid," *Revue d'histoire de la philosophie,* 1938, 29-52; M. Sedgwick, "Richelieu and the 'Querelle du Cid,'" *Modern Language Review* 43 (1953): 143-50.

82. Chapelain, correspondence, letter CXI.

83. Ibid., letter CXII. It is Chapelain who had sent the *Cid* to Balzac on Corneille's behalf and then the *Observations sur le Cid* (but Scudéry himself sent a copy of it to Balzac). To complicate the game even further, Chapelain had to face the impatience of Scudéry, who expected a prompt judgment of the *Cid.* On August 20 Scudéry conceded to him that Corneille had "obliged [him] to lower his vainglory" (letter CXIII).

84. Ibid., letter CXV.

85. Ibid., letters CXXI, CXXX, CXXXVII, CXLIV, CXLVIII, CLVII, CLVIII.

86. Pellisson, *Relation*; Colbert Searles, ed., *Les Sentiments de l'Académie française sur le Cid,* University of Minnesota Studies in Language and Literature (Minneapolis, 1916); A. Hunter, *Opuscules critiques,* 153-97; Gaste, *La Querelle,* 355-417.

87. Searles, *Sentiments,* 105-12 (in this edition the texts of the various versions are set up opposite each other); Hunter, *Opuscules critiques,* 193-97; Gaste, *La Querelle,* 413-17.

88. If, at the moment of his greatest fear of the consequences (in August), Chapelain seemed to wish that the academy would be dispensed from the investigation of the *Cid,* the idea, on the contrary, that he alone and not the academy might be relieved of it, and that he would share thus only a distant responsibility, did not faze him!

89. Léopold Lacour, *Richelieu dramaturge et ses collaborateurs* (Paris: 1926); H. Lancaster, *A History of French Dramatic Literature,* part 2 (vols. 3 and 4), *The Period of Corneille* (Baltimore-London-Paris: 1932); Jean Mesnard, "Richelieu et le théâtre," *Richelieu et le monde de l'esprit,* 193-206; Georges Couton, *Richelieu et le théâtre* (Lyon: Presses Universitaires de Lyon, 1986); Rene Kerviler, *Jean Desmarets Sieur de Saint-Sorlin, l'un des quarante fondateurs de l'Académie française* (Paris: 1879). Chapelain was part of the team of "five authors" of *La comédie des Tuileries, La grande pastorale,* and *L'aveugle de Smyrne.*

90. The question of Richelieu's "taste" remains at the center of the contributions of P. Mesnard and G. Couton cited in the preceding note; it seems that it has replaced the even more futile (and so poorly posed) question of whether Richelieu was himself tempted to write for the theater (this inclination would, moreover, engender in him an author's jealousy).

91. Timothy Murray, "Richelieu's Theater: The Mirror of a Prince," *Renaissance Drama*, 1977, 275-98, and *Theatrical Legitimation: Allegories of Genius in Seventeenth-Century England and France* (New York and Oxford: Oxford University Press, 1987).

92. *Memoires de Michel de Marolles, abbé de Villeloin, divisés en trois parties contenant ce qu'il y a de plus remarquable en sa vie, depuis l'année 1600, ses entretiens avec quelques uns des plus savants hommes de son temps et la généalogie de quelques familles alliées dans la sienne, avec une brève description de la très illustre Maison de Mantoue et de Nevers* (Paris: Sommaville, 1656), 125-26.

93. *Gazette*, 1641, no. 7, account dated January 19, it ends thus: "Finally, if I have difficulty ending this narration, judge how difficult it was for the spectators of so fine an action to leave a place in which they believed themselves to have been enchanted through the eyes and the ears: which ravishment was not for the French alone, the generals Jean de Wirth, Enkenfort and Don Pedro de Leon, prisoners of war, shared in it, having been led there from the bois de Vincennes."

94. Pellisson, *Relation*, 81.

95. Dotoli, *Littérature et société,* Georges Forestier, "Du côté du plaisir: La naissance de la critique dramatique moderne au XVIIe siècle," *Storiografia della critica francese nel seicento, Quaderni del Seicento Francese* 7 (1986): 13-29: in the appendix is a chronology of texts of drama criticism before 1640.

96. *Discours de la poésie représentative,* in *Opuscules critiques,* ed. Hunter, 127-31.

97. Searles, *Sentiments,* 22.

98. Ibid., 27.

99. François Hedelin abbé d'Aubignac, *La pratique du théâtre, oeuvre très nécessaire à tous ceux qui veulent s'appliquer à la composition des Poèmes Dramatiques, qui font profession de les réciter en public, ou qui prennent plaisir d'en voir les représentations* (Paris: 1657); for him (book 2, chapter 2), the probable is "the essence of the dramatic poem without which nothing reasonable may be said or done upon the stage." Robert Morrisey, "La *Pratique du théâtre* et le langage de l'illusion," *XVIIe siècle* 146 (1985): 17-28. Murray, "Richelieu's Theater." Charles Arnaud, *Etude sur la vie et les oeuvres de l'abbé d'Aubignac* (Paris: 1887).

100. Cf. Jean-Marie Apostolides, *Le roi-machine. Spectacle et politique au temps de Louis XIV* (Paris: Minuit, 1981) and *Le prince sacrifie. Théâtre et politique au temps de Louis XIV* (Paris: Minuit, 1985).

101. Jouhaud, "Histoire et histoire littéraire." See also "Lisibilite et persuasion: Les placards politiques" and "Imprimer l'événement: La Rochelle à Paris," *Les usages de l'imprime (XVe-XIXe siècles),* under the direction of Roger Chartier (Paris: Fayard, 1987), 309-42, 381-438; translated into English as *The Culture of Print* (Cambridge: Polity, 1989).

102. Gabriel Naude, *Considérations politiques sur les Coups d'Etat,* preceded by Louis Marin, *Pour une théorie baroque de l'action politique* (Paris: Editions de Paris, 1988).

103. Roger Chartier, "Le monde comme représentation," *Annales ESC,* 1989, 1505-20, especially 1514-16.

104. Michel Prigent, *Le héros et l'Etat dans la tragedie de Pierre Corneille* (Paris: PUF, 1986) proposes thus to answer two questions: Why is tragedy necessarily political? Why is

politics necessarily dependent on tragedy? And, for a different point of view, see Apostolides, *Le prince sacrifie*, especially 28.

105. See the letter to Boisrobert of December 23, 1637.

106. Corneille, *Oeuvres complètes* vol. 1, *Horace*, dedicatory Epistle to Richelieu, 833-35; Louis Marin, "Théâtralité et politique au XVIIeme siècle: Sur trois textes de Corneille," *La France et l'Italie au temps de Mazarin* (Grenoble: Presses Universitaires de Grenoble, 1986), 399-407.

107. Chapelain, correspondence, letter IX.

108. To speak of a cultural field in the seventeenth century is immediately to evoke an imbrication with political bodies and the church. From another perspective, concerning the autonomy of authors, we must emphasize that Chapelain entered into Longueville's service *after* having become a creature of Richelieu: one may not thus consider that autonomy is gained by passing from an aristocratic clientele to a dependence on the state (according to the schema of Alain Viala); it is a matter rather of a subtle play with a whole set of forces (and it is, in this way, political).

109. It is against this solidarity in the practice of the illusion that the Jansenists took aim in their attacks against the theater. From 1637 to 1640 the withdrawal from the world of Antoine Lemaitre, then the arrest of the abbé de Saint Cyran, are discussed at great length by Chapelain in his correspondence. He was very close to the Arnauld family but miles away from the genuinely subversive reexaminations of the Jansenists.

Flower Power: Shakespearean Deep Bawdy and the Botanical Perverse
Donald Hedrick

I am very happy to see so many flowers here and that is why I want to remind you that flowers, by themselves, have no power whatsoever, other than the power of men and women who protect them and take care of them against aggression and destruction.

—Herbert Marcuse, "Liberation from the Affluent Society"[1]

What the Fuck?

Given contemporary pressures to return humanistic studies to their traditional content and practices—pressures often brought to bear without acknowledging exactly what the earlier content and practices were—it may be time to comply by returning Shakespeare studies to a formerly perennial topic, lamentably absent today: namely, Shakespeare's deep knowledge of plant lore, gardening, and flowers. It would be instructive should we discover that the topic is not yet exhausted.

By introducing what might be termed a "police perspective" into consideration of Shakespeare's flower imagery, I may further the politicization of the pastoral conducted by Annabel Patterson, James Turner, and others.[2] In so doing I suggest the possible shape of a "new imagery study," expanding the range of answers to the traditional question about what "associations" a particular aesthetic image had for Shakespeare.[3] In exploring some Shakespearean habits of art, I want also to explore mechanisms of censorship, self-censorship, and decensorship, using the least likely case of the censorship of flowers. If the a fortiori form of the argument holds, it may be extrapolated into the general possibility of oppositional tactics against a hegemonic censorability, including tactics of "deep bawdy" and a pedagogy of the perverse. Toward such generalization I will introduce some historical range, looking at Shakespeare, at readers of his "naturalness," at his nineteenth-century editor Thomas Bowdler, and, briefly, at the controversial contemporary photographer of flowers, Robert Mapplethorpe.

Traditionally, Shakespeare has often been thought of as a lover of nature. Indeed, the sheer force and prevalence of representations of nature, perhaps less apparent in the current climate of political criticism, are striking throughout the plays. This view of Shakespeare as loving nature, often presuming his nostalgia for Stratford-upon-Avon and a rural upbringing, has been acccompanied at times by a related speculation that he was sophisticated in knowledge of plants and gardening. As one nineteenth-century Shakespearean asserted, "A lover of flowers and gardening myself, I claim Shakespeare as equally a lover of flowers and gardening."[4] Although one does not encounter in scholarship now many of the claims that used to proliferate about Shakespeare's presumed expertise in a variety of fields (law, navigation, etc.), it does seem as if the natural world was a place of especially "thick description" for Shakespeare, and that he knew it, or parts of it, intimately. Indeed, botanists offer astonished praise of Shakespeare's almost scientific powers of observation. Mats Ryden, for instance, finds it remarkable that Shakespeare notices a small orange-red patch at the base of each lobe of the corolla of the cowslip (thus, "freckled"), as when Iachimo observes on sleeping Imogen's left breast "a mole, cinque-spotted, like the crimson drops / I'th' bottom of a cowslip" (*Cymbeline* 2.2.38–39).[5] Was Shakespeare primarily a lover of nature or rather its objective describer? Or does he combine the two, namely, as a *fetishist*? I believe that fetishism, in both erotic and economic senses, captures much of what is helpful in order to understand imagery here.

Whether or not, as has been suggested, Shakespeare actually read Henry Lyte's herbal, he was interested enough in plant lore to have centered *A Midsummer Night's Dream* on the plant "love-in-idleness" or pansy, whose magical properties drive and connect the action. Its name in Gerard's herbal is somewhat less romantic: "live-in-idleness" (a variant adding economic undertones of vagrancy or masterlessness). The image of a nature-loving or "natural" Shakespeare often depends on the assumption that gardening and theater are distinct and complementary activities and that nature might serve as "recreation" to Shakespeare's cultural work. It may be a corrective to think of the nature represented in, for instance, *A Midsummer Night's Dream* in the terms of Jan Kott's infamous interpretation of the play stressing the bestiality and decadence of a drunken orgy.[6] Despite Kott's rhetorical overkill, his reading suggests how natural imagery, readily linked with an implicit sexuality, may become political and oppositional, entangled as it is with the conditions and practices of a dominating "culture."

"Is there fucking going on in there?" The policeman's question, much the same question as the censor's, may be valuable for more fully understanding the potential cultural force of *A Midsummer Night's Dream*, though it is a question itself often censored or repressed in criticism. William Empson unpacks such critical self-censorship in the Arden edition of the play, where the editor, Harold Brooks, speaks of Bottom as "quite unsusceptible to the romance of fairyland." A shrewd analyst of critical tone, Empson suggests that the "real feeling" of this remark is "thank God we don't have to watch a lady actually giving herself to a stinking hairy worker. 'Even a controlled suggestion of carnal bestiality is surely impossible,' he [Brooks] remarks."[7] Empson proceeds to unearth the "concealed struggle" of such provocative remarks in the "real opponent" of Brooks, namely, Jan Kott's reading of the play. Empson's critique and usual stance against "moralistic" criticism do not, however, induce him to side with Kott, for he announces that on the question of whether or not sex occurs in the play, he sides with the "old buffers," calling Kott's misreading "wild" and declaring bluntly that "no act of sex takes place on the fierce Night, and there is never anything to drink" (230).

But this is not where the matter stops for Empson. It is important, I believe, that Empson arrives at the useful policeman's question and subsequent denial of copulation not by prudery but by decensoring criticism itself, basing his conclusion in part on an imaginatively "wild" reading of his own that highlights rather than occludes sex. Thus, he asserts:

> As to whether it is "bestiality" to love Bottom, many a young girl on the
> sands at Margate has said to her donkey, unblamed: "I kiss thy fair large
> ears, my gentle joy." If the genital action is in view, nobody denies that
> the genitals of Bottom remained human. (229)

He then proceeds by closely reading the action, suggesting that Bottom's possibly misspoken "I have an exposition of sleep come upon
me" is greeted by "immediate connivance" as Titania explosively dis-
misses her fairies, followed by

> time for exploring fingers to enquire whether she is solid enough for
> the purpose, and also whether he is genuinely welcome. This groping
> process could be made obvious and entertaining, but then the lurking
> husband comes forward and performs an act of magic. (229-30)

For Kott the text or play is a space limited to a literal sexuality,
played for shock value, while for Empson, despite his denial of
fucking going on in there, it is a space where anything goes, actors
exploring fairy genitalia, perversions on perversions. In both there
are elements of what I describe as policeman's or censor's sensibilities. But Empson's deeper bawdy may have a more progressive
political leverage, in gaining access not merely to social relations but
also to the codes of social relations, and in thereby disturbing censorability itself; whereas mere transgressing—whether it is Kott's sort
of reading or the use of the word *fuck* in serious scholarship—may
not.

The apparently progressive cast of a sexually alert ideological criticism may be sacrificed, then, if a different form of impulse to censor reads sex largely as abstract idea or symbol. Unlike Empson's
review, Louis Montrose's well-known and influential essay on the
play does just that, by structurally or theoretically suppressing the
policeman's question.[8] In effect, Montrose implicitly revises Foucault's famous question, "What does it matter who's speaking?" into
another: What does it matter who's fucking? Refusing to play policeman, Montrose inadvertently reduces sex to the merely indexical.
For an essay ostensibly about "the erotic," there is a surprising absence of actual, or at least completed, sex. Accordingly, Simon Foreman's suggestive dream about Elizabeth breaks off after her seductive remarks and kisses, the play is shown to be intertextually linked
to stories of sex and bestiality and violence *outside* it, and Elizabeth's
"dalliances" (Bacon's own weasel word) are alluded to without di-

rect consideration of the question of what, if anything, she actually did to provoke courtly erotic interest—as if the criticism embodied here is a criticism of romantic frustration, like the kind of literature D. H. Lawrence would inveigh against as "masturbatory."

Suppressing the police perspective, moreover, even leads to methodological contradiction. Thus, by skirting any interest in whether Bottom did it with Titania (or rather, as I will suggest the locution makes some difference, did it *to* Titania), Montrose refuses the force of his earlier claim that in the play "the female body is a supreme form of property and locus for the contestation of authority" (68). If this is true, what happens to Titania's body, it would seem, matters at the level of theory but then, as we proceed through the study, turns out not to matter at all at the level of material fact, hence weakening or undermining the theoretical claim. On this site is staged a contest and no contest, or rather a contest in which no one—and this is where the often criticized political limitation of the new historicism becomes manifest—can win. Or rather it is a story in which the forces of containment "win" if they succeed in containment—a "poetics of culture" that is always and only a zero-sum poetics.

If Bottom did indeed fuck Titania, the story of at least that particular female body is a different one, and the claim about the play's containing or "socializing" the libido through final marriages rather than through "sacrimentalizing" (69) would require a rethinking I can only suggest here. If Bottom fucked Titania, this is a "socialization" with a political and class edge, a significance we might detect from Montrose's perceiving Bottom to be merely in a "childlike" (85) relation to his social superiors such as Titania. What we see, then, in the essay's evasion of one kind of deeper bawdy in Shakespeare, is a critique of containment tending itself to replicate containment, maintaining Bottom's position as always beneath a queen. This is not, however, to read the significance unproblematically, as a kind of class victory, for it simultaneously involves a gender defeat, at another level of bawdy. At all events, it is through a superficial question that one arrives in this case at a deeper level of bawdy and an evasion of the censor's oversight.

To oppose this structural censorship, whether or not one concludes that Bottom and Titania actually do it, is to recast the play, as both Empson and Kott do (despite their mutually exclusive read-

ings), in terms of sex rather than of abstracted sexuality, and perhaps to think of the sexual imagery of Shakespeare's language in
somewhat different and more vulgar terms. In doing so, what becomes striking is the pervasiveness of the sex of the play. For even if
we accept the blanket assertion that "no act of sex takes place"
during that night, what is extraordinary is how the order of night
is structurally drenched by acts of sex, and not just intertextually
through classical allusions. There is, it seems, sex before the play
among the fairies, afterward among the humans; before and after
the performance, as the antitheater tracts complained, among the
corrupted members of the audience, and more—illicit heterosexual
sex downstage, toward the pit with its groundlings and circulating
prostitutes; illicit homosexual sex upstage, toward the tiring house
with its men and boy actors; and in many other forms outside in the
brothels and taverns of the liberties. (And I am not counting what
goes on in dreams.) In such a context, every piece of mere "imagery"
is especially charged, and all the more so if actual sex, absent in the
play, is thus radically *in potentia*. The overall configuration of an
"always already" sex—a censor's nightmare, like an interpretive community for whom every referent is sexual—is one inviting an
imagery of "deep bawdy" beyond a literal one easier to gloss or to
censor. It is a flexible bawdy, more likely to evade a censor's gaze,
and associated with unfixed social relations. The nature of that gaze
will, of course, be historically relative; the bawdy of the Victorian
era, as we shall see, and that of Shakespeare's era are not identical,
and flowers therefore are a different sort of issue for each. Furthermore, although moral grounds for censorship could be offered,
plays in Shakespeare's time were censored primarily on political or
religious grounds.[9] In any case, however, the potential within a text
or image for radically altered social relations can produce an
ambiguous space for a deeper bawdy, a space produced in this play,
as it happens, by a not entirely natural flower, a hybrid, as it were,
color-changed by "love's wound" from an arrow.

Floral Policy

For Shakespeare, as for Jacques Derrida in "The Double Session," the
comprehensive analogue for the curious opposition of the natural

and the artificial is the concept of the *graft*, etymologically linked to writing and the *graph*, that link not my subject here.[10] Shakespeare, of course, explores the topic in a much-discussed passage in *The Winter's Tale*, when Perdita and Polixenes debate the value of hybrids and of "marrying a gentler scion to the wildest stock, / And make conceive a bark of baser kind. By bud of nobler race"—an image, ironic in the dramatic context, drawn from an ordinary Shakespearean association of grafting with class mixing. Often taken as self-referential for Shakespeare's art, the debate includes the claim that for grafting "the art itself is nature" (4.4.92-97). While Kermode's edition of the play discusses the passage primarily in terms of natural nobility,[11] it is Shakespeare's deconstructive fascination with an entangled opposition and the fact that the passage is actually an overt debate about the censorship of flowers that interest me here.

As if by historical coincidence, the flourishing of the institution of theater in the 1590s was paralleled by a flourishing of the institution of gardening, and it has been suggested by Keith Thomas that to the other revolutions of the early modern period be added a "gardening revolution."[12] Although we might expect theater and gardening to inhabit separate or autonomous cultural spheres, as suggested earlier, they could in fact be related in historically particular ways. An opposition of gardening and theater was, as it happens, available for Shakespeare the presumed nature lover; it was available, moreover, in the very gardening treatises on grafting that had become so popular in the latter sixteenth century, as the cult of the private garden and the controversial importation of exotic plants began to increase. We find this in the dedication by the translator L. Mascal of one popular grafting treatise by D. Broussard (1569 edition), urging his readers to give up games and pastimes for nationalist reasons ("the good of the commonwealth"); and he observes approvingly that many noble lords have, in fact, left the "Theatres, pleasaunt stages, goodly pastimes" for this hobby.[13] But the garden, as we shall see, offered no true insulation from the theatrical.

The *Winter's Tale* passage defending "nature's bastards" has its source in Montaigne, but implicitly questions that source, where the hyperrefinement of corrupted European taste is negatively opposed to "wild" fruits of the American Indian. Jonathan Dollimore cites this in his argument about a "perverse dynamic" implicit in social relations, noting that Montaigne does not exactly invert the opposition

of natural and unnatural, but rather reverses the "conventional position of groups governed by it."[14] The Shakespeare passage, then,
opens the possibility of what might be termed a radical "theater of
gardening" in grafting, a fetishized and cultivated decadence at the
intersection of the commercial, the sensual, the artistic, and the
national. Grafting is later assigned the derogatory term "curious" by
Francis Bacon, who in *Sylva Sylvorum* condemns the practice even
as he gives gardening tips for carrying it out.[15] This fetishization of
nature, like Shakespeare's fetishized observation, apparently grew
from the previously mentioned surge of popularity of private gardens among the nobility. Its connection to the theatrical is even
more evident when one surveys the list of what Mascal's treatise
terms the "straunge and subtile ways" of doing things, such as how
"to make an Oke (or other tree) as greene in Winter, as in Sommer"—
a grafting practice allegorizing, as it were, Shakespeare's late ro-
mances. These lists are lists of wonders, but as political images they
suggest the wild possibilities of social relations that Christopher Hill
has shown to have collectively blossomed in the thinking of seventeenth-century radical groups such as the Diggers and Levellers.[16] In
this textual theater we learn how to "alter fruit," "to helpe barren
trees," "to colour Apples, what colour ye lyst," "to make an Apple
grow in a glasse," "to graffe many sortes of Apples on one tree," "to
helpe frozen Apples," "to make Cherries and Peaches smell, and tast
like spyce," "to have Nuttes, Plummes, and Almondes, greater and
fayrer than others," and "to graffe the Holy that his leaves shall kepe
all the yeare greene."[17]

If, following Spurgeon but with an ideological orientation, I were
to stipulate in a single phrase Shakespeare's chief conceptual association of flowers, it would be the following: *radical arrangeability.*
Ideology applied to imagery study means simply that images
embody social relations. The botany of the time made its own gesture in this direction, in the Latin tag cited by Bacon: "Homo est plan-
ta inversa" (432). While its point is that the human shape is like a
forked plant upside down, an idea pursued on a scientific level by
Bacon and others, the analogy points out how social relations themselves may become constellated within plant imagery, following
Marx's notion that ideology, construed negatively, acts like a camera
obscura that turns images on their head.[18]

For James I, the image, if not of hybrids at least of mixing cultivated plants with wild ones, had some positive political valence as an art of the political power of flowers. We find this imagery in *Basilikon Doron*, where it is employed in colonialist terms in the king's distinguishing two kinds of barbarism among the inhabitants of the Scottish highlands—the one amenable to civilization and the other not. For the intractable savages, he advises colonization to "root out and transport the barbarous and stubborn sort, and plant civilitie in their roomes."[19] Theatrical gardening was soon institutionalized and given state legitimation when in 1606 James established as royal botanist the noted Matthias DeL'Obel, a native of Lille who had come to London in 1569. A chief participant in the institutionalization of the natural, DeL'Obel furthered the systematization of plants. In the new political role of plant policeman, he was occasionally called on to testify to the presence of plants identified in the catalogs of the private gardens of nobles.[20] Given a larger historical context of this sort, the entire debate between Perdita and Polixenes can be simultaneously understood as just the sort of issue of taste that would increasingly appeal to James and other participants in the new cult of private gardens. In a nascent capitalism, nature itself was becoming subject to the processes of what Pierre Bourdieu analyzes as the making of refined distinctions.[21] The particular issue of the debate is therefore less important than the production of a discourse of fetishized refinements and the subtly perverse. "Radical arrangeability" would reflect the logic of the new market economy and its own rearrangements of the social and natural.

The production of taste and refinement occurred through not only the collecting but also the naming of flowers, and it is significant that there began to be admonitions against overly "theatrical" gardeners who, in order to make a profit, would simply invent or give false names, "to deceive men and make them believe they were the finders-out or great preservers of rarities."[22] Naming flowers, moreover, had a political association in nationalist terms, since a botanical issue of the time was the use of vernacular as opposed to technical names for flowers and plants. The important herbal of Dodoens, dedicated to Princess Elizabeth in 1619, claimed as one of its benefits to the nation that inhabitants would become familiar with plant names, and could thereby, even if they were not wealthy enough to afford a physician, help heal themselves. Such treatises provided a direct link between plants and sexuality, listing plants that would provoke "fleshly desire" and, on the other hand, plants that were "very good against Venus," enforcing chastity by taking desire away,[23] and offered ways of wresting sexual control away from ideological apparatuses for private use. James's expert in naming, as it happens, was also a specialist in a flower with special sexual connotations, namely, the orchid, to which I now turn in the context of bawdy and censorship.

Is there fucking going on in *Hamlet*? Overall, the sex of the play seems less anticipatory than long ago completed, in keeping with the sexual loathing at the heart of the story. That theme, as it happens, links the two deep images of the play: Hamlet's skull and Ophelia's flowers, the latter once again in an oblique relation to sexuality. In the passage on Ophelia's death (4.7), Gertrude's catalog of her garland flowers growing "askant" (or "aslant") the brook includes the "long purples, / That liberal shepherds give a grosser name, / But our cold [cull-cold in the Folio] maids do dead men's fingers call them" (168–70). The passage about "dead men's fingers" has naturally attracted the attention of both the Shakespeare-as-nature-lover and Shakespeare-as-naturalist camps, the latter generally concerned with identifying the "long purple," first mentioned in Shakespeare (possibly like a few others his own creation, in his typical mode of linguistic grafting) and mentioned by Middleton in a comparable euphemism. It may be the *orchis mascula*, well known and with at least three names to it; its grosser names include the various references to testicles associated with orchids, such as ballock, cod, cullion and stone (e.g., priest's pintle, standergrass, sweet ballocks, sweet cods, dog's cods, fool's cullions, and the like). Glossarial delicacy is accomplished in various ways, usually stressing the phallic character of the plant's central spike, but sometimes, as in an earlier book on Shakespearean gardens, by choosing the least gross of the grosser possibilities, namely, "cuckoo-pint."[24] Alan Dent's book on Shakespeare's plants simply cites a British wildflower guide that identifies the plant as wild arum, "whose tiny green flowers are densely packed in a stout spike projecting upwards."[25]

One nineteenth-century admirer of Shakespeare thought the writer should be praised for his "manly delicacy" in withholding such common names from "the lips of the queen."[26] But the self-censoring impulse is not limited to that era; we find a more recent version of it in the modern scholarship of Robert Speaight, who reads the speech as Ophelia's innocent return to nature, her earlier scenes exemplifying her connection to the "flowers of the uncorrupted fields."[27] To preserve the "natural" Shakespeare, an enemy of theatricalized grafting, one must suppress the bawdy side of the speech, and most of all of its flowers, or at least suppress the possibility of its having any effect on the audience.

Even E. A. M. Colman in his exploration of how Shakespearean bawdy may be thematically functional—an argument whose logic points toward the present claim that a "deeper" bawdy might operate beyond the functional or censorable—finds the tone of the speech disturbingly problematic. Colman's grasping hypothesis of an "ambiguous bawdy" in Shakespeare is implicitly subject to a policing convention, since we are told that we must be vigilant not to activate such references too readily with bawdy interpretation.[28] But what if the reference, through its very censorship, is placed so as to invite bawdy interruption, if not verbally among the spectators imbued with new-found plant lore and issues of popular identification and naming, at least within their imaginations? This leering "deep bawdy," as I would term it, would then serve not thematically but rather as an undermining carnivalesque, much as Michael Bristol argues that the gravedigger might do by hanging around onstage during Ophelia's funeral.[29]

The danger for the interpretive community in this case is a kind of contagion, a shuffling from one bawdy object to another, either from a literal kind of bawdy to a less obvious one, or, more disturbingly, from one object of prohibition to another. This latter displacement, I believe, may offer the most potentially valuable cultural tactic. Its mechanism was partly explicated by Freud in *Totem and Taboo*, where he identifies a possibility of the contagious violation of prohibitions,[30] reminding one of his comparable analysis of the infectious character of jokes in *Jokes and Their Relation to the Unconscious.* What cultural critique could use, then, is an account of the process of taboo shifting, which I suggest is promoted rather than curtailed by a contagious, sustained practice of censorship that is trained to detect, through aesthetic nuance, the evasion of the policeman's gaze.

I turn now to an exemplary practice of the aesthetics of administering policemanship. The powerfully corrosive effect of a "deep bawdy" of flowers would require the vigilance of the resistant reader, as it must have for Thomas Bowdler in his nineteenth-century editions of *The Family Shakespeare*.[31] Although we tend to place the work in the tradition of censorship, its originary mode was rather like the sort of self-censorship natural to artistic endeavors, for Bowdler tells us that his project for a Shakespeare suitable to be read to the family (especially when young ladies are present) was simply the extension of a family tradition: his father, reading aloud to the family from Shakespeare on winter evenings, had found it necessary to check his own speech scrupulously as he proceeded through the text.[32] What is interesting about the son's project is that, as we observe in successive editions of this enormously popular text, Bowdler's eye for bawdy and his sense of potential bawdy interpretation become increasingly refined, and, as a result, he too would censor flowers for sexual association and invent different means for doing so.

It should be understood that just as literal "bawdy" may vary historically, the sexual association of flowers was not the same for Shakespeare as it was for Bowdler, for whom botanical perversity was in a sense more "graphically" imaginable. The difference is that in Shakespeare's time literal sexuality for plants was not known among botanists, for whom Bacon may be taken as representative in his explicit denial of generation by "copulation among plants" (though allowing gendered anomalies, as he notes for he-palms and she-palms) even as he viewed human-plant analogies.[33] The sexuality of plants was not fully accepted until the mid-eighteenth century, when the new knowledge was accompanied by a new topic for bawdy, as some botanists began to crack leering jokes in their lectures and others declared the idea to be both unconvincing and morally revolting.[34] What this means is that, to borrow Pierce's semiotic distinctions, flowers had a symbolic relation to sexuality in Shakespeare's time, whereas they had an indexical, if not iconic, relation to sexuality in Bowdler's time. In a sense, however, of these historical alternatives the more powerfully sexual image, more capable of shifting taboos and resisting censorship, may be Shakespeare's, loosened as it is from literal referentiality and based merely on sensual features of shape, hue, texture, and smell rather than on biology itself.

In his earliest (1807) edition, Bowdler simply excises the entire flower list, grafting the line "Therewith fantastic garlands did she come [*sic*]" to the line "And on the pendant boughs her coronet weeds."[35] By the 1818 edition, somewhat surprisingly, he reintroduces the list that includes "crow-flowers, nettles, daisies, and long purples," censoring the two bawdy lines but policing the possible bawdy association of the remaining bawdy reference in another way. He does this by footnoting the offending phrase and adding the sobering Latin plant name, *orchis morio mas*, abbreviating the telltale Latin word of gender. Apparently, he has learned what Shakespeare must have known from the start—that the bawdy allusion is effected not merely textually, but, as I suggested earlier, as a result of a bawdy interpretive community, just as Freud indicated that a comic community provides the requisite atmosphere for a successful joke. The glossarial impulse precludes such a community.

Police/Academy Deviance Training

An unintentional member of the bawdy interpretive community by virtue of his *Family Shakespeare* project, and having acquired the bawdy habits of mind that Bertrand Russell would later spoof in his short story about the Shakespeare editor, Bowdler manifests police mentality in a productive reciprocity with the mentality of the creative artist. The dynamic here has been brilliantly unpacked by the sociologist Harvey Sacks in his analysis of police training in perception and assessment of moral character. Sacks claims that the effective police officer—or perhaps more appropriate for present purposes, *policeman*—must develop, through a variety of "observation games" involving the "territory of normal appearances," a decidedly perverse imagination, exactly that of the pornographer or child molester, in order to observe everything with practical suspicion: "The novice is shown how to see the streets as, so to speak, scenes from pornographic films." A playground, for instance, is a place for child molesters; stores are places where shoplifters go, and so on.[36]

The general form of the problem facing the policeman, as described by Sacks, might be identical to that of the censor's, namely, to "maximize the likelihood that those who will turn out to be criminals and who pass in view are selected, while minimizing the likelihood that those who would not turn out to be criminals and who pass in view are selected" (282).[37] Clearly, this is important to the idea of a deep bawdy, for it outlines the reciprocal relation of the artist/ criminal whose task is to avoid appearances that would warrant investigation in order to "assure safe passage across the policeman's line of vision" (284). What is especially significant for the present purposes is the antimethodological character of this reciprocity and of the maintenance of appearances, for if the codes are methodized and announced in advance (from the perspective of judicial codes this would seem desirable), then the means of evasion are immediately evident. (This is somewhat different from Leo Strauss's idea of a writer's dodging censorship by conveying meaning through an esoteric text meant for the knowing audience.)[38] In the present terms of "deep bawdy," to play at policing, cultivating the antennae for deviance, is itself to complicate or disrupt the more straightforward logic of the "natural," in turn testing censorability and encouraging taboo shifting.

Bowdler's treatment of the Perdita's flower passage is also instructive. Perdita has complained of not having the right flowers with which to make Florizel garlands, and he jokingly asks if that makes him a corpse:

FLO. What, like a corse?
PER. No, like a bank for love to lie and play on,
    Not like a corse; or if, not to be buried,
    But quick and in my arms. Come, take your flowers.
    Methinks I play ... (4.4.130–33)

In the 1807 Bowdler edition, Perdita responds:

No, like a bank, for love to lie and play on;
Not like a corse. Come, take your flowers.

Thus, the indelicacy of the more directly bawdy physical scene itself, "quick and in my arms," is the immediate object of the erasing gaze of the editor. But after reflection and interpretive refinement, it is once again the flowers that become problematic, in the metaphor of Florizel's body as a bank of flowers. Bowdler has accurately sniffed out the disruptive implications embodied here, namely, a masculinity eroticized and aestheticized in conjunction with a woman aggressively on top. More deviant than transgressive, this "grafted" image, as it were, contains the deeper bawdy that only the most proficient of censors might detect. That Bowdler's interpretive sophistication developed such a refinement might be apparent from his nonsexual censoring, as in his edition of Gibbon's history of Rome, where he assures the readers that not only indecency but also "Allusions of an Irreligious Tendency" are excised "by the Editor of the Family Shakespeare."[39] Once again, it is a censorship of great delicacy, an aestheticized policing, that is most likely to reach the deeper levels where shifting of taboos, from religious to erotic heterodoxy, can more readily occur.

If "radical arrangeability" is the characteristic force of the flower image for Shakespeare, the sensual photographs of orchids by Robert Mapplethorpe, theatrical in their black-and-white posings, provide an interesting transhistorical analogy that itself might illuminate censorship's more immediate access to a deep bawdy of artistic imagery. Like the flowers of Georgia O'Keeffe, they are readily visualized in erotic terms, though for O'Keeffe the erotics is female, if not implicitly antimasculinist. Mapplethorpe's photographs, often described as being as erotically charged as his controversial, explicitly sexual counterparts, provide an immediate analogue to the genital imagery of some of Shakespeare's flowers. In order to consider censoring Mapplethorpe's flowers, one would have to experience their implicit intertextual connection with his sadomasochist and other images conventionally marked as unnatural, a connection that again opens up the possibility of an implied radical arrangeability of social relations. Difficult to domesticate, Mapplethorpe's images continually anticipate the pressure of appropriation and naturalization.[40] Richard Howard alludes to this displacing character of the images in his introduction to the photographs, where he writes, "What is spoken, Heidegger says, is never—and in no language—what is said. And I might add: not even in the language of flowers."[41] If, as I have argued, the oppositional character of grafting is an important notion for unpacking flower imagery in Shakespeare, for experimenting with the domination of nature over culture, the comment Mapplethorpe is said to have made about the look of his flowers—that these are *New York* flowers—may be apropos. In order to understand Shakespeare's implied attitude toward nature as more tough-minded and radical than that of a nostalgic ruralist, it might be apt to think of his flowers as, say, quintessentially *London* flowers, and therefore part of a new sexuality and a new market, fetishized in the double, economic-erotic sense of the term. If so, the image of flowers in Shakespeare is an example of what Trotsky understood as capitalism's chief social consequence, the victory of town over country. Socialized, theatricalized, fetishized, and nationalized, Shakespeare's flower images are miniatures of ideology in their historical moment.

Class Performance: Toward an Oppressive Pedagogy

If Noam Chomsky is correct in seeing self-censorship as a chief mode by which consent is manufactured in U.S. society today, then it may be that an understanding of this process is a political project of some urgency.[42] And it may be that since for Shakespeareans the most immediate and direct political act is teaching, a pedagogy that subverts social decorum, perhaps through an access to deep bawdy learned from the practices of censorship, may help provide a corrective through the humanities to our impoverished political culture. I want, then, to conclude by reflecting on the teaching of Shakespearean bawdy as a possible oppositional practice, and to suggest the shape though not necessarily the particulars of such a practice.

I will begin by noting that the form of teaching practice I propose adopts a model different from the one that is usually assumed in studies of theory in the classroom—of which there seem to be increasing numbers now, perhaps in response to the narrowing of the possibilities of effective political practice in U.S. culture. A recent anthology, *Theory in the Classroom*, shares some assumptions with traditional teaching models.[43] Even though the goal is a critical understanding of the nature of interpretation itself, rather than understanding of some transcendent humanistic content, the end of pedagogy nevertheless is still primarily understanding. An alternative or at least a supplement would be a "performative" model, not in the sense of play performance but in the sense of the ordinary language philosophy as formulated by J. L. Austin, who founded speech act theory on the case of language use in which something is done even *in* the saying of it, as in the classic examples of advising, warning, thanking, requesting, and the like.[44] Speech act theory, because its roots are largely in the traditional study of stylistics with its attention to the wide differences of meaning that slight nuances of usage produce, is a field defined, as it were, by deviance. In a performative pedagogy, by analogy to linguistic performativity, what is taught as knowledge would occur simultaneously with experience. It might be both oppositional and antimethodological.

As a kind of poststructuralist performative in Shakespearean teaching, for example, I have adopted the practice of having students memorize long passages, a "residual" if not actually "archaic" teaching device, to use the distinctions of Raymond Williams.[45] One of the passages is Kate's submission speech from the conclusion of *The Taming of the Shrew*, which is "memorable" in a traditional way, but it fails to conform to the traditional requisite of providing general and timeless truths from the cultural warehouse (unlike, say, Jacques' ages of man speech)—unless abject social submission is regarded as a timeless value. That failure is precisely the point. As intriguing as the speech may be, it is certainly not one that could ever be mustered as evidence for Shakespeare's transcendent wisdom, which is why I would have it inscribed in a student's memory in the first place. Lodged there, it will always disturb any impulse to assent automatically to warm claims about the universal truths flowing from Shakespeare's great pen. This innoculated student would be wary of such a claim, without necessarily being able to articulate why. In short, the exercise is a performative practice designed to produce not understanding but rather a certain cultural dysfunctionality. It is a pedagogy more directly aimed at discursive practices and their undoing.

The experience of bawdy language in Shakespeare offers insight into a performative pedagogy. Despite the fact that the subject of bawdy has maintained perennial interest among Shakespeareans, one does not hear about the teaching of it as often as one might expect in a liberal academic climate. The bias about teaching may stem from the privileged status of editing in Shakespeare studies, conveying the expectation that what one does when one gets a bawdy passage is essentially what an editor would do, namely, *gloss* it—a mode that is, as we have seen, one of the police modes examined in the case of botanical bawdy. And, while the current theoretical interest in the social formations associated with the body encourages a more untrammeled pedagogy, even such a theoretical interest may itself come to be policed by the glossarial—tending to replace textual gloss with ideological gloss. But for students, I suspect that any glossarial approach would fail even in terms of understanding, unless an attempt is made to historicize the language adequately, a historicization that I suggest might be more directly accomplished through a performative pedagogy.

An example of a performative pedagogy for Shakespearean bawdy might be teaching the significance of cuckoldry, which makes little sense as a definition without a more elaborate explication of its context in the history of familial and gender relations. In short, students just don't get it. But a performative pedagogy might try a more direct route to the performative experience of the term, as I have attempted when I ask all the men in class to laugh out loud, uproariously if they like, when I read any allusions to "horns" in reciting passages and lines. (The "horn" song from *As You Like It* works well.) I ask the women to laugh if they feel like it. (The different instructions are intended to reproduce the historical asymmetry of gender relations.) What is remarkable is that quite soon the "canned" laughs appear "naturalized" and unforced, and some students even guffaw uncontrollably at something that moments earlier they did not find in the least amusing. Among other things, such an exercise in contagious bawdy construction becomes a demonstration of the potential for instant enculturation in social relations, and bypassing the means of censorability. (Further study would explore the gender asymmetries both of the exercise and of the bawdy response—perhaps generalizing to asymmetries of the concept of "bawdy" itself.) After this exercise, when students encounter allusions to cuckoldry, they may be *feeling* bawdy before *thinking* it, perhaps inviting a more accurate registering of the emotional logic of a passage. Once again we might appropriate Freud's account of the contagious nature of both humor and taboo violation, in understanding how either might be enacted in a pedagogy of deep bawdy. Mere lewdness is not enough.[46]

A performative pedagogy, then, would need to be wary of the glossarial impulse, understood as the combination of interpretive and pedagogical controls. Its opposite would be the sort of experience we might recall from occasions in secondary school when, despite, or rather because of, a teacher's rigor—the more rigor the better—everything whatsoever acquires sexual innuendo for the students. In fact, the further the subject is from the sexual (a music teacher, say, explaining how to "finger your instrument"), the more powerful is the activation of the bawdy (more so than in, say, a health class talk on sexuality). It is, of course, just such sniggering that a glossed reference usually impedes, as Freud explains that analysis diminishes the affective response to a joke. The same anxiety informs the analysis of Shakespearean bawdy by Colman, whose openness to the possibilities of bawdy finds much more of it in Shakespeare than previous dictionary-based approaches would suggest, but whose arguments about the thematic functioning of bawdy references nevertheless stumble, as we have seen, on the significant case of "ambivalent bawdy." This category of a certain bawdy that seems present but lacking evident purpose causes Colman to throw up his hands, merely urging interpretive prudence. Perhaps what lurks behind the methodological stricture here is not so much fear of reader empowerment with its attendant interpretive anarchy but the fear of a free-floating prohibition leading to just as radical a taboo shifting.

I am suggesting here the shape but not the details of such a performative pedagogy. My own experiences in teaching bawdy, ranging from the glossarial to the leering, have been decidedly mixed successes.[47] To make the class into a single interpretive community, moreover, may risk other possible "communities," and I do not presume to suggest that the notion of community here should suppress differences in gender or orientation. The discomfort for at least some students would argue real limits to such performativity.[48] It must be noted that, even allowing for Constance Penley's and others' claims about the "basically eroticized nature of learning,"[49] a pedagogy of deep bawdy might assume the form, if not the ends, of sexual harassment. Regardless of the particulars of such a pedagogy, however, it may be an important strategy for reaching the territory of censorability itself.

Finally, one might ask, in keeping with radical political theorizations of educational practice such as that of Paulo Freire in *Pedagogy of the Oppressed*, whether the goal of such performativity would be a form of "empowerment" of students.[50] Unfortunately, this progressive cliché of "empowerment," sometimes inappropriately transferred from the specifics of an oppressed population of Latin America, conceals the actual political subject positions of our students in most present situations in the United States, as well as limits notions of political value to the private and the personal, in keeping with the impoverished political discourse here. Even when one grants the general value of empowerment, however, one must ask, empowerment for whom? Do all students need a supplement of power? It may be instead that what is called for is a tactic or a flexibility that simultaneously empowers and disempowers—that offers empowerment for some students in the class but disempowerment, or more accurately the *performance* of disempowerment, for others. More specifically, it may be important to disempower American students with respect to the "third world" and at the same time to empower the same students, if they are women, with respect to the men. The same student, in effect, might be both empowered and disempowered according to class, gender, and race. A performative pedagogy, as in the example of teaching bawdy and the natural, might be designed to encourage both these contradictory effects at the same time. It could be a pedagogy of conscious bifurcation whose minimal unit of community would be playing cops and freaks together.

NOTES

I would like to thank Lena Cowen Orlin and the members of the Folger Institute Evening Colloquium series of the Folger Shakespeare Library for their energetic and useful responses to this paper, an earlier version of which I was invited to present at the colloquium on March 3, 1993. I especially thank Michael Bristol and Denise Albanese for their troubling questions.

1. Herbert Marcuse, "Liberation from the Affluent Society," in *Critical Theory and Society: A Reader*, ed. Stephen Eric Bronner and Douglas MacKay Kellner (New York and London: Routledge, 1989), 276.

2. Annabel Patterson, *Pastoral and Ideology: Virgil to Valery* (Berkeley: University of California Press, 1987); James Turner, *The Politics of Landscape: Rural Scenery and Society in English Poetry, 1630-1660* (Cambridge, Mass.: Harvard University Press, 1979).

3. Caroline Spurgeon, *Shakespeare's Imagery and What It Tells Us* (Cambridge: Cambridge University Press, 1952). While it might be thought that an ideological imagery study would in no way be indebted to Spurgeon's generally disregarded work, it should be mentioned that Spurgeon's work itself had an unacknowledged progressive side to it, since it quietly violated New Critical strictures against extrinsic criticism by allowing for a referentiality outside the text.

4. Henry N. Ellacombe, *The Plant-Lore & Garden-craft of Shakespeare* (Exeter: William Pollard, n.d.), 1.

5. Mats Ryden, *Shakespearean Plant Names: Identifications and Interpretations* (Stockholm: Almquist and W. Krell, 1978), 25. Citations to Shakespeare are from *The Complete Pelican Shakespeare*, ed. Alfred Harbage (Baltimore: Penguin, 1969).

6. Jan Kott, *Shakespeare Our Contemporary* (London: Methuen, 1964).

7. William Empson, "Fairy Flight in *A Midsummer Night's Dream*," in *Essays on Shakespeare* (Cambridge: Cambridge University Press, 1986), 223-24.

8. Louis Adrian Montrose, "'Shaping Fantasies': Figurations of Gender and Power in Elizabethan Culture," *Representations* 1 (1983): 61-94.

9. Christopher Hill, "Censorship and English Literature," in *The Collected Essays of Christopher Hill*, vol. 1 (Sussex: Harvester, 1985), 32.

10. Jacques Derrida, *Disseminations* (Chicago: University of Chicago Press, 1982), 202.

11. Frank Kermode, ed., "Introduction," William Shakespeare, *The Tempest* (Cambridge, Mass.: Harvard University Press, 1954), liii.

12. Keith Thomas, *Man and the Natural World: A History of the Modern Sensibility* (New York: Pantheon, 1983), 224. See also Blanche Henry, *British Botanical and Horticultural Literature before 1800* (London: Oxford University Press, 1975), 8 and passim.

13. Leonard Mascall, *A booke of the art and maner, howe to plante and graffe all sortes of trees . . .* (London, [1569]), A4, A3.

14. Jonathan Dollimore, *Sexual Dissidence: Augustine to Wilde, Freud to Foucault* (Oxford: Clarendon, 1991), 115.

15. Francis Bacon, *Sylva Sylvarum; or, a Natural History*, in *The Works of Francis Bacon*, ed. James Spedding, vol. 4 (New York: Hurd and Houghton, 1864), 392 ff.

16. Christopher Hill, *The World Turned Upside Down: Radical Ideas during the English Revolution* (New York: Viking, 1972).

17. Mascall, *A booke*, C3-C4.

18. Karl Marx, *The German Ideology*, in Karl Marx and Friedrich Engels, *Basic Writings in Politics and Philosophy*, ed. Lewis S. Feuer (Garden City, N.Y.: Doubleday, 1959), 247.

19. James I of England, *A Royal Rhetorician* (Westminster: A. Constable, 1900), xvi. A contemporary analogue of social bifurcation is former president George Bush's "weed and seed" policy, proposed in response to the worst urban riots in U.S. history in South Central Los Angeles in 1991. But the governing metaphor of the Bush administration was not so much the garden as the suburban lawn or golf course, an interpretation for which I am grateful to Jonathan Holden.

20. Edward Lee Green, *Landmarks of Botanical History, Part II* (Stanford, Calif.: Stanford University Press, 1983), 883.

21. Pierre Bourdieu, *Distinction: A Social Critique of the Judgement of Taste* (Cambridge, Mass.: Harvard University Press, 1984).

22. John Parkinson in 1629, as cited in Thomas, *Man and the Natural World*, 224.

23. R. Dodoens, *A New Herbal, or Historie of Plants* (London: Edward Griffin, 1619).

24. Esther Singleton, *The Shakespeare Garden* (New York: Farquhar Payson, 1931), 208-9.

25. Alan Dent, *World of Shakespeare: Plants* (New York: Taplinger, 1973), 99.

26. Leo Grindon, *The Shakespeare Flora*, 2nd ed. (Manchester: Palmer and Howe, 1883), 129.

27. Robert Speaight, *Nature in Shakespearian Tragedy* (London: Hollis and Carter, 1955), 41.

28. E. A. M. Colman, *The Dramatic Use of Bawdy in Shakespeare* (London: Longman, 1974), 169.

29. From an unpublished talk given at the Central Renaissance Conference, St. Louis, Missouri, in March 1987.

30. Sigmund Freud, *Totem and Taboo: Some Points of Agreement between the Mental Lives of Savages and Neurotics* (New York: Norton, 1950), 34-35.

31. Noel Perrin, *Dr. Bowdler's Legacy: A History of Expurgated Books in England and America* (New York: Atheneum, 1969).

32. Introduction, Thomas Bowdler, *The Family Shakespeare* (London, 1818).

33. Bacon, *Sylva Sylvarum, 432.*

34. A. G. Morton, *History of Botanical Science* (New York: Academic Press, 1981), 239.

35. Thomas Bowdler, *The Family Shakespeare* (London, 1807).

36. Harvey Sacks, "Notes on Police Assessment of Moral Character," *Studies in Social Interaction,* ed. David Sudnow (New York: Free Press, 1972), 285.

37. Of course, in proposing this reading of the "problem" for the policeman, one must in practice take account of specific political contexts, for the interest of the state apparatus might be precisely the opposite; that is, to select out those who are *not* criminals, while an "error" of the policeman, may clearly serve state interests by creating an overall atmosphere of coercion and compliance. That lack of inclusion of the state apparatus in the consideration of the ethnomethodologist suggests a certain systematic distortion within the discipline as usually practiced.

38. Leo Strauss, *Persecution and the Art of Writing* (Glencoe, Ill.: Free Press, 1952).

39. Perrin, *Dr. Bowdler's Legacy,* 85-86.

40. For a corresponding account of Mapplethorpe's built-in anticipation of the discursive appropriation of the perverse, analogous to the concept of "deep bawdy," see Paul Morrison, "Coffee Table Sex: Robert Mapplethorpe and the Sadomasochism of Everyday Life," *Genders* 11 (1991): 17-36.

41. Richard Howard, in *Robert Mapplethorpe,* ed. Richard Marshall (New York: Whitney Museum and New York Graphic Society, 1988), 153.

42. Edward S. Herman and Noam Chomsky, *Manufacturing Consent: The Political Economy of the Mass Media* (New York: Pantheon, 1988).

43. *Theory in the Classroom,* ed. Cary Nelson (Urbana and Chicago: University of Illinois Press, 1986).

44. J. L. Austin, *How to Do Things with Words* (New York: Oxford University Press, 1965).

45. Raymond Williams, *Marxism and Literature* (Oxford and New York: Oxford University Press, 1977), 121 ff.

46. I want to thank Denise Albanese of George Mason University for pointing out the asymmetry of her assuming a "bad girl" teaching persona, radically complicating the question of standpoint here. I can report from my limited classroom experience that the performativity I describe seems not to repress but on the contrary to encourage responses from women students, and to elicit productive rather than unproductive confrontation, though in turn one might ask how I would know that for sure. And, aside from the classroom limitations, I am aware that despite the use here of a "leering" pedagogy for momentary political purposes, the larger inescapable context remains that of U.S. media culture, in which bawdy and outrage are increasingly packaged and marketed, though less often in the form of "deep" bawdy. A glance at the television show "Studs" would confirm this.

47. In one instance of failure, attempting to explicate the "long purples" passage with leering indirection and innuendo, I managed to have most of the students "get it," or pretend to; but one student, who may have misperceived the referent for racial reasons, was awkwardly disconcerted. At that moment, one could hardly have imagined a worse scene of pedagogy.

48. I accept the objection that there might be an implicit claim here about a different *capability* of women's response. I think the objection could open up other difficulties with a performative pedagogy, which becomes a question of the relation of pedagogy to

models of hegemony. I wish to thank Professor Susan Green and her students at the University of Oklahoma for these comments.

49. Constance Penley, "Teaching in Your Sleep: Feminism and Psychoanalysis," in *Theory in the Classroom*, 138.

50. Paulo Freire, *Pedagogy of the Oppressed* (New York: Continuum, 1990).

Jean-Jacques Rousseau: Policing the Aesthetic from the Left

Dennis Porter

If one major task of the present volume is to question our current understanding of the concept and practice of censorship by means of a series of discrete historical probes, then an exploration of Jean-Jacques Rousseau's contribution to the debate is a crucial one. Twentieth-century history is still too gruesomely familiar for anyone to believe that there is a simple narrative of progressive elimination in which, from roughly the seventeenth and eighteenth centuries on, conservative and reactionary forces affirmed the need for censorship and democratic and revolutionary movements opposed it. As Michel Foucault might well have said, censorship comes from everywhere (although it varies enormously in its institutionalized practices, its objects, and its effects).[1] If there is any doubt that this is the case, a return to the works of Rousseau and to the prerevolutionary moment of mid-eighteenth century France is an instructive experience.

Rousseau's relationship to censorship is especially illuminating because he is widely regarded as the first major theorist of political democracy in the modern West and the French philosopher of his age to exercise the greatest influence over French revolutionary discourse in its Jacobin phase or what Keith Baker among others has referred to as "revolutionary republican ideology."[2] At the same time, along with other eighteenth-century philosophes, Rousseau was himself the victim of ancien régime censorship.[3] As a result, Rousseau's formulation of the issues takes us back to the beginning of the tangled and frequently oppositional relationship between aesthetic practice and political power that took a decisive new turn with the events of the French Revolution.

To understand why Rousseau argued in favor of censorship—in spite of his own harrowing experience of persecution, flight, and exile—there is no better place to begin than with his first published work of critical philosophy cum cultural criticism, the so-called *Discourse on the Sciences and the Arts* of 1750. I shall concentrate here on that work and on the *Letter to D'Alembert on Theater* of 1758 because in the authoritarian revolutionary tradition of censorship, which holds that republican virtue and good citizenship can be legislated, they have something of the status that Milton's *Areopagitica* and John Stuart Mill's *On Liberty* have among political liberals.

The First Discourse was, of course, written as a response to a question posed by the Academy of Dijon for an essay competition on the question of "whether the reestablishment of the Sciences and the Arts have contributed to the purification of manners" (*épurer les moeurs*).[4]

As posed, the subject is tendentious enough; it invites a response that assumes a moral function for art and learning and foregrounds a highly charged word, *épurer*, that already had long-standing ethical and aesthetic as well as medicinal connotations. One can only suppose that the provincial academicians from Dijon who asked the question were probably expecting the answer "yes, but ... " to their question. Yet with a symptomatic gesture that can, in retrospect, be perceived as an opening onto Rousseau's whole future career as moral philosopher and political thinker, he reposes the question in his opening sentence with a notable addition: "whether the reestablishment of the Sciences and the Arts have contributed to the purification *or the corruption* of manners."[5]

The effect of Rousseau's metonymic slide is to highlight what was to become for him the kind of master signifier that stabilizes an ideological field, fixes meanings, and mobilizes interventionist energies. Surrounded by "corruption," he will make "purity," or its virtual synonym in the context, "virtue," the goal to be pursued throughout his life, on both the individual and the collective level, even when, as is sometimes the case, he is also succumbing to the temptations of the world.

Moreover, to move from the title to the text of Rousseau's first important work is to realize how a whole critical essay is organized in terms of a series of equivalences and oppositional terms centered on "corruption" and "purity" as a kind of nodal point: nature, being, freedom, virtue, truth, vigor, manliness, simplicity, utility, and industriousness line up against civilization, appearance, enslavement, moral corruption, deception, masquerade, degeneration, effeminacy, politeness, luxury, leisure, philosophy, literature, the arts, and even learning (in the form of "the sciences").

Further, what the former set of equivalences presupposes in comparison with the latter is a spirit of sacrifice: whereas the latter may be said to be associated in one way or another with the Freudian pleasure principle (although some of them are clearly at its destabilizing outer limit), the former have the quality of an ethical imperative; they smack of "duty" and "responsibility," of a giving up of self to that which, whether within or without (God, nature, empire, nation, class, leader, or, in Rousseau's case, "Geneva") transcends the self. It is the spirit of sacrifice in a noble cause that gives rise to the militant tone of the First Discourse: the essay is the kind of moralistic and civic call to order familiar enough from the tradition of republican Roman discourse but decidedly out of place in the Paris of Louis XV, as Rousseau himself was aware. It is, therefore, characteristic of the moral ethos and argument of the First Discourse that it should end with a comparison between "two great Peoples," namely, Athens and Sparta, the first of which "knew how to speak well [*savait bien dire*], and the other to act well [*bien faire*]."[6] From the beginning, then, (political) action is elevated above (aesthetic) performance.

As for the relation of such a set of attitudes to the specific question of censorship, one does not have to read very far into the text of the First Discourse to realize that at its heart is a fierce and generalized suspicion of the pursuit of knowledge for its own sake, and especially of art and literature. Moreover, art and literature are required to justify themselves on grounds that transcend the aesthetic in the direction of morality and politics.

In this connection it is interesting to note that, in his posthumously published autobiography, Louis Althusser praises Rousseau for his understanding of the important connection between art and ideology.[7] The most influential Western Marxist theorist of his generation clearly shared his eighteenth-century predecessor's suspicion of the sphere of the aesthetic and asserted that Rousseau was one of the earliest thinkers to formulate the concept of hegemony, although the Enlightenment philosopher does not, of course, use that Gramscian term: "I take Rousseau to be the first theorist of hegemony—after Machiavelli."[8]

Althusser claimed to have discovered the theory of hegemony laid out in Rousseau's Second Discourse, *On the Origin and Foundation of Inequality among Men* (1755), but the First Discourse is, in fact, even more explicit on the subject:

> Whereas the Government and Laws provide for the security and the well-being of the collectivity of men, the Sciences, Letters and the Arts, though perhaps less despotic and less powerful, hang their garlands of flowers over the iron chains that weigh men down, stifle in them the feeling for the original liberty they seemed born for, make them love their slavery, and turn them into what are known as civilized Peoples.[9]

In short, the sciences, literature, and art are a crucial factor in seducing humanity into overlooking the lack of freedom and the injustices of its sociopolitical condition.

From the point of view of twentieth-century Marxist theory, the concept of hegemony, along with Althusser's revisionary theory of the functioning of ideology,[10] forced attention on cultural production as, in spite of appearances, itself a site of political conflict, as a relatively autonomous practice characterized by fundamental class antagonisms. Two centuries earlier Rousseau had already understood that to take hegemony seriously is to believe in the necessity, under certain conditions, of banning books or policing thought; in a conflict between artistic freedom and social justice, there is no doubt where either Rousseau or Althusser stood. Moreover, Rousseau's writings may be regarded as the site in which the connection is made between *censor* in the antique republican Roman sense and the modern meaning of the term.[11]

The great originality of Rousseau's opening pamphlet in what was to be his lifelong adversarial relationship with Enlightenment culture appears not only in the fact that he anticipates the twentieth-century concept of hegemony, but also in the fact that the First Discourse as a whole has the character of what, after Nietzsche and Foucault, would come to be known as a "genealogy," or critical counterhistory. The First Discourse is, in effect, a genealogy of science, literature, and art that is probably closer to the Nietzsche of *Genealogy of Morals* than to Foucault insofar as Rousseau finds the masked origins of the arts and sciences in vice and amour propre as well as in a will to power:

> Astronomy is born of superstition; Eloquence of ambition, hatred, flattery, deceit; Geometry of avarice; Physics of a vain curiosity; and all of them, including Morality itself of our vices: we would have fewer doubts about their advantages if they owed them to our virtues.[12]

Hence Rousseau concludes that the arts and sciences are corrupt in their origins, in their objects of study and representation, and in the negative influence they exercice on politics and morals. In this and other of Rousseau's works, then, it is clear that the critique of the Enlightenment associated with a central strain in twentieth-century Continental thought—I am thinking of the Frankfurt school as well as of the "genealogists"—itself had its origin in the Enlightenment.

The most notable aspect of the First Discourse is, however, that Rousseau justifies his attack on Enlightenment culture broadly speaking on political as well as moral grounds; the fact that, in lieu of the author's name, the title page originally bore the clearly honorific phrase "By a Citizen of Geneva" immediately alerts the reader to the political dimension of the work, as well as to its character as a demand for acknowledgment from a homeland that he had left at the age of fifteen. In any case, the human virtue Rousseau chiefly celebrates in the First Discourse is civic virtue; that is, the kind that makes for the social order, power, and stability of states and empires. The point of view is that of state or polis and not that of the individual, in spite of his references to the loss of individual freedom that characterizes those states in which learning, literature, and the arts flourish.

Consequently, it is not surprising if Rousseau's ideal states should turn out to be Sparta and republican Rome, where ascetic values virtually exclude aesthetic ones. "Oh! Sparta," he eulogizes:

> the eternal opprobrium of a false doctrine! Whereas the vices produced by the fine arts entered Athens, whereas a Tyrant there assembled with great care the works of the Prince of Poets, you banished from within your walls Arts and Artists, Sciences and Scientists.[13]

Rousseau goes on to endorse the affirmation of the third century B.C. Roman general and censor, Fabricius Luscinus, who was famed for his poverty, austerity, and incorruptibility, that the mission of Rome was to subdue and impose morality: "Let others distinguish themselves with their vain talents; the only talent worthy of Rome is to conquer the world and to make virtue reign."[14] This is "virile virtue" indeed.

The open *Letter to D'Alembert on Theater* of 1758 effectively consecrated Rousseau's break with his erstwhile friends and collaborators, the philosophes, including in particular Denis Diderot and Jean Le Rond D'Alembert, the coeditors of that *summum* of Enlightenment thought, the *Encyclopédie* (1751–1765). In his open letter, Rousseau, in effect, gives his most complete response to the question posed in Sartre's best-known work of literary theory, *What Is Literature?* The answer is, of course, that it is not much or, at least, not much that is good.[15] The *Letter* is Rousseau's longest sustained attack on the most social and urbane form of literary expression. It is significant because in refuting D'Alembert's mild plea, in his article on Geneva in the *Encyclopédie,* that the Calvinist republic allow theatrical productions for the sake of "urbanity" and the improvement of taste, Rousseau develops further the themes of his First Discourse of almost a decade earlier.

Given the character of his writings in the intervening years, the fervor of his refutation of D'Alembert hardly constitutes a surprise, especially in light of the fact that Voltaire, who was a devotee of theater and was living nearby at Saint-Jean, was an interested party. From Rousseau's point of view, D'Alembert's inconsiderate proposal amounts, in effect, to an assault on the Geneva of his own fantasy scenario; that is, on the utopian idea of a republican city-state characterized by virtue, egalitarianism, unity, and faith, and consequently without the inequities and ostentation of ancien régime monarchy. To admit theatrical performances into such an achieved social totality was once again for Rousseau to introduce the vices of representation, critical worldliness, irony, detachment, doubt, pleasure, and play on the part of the authors; masquerade and immorality on the part of actors and actresses; and leisure, luxury, display, and effeminacy on the part of the audience. Perhaps even more than the other arts discussed in the First Discourse, theater and all those associated with it (from playwrights and actors and actresses to its philosophical apologists and the members of the public who constituted its audience) were in their way the agents of such "corruption."

The *Letter* makes clear that for Rousseau, no figure exemplified so notoriously the dangerous, seductive power of theater as Molière—who was preeminently "a man of the theater," who virtually alone created French classical comedy, whose patrons were Parisian salon society and the court. Molière's comedies constituted the most compelling of evidence against theater for "the citizen of Geneva" insofar as an enormous talent can be seen to have been put in the service of wit and worldliness and a skeptical ethic of accommodation that undermines the very idea of a nonalienating society characterized by political virtue, moral seriousness, natural hierarchy, and social harmony.[16]

At the heart of Rousseau's polemical essay, there is, of course, the celebrated defense of the character of the Misanthrope against his author. The section is illuminating, in the first place, for the obvious way in which Rousseau identifies with Molière's comic hero and, in particular, with the cleansing energy of his "hate":

> What is Molière's Misanthrope then? A good man who hates the morals of his time and the wickedness of his contemporaries; who precisely because he loves his fellow men hates in them the evils they do to each other and the vices these evils cause.[17]

In the second place, the passage is suggestive insofar as it throws light on the phantasmatic character of Rousseau's reasoning and the connection made between the private man and his social world.

On the level of the social world, to identify with the Misanthrope is to believe in the possibility of a homogeneous and transparent society[18] characterized by total honesty, complementarity, and reciprocity in its relations—in other words, an impossible and probably totalitarian society or one that can only exist as social fantasy.

On the level of the private man, to identify with the Misanthrope is to fail to appreciate the underlying comic structure of the character, that is to say, the way in which Alceste lives a contradiction; Alceste is a comic character, not a model of moral rectitude in a hypocritical world, because of the antagonism he embodies between a dogmatic moral stance and passion, between contempt for the insincerity of human social relations and desire for a coquette who is a living incarnation of that insincerity. As he indicates in a brilliant sentence, Rousseau was aware of this: "Making his Misanthrope fall in love was nothing, the stroke of genius was in making him fall in love with a coquette."[19] But he resents the resulting ridiculousness of the figure. It is as if Rousseau, in this case at least, wants to deny the possibility of the divided self or subjectivity in the modern psychoanalytic sense of the word; in the face of so much evidence in himself and others, Rousseau clings to the dangerous illusion of homogeneity and transparency within and without, of full accessibility of self to self and of self to others.

It is for similar reasons that he also indignantly condemns the art of acting; there is for him an implied connection between the social role playing of the characters who surround Alceste in Molière's play and those who earn a living from pretending to be what they are not:

> In what does an actor's talent consist? It is in the art of counterfeiting himself, of donning another character than his own, of appearing different from what he is, of pretending passion when he feels none, of saying something different from what he thinks just as naturally as if he really thought it, and, finally, of forgetting his own situation by dint of imitating that of others.[20]

Actors are the incarnation of masquerade and nontransparency; acting is an art that makes a virtue of the human capacity to appear to be what one is not and is, therefore, the worst possible model for citizens in an ideal republic.

If one follows Slavoj Žižek's advice in the sphere of "the criticism of ideology,"[21] namely, to locate "the symptom" that explains the logic of enjoyment, one finds that the particular "symptom" that provides the clue to an understanding of Rousseau's ideological fantasizing is precisely the identification of the sciences and the arts, including preeminently literature, with "corruption"; the sciences and the arts pursued as an end in themselves in the First Discourse are represented as, to a significant degree, both cause and effect of the decadence of the modern European monarchies, as the locus of an inadmissible form of pleasure, and hence as obstacles to the making of a new society on sound moral and political principles.[22] Perhaps the most disturbing part of Rousseau's argument in his early writings, in fact, is the implication that a just and egalitarian republic can only be created by exclusion and censorship; its founding act virtually expels certain classes of people such as writers, artists, thinkers, and performers and suppresses their works.[23]

Rousseau's ideal society is, in fact, associated crucially with homeostasis, and it is notable for largely having been inspired by the models furnished by classical antiquity, including in particular Sparta, and by classical writers from Plato to the second-century Roman, Cato the Elder. His goal was above all to "purify" contemporary morals and manners, and in order to achieve that he was ready to eliminate from the social order a great many of the activities we normally associate with the idea of civilization and "the public sphere" in Habermas's sense along with those who, whether actively or passively, engage in them.

Moreover, the motivation both for the condemnation of certain classes of artists, writers, and thinkers in Rousseau's writings and for his own retreat from contamination by them is in many ways similar to that of antique Roman censor, traditional church moralist, or modern party ideologue of either left or right; they are all animated by the conviction that those they condemn (sophists and epicureans; dramatists, artists, and actors; aristocrats, bourgeois, or Jews, as the case may be) are an intolerable race of *jouisseurs*—of those whom Žižek, in his extension of a familiar Lacanian concept, has called "the subject(s) presumed to enjoy," and, therefore, subjects who should be saved from such scandalous enjoyment for their own sake as well as society's—even if it costs them their lives.[24]

There are in this connection two important points to be made: one relates to the idea of political will and the other to cultural revolution. First, more than two hundred years before Mao Tse-tung, Rousseau was advocating putting "the polis (if not politics) in command." Confirmation of this attitude is, in fact, to be found in one ringing sentence in the *Confessions* at the point where Rousseau is discussing the themes of his projected work on political institutions, of which *The Social Contract* was in the end to be the only substantial result: "I had understood that everything at bottom depended on politics [*tout tenait radicalement de la politique*] and that, however one approached the question, a given people would only ever be what the nature of its government made it."[25] Even if one makes allowance for the fact that Rousseau is specifically focusing on political institutions here, the formulation of the problem of moral virtue and human well-being in purely political terms is striking.

There is, then, at the core of his political theory a logic that elides the very notion of civil society and points to Jacobin revolutionary politics at their most radical, even if one finds in his works no apology for revolutionary violence. It would be inaccurate as well as unfair to affirm a direct link between Rousseau's Discourses and the Terror, but he did prepare the discursive ground. Paraphrasing François Furet in this connection, Lynn Hunt points to the dangerous confusion among the Jacobins of which Rousseau was guilty first:

> The Terror was the logical consequence of the revolutionary distortion of the normal relationship between society and politics; politics was no longer the arena for the representation of competing social interests, but rather a terrorizing instrument for the reshaping of society.[26]

Along with a new conception of "political will," what Rousseau's Discourses and the *Letter to D'Alembert* also make explicit is that to obey the Maoist injunction and "put politics in command" is to subject civil society to the kind of total transformation of its values, institutions, and practices that we have come to call cultural revolution and that we associate with almost all the major political revolutions of the modern world, starting with the French on down through the Bolshevik, Chinese, Vietnamese, and Cuban ones.[27]

In short, in old regime Europe, Rousseau was the first to argue so powerfully for the policing of the aesthetic in the cause of a new radical politics. It is thus fully consistent with his developed political position that he should seek to replace the decadent, cosmopolitan theater of eighteenth-century European high culture with a kind of communitarian "people's theater." In lieu of alien forms of theater in his native Geneva, Rousseau argues for festivals based on indigenous popular culture and for communal balls that have the great virtue of putting the contented and virtuous populace itself on display to itself; in place of the separation between active performer and passive spectator associated with theater, such spectacles, properly supervised, would reaffirm the familial oneness of the collectivity: "These balls ... would resemble less a public spectacle than the reunion of a great family, and from the midst of such joy and pleasure there would be born the preservation, unity, and prosperity of the Republic."[28] One finds anticipated here the kind of mass public festivals that, first organized by the revolutionaries in the 1790s, were to become a central feature of the French republican tradition and to be taken up by the various twentieth-century revolutionary movements.

It is in his discussion of public festivals, in fact, that Rousseau evokes a Genevan at play and comes closest to presenting a portrait of his ideal happy, animated citizen in whom, unlike the actor, there is no gap between appearance and being:

> He is lively, gay, warm; at such moments his heart is in his eyes as it is on his lips; he seeks to communicate his joy and his pleasures; he invites, he presses, he forces himself upon those who come by, he disputes their company. All the different circles become one; everything belongs to everyone.[29]

In a passage such as this, one recognizes the emergence of the politicizing of sentiment that at certain moments of high revolutionary fervor was to raise the idea of fraternity to equal status with liberty and equality.[30]

In any case, the kind of socially induced happiness Rousseau imagines in collective popular events requires that modern Western civilization be "purified," or as we might say now in the wake of bolshevism, "purged" of divisive and subversive institutions such as theater. And in such a cause, Rousseau has no qualms about wanting to impose the Spartan spirit of duty and self-sacrifice on his ideal republic. At the same time, he recognizes that, if he expects to be followed, a call for general denial must be preceded by his own example of self-denial. As his autobiography makes clear, his way of responding to the desire of the Other—which in his case is associated with the Calvinist God and the Republic of Geneva—is, on the one hand, to affirm the vanity of all those morally ambivalent achievements in the sciences and the arts celebrated by his contemporaries and, on the other, to explain how he came to see the error of his ways and find the path back to truth and the kind of "virile virtue"[31] that was to be the legacy he was to pass on to the Jacobins and, through them, to revolutionary parties down into our own time.

That Rousseau's suspicion of the aesthetic in general and of literature in particular extended to all genres is confirmed by his famous comments on the novel and by his theory of pedagogy as laid out in

Emile; or, On Education. When, in spite of his distrust of the novel, he did indulge himself by writing one, *Julie; or, The New Heloise* (1761), it turned out to be a utopian and sentimental romance in letter form in which one correspondent ostensibly addresses his intimate thoughts directly to another. And even then, in the opening lines of his preface, he finds it necessary to place the blame for his recourse to the genre on the immorality of his time: "Cities need theatrical performances and corrupt nations novels. I have observed the manners of my time and have published these letters. If only I had lived in an age when I should have thrown them into the fire" (3).[32]

If *Emile* is significant in the context of a discussion of censorship, it is because Rousseau's programmatic faith in "natural" or "negative" education means that, through infancy and adolescence, the pupil is deliberately isolated from virtually all contact with the wider and supposedly corrupt social world. The tutor conducts his model education in a totally controlled environment remote from the temptations of urban life. What this means, among other things, is that in opposition to the practice of the age, Rousseau delays teaching Emile to read and argues against giving him a literary education—including exposure in childhood to that professor of cynicism, La Fontaine. Until late adolescence at least, Emile is to be the student of only one book, *Robinson Crusoe*, whose function is to demonstrate the uselessness of books for a solitary, virtuous, and self-sufficient man living in an approximation of the state of nature. The great merit of Defoe's novel for Rousseau is that it teaches the lessons of nature and not those of society.

Rousseau's championing *Robinson Crusoe* in *Emile*, coupled with the virtual ban imposed on all other works of literature, is also a reminder that those who believe all wisdom and all essential knowledge is to be found in a single book—the Bible, the Koran, *The Communist Manifesto*, Mao's little red book—typically find no use for other books.

With the hindsight of more than two centuries, we can more easily see the dangerous archaic tendencies at the core of Rousseau's political thought. His opposition was not simply to the politics and institutions of ancien régime absolutism but also to the recognizably modern trends associated with the new literary, philosophical, and political culture of the eighteenth century. Had what Habermas calls "the public sphere" been formulated in such terms in his time he would have disapproved of it and of "the ideal of communicative rationality among free and equal human beings" even as a normative idea, for reasons that Keith Baker helps make clear: "Participants in this modern public sphere were to be conceived not as citizens of an ancient polis assembling together to engage in the common exercise of political will but as the dispersed members of a 'society engaged in critical public debate.' "[33]

The problem for Rousseau would clearly be focused on that notion of dispersal, for it implies distance between members of a social formation, "mediacy" rather than immediacy, or what Jacques Derrida famously called *différance.*[34] Given Rousseau's suspicion of indirection and re-presentation in the linguistic and artistic spheres as much as in politics, it is to be expected that only the direct democracy of classical republicanism was good enough for him. The circuits of correspondence and communication associated with enlightened salon society, "the republic of letters," publishing, and the print media in the middle decades of the eighteenth century in France were remote from the kind of direct, sentient exchange between assemblies of citizens of which he so nostalgically dreamed.

Baker might well have Rousseau in mind, in fact, when he points out that the Habermasian idea of the public sphere, whether as a discursive category or a once and future social reality, "is altogether antithetical to the classical republican conception of the public political realm as the domain in which independent citizens participate in the common exercise of a sovereign, political will."[35] And once again this last phrase, "sovereign political will," has a specific resonance in connection with Rousseau, since he was the inventor of the concept of "the general will"—to which, under any legitimate social contract, once it is entered into, all particular wills are subordinated.

In this respect, it is important to note that the treatise in which Rousseau lays out the concept and gives the fullest account of his ideal polity, *The Social Contract* (1762), is characterized in part by what it lacks, namely, a bill of rights—including, of course, the right to freedom of speech and of the press. Rousseau apparently assumed that if the principle of the general will were functioning properly, there would be no need to set down constitutionally guar-

anteed limits to a state's power over a citizen's life. The purpose of
the work in which the general will played such a key role was, after
all:

> to find a form of association that defends and protects with all its collec-
> tive force the person and the possessions of each member, and, as a
> result of which, everyone being united with everyone else, only obeys
> himself and remains as free as he was before.[36]

And, as Rousseau puts it in a famous and disturbing formula that has
come echoing down the centuries, in practice this meant that the
tacit commitment embodied in the social compact was "whoever
refuses to obey the general will will be obliged to do so by the social
body; which means nothing less than that he will be forced to be
free"—a formula that seems to leave precious little space for dissent
let alone for such practices as civil disobedience.[37]

The reconstituted polis of which, in effect, Rousseau had always
dreamed is then resolutely "unmodern," if by modern one means,
first, the kind of public sphere in which "private individuals dispersed throughout society ... participated in the critical discussion
leading to the formulation of a rational, consensual judgment," and,
second, the kind of political culture that Baker defines elsewhere as
follows:

> It [political culture] sees politics as about making claims; as the activity
> through which individuals and groups in any society articulate, negoti-
> ate, implement, and enforce the competing claims they make upon one
> another and upon the whole. Political culture is, in this sense, the set of
> discourses or symbolic practices by which these claims are made.[38]

To function openly and to the relative satisfaction of all, such a
political culture presupposes a form of Habermas's public sphere or
at least a liberal free exchange of ideas, including potentially dangerous and destabilizing ideas. But that is not, of course, what Rousseau
had in mind for his polis. Nor was it what the great majority of
champions of the so-called bourgeois and socialist revolutions—who,
however indirectly, drew on him—had in mind over the two centuries since Rousseau published his works.

In sum, one might say that more or less at the beginning of what
we like to think of as modernity, Rousseau presents us with a reversal of the opposition referred to in the introduction to this volume

between "right-wing censors and left-wing critics." Rousseau's is a case of a "left-wing censor," whose critics, if not "right wing," were definitely "liberal" in the eighteenth-century meaning of the term—that is, if the opposition between left and right is still meaningful now that the revolution that first invented it is indeed over.

NOTES

1. In a paper delivered at Mount Holyoke College on October 22, 1992, "Censorship, a Comparative View," Robert Darnton defined censorship as "an ingredient in authoritarian political cultures." In comparing the two regimes of censorship practiced in ancien régime France and communist East Germany in the 1980s, he identified their organizing principles as "privilege" and "planning," respectively.

2. See, for example, his recent article "Defining the Public Sphere in Eighteenth-Century France: Variations on a Theme by Habermas," in *Habermas and the Public Sphere*, ed. Craig Calhoun (Cambridge, Mass.: MIT Press, 1992), and "On the Problem of the Ideological Origins of the French Revolution," in *Inventing the French Revolution: Essays on French Political Culture in the Eighteenth Century* (Cambridge: Cambridge University Press, 1990).

3. Most notable among his censored works, especially for the effect on him, were *The Social Contract* and *Emile; or, On Education*, both of which appeared in 1762. The former was banned from being imported into France from Holland, and the latter was condemned by the Parlement of Paris to be burned and its author to be arrested. Both works were also banned in Rousseau's homeland, the Republic of Geneva.

4. *Oeuvres complètes*, vol. 3 (Paris: Pléiade, 1964). Unless otherwise noted, translations from the French are my own.

5. *Sciences*, 5 (emphasis added).

6. *Sciences*, 30.

7. *L'Avenir dure longtemps suivi de Les Faits* (Paris: Stock/IMEC, 1992).

8. *L'Avenir*, 212.

9. The phrase in Rousseau's French is "Peuples policés," which, before the age of modern "policing," conflates without apparent ironic intention the ideas of "polis," "polite," and "police" itself. *Oeuvres complètes*, vol. 3, 6-7.

10. The highly influential text here is, of course, "Ideology and Ideological State Apparatuses" in *Lenin and Philosophy and other Essays*, trans. Ben Brewster (London: Monthly Review Press, 1971).

11. The First Discourse pays particular homage to the great classical orators and incorruptible guardians of public morality from Socrates and Demosthenes to Fabricius Luscinus and Cato the Censor.

12. *Sciences*, 17.

13. *Sciences*, 12.

14. *Sciences*, 15.

15. It is noteworthy in the light of recent debates that, in a sympathetic reading of the *Letter* in an introduction to his own translation of the work, Allan Bloom points out that Rousseau belonged to the classic tradition of political philosophers who assumed that, in order to survive, republics required a more virtuous and more self-disciplined citizenry than other forms of government. Furthermore, Bloom describes Rousseau as "one of the last great voices in favor of censorship" and makes the rather extravagant claim that the

Letter is "as complete a treatment of the arts in relation to politics as has ever been produced." *Politics and the Arts: Letter to D'Alembert on the Theater* (Ithaca, N.Y.: Cornell University Press, 1960), xi-xvi.

16. "Notice how in order to elicit laughter this man disturbs the social order; how scandalously he overthrows all those sacred relations on which it is founded; how he makes fun of the respected rights fathers have over their children, husbands over their wives, masters over their servants." Ed. M. Fuchs (Lille: Librairie Giard, 1948), 46.

17. *Letter*, 49.

18. The classic work on this concept relative to Rousseau is Jean Starobinski's *Jean-Jacques Rousseau: Transparency and Obstruction*, trans. Arthur Goldhammer (Chicago: University of Chicago Press), 198.

19. *Letter*, 75.

20. *Letter*, 106.

21. See, in particular, the chapter entitled "Che Vuoi?" in *The Sublime Object of Ideology* (London: Verso, 1989).

22. The idea of the libidinal and even transgressive character of cognitive inquiry is given a particularly lapidary formulation in the *Discourse on the Origin of Inequality among Men*: "We only seek to know because we desire to take our pleasure [*jouir*]." *Oeuvres complètes*, vol. 3, 143.

23. "What! Plato banished Homer from his Republic and we should tolerate Molière in ours!" *Letter*, 157.

24. *Sublime Object*, 185-87.

25. (Paris: Garnier, 1964), 480.

26. Lynn Hunt, *Politics, Culture, and Class in the French Revolution* (Berkeley: University of California Press, 1984), 11. There is more than a suggestion of such an attitude in the *Letter* in the idea of censorship itself as a form of civically responsible mutual surveillance. With reference to the institution of women's circles or clubs in Geneva, Rousseau comments that those involved "have as it were the function of Censors in our town. In a similar way in Rome's great age Citizens observed each other closely and accused each other out of a zeal for justice." *Letter*, 143.

27. Part 1 of Lynn Hunt's *Politics, Culture, and Class*, "The Poetics of Power," is particularly suggestive of the form "cultural revolution" took during the course of the French Revolution.

28. *Letter*, 176.

29. *Letter*, 170.

30. In an article entitled "Fraternity," Mona Ozouf notes that fraternity "made its entry into official language through the back door, in a supplementary article to the Constitution of 1791, which envisioned fraternity as a remote product of future national holidays. Those holidays were instituted in order to 'foster' fraternity, which was thought of as the goal of a long-term project to shape the civic spirit." *A Critical Dictionary of the French Revolution*, ed. François Furet and Mona Ozouf, trans. Arthur Goldhammer (Cambridge, Mass.: Harvard University Press, 1989), 694.

For Rousseau the idea is already represented by the seductive power of a memory from childhood: "Oh! where are the games and the festivals of my youth? Where is the concord among citizens? Where is public fraternity? Where is pure joy and true merriment? Where are peace, liberty, equity, innocence?" *Letter*, 178-79.

31. Robert Darnton evokes the moral temper of the French revolutionaries in this respect in terms that are decidely Rousseauist: "At the height of the Revolution, however,

from mid-1792 to mid-1794, virtue was not merely a fashion but the central ingredient of a new political culture. It has a puritanical side, but it should not be confused with the Sunday school variety preached in nineteenth-century America. To the revolutionaries, virtue was virile. It meant a willingness to fight for the fatherland and for the revolutionary trinity of liberty, equality, and fraternity." "The Kiss of Lamourette," *The Kiss of Lamourette: Reflections in Cultural History* (New York: Norton, 1990), 10.

32. The preface goes on: "No chaste girl has ever read a novel, and I gave this one a clear enough title so that when one opened it, one knew what to expect. She who in spite of the title dares to read a single page is a lost girl." (Paris: Garnier, 1960), 3-4. See also Rousseau's much longer "Préface de *Julie* ou Entretien sur les Romans," which is usually published as an appendix to the novel. For a recent discussion of these and related issues, see Joan De Jean "*Julie:* The Well-Ordered House," in *Literary Fortifications: Rousseau, Laclos, Sade* (Princeton, N.J.: Princeton University Press, 1984).

33. "Defining the Public Sphere," 183.

34. The by now classic references are, of course, "Différance," in *Speech and Phenomena* (Evanston, Ill.: Northwestern University Press, 1973) and, with specific reference to Rousseau, "Nature, Culture, Writing," in *Of Grammatology*, trans. Gayatri Chakravorty Spivak (Baltimore: Johns Hopkins University Press, 1976).

35. "Defining the Public Sphere," 187.

36. *Oeuvres complètes*, vol. 3, 360.

37. *Social Contract*, 364.

38. *Inventing the French Revolution: Essays on French Political Culture in the Eighteenth Century* (Cambridge: Cambridge University Press, 1990), 4.

Part II

Censorship and Modernity

Ulysses on Trial: Some Supplementary Reading

Brook Thomas

A text of *Ulysses* is on trial again, but the nature of the trial is quite different from the one that allowed *Ulysses* to enter the United States legally. In fact, one reason that the present text is on trial is that it is not the same as the one tried, or at least presumably tried, in 1933.

In the 1933 trial everyone involved assumed that they were prosecuting or defending the text of *Ulysses* corresponding to the one published in Paris in 1922 by Shakespeare and Company. The courts were asked to decide whether that text was morally corrupting. Random House, Joyce's publisher in the United States, successfully defended *Ulysses* against obscenity charges, and prevailed in court again when the 1933 decision was appealed. Even so, the book that it circulated turned out to have numerous corruptions—of the textual, not moral, variety. The 1934 edition was so corrupt that the text was completely reset in 1961. But even the reset edition oozed with corruptions, as did the Bodley Head and Penguin editions published in Great Britain. As a result, an international team headed by the German scholar Hans Walter Gabler began work on a massive edition designed to record the numerous stages of Joyce's revisions on his masterpiece, revisions that had contributed to the corrupt state of the existing texts. In 1986 all three publishers adopted Gabler's reading text for paperback editions. This is the text currently on trial. The 1934 *Ulysses* faced the threat of withdrawal because it was the notorious text penned by James Joyce; the 1986 *Ulysses* faces the threat of recall because some scholars say that it does not come close enough to what they consider to be an almost sacred text.[1] As a result of the current controversy, Random House has made its paperback 1961 reset of the 1934 edition available again, giving the public a sort of new Coke/Coke Classic option. Concerned that neither one is Joyce's legitimate classic, others have published a do-it-yourself editing kit, allowing readers to correct their editions in order to produce yet another version claiming to be the real thing.[2]

To compare *Ulysses*'s current textual trial with its days in court in the early 1930s is to provide a fascinating insight into the relations between law and literature as well as the role that both legal and nonlegal forces can play in the production of a literary text. The comparison also raises crucial questions about constructs such as "classic," "authorship," and "the normal reader" that play an important role in current debates about how to read. Finally, it complicates the opposition that some have drawn between the close reading of texts and the sort of political readings that bring legal issues to bear on the interpretation of literature. I plan to touch on all of these issues.

Classic Authorizations

The most hotly debated change made by Gabler is to have provided an answer to Stephen Dedalus's question about a "word known to all men" (*U* [1961] 49, 581). By leaving Stephen's question unanswered, all previous editions allowed readers room to speculate. Relying on an early manuscript version of the text, Gabler has restored a passage identifying the word as *love*. This may be the most publicized change, but many others have caused heated debate among Joyce's loyal readers. Without minimizing the importance of those debates, I want to shift their focus by concentrating on a substantial change that no one has mentioned, a change that has nothing to do with the words of *Ulysses* itself, but everything to do with the supplementary material accompanying it.

The 1961 Random House edition that I read as a student reset the 1934 Random House edition, but retained the original introductory material: a foreword by Morris Ernst, the attorney who engineered the strategy to legalize *Ulysses* in the United States, Judge John M.

Woolsey's decision lifting the ban on *Ulysses*, and a letter from Joyce to Bennett Cerf. There is no afterword. In the 1986 edition of "the corrected text," Ernst's foreword, Woolsey's decision, and Joyce's letter have been replaced by a preface by Richard Ellmann, Joyce's prize-winning biographer. An afterword by Gabler has been added.

These changes dramatize changes in *Ulysses's* institutional status. For instance, there are few better measures of how we regard *Ulysses* today than the displacement of a legal document concerned with Joyce's inclusion of four-letter words that, as Woolsey put it, are "known to almost all men and, I venture, to many women" (*U* [1961] x) by Ellmann's homage, which spends considerable time discussing Gabler's inclusion of that four-letter "word known to all men" (*U* [1961] 49, 581). If there *is* a better measure of *Ulysses's* firmly entrenched institutional status, it might be the inclusion of Gabler's afterword. Representing the vast amount of labor, resources, and time devoted to coming up with the corrected text, this afterword indicates the value placed on a book that only half a century ago was banned in the United States and Britain. That the text was produced by a German scholar also indicates the international scope of *Ulysses's* institutionalization.[3] One reason that Gabler's text was initially so welcomed is that it standardizes the texts of *Ulysses* across national boundaries. With the Random House, Bodley Head, and Penguin editions all essentially the same, it is easier for an international community of scholars to have free trade in ideas about their object of study.

Ulysses's international institutionalization puts to rest some controversies and sparks others. In the 1933 trial an important question was whether *Ulysses* was a modern classic or not. Although the defense did not hinge on proving classic status, doing so could make the case much easier. The tariff act of 1930 under which *Ulysses* was prosecuted allowed the secretary of the treasury discretionary authority to admit recognized classics for noncommercial purposes, even if they might otherwise be prohibited. Unknown to the prosecutors, Random House's attorneys had received a letter from the collector of customs agreeing that *Ulysses* was a "classic and therefore comes within the purview of the Secretary's discretionary authority."[4] Given this ruling, the attorneys went on to cite *Webster's* definition of a classic in support of their argument that the words "classic" and "obscenity" represent polar extremes. They are mutually antagonistic and exclusive. That which is obscene, corrupts and depraves—it cannot be "of the highest class and of acknowledged excellence." (*One Book* 256)

Liberating in the sense that it could help clear *Ulysses* of obscenity charges, this definition of a classic was constricting in another, for it dictated how *Ulysses* was to be read. Since by definition a classic could not be corrupting or depraved, the defense could not offer a reading in which *Ulysses* condoned the "unseemly" side of life that it presented. For instance, it quoted the critic Paul Jordan Smith, who asserted that *Ulysses*'s "universal message" is "a weird cry from the very depths of Dublin to the rim of the world—the cry of tortured conscience, 'agenbite of inwit'" (*One Book* 268). In his decision, Woolsey basically accepted this reading. He distinguishes between Joyce's description of a world and his celebration of it. Passages considered obscene are excused because they are necessary to fulfill Joyce's purpose of drawing "a true picture of the lower middle class in a European city." Obscene words are allowable because they are "such words as would be naturally and habitually used...by the types of folk whose life, physical and mental, Joyce is seeking to describe." Joyce's realism produces a "very powerful commentary on the inner lives of men and women," Woolsey concludes, even if it is a "somewhat tragic" one (*U* [1961] x–xi).

In arguing that the defense's and Woolsey's reading of *Ulysses* was restricted, I do not mean to belittle it, for their reading is not only a symptom of *Ulysses*'s institutional status in the 1930s, it is one of the clearest examples we have that persuasive readings can alter the institutional status of a book. Limited as the reading might have been, in giving legal sanction to *Ulysses*'s status as a modern classic, it allowed future critics to use *Ulysses*'s stature to question what is considered corrupt and depraved.

Few have been more persuasive than Ellmann in making this argument. Allusions to Virgil and Dante in his preface place *Ulysses* in a classical tradition—but a comic, not a tragic, one. As he writes elsewhere, "The courts demanded high seriousness...and found enough to satisfy them. Fortunately, we need no longer be so glum" (*One Book* xxii). Thus Ellmann argues for a comic *Ulysses*, whose celebration of "love in its various forms, sexual, parental, filial, brotherly, and by extension social" (*U* [1986] xiv) expands our vision of life.

If *Ulysses's* original legal defenders adopted a somewhat tragic reading in order to assure its respectability and Ellmann a comic reading to show how it expands accepted boundaries of respectability, some contemporary critics argue that Ellmann's moral, humanistic reading places boundaries of its own on the text. Indeed, given today's war over the canon, classical status is not necessarily desirable, and controversy has arisen over whether *Ulysses* is representative of a Eurocentric, patriarchal modernism or is a precursor to postmodern subversions of phallogocentric norms and authority. Whereas in 1933 *Ulysses's* supporters tried to deny all charges of subversion, the 1986 edition appeared in a climate in which many of *Ulysses's* supporters actively advocated its subversive qualities. That changed climate invites comparison between Joyce's letter to Cerf and Ellmann's preface.

As different as they are, the two serve a common function, that is, to authorize the texts of which they are a part. Both in fact do so by appealing to the authority of Joyce, the author. But that appeal is directed against different challenges to *Ulysses's* authority. Because *Ulysses* was banned in the United States, Joyce could not comply with its copyright laws. As a result, people like Samuel Roth had produced pirated editions. Joyce's letter is directed against such an "unscrupulous person" and assures "American readers" of the authenticity of the Random House text by asserting his "moral ownership over it" (*U* [1961] xv).

Ellmann did not need to worry about pirated editions, but he was aware of critics arguing that *Ulysses's* language undercuts claims to authorial authority over it, making it a world without end created and recreated by every act of reading. Ellmann ends his preface by taking issue with the morally subversive notion that *Ulysses* is "unfinished." Positing an author whose stylistic experiments have allowed him to embody the powerful moral vision of love, Ellmann writes, "Because Molly Bloom countersigns with the rhythm of finality what Stephen and Bloom have said about the word known to all men, *Ulysses* is one of the most concluded books ever written" (*U* [1986] xiv). *Ulysses* is not only "finished," discovery of "the word known to all men" should put an end to the critical controversy about how to read it.[5] By asserting the concluded nature of *Ulysses,*

Ellmann implies that the reader's task is to recover the moral vision that Joyce embodied through his authorial control over the text. Arguing that "the corrected edition" most accurately reproduces Joyce's intention, Ellmann's preface authorizes the text of which it is a part.

As the current textual controversy indicates, however, Ellmann is not completely persuasive. In the preface Ellmann confidently claims that "Professor Gabler has been able to settle" (*U* [1986] xii) the debate over the word known to all men, a word that proves the concluded nature of *Ulysses*. What that preface does not tell us is that prior to its appearance Ellmann himself had reopened the question of whether the debated passage should be included.[6] To have included those doubts in his preface might well have given readers a different sense of the "concluded" nature of the text that they are about to read, causing them to raise questions about its status as "*the* corrected text*." Indeed, a close comparison of the 1934 and 1986 Random House editions does not necessarily substantiate Ellmann's claims about the text. Instead, it plunges us into the current critical debate over whether an author is wanted, dead or alive.

Legal and Aesthetic Authors

In recent years powerful voices from France have declared the "death of the author." By this they do not mean to deny the existence of someone who put pen to paper, nor are they talking about the New Critics' "intentional fallacy," which insists that a text should not be judged by a writer's intention, because that intention is not always realized. Instead, they argue that "authorship" is a social and linguistic construct.[7] Whereas even the New Critics admit that a poem is caused by the author's "designing intellect,"[8] critics like Roland Barthes and Michel Foucault deny that an author is the source of a poem because an "author" does not exist prior to language, but is instead a socially constructed role created by language. In the act of writing, a writer submits to the role of author, so that when we speak of an author we speak not of the empirical self who put pen to paper but of a role defined by texts, both literary and legal, that have defined the function of "author." Joycean texts, with their linguistic play that continues beyond control of the author, are often cited to illustrate the death of the author.

In contrast, Ellmann's argument about the completed nature of *Ulysses* depends on an appeal to "Joyce," an author very much in control over his work. As a result, Ellmann's argument would seem to confirm Joyce's claim to have "moral ownership" of the authentic version of *Ulysses*. Nonetheless, by displacing Joyce's authenticating letter in the Random House edition with his own preface, Ellmann undermines the very authority that he wants to grant to Joyce.

Joyce's letter resulted from his negotiations with Cerf, which resulted in a contract permitting a foreword by "another author" (*One Book* 106). An author for Joyce, however, was not a critic, and Cerf assured him that such a foreword would "be in no sense a criticism of *Ulysses*" (103). It was further agreed "that there will be no preface by the Author" (105). In place of an authorial preface, Joyce agreed to write his own authenticating letter. In replacing that letter with Ellmann's preface, the 1986 Random House edition provides the very sort of critical introduction that Joyce objected to. So much for "the corrected text."

As if this were not enough, the displacement of Joyce's letter by Ellmann's preface undercuts Joyce's authority in a much more basic sense, for it reminds us that Joyce himself no longer has the power to authenticate "the corrected text." That power is now the property of the community of Joycean critics, even if some members of that community, like Ellmann, will appeal to the construct of "the author" to substantiate their claims.

At this time I can imagine a skeptic objecting: to be sure, there has been a change in authority over the text, but that change has more to do with the death of a real author—that is, the historical James Joyce—than with the death of a mystifying notion of authorship evoked by contemporary critics. After all, if Joyce were still alive he would retain the power to authorize his own text. Indeed, legally that power now rests in the hands of the trustees of his estate, whose copyright of the 1984 reading text produced by Gabler is inscribed in the 1986 Random House edition.

This objection has the overwhelming strength of logic behind it, and thus forces a more precise articulation of what we mean by authorship. To do so is, on the one hand, to confirm the poststructuralist argument that authorship is a construct, and, on the other, to pose a challenge to those who make such proclamations by asking them whether they are willing to unwind completely all that our culture has constructed in terms of authorship.

The controversy over *Ulysses* in the 1920s and 1930s stresses the importance of distinguishing between two constructs of authorship: the legal and the aesthetic.[9] Although they are not totally separable from one another, they are not identical, either. For instance, whereas Ellmann evokes the authority of Joyce, the author, in an aesthetic sense, his very appeal cannot evoke the authority of Joyce, the author, in a legal sense. To do so would be to authorize both the 1922 and 1934 editions legally sanctioned by Joyce, texts that the 1986 edition hopes to replace. Indeed, the undeniable existence of Joyce's assertion of "moral ownership" in his letter to Cerf would seem to cause a bit of embarrassment for poststructuralists who insist that his texts undermine notions of authorship. But, as Joyce well knew, denying paternal guardianship over his works in an aesthetic sense had consequences very different from those of doing so in a legal sense.

The correspondence between Joyce and Cerf makes clear how much Joyce adhered to the modernist notion of an autonomous work of art. For instance, at one point Cerf tried to convince Joyce, through Joyce's friend Paul Léon, to include the celebrated chart of chapter correspondences that Herbert Gorman had gotten ahold of for his proposed biography. Joyce was so upset that he temporarily canceled his authorization for the biography, and Cerf had to assure him that Gorman had not been the one to release the chart. Obviously, Cerf never got the permission he sought. According to Léon, the reasons why were clear: "[W]e should not forget that *Ulysses* is a piece of belles lettres, i.e. pure literature; if it needs explanations these belong to the class of critical and historical writings, not to the book itself" (*One Book* 278). To Cerf's further insistence, Léon responded, "Mr. Joyce's decision is absolutely definite. *Ulysses's* text must stand on its own feet without explanation" (280). The matter decided, Léon later assured Cerf that

> Mr. Joyce will see no objection to the incorporation of the chart in any publication you might envisage about *Ulysses*, i.e. in any criticism or history of *Ulysses* you may be interested in publishing, except in the text of *Ulysses* itself. (*One Book* 307)

If Joyce was so adamant about *Ulysses* standing on its own, we might wonder why he agreed to have any prefatory matter at all. But he was aware that, whereas aesthetically it was desirable to have *Ulysses* stand on its own, to do so legally was a disaster. As he wrote to Cerf, the complications he faced in publishing *Ulysses* in America had, to his detriment, "given my book in print a life of its own" (*U* [1961] xiii)—a life, that is, of pirated editions. If prior to Woolsey's decision Joyce could not obtain a United States copyright for *Ulysses*, he did try to forbid pirates from using his name. In 1928 Joyce had even obtained an injunction against Samuel Roth, forbidding his "publishing, printing, stating or advertising, or otherwise disseminating the name of the plaintiff in connection with ... the book *Ulysses*" (*Ub* 747). Aimed at protecting Joyce, this injunction raises questions about the legal consequences of having *Ulysses* stand on its own.

We often think that a forgery, copying an original, can be detected by some flawed act of imitation. But what are we to do with the authorized 1934 text? Rushing to get the text out as soon as possible after the 1933 trial, Random House based its authorized version on' one of Roth's pirated editions. What distinguished the authentic copy was, therefore, not something *in* the text but an invisible act of authorization, made visible by Joyce's signature or, in the case of the 1934 edition, Joyce's letter.

The importance of Joyce's letter was not lost on Cerf, who had it copyrighted. Thus we have a bizarre situation in which the letter authenticating the Random House edition itself required authorization. Furthermore, whereas the value of the letter is that it is signed by the author Joyce, in one sense the hidden "author"—or at least originator—of the letter was Cerf, who contracted for it. Cerf was so intent on getting Joyce's letter that he refused to send Joyce's initial payment until the letter was in hand (*One Book* 102). Cerf's reasons are instructive.

Not only would Joyce's letter establish the Random House edition as an authorized one, it would also "give a certain first edition value" (*One Book* 102) to the Random House edition, an edition that copied a forged text! Cerf's desire for "first-edition value" accounts for another difference between the 1934 and 1986 editions. The 1986 edition, like the Bodley Head edition first published in England, lists the previous editions of *Ulysses*, which makes perfect sense given its claim to be "the corrected edition." In the 1934 edition, with its efforts to appear to be a first edition, this list is absent. To be sure, Joyce mentions the book's publishing history in his letter, but that letter is Cerf's major claim to first-edition status. There was, however, another reason for copyrighting Joyce's letter.

As Cerf knew, the more copyrighted material that he could include, the less the possibility of a successful pirate of his edition. Even if legal difficulties over *Ulysses* remained, complicating efforts to procure a copyright, Joyce's *letter* would be copyrighted. Indeed, the need to have copyrighted material was one reason that Cerf argued for inclusion of the correspondence chart. Of course, Cerf could not copyright Woolsey's decision, but he could copyright Ernst's foreword introducing it. Ernst's letter further complicates notions of authorship, since it was not only initiated by Cerf, but actually composed by Ernst's law partner, Alexander Lindey, who based it on Ernst's press statement after the victorious trial (*One Book* 317, 334).

One reason for including both Ernst's preface and the court decision was to capitalize on the publicity of the trial, which caused Cerf to rush the book to print. But from the start Cerf had anticipated the advantages of replacing the proposed preface by another author with a "brief note by a prominent attorney embodying the decision of the judge who legalizes the book" (*One Book* 103). Cerf worried that there might be future actions against *Ulysses* and that evidence from the original trial would not be allowed. By including Woolsey's decision, Cerf provided Random House with a solid defense. Any action against the 1934 edition would place on trial more than the text of *Ulysses*: on trial would be a text that included the decision legalizing the very work in question.

Emphasizing the historic importance of the 1922 edition in his afterward, Gabler describes it as the *Ulysses* "Joyce allowed to go before the public" (*U* [1986] 649). In his correspondence with Cerf, Joyce makes it clear that he wanted *Ulysses* to go before the public on its own. Part of the historic importance of the 1934 edition is its dramatic illustration that in order to go before the American public an authorized *Ulysses* could *not* stand on its own.

In a fascinating way, then, the supplementary material to the 1934 edition confirms the poststructuralist argument that the notion of private, creative authorship is a construct. Ellmann's preface may try to reassert the importance of authorial control against poststructural-ist attacks, but its very existence serves to undermine its claims. Fur-thermore, it is at odds with Gabler's afterward, which posits a differ-ent sense of authorship. Gabler never claims to have embodied Joyce's intention.[10] His is "an edited, and not a definitive text" (*U*[1986] 650). Even the label "the corrected text" was the publisher's, not Gabler's. Gabler writes that "no text written or edited can be wholly divorced from the processes of writing and editing and the decisions and judgments that they entail" (*U*[1986] 650). The legal decision and judgment included in the 1934 Random House edition remind us that the process of writing and editing involves more than writers and editors: Random House's lawyers and Judge Woolsey also played a role in placing *Ulysses* before the United States public. But if the texts of *Ulysses* on trial confirm that private authorship is a social con-struct, they also force us to face the consequences of abandoning that construct in a legal rather than an aesthetic realm.

Joyce's works, as much as any, demonstrate the problematic na-ture of distinctions between the real and the counterfeit that depend upon the legal fiction of an invisible authorizing act by an author. To challenge the distinction between the real and the coun-terfeit seems to have a revolutionary potential because, as Walter Benjamin pointed out, it demystifies the aura of an original work of art.[11] If, in an age of mechanical reproduction, the distinction be-tween the original and copies that imitate it collapses, the very possi-bility of ownership over an authentic text is called into question. Such a challenge to ownership would seem to give art an important role to play in moving toward an egalitarian socialist state. But the notion of the death of the author has an important flaw. It assumes a utopian moment of the free play of the signifier in which no one else will come forward to claim authority over the words of the text. In the historical actuality of 1933's capitalist world, though, someone was always there to claim the profits from an uncopy-righted text. To give up the legal construct of authorship in the case of *Ulysses* was to side with an "unscrupulous person" like Samuel Roth against Joyce.

My point is not to dispute the claim that authorship is a construct. It is merely to stress that to expose various notions as constructs is only part of the task at hand, for we still have to decide whether or not we want to advocate their overthrow. After all, there is no law proclaiming that all constructed institutions are inherently bad. Some might, at this particular historical moment, be worth defending; others might be deserving of attack. In terms of legalizing *Ulysses*, one construct that needed to be attacked was the law's definition of who represented the public in obscenity cases. Woolsey's redefinition did not abandon all constructs, but appealed to a different one, that of the normal reader, a construct as problematic for some critics as authorship.

Normal and Supersensitive Readers

Woolsey's willingness to determine obscenity according to a book's effect on "a person with average sex instincts"—what the French would call "l'homme moyen sensuel" (*U* [1961] xi)—was extremely important. For instance, the 1921 trial that declared *Ulysses* obscene was sparked when the daughter of a prominent New York attorney was offended at reading an excerpt in the *Little Review*. The 1921 court operated according to the standard set by the 1868 English case of *Regina v. Hicklin*, which determined obscenity according to a work's capacity "to deprave and corrupt those whose minds are open to such immoral influences and into whose hands a publication of this sort may fall" (*One Book* 249).[12] According to Ernst:

> Such a criterion was patently unfair, unreasonable and unsound, because it sought to gauge the mental and moral capacity of the community by that of its dullest-witted and most fallible members, and because it sought to withhold from society any material which might conceivably injure its lowest and most impressionable element. (*One Book* 249-50)

How unreasonable this criterion could be was illustrated at the 1921 trial. When allegedly offensive passages were about to be read out loud, one of the three judges refused to allow the reading because of the presence of an attractive woman in the courtroom, a woman who turned out to be Margaret Anderson, one of two editors of the *Little Review*. The judge replied that she certainly could not have known the significance of what she had printed. In contrast, Anderson felt that "judgment on what is obscene in literature should be left to us experts."[13] Or, as her fellow editor Jane Heap was reported to have remarked, "If there is anything I fear it is the mind of the young girl."[14] In 1933 Ernst worked extremely hard to have "the experts," not society's "lowest and most impressionable element," speak for the public on matters of obscenity. For it was experts who could speak for the normal, not the abnormal, reader.

Ernst's defense relied strongly on the philosophy of legal realism that was gaining ground in U.S. courts in the 1930s. One premise of legal realism was that moral standards change with the times. Thus, in its brief to the court, the defense's first point was that "the test of obscenity is a living standard, and *Ulysses* must be judged by the *mores* of the day" (*One Book* 244). Furthermore, as Ernst argued, quoting Justice Cardozo, "Law accepts as the pattern of its justice the morality of the community whose conduct it assumes to regulate" (245). But how, we might ask, are we to determine that morality? The realists' answer, which influenced New Deal institutions such as Franklin Roosevelt's "brain trust," was through the scientific work of experts. Drawing on all of these assumptions, the defense concluded:

> Public opinion furnishes the only true test of obscenity. Such opinion is definitely ascertainable. It is true that people as a mass are inarticulate. The body politic registers its will through representatives chosen at the polls. By the same token the community makes its moral reactions felt and its judgments pronounced through responsible men, who, by reason of their respective endeavors, furnish an accurate social mirror.
>
> When newspapers, college professors, critics, educators, authors, librarians, clergymen and publishers rally to the defense of a book, they do more than express their personal views. They speak for the body social. (*One Book* 264)

Accordingly, the defense submitted to the court testimony of many such experts. In addition, it appended a map of the United States indicating the "cities in which city or university librarians have stated that they either have copies of *Ulysses* or would place the book on their shelves if it were made available" (*One Book* 421). Here was proof that *Ulysses* had already been accepted by the general public. The court would simply be bringing the law into conformity with the voice of the public.

Woolsey's decision does not explicitly endorse the claim that experts can speak for the "body social," but in accepting the defense's argument that obscenity must refer to effects on a "normal person," he essentially defers to expert authority. Experts were less important when the *Hicklin* criterion was observed because it was merely necessary to prove that various concrete individuals had been depraved or corrupted by a particular work. But once the standard of normalcy was evoked, the defense could always object that those upset by the book were one of "two kinds of abnormal persons: The morally weak and the prudishly supersensitive" (*One Book* 271). Woolsey agreed that such people should not speak for society as a whole. Nonetheless, the court still needed some method to gauge the response of that legal fiction, the normal person. Woolsey's method of doing so is revealing.

Having already admitted that the length of the book and the difficulty of reading it would make a jury trial "extremely unsatisfactory" (*U*[1961] viii), Woolsey chose for his "literary assessors" (a phrase he gets from the defense's brief) two friends "whose opinion on literature and life I value most highly" (xi). Allowed to speak for the "normal person," these two friends, not surprisingly, agreed with Woolsey that the book was not obscene. Indeed, the opinion of one of the two, Henry Seidel Canby, editor of the *Saturday Review of Literature*, had been included in the defense's list of experts testifying to *Ulysses's* literary merit (*One Book* 190, 317)!

Today such a casual determination of the "normal" reader's response would not be allowed. Even so, in recent criticism the construct of the normal reader has come under attack for being as politically repressive as that of authorial authority. *Ulysses*, after all, can be said to call into question notions of normalcy, whether a stylistic norm from which *Ulysses's* experimental chapters deviate or ethical and sexual norms that its actions violate. Listen, for instance, to Jules David Law in a recent essay on pornography in "Nausicaa," the chapter that provoked the 1921 *Little Review* trial. Citing Woolsey's decision, Law writes:

> The law is concerned only with the forensically "normal"—that is, the masculine—response to pornography. What is clear, finally, is that feminine ignorance of the obscene is both a presupposition and an intended effect of the law. The law, in patriarchal culture, assumes that in the course of "normal" sexuality women are only the objects of, and not the consumers or producers—in other words, not the subjects—of sexual fantasy.[15]

Law's exposure of the gender bias in Woolsey's definition of the normal reader is hard to dispute. In fact, Woolsey's norm also carries with it a class and perhaps an ethnic bias. As I pointed out earlier, *Ulysses*'s respectability was in part ensured by Woolsey's assumption that Joyce does not celebrate the "persons of the lower middle class" that he represents. Woolsey admits that one may "not wish to associate with such folk as Joyce describes"; nonetheless, an artist has a right "to draw a true picture" of their lives "physical and mental," especially when the net effect of that picture on the normal reader is "somewhat tragic" (*U* [1961] x-xi). Woolsey's possible ethnic bias surfaces in a remark once praised as a fine example of judicial humor. Admitting to the "recurrent emergence of the theme of sex in the minds of [Joyce's] characters," Woolsey reminds us that "his locale was Celtic and his season Spring" (x). If citing this remark seems to be pushing charges of bias too far, to identify the second friend allowed to speak for the normal reader is not.

Choosing one "literary assessor" from the literary world, Woolsey chose the other from the business world in the person of Charles E. Merrill, Jr., who is most likely the Charles E. Merrill who cofounded the investment firm of Merrill Lynch and the Safeway stores (*One Book* 317). Merrill was an amateur man of letters and the father of poet James Ingram Merrill. A year before the *Ulysses* trial, Merrill also founded *Family Circle* magazine, sold at Safeway checkout stands; the juxtaposition suggests how the period's elite arbitrated taste along gender lines.

To allow Merrill to speak for the "normal reader" hardly seems fair. Nonetheless, the fact that he proved to be bullish on *Ulysses* fits perfectly with his strong belief in free trade. Indeed, one of the most famous pronouncements defending the value of the First Amendment came from Justice Oliver Wendell Holmes: "The best test of truth is the power of thought to get itself accepted in the competition of the market."[16] Holmes's own background (his father coined the phrase "Boston Brahmins") might turn Ernst's comparison in his preface of Woolsey to Holmes "as a master of juridical prose" (*U* [1961] v) into more evidence of the defense's class bias. After all, who has the power and money to get ideas into public circulation in the first place?

But even though my concrete historical analysis can outdo abstract theoretical efforts to expose the biases inherent in Woolsey's

construction of the normal reader, that analysis also undoes the conclusions that Law draws about the law. Faulting Woolsey's representation of the normal reader, Law is himself flawed when he general-
izes about the law in "patriarchal culture." Far from being concerned
"only with the forensically 'normal,'—that is, the masculine—response
to pornography," the law under the *Hicklin* standard was concerned with what the defense lawyers claimed was the "abnormal"
response of the most susceptible to the potentially harmful effect of
a book. In the eyes of the law at that time, such a response was usually that of women or adolescent girls, such as the one that provoked the 1921 trial of *Ulysses.* Whereas Law claims that the construction of a masculine norm is typical of pornography law in a
patriarchal society, in fact, the acceptance of the normal reader as a
standard marked a move away from the paternalistic attitude
embodied in the *Hicklin* standard, in which the law tried to protect
the susceptible.

Confirming the gender bias of constructions of the normal reader,
the legal material supplementing the 1934 *Ulysses* should also alert us
to the important function that the construct served. It is, as I pointed
out, tied up with progressive thought that led to important reforms
in the first half of the twentieth century. Ernst begins his foreword,
"The new deal in the law of letters is here," adding later that "the first
week of December 1933 will go down in history for two repeals,
that of Prohibition and that of the legal compulsion for squeamish-
ness in literature" (*U* [1961] v-vi). In retrospect we can feel the limits
of his boast that "we may now imbibe freely of the contents of bot-
tles and forthright books" (vi). Aware of those limits, we find it difficult to share the optimism that allowed Ernst to call the "victory" of
Ulysses "a fitting climax to the salutary forward march of our courts"
(vi).[17]

A major dilemma facing many politically engaged literary critics is
what to do once they have questioned such progressive assumptions. Scapegoating the New Critics is not only fun but also fairly
painless, because it is so easy (perhaps too easy) to link their aesthetics to a conservative political program. But for leftist intellectuals in
the United States to undermine progressive assumptions is to leave
them facing the unusability of their own past. It is also to leave them
without a concrete political program, since the liberal wing of the
Democratic party has yet to come up with a convincing alternative

to those seemingly outmoded progressive assumptions. How we respond to Woolsey's notion of the "normal reader" is a minor, yet instructive, example of what is at stake in that dilemma.

For very good reasons, many of today's critics question the construct of a "normal" reader that denies legal voice to responses considered abnormal. Rather than, like Jane Heap, fearing the mind of the young girl, they recognize the need to take that mind seriously, while simultaneously adopting a healthy skepticism toward the judgments of experts. We should not forget, however, that it was precisely the refusal to accept the legal fiction of a normal reader and the insistence on taking seriously individual responses that contributed to stringent standards of literary censorship. It would be unfair to identify today's political criticism with what Ernst calls "the days of Bowdler and Mrs. Grandy and Comstock" (*U* [1961] vi). Nonetheless, recent attacks on some books (more often than not classics) for presenting material unsuitable for specific audiences might remind us of the dangers involved in turning Comstock's slogan of "Morals, Not Art or Literature" into "Politics, Not Art or Literature."[18]

The Politics of Reading Aids

If comparing the textual trials of the 1934 and 1986 Random House editions warns us against making hasty political judgments, the lesson is not to deny the importance of the sort of political criticism that links legal and literary issues. On the contrary, it points to the inadequacy of at least some of those who have responded to the recent political turn in literary criticism with calls to return to close readings of texts themselves. One example pertinent to discussions of how to read *Ulysses* is Richard Poirier's nostalgic celebration of how reading used to be taught at Amherst College and in Harvard University's Humanities 6. According to Poirier, students privileged to be taught in those institutional settings learned to read, as Reuben Brower put it, in "slow motion." Opposing recent claims that such close readings can be politically subversive, Poirier claims that reading "can be subversive only to the extent that it encourages us to get under and turn over not systems and institutions, but only words." Not a political activity, reading as Poirier was taught it and as he would teach it is a "lonely discipline that makes no great claims for itself."[19]

Poirier, however, is not above making claims for "Hum 6" as part of an American tradition of reading running from Ralph Waldo Emerson through William James, Kenneth Burke, and Robert Frost. When he pits this native American tradition against the modernist one that runs through T. S. Eliot and institutionalized itself at Yale, it is clear that he is making political claims as well, even if they are of a limited sort. For Poirier the way a generation was taught to read *Ulysses* plays an important role in the battle over how to read.

Commenting on the injury committed to the body literate, he laments:

> Eliot's exultation of the so-called "mythic method"—along with Joyce's notes on *Ulysses*, which to the book's misfortune still dominate readings of it—can be shown to have had a profoundly damaging effect on the reading of modern and therefore of other literatures. ("Hum 6" 26)

I assume that when Poirier refers to "Joyce's notes" he means the infamous chart, and no doubt he would be pleased to learn that Joyce resisted Cerf's efforts to include it as part of the American edition. Nonetheless, Poirier's example of *Ulysses* along with the opposition he forges between American and modernist traditions of reading suggests that there is more at stake than an institutional squabble between Yale and Harvard, for he raises questions about the role of reading in a republic of letters.

Poirier's claim that reading "encourages us to get under and turn over not systems and institutions, but only words" ("Hum 6" 30) betrays his own desire to get under institutions. Lodged, as he acknowledges, within an Emersonian tradition, he posits the ideal of self-reliant, critical readers who eschew institutionally mediated ways of reading in order to confront directly the text at hand. Indeed, as much as Poirier disagrees with those who worry about the ideological implications of constructs like the "normal reader," he shares their distrust of such categories and especially the suggestion that we should rely on experts to guide our reading. That distrust leads to contradictions that are central to the tradition that he embraces. First, the very nature of reading rules out the possibility of truly self-reliant readers. After all, reading cannot take place without books to read. Furthermore, reading by its very nature has to be

taught, and teaching almost always takes place within an institutional setting—such as the once all-male Amherst College attended by
both Merrill and his son, for example. Finally, even if we were to
grant Poirier's argument that Amherst and Harvard's Hum 6 produced more self-reliant readers than other institutions, he would not
feel compelled to make his argument if all read as he proposes. But
in fact so few learn the skills that he advocates that they establish
themselves as a new elite of experts rather than provide a foundation for a democratic republic of letters.[20] The political dangers of
such elitist notions of reading are illustrated by Ezra Pound.

A central figure of modernism, Pound was one of the most important early readers of Joyce, helping him to find publishers and financial support to continue work on *Ulysses.* He also wrote *ABC of
Reading,* which is an essential part of the tradition that Poirier traces
from Emerson to himself. Poirier's failure to mention Pound makes
sense, since to include him would complicate the opposition that
Poirier constructs between American and modernist ways of reading. It would also cause political embarrassment, since Pound responded to the elitist consequences of his democratic desire for
every reader to become self-reliant by embracing fascism. By no
means does Poirier embrace fascism. Instead, he retreats from facing
the contradictory political consequences of his position by making
claims for a way of reading "that makes no great claims for itself"
("Hum 6" 30). Neither too hastily trying to resolve those contradictions nor retreating from them, the trials that the text(s) of *Ulysses*
have had to undergo in the United States neatly illustrate them. As I
have tried to demonstrate, the trials are not only legal ones, although
they play an important role.

The ideal that readers should read on their own is tested by the
acknowledged difficulties of reading *Ulysses.* In the 1921 trial, John
Quinn, the lawyer for the *Little Review,* tried to turn those difficulties to his advantage: he argued that *Ulysses* could not corrupt the
average reader because the average reader could not understand it.
As defense witness John Cooper Powys testified, "*Ulysses* is too
obscure and philosophical a work to be in any sense corrupting."
Quinn put it this way: "The average person would either understand
what it meant or would not. If he understood what it meant, then it
could not corrupt him, for it would either amuse or bore him."[21]

Not content with confining the importance of *Ulysses* to the few who could understand it, Cerf faced a dilemma central to those who want the benefits of difficult books to be distributed democratically. On the one hand, he hoped for as many individual readers—and sales—as possible. On the other, he had to acknowledge that the normal reader would face uncommon reading difficulties. One attempted solution was to include in the text the correspondence chart Poirier so loathes. "Thousands of people," Cerf wrote to Joyce through Léon, "will want to know about *Ulysses*, especially if we win our legal fight, and they will buy the book if there is some key that will enable them to understand the more obscure portions of the book. Without some guide for their enlightenment, you must know as well as I do that *Ulysses* is not for the general public" (*One Book* 279). A reading aid, Cerf insisted, would be "a tremendous service to the reading public" (234).[22]

As a teacher who has struggled to get students to read *Ulysses* itself rather than to rely on the numerous aids designed to minimize its difficulty, I share Poirier's concern about such aids. *Ulysses*, after all, is a text crying out to be read in slow motion. Nonetheless, if I am honest with myself and my students, I have to admit that my own efforts to read it in slow motion have been aided by the entire institutional apparatus that has grown up around the text, including its community of experts. Indeed, without such aids I would not have been able to develop my own point of view on the text, one that now allows me to disagree with the readings of some of those experts, like Ellmann. Nor can I forget that it was precisely such aids that enabled Woolsey's reading, a reading that made it possible for *Ulysses* to be legally available to the public in the first place. "*Ulysses*," Woolsey writes,

> is not an easy book to read or to understand. But there has been much
> written about it, and in order properly to approach the consideration of
> it it is advisable to read a number of other books which have now
> become its satellites. (*U* [1961] viii)

"Americans," Cerf noted, "are notorious seekers of short cuts to culture" (*One Book* 279). An often-lamented result of their quest is the widespread availability of reading guides designed to help students and the public "get through" the classics. One less noted is the importance some of our educators place on the classics themselves. Yet a case can be made that Americans, more than others, want a set number of classical works to embody everything they want to know about Culture, because they are afraid to ask for more. Series like the Harvard Classics, the Great Books of the Western World, and the Library of America result from this desire for a select group of texts that represent the body of culture, just as *Ulysses*'s lawyers claimed that experts could represent the body social. There is no need to take the extreme stand that "a classic" is inherently an ideologically corrupt category to recognize that the body social will not be turned into a cultural body merely by reading someone's top-forty list of the classics. Indeed, those who attempt a close reading of the modern classic *Ulysses* soon realize that it is impossible without supplementary reading on all sorts of subjects, large and small.

To do justice to Poirier, I need to make clear that his response to "political" criticism is not to advocate a return to a set body of works. What he resists is the tendency of critics to impose their theoretical and political beliefs onto texts. In contrast, he insists on the need to pay close attention to the text at hand, whatever it may be. That is, no doubt, a noble goal. Nonetheless, by examining closely the supplementary reading contained within the covers of the 1934 and 1986 Random House editions of *Ulysses*, which even those who advocate a return to the "text" often neglect, I have tried to suggest the limits of that goal. Before ending my reading (so that you can get back to reading *Ulysses*), I want to take a final look at the authorizing letter included in the 1934 edition.

Directly after remarking that the complications of its history in print in the United States have given *Ulysses* a life of its own, Joyce cites the Latin phrase "Habent sua fata libelli" (little books have their own fate)! Often attributed to Martial or Horace, the phrase comes from "Carmen Heroicum" by the third-century grammarian Terentianus Maurus. As quoted by Joyce, the words support notions of textual autonomy. But Joyce does not cite the entire sentence, which reads: "Pro captu lectoris habent sua fata libelli" (only through the constructive power of the reader do little books have fates of their own). Books do not simply exist to be read; reading is a constitutive part of their identities. Few texts better illustrate how reading can determine a book's fate than the 1934 Random House edition of *Ulysses*, whose very existence depended upon the powerful judicial reading that is an integral part of it. Eliminating the legal decision from within its covers, the 1986 edition might seem to have avoided the social control that played such a role in the production of the 1934 text. But a close scrutiny of the new edition's accompanying material reveals that those controls have been transformed, not eliminated. As we debate the merits of the new edition, it would be wise to submit that material to a judicious reading as well. To compare it to the supplementary material of the 1934 edition is to remind ourselves that, try as we might, we cannot divorce our close readings from the politics that helped to produce the very texts that we are reading.

NOTES

1. The first public attack on the Gabler edition was John Kidd's "Errors of Execution in the 1984 *Ulysses*," delivered to the Society for Textual Scholarship, New York City, April 26, 1985. The controversy was brought to wide public attention by Kidd's "The Scandal of *Ulysses*," *New York Review of Books*, June 30, 1988, 32-39. For a bibliography of the controversy to date, see Charles Rossman, "The 'Gabler *Ulysses*': A Selectively Annotated Bibliography," *Studies in the Novel* 22 (1990): 257-69. This entire issue, edited by Rossman, is devoted to editing *Ulysses*. It includes the Kidd address mentioned above, as well as Gabler's reply.

2. Philip Gaskell and Clive Hart, *"Ulysses": A Review of Three Texts: Proposals for Alterations to the Texts of 1922, 1961, and 1984* (Totowa, N.J.: Barnes and Noble, 1989). The texts of *Ulysses* that I will cite parenthetically are James Joyce, *Ulysses*, ed. Hans Walter Gabler et al. (New York: Random House, 1986): *U* [1986]; James Joyce, *Ulysses* (New York: Random House, 1934, reset and corrected 1961): *U* [1961]; and James Joyce, *Ulysses* (London: Bodley Head, 1937): *Ub*.

3. Michael Groden emphasizes the international scope of the editorial work in "Editing Joyce's 'Ulysses': An International Effort," *Scholarly Publishing*, October 1980, 36-41.

4. *The United States of America v. One Book Entitled "Ulysses" by James Joyce. Documents and Commentary—A 50-Year Retrospective*, ed. Michael Moscato and Leslie LeBlanc (Frederick, Md.: University Publications of America, 1984), 255. References to this book will be referred to parenthetically in the body of the essay as *One Book*. The introduction is by Richard Ellmann (misspelled Ellman). For an excellent short review of the collection, see Allen Boyer, "Review," *James Joyce Quarterly* 21 (1984): 373-75.

5. Ellmann's attempt to associate *Ulysses*'s finished nature with "the corrected text" as well as to imply that Gabler's discovery of the word known to all men should end critical controversy over how to read *Ulysses* is even more obvious in the title of a review adapted from his preface: "Finally, the Last Word on 'Ulysses': The Ideal Text and Portable Too," *New York Times Book Review*, June 15, 1986, 3, 37.

6. Richard Ellmann, "A Crux in the New Edition of *Ulysses*," in *Assessing the 1984 Ulysses*, ed. C. George Sandulescu and Clive Hart (Totowa, N.J.: Barnes and Noble, 1986), 28-34. Ellmann delivered the essay at a conference in Monaco in May 1985.

7. See Roland Barthes, "From Work to Text," and Michel Foucault, "What Is an Author?" in *Textual Strategies, Perspectives in Post-Structural Criticism*, ed. Josué Harari (Ithaca, N.Y.: Cornell University Press, 1979).

8. W. K. Wimsatt, Jr., and Monroe C. Beardsley, "The Intentional Fallacy," in *The Verbal Icon* (Lexington: University of Kentucky Press, 1954), 4.

9. For important work *linking* legal and aesthetic notions of authorship, see Martha Woodmansee, "The Genius and Copyright: Economic and Legal Conditions of the Emergence of the 'Author,'" *Eighteenth-Century Studies* 17 (1984): 425–48, and Mark Rose, "The Author as Proprietor: *Donaldson v. Becket* and the Genealogy of Modern Authorship," *Representations* 23 (1988): 51–85. My distinction between legal and aesthetic authorship supports the sophisticated historical work done by David Saunders and Ian Hunter, "Lessons from the 'Literary': How to Historicise Authorship," *Critical Inquiry* 17 (1991): 479–509. It should be noted that the Gabler edition of *Ulysses* involved revisions substantial enough to receive a new copyright. The 1961 reset of the 1934 Random House edition did not.

10. For a fascinating discussion of Gabler's complete edition as a postmodern text, see Jerome J. McGann, "*Ulysses* as a Postmodern Text: The Gabler Edition," *Criticism* 27 (1985): 283–305.

11. Walter Benjamin, "The Work of Art in the Age of Mechanical Reproduction," in *Illuminations*, trans. Harry Zohn (New York: Schocken, 1969), 217–52.

12. Ernst's argument against the Hicklin standard can be traced to a 1913 decision by Judge Learned Hand, who, even while feeling obliged to uphold it, remarked, "To put thought in leash of the average conscience of the time is perhaps tolerable, but to fetter it by the necessities of the lowest and least capable seems a fatal policy." *United States v. Kennerley*, 209 Fed. 119 (S.D.N.Y. 1913) at 121. Hand ended up hearing the appeal to Woolsey's decision, which was upheld by a two to one majority.

13. Quoted in Jackson R. Bryer, "Joyce, *Ulysses*, and the *Little Review*," *South Atlantic Quarterly* 66 (1967): 161, 158. My argument should help correct Bryer's claim that "Ernst's arguments . . . were not very different from those of John Quinn [the *Little Review*'s lawyer] in 1921" (160).

14. Quoted in *Mediator* 9 (1990): 1.

15. Jules David Law, " 'Pity They Can't See Themselves': Assessing the 'Subject' of Pornography in 'Nausicaa,' " *James Joyce Quarterly* 27 (1990): 219.

16. Holmes, dissenting, *Abrams v. US* 250 US 616 at 624 (1919). The defense tried to get Holmes, recently retired, directly involved in the case. Wanting to have *Ulysses* go to trial before Random House spent considerable money publishing it, the defense arranged to have a copy sent from Europe and seized by customs. Ernst and his partner Lindey gave "some time to choice of a sendee" (*One Book* 109). On March 30, 1932, Cerf wrote Holmes asking if he would agree to play that role. Lindey felt that Holmes's consent would be "a substantial step forward" (*One Book* 114), but he refused. As his secretary wrote, "Regardless of his opinion of the book, the Justice thinks that taking part in the controversy over it, even so slightly as you suggest, would break in upon the complete withdrawal from affairs which he intended by his resignation from the Supreme Court" (*One Book* 115). Holmes was familiar with Joyce's work. In a March 1917 letter to Harold J. Laski, he mentions reading *A Portrait of the Artist as a Young Man*. There is even evidence that he might have been reading serial publication of *Ulysses*. In a September 6, 1920, letter to Morris Cohen he mentions "Agen Bite [*sic*] of Inwit," for "remorse of conscience," which he might have gotten from the first chapter of *Ulysses* (*U* [1961] 16) in the *Little Review*.

17. Despite Ernst's rhetoric, it would be a mistake to identify Woolsey's decision completely with New Deal progressive politics. Woolsey himself was a Republican, as was Merrill. Progressivism, after all, was not a Democratic invention. A particular version of it did, however, achieve Democratic embodiment with the crisis of the Great Depression. Nonetheless, the link between progress in literature and society was an article of progres-

sive faith. In denying the appeal to overturn Woolsey's decision Judge August N. Hand writes, "Art certainly cannot advance under compulsion to traditional forms and nothing in such a field is more stifling to progress than limitation to experiment with a new technique" (*Ub*, 758).

18. On Comstock, see Heywood Broun and Margaret Leech, *Anthony Comstock: Roundsman of the Lord* (New York: Boni, 1927).

19. Richard Poirier, "Hum 6; or, Reading before Theory," *Raritan* 9 (1990): 30.

20. For a very different sense of English instruction at Amherst College, see H. Bruce Franklin's "Amherst and Empire," in *Back Where You Came From* (New York: Harper's Magazine Press, 1975), 63–73. Franklin entered Amherst in September 1951. On the course that Poirier says was the model for Hum 6, he writes, "Amherst had just developed a freshman English course that was becoming widely known as a model of sophistication and ingenuity. English 1 was designed to indoctrinate us into a set of beliefs based on the premise that only a highly select and rigorously trained intellectual elite could glimpse the essence of 'reality,' which lay in the total dependence of the objective world on the subjective. . . . We soon learned our first lesson, that our teachers were brilliant, that they were in possession of some great mystery, and that they were to lure us into this inner sanctum with sly looks, bizarre questions, a thousand little suggestive ironies, cryptic comments on our papers, and very occasionally a dramatic physical act in the classroom" (66–67). Nonetheless, Franklin admits that English 1 did him "some good, mainly by letting me in on the ways the cynical ideologues of the empire could manipulate language" (67–68).

21. Quoted in Bryer, "Joyce, *Ulysses*, and the *Little Review*, 163.

22. As Kevin Dettmar pointed out to me, the publisher's ads for *Ulysses* in the *Saturday Review of Literature* include the sort of aids that Joyce refused to allow Random House to include in the book. Stuart Gilbert had already published (and copyrighted) his version of the correspondence chart, but since it was in a book of criticism, it did not bother Joyce, who merely insisted that it be separate from the text of *Ulysses.*

Whistler v. Ruskin:
The Courts, the Public, and Modern Art
Stuart Culver

> *Indeed, among the dangers threatening modern art, not the least is that it is becoming inoffensive.*
>
> —Theodor Adorno, *Aesthetic Theory*

At almost the same time Theodor Adorno was reaching this conclusion in his *Aesthetic Theory*, the Congress of the United States was establishing the National Endowment for the Arts (NEA), which could be described as a contributor to the administered culture Adorno distrusted. In an effort to secure the place of art in the nation's public sphere and believing that the arts required public funding because the values they represented were at once too crucial and too tenuous to be trusted to the vagaries of the marketplace, Congress proposed to help finance projects that a panel of experts deemed worthy. These experts would be indifferent to the pressures of the marketplace, popular taste, and political constituencies and, Congress assumed, would judge each proposal solely on the basis of its artistic merit. This assumption of the radical autonomy of art seems naive today; and if we take seriously Adorno's critique of administered culture, we can say that the ideological function of the NEA lies precisely in its claim to have cordoned art off from politics by defining the projects it chooses to fund as timeless, priceless masterpieces bearing a purely aesthetic value.

If the NEA seems theoretically committed to the autonomy of the aesthetic realm, it is because the agency is itself an institutionalization of a modernist conception of art that insists on distinguishing authentic works of art from the consumer-oriented products of the entertainment industry on the one hand and blatant propaganda on the other. Art, in this official view, is somehow essential even though it is neither what people want nor what they need to know. But if the NEA has always been in theory modernist, in fact the agency has been willing to fund recent, postmodern projects that claim to challenge both the elitism and the formalist or nonrepresentational bias of high modernism. Despite Adorno's warning that art might lose its critical power once it comes to rely on such agencies, the NEA has managed to fund projects that seem to stand at odds with the theory justifying the agency in the first place simply by refusing to be detached or autonomous enough.

These grants seem to have gone unnoticed until 1989, when the Corcoran Gallery of Art felt compelled to cancel its scheduled showing of photographer Robert Mapplethorpe's The Perfect Moment. In the ensuing months conservative politicians and cultural critics rummaged through the agency's files to discover more outrages against the values and tastes of typical Americans, funded by their own tax dollars. The conservative critics of the NEA share with postmodern artists a distrust of the notions of autonomy and expertise that underlie the NEA's modernist ideology of art. The conservatives, of course, do not just distrust modernist theory; they also believe that postmodern art is itself produced by and for a cultural elite whose tastes not only differ from but actually subvert the values that hold the American people together across racial and economic divisions. In its more paranoid moments, this brand of cultural criticism argues that a leading cause of contemporary social problems is the art that caters to degenerate tastes and prevents the honest expression of "traditional" values. The target of this attack is not just the modernist mechanism for determining which projects ought to be funded but also the very notion that the government should fund art when it cannot guarantee either the social utility or general comprehensibility of the work it sponsors.

One could say that the controversy has its benefits: art has clearly regained its power to offend, and people are being forced to debate the meaning of free speech and to question their own assumptions about what art is and can do. There are, however, more ominous consequences and none more ominous than the fact that some people have been put on trial for displaying or selling suspect works.

The most noteworthy case was the arrest of Dennis Barrie, the curator of Cincinnati's Contemporary Arts Center, who was willing to show the Mapplethorpe photographs when the Corcoran would not. In October 1990 a Cincinnati jury surprised and frustrated the conservatives by acquitting Barrie of all the charges brought against him. By insisting on the autonomy of art and the sanctity of the gallery, the jurors assented to the modernist notion that art is fundamentally different from pornography because the true work of art is not reducible to its content. More significantly, they refused to decide among themselves what counts as a work of art and placed the testimony of the art expert above the concerns of local citizens. As one juror put it, "It's like Picasso. Picasso from what everybody tells me was an artist. It's not my cup of tea. I don't understand it. But if people say it's art, then I have to go along with it."[1] It is crucial to recognize that the acquittal in Cincinnati was less a victory for free speech than a triumph of what I would call the modernist approach to legitimating art, a mode of legitimation that preserves the distinction between art and obscenity by rewriting it as the critical difference between works of art—distinguished by formal qualities established by the testimony of experts—and pornographic commodities, which appeal more immediately to the senses and are never admitted into galleries or museums.

What the Cincinnati verdict lets us see is just how deeply this modernist conception of art has penetrated both legal and popular conceptions of aesthetic value and significance despite—or, rather, because of—its refusal to be responsive to the interests and concerns of the average citizen. In the pages that follow I want to explore how exactly this approach to the regulation of artistic production and consumption came into being and how the contradictions implicit in it first appeared in the public eye. I want to do this by looking at a trial that took place in London more than a century ago, when the modernist ideology of art was first being articulated. The trial is James McNeill Whistler's 1878 libel suit against John Ruskin. In that London courtroom, as in Cincinnati, a panel of jurors was asked to decide what counted as a work of art and who had the right to police the country's galleries and museums. I want further to underscore the implications of the trial and its aftermath by looking at how it affected the critical theories and practices of one particularly interested observer, Henry James, who reported on the trial for the

Nation. James's brief notes on the affair register its impact as both a minor cultural trauma and an embarrassing media event that confused the public about the process of artistic production and the role of critical commentary as it introduced them to the new theories and practices of modern art.

The dispute began in 1877 when, reviewing an exhibition at the recently opened Grosvenor Gallery, Ruskin singled out Whistler's *Nocturne in Black and Gold* as a particularly egregious example of the worst tendencies of modern art:

> For Mr. Whistler's own sake, no less than for the protection of the purchaser, Sir Coutts Lindsay ought not to have admitted works into the gallery in which the ill-educated conceit of the artist so nearly approached the aspect of willful imposture. I have seen and heard, much of Cockney impudence before now; but never expected to hear a coxcomb ask two hundred guineas for flinging a pot of paint in the public's face.[2]

The review, which appeared in Ruskin's *Fors Clavigera*, argued that the "forced eccentricities" of the murky, bewildering painting amounted to a fraud perpetrated against the British public because the artist refused to take seriously the aims of artistic representation. Whistler, Ruskin suggested, was offering up for sale paintings that were merely novel and obscure in an effort to see what the public could be made to buy.

The artist won his suit. The jury found that Ruskin had unfairly damaged Whistler's reputation when he attacked his motives but awarded Whistler only a farthing in damages. In what is usually described as a Pyrrhic victory, the jury granted the artist the right to call whatever he produced a work of art but refused to assign any real value to that work. At the same time, the free speech of the critic was restrained in order to ensure the autonomy of artistic production. By appealing to the law of libel, Whistler managed not only to limit the authority of the nation's leading art critic but also to establish art's independence from bourgeois notions of meaning and value, an independence so absolute that the painter's work was dismissed as essentially without economic value. *Whistler v. Ruskin* should be recognized as a crucial moment in the formation of the modernist ideology not because the *Nocturne in Black and Gold* represents a critical turning point in the tradition of oil painting, but rather because the testimony in court (together with the ensuing battle of words between Whistler and the established art critics of England and the United States) marks a turning point in the way artists sought to justify their work and envision their place in cultural institutions. Anticipating the Mapplethorpe verdict, Whistler's jury abdicated any role in determining aesthetic value; if they were willing to say that the *Nocturne* was probably a work of art, the jurors refused to decide whether or not it was good as art and good for them.

Like the conservative critics of culture today, Ruskin believed that bad art posed a real threat to social values in general, and he demanded a more legible kind of painting than Whistler's. To his mind, the muddled nocturnes appealed only to the decadent tastes of an emerging cultural elite who cultivated superficial pleasures that had little to do with the public good. Yet, unlike Jesse Helms and Patrick Buchanan, Ruskin did not simply identify the significance of a work with its content, and he had been an aggressive advocate of other brands of artistic innovation. Moreover, he was deeply committed to conceiving art as a powerful critique of existing social values and economic practices. What he saw in Whistler was a decadent aestheticism that failed to be offensive in the correct, politically productive way.

The London jury was actually confronted with two competing accounts of how art resisted dominant social values and with two ways of differentiating works of art from the mass-produced articles of everyday use. Ruskin imagined that art could serve as a model for what all forms of manufacture could and should become. Regarding the artist as a craftsman absorbed in his work, he argued that art offered an alternative to the alienated labor of the factory and a way of reconciling the equally crucial values of beauty and utility. Whistler, conversely, believed that beauty had nothing whatsoever to do with utility and was unwilling to think of himself as either a medieval craftsman or just another factory hand; he presented himself to the jury instead as a professional, an expert whose competence derived both from his practical experience in the studio and his familiarity with the great works of art history and crucial documents of art theory. His paintings, therefore, could be judged only by those who understood not only how they derived from and participated in a worldwide tradition, but also how he conceived and executed them. Whistler asked the jurors to think of every artistic practice as a self-regulating profession that provided the public a service that only another artist could appreciate or evaluate. Like that of the doctor administering a dose of medicine, the professional artist's concern is not what people want but what, given his specific theoretical and practical knowledge, he thinks they ought to have. Arthur Symons described Whistler's art as just this effort to prescribe: "He had shown them a glimpse and they wanted a gulp."[3] If Ruskin saw Whistler asking the public to purchase what they could not understand, Symons suggested that this art was in fact a willful rejection of normal modes of consuming art; these were paintings that withheld themselves from the untutored eye.

The Grosvenor Gallery opened in June 1877 as a self-consciously modern alternative to the Royal Academy. It was intended to provide new conditions of display that were uniquely suited to contemporary experiments in painting. The gallery's owner, Coutts Lindsay, described the Grosvenor as

> an entirely independent picture gallery, where distrust of originality and imagination would not be shown, delicate workmanship would not be extinguished, and the number of pictures displayed would not be too large for the wall-space. (cited *CW* 29.158)

Independent of government control, open to innovations, allowing its visitors to confront each image on its own terms, the modern gallery promised to give the public the best possible access to the new art. But what made the gallery popular in its early years was just the fact that it seemed thoroughly novel and wickedly transgressive. In a review of the second Grosvenor exhibition, Henry James suggested that the gallery's visitors were all too willing to be shocked by the new in art. He claims to have overheard one woman complain that the exhibition was not "peculiar" enough: "I am rather disappointed, you know; I expected the arrangement of the pictures would be more unusual." James wonders if she would have been satisfied if the pictures had been "hung upside down or with their faces to the wall." The woman was not a dadaist *avant la lettre*; she merely exemplified the appetite for "something very strange and abnormal" that brought the London crowds to the Grosvenor.[4] James shared Ruskin's distaste for this desire, which seemed vulgarly to commodify modern art as novelty for novelty's sake.

Ruskin was troubled in two distinct ways by Whistler's prominence in the gallery's first exhibition. The Grosvenor announced itself as both the definitive display of modern masterworks and a way of inserting the new painting into the marketplace. The paintings were, after all, for sale. Yet, Ruskin charged, this odd mixture of museum and shop kept Coutts Lindsay from recognizing his responsibilities as a shopkeeper. Speaking as a sort of consumer advocate, Ruskin chastised the would-be curator for not ensuring the quality of his merchandise, arguing that "just as the dealer in cheese or meat answers for the quality of those articles" so too must the art dealer (*CW* 29.155). To the critic, the *Nocturne* seemed, like so much tainted meat, potentially a threat to the health of everyone passing through the doors of the Grosvenor.

Ruskin was, however, more deeply disturbed by the way in which Whistler's self-promoting modernity pandered to the appetite for novelty and peculiarity that brought so many Londoners to the gallery. Whistler seemed to be exploiting the troubling desire for images that viewers can neither use nor comprehend; hence his pictures opened up a gap between their market value and their utility. Unconcerned with her own perception of the *Nocturne*, Whistler's hypothetical buyer treasured the canvas because it seemed to have value in the eyes of others if only by virtue of its outrageous defiance of representational standards. The *Nocturne*'s purchaser could not help but be a speculator, but Ruskin wanted an art shopper to "buy nothing with intent to sell again" and, if at all possible, to "buy it of the artist only, face to face" (*CW* 29.154). The clarity of values in exchange was crucial in Ruskin's political economy. In *Unto This Last* he had defined wealth as "the possession of useful things, which we can use." Whistler's nocturnes proved that this is no tautology; people could indeed be made to buy things the use of which they could never really know. Economics properly understood recognizes that "consumption is the aim and end of production," but Whistler's brand of modernism encouraged and exploited the gap between buying and using, mystifying value where Ruskin expected it to be most clear (*CW* 9.104).

Ruskin had begun his career in art criticism by trying to convince the British public that another painter whose works appeared illegible and poorly crafted was in fact producing works they could use. *Modern Painters* was devoted to showing exactly how Turner's departures from conventional realism were in fact what gave his paintings their value. If Turner's more eccentric landscapes did not delineate objects clearly it was because they captured the violent movements of nature. Ruskin argued that this approach to "modern" painting forced the viewer to reconceive nature as a force or power and not just a collection of objects. The trouble with conventional landscapes in the tradition of Claude, he argued, was just that they blinded the viewer to nature by confronting her with objects too clearly delineated under atmospheric conditions too transparent to be real: "It cannot, I think, be expected that landscapes like this should have any effect on the human heart, except to harden or degrade it" (*CW* 3.125). Ruskin wrote the five volumes of *Modern Painters* in the hope that he could educate the typical British eye to the point that it could take in both the scientific accuracy of Turner's landscapes and the moral lesson implicit in each canvas. In Ruskin's aesthetics, good taste was just the ability to see accurately and hence was inextricably bound up with moral vision. Bad art and good were both symptoms and causes of an individual's—and a nation's—moral and political condition. By learning how to read pictures like Turner's and in turn fostering the production of such images, the nation could provide itself with the means of self-improvement. Ruskin's defense of Turner can be seen as both a repudiation of sentimental tastes in landscape painting and a recuperation of the popular demand for both narrative and moralism in art.

Still, to an untrained eye, Whistler's nocturnes might seem to be merely a darker version of Turner's more extreme landscapes, and so Ruskin needed to establish an objective criterion that average viewers could use to determine whether they were being visually assaulted or not. He found it in what he termed the painting's composition, which he considered both a moral and a formal quality. In the final volume of *Modern Painters* he defined composition as "the help of everything in the picture by everything else" (*CW* 7.205). The well-composed painting mimes the interdependence or organic integration of the natural world and is the result of both the artist's perception of the law of cooperation at work in the phenomena of the world and a conscientious effort to make that vision of integration visible to others. The successful artist is, therefore, equal parts visionary and craftsman; and the composition that distinguishes his paintings is both a formal quality and the moral tale he has to tell. When Ruskin looked for an analogy for poorly composed pictures, he turned to the denaturalized landscape of industrial England: "the mud or slime of a damp, over-trodden path in the outskirts of a manufacturing town" is an instance of an unhelpful or disintegrated mixing of parts (*CW* 7.207). It is as though the social relations surrounding industrial production had actually contaminated nature. Whistler's uncomposed *Nocturne* with its violent and unnatural mixture of colors seemed to Ruskin to be an example of an art that colludes with industry in the destruction of nature's moral example.

Ruskin found an alternative to Whistler's modernism in the Pre-Raphaelite paintings of Edward Burne-Jones also on display in the Grosvenor. The critic noted the "utmost conscience of care" visible in Burne-Jones's work; where Whistler seemed to have quickly flung paint onto his canvases, these paintings palpably displayed the expense of effort that went into their making (*CW* 29.160). In praising Burne-Jones, however, Ruskin had little to say about his moral vision or his scientific accuracy. Ruskin was beginning to consider composition merely a formal property—the presence of craft but not vision—and to identify the use value of a painting with the spectacle of devoted labor it presented rather than the grand narrative it related.

Thus the case for the defense in the libel suit raised two related questions: Was Whistler's *Nocturne in Black and Gold* "composed"? Did he put any serious effort into its making? Ruskin's attorney noted that his client required from every artist "a laborious and perfect devotion to art" and expected to see the signs of that devotion inscribed on the canvas.[5] Testifying for the defense, Burne-Jones suggested that, though the nocturnes were "good in colour," they were "bewildering in form" and, as a group, represented just "one of a thousand failures to paint night." Whistler, he went on, "evaded the great difficulty of painting" when he passed these sketches off as finished work.[6] Ruskin's favorite described the work of his rival as arty but uncomposed, demonstrating a sense of visual values like color and atmosphere but lacking any deep-seated devotion to the craft of painting.

Whistler seemed to have helped the defense when he confessed in court that he could "knock off" a nocturne in a day or perhaps two. Indeed, what Ruskin called his "Cockney impudence" was in part his refusal to be the sort of craftsman Ruskin wanted all artists to be. Instead of insisting on the amount of conscientious care and labor that went into each of his works, Whistler explained that his paintings were worth two hundred guineas because each of them had "the knowledge of a lifetime" behind it (*GAME* 5). To his modernist sensibility, art was not a labored production but a scientific experiment. As Whistler's lawyer described his client's practices, the painter had come up with "a theory of his own" that he followed "with earnestness, industry, and almost enthusiasm."[7] Each of his paintings, therefore, had value in relation to other works and to the possibilities of the medium in general. Values of this sort, Whistler maintained, appeared "only to those who understand the technical matter" (*GAME* 8).

The instructions the jurors were given made the verdict inevitable: "A critic should have full latitude to express the judgments he has formed" and can even use ridicule to make his point, the judge declared, but no one can use criticism as "a veil for personal censure" or criticize "merely for the love of exercising his powers of denunciation" (Adams 24). There may be art for art's sake, but not criticism for its own sake. Following the logic of libel law, the judge distinguished legitimate criticism that attended only to the work itself from the illegitimate effort to criticize the motives and character of the person behind the work, making clear to the jury that they were not just to determine the relative authority of two different varieties of expertise but that they were implicitly defining the kind of activity criticism properly is. The notion of criticism as merely the analysis of a work's objective features is at odds with Ruskin's belief that, at bottom, art is both a reflection of and an operation on a society's moral condition. It was inevitable that Ruskin would transgress the boundaries libel law establishes between private individual and public expression, person and work. The legal formalism that recognized an irreducible gap between alienable property and the individual ultimately limited the range of critical commentary.

Believing that every work was a performance the public could not understand much less objectively analyze, Whistler testified that "none but an artist can be a competent critic of art." Criticism is indeed necessary but its scope should be restricted to "technical criticism by a man whose life is passed in the science which he criticizes" (*GAME* 6). If Whistler's theoretical approach to painting requires critical, rather than popular, appreciation, it nonetheless reduces the range of critical activity to the mere second-guessing of strategies and techniques. The artist refused to let the critic broach any of the larger questions about art's final purpose or social role. As a proponent of Gautier's *l'art pour l'art*, Whistler held that artists should never worry about what use their paintings may serve as they strive after purely aesthetic effects; thus, in his most radical description of the nocturnes as a group, he suggested that these paintings succeed in appealing to the viewer's visual sense without engaging the intellect. He told the jurors that his *Nocturne in Blue and Silver* was not intended to be a correct representation of Battersea Bridge by moonlight. "My whole scheme," he insisted, "was to bring about a harmony of color" (*GAME* 8). According to his testimony, the artist was never interested in clearly delineating objects in the real world, nor was he concerned to reproduce a prior act of vision; rather, he wanted to construct a visual experience for the viewer, performing a service that the viewer would in all likelihood never notice.

Whistler, consequently, had a very different understanding of the place of nature in the visual arts. The objects and phenomena of the natural world could no longer be considered art's privileged subject matter; they were instead a collection of raw materials the painter could use to bring off highly artificial visual effects. "Seldom does nature succeed in producing a picture," Whistler noted, and so the modern painter should take an anti-organic approach to composition rather than seek only to copy how colors and forms are organized in nature (*GAME* 143). In effect, Whistler was converting what Ruskin saw as the end of painting into its means and vice versa. He extended this reversal of purpose and instrument even to the human subjects of his canvases: "I care nothing for the past, present, or future of the black figure, placed there because black was wanted at that spot" (*GAME* 126). This seems to approach a dehumanizing technological appropriation as the human figure becomes merely a tool for distributing color around the canvas; thus he called his famous portrait of his mother *An Arrangement in Black and Gray.* Of course, that painting points to a gap between Whistler's theoretical claims about nonrepresentational art and his actual practice, which, even in the nocturnes, never dispensed with the subject. The painter was not so much giving up representation as he was distorting its purpose and complicating the public's access to the object behind the image.

Whistler was in fact engaged in a struggle against what he understood as the dominant mode of reception and criticism, the literary interpretation of painting. Looking past the formal elements—the painterly concerns of color and mass—the typical critic saw only the story behind the picture. Whistler was willing to risk being entirely misunderstood in order to prevent his paintings from being so easily read. Recognizing this reduction of image to narrative as the repression of painting's real power, the artist claimed to "divest the picture of any outside anecdotal interest" (cited in Merrill 144). The nocturnes, therefore, are intended to make the viewer experience the difference between looking through a painting and actually seeing it as a work of visual art. What could be called the aura or form effect of one of Whistler's modern paintings is just its resistance to any easy translation of pictures into words or visual sensations into moral concepts. In this gap between looking through and truly appreciating pictures, another tension becomes evident. We see the hedonism of the modernist call for a purely visual pleasure and the abstract intellect at work in its means of production. The modern painting will immediately and physically gratify the eye even as its techniques and aesthetic merits remain inexplicable to the average viewer. If painting does perform a public service, it seems to be a sort of physical therapy that acts subliminally on its patient.

Ruskin's mistake, Whistler believed, was to imagine that by teaching the public how to read moral allegories into paintings, he could bridge the gap between the painter's intentions and the public's reception. "The gentle priest of the Philistines," writing as an unlicensed and uninitiated middleman, actually "widened the gulf between the people and the painter" (*GAME* 150). The artist felt that the gap could never be bridged and assumed it was his responsibility to disabuse the public of any illusion that it had been: art was something the typical person would never really understand.

To this end, in his "Ten O'Clock Lecture," delivered in the aftermath of the libel suit, Whistler attacked the central premises of Ruskin's approach to art history: "There never was an artistic period. There never was an art-loving nation" (*GAME* 139). If Ruskin hoped to create another golden age for art by educating the public eye to the standards of the best art, Whistler was resigned to the fact that artists would never give the people what they wanted. Throughout the course of history the artist stood in the same alienated relation to society. The first artist, according to Whistler's theory, was a nonproductive, feminine figure who "stayed by the tents with the women and traced strange devices with a burnt stick on a gourd" (*GAME* 139). Investing useful objects with a supplementary value that is unnecessary and largely unnoticed, this primordial artist—and anyone who follows in his path—stands at odds with the interests of the tribe. Therefore we can assume no necessary relation between a given form of society or mode of production and the making of interesting art. As Whistler put it, "Art happens. No hovel is safe from it, no Prince may depend upon it" (*GAME* 150). It is an ahistorical, universal resistance to notions of utility and instrumentality.

Whistler, of course, anticipated the founding gesture of the NEA by imagining a barrier separating art from ideological argument even as he suggested that governments can never really subsidize art. The artistic masterpiece is, he insisted, "no more the product of civilization than the scientific truth is dependent upon the wisdom of a period" (*GAME* 155). Whistler presented himself as the consummate professional, a master of all studio techniques who was accountable for every step in the composition process. He made his own brushes and frames and attempted to govern exactly where and how his pictures would be shown in an effort to make every step count as a clear, consciously considered choice. The difficulty of the artist's job is precisely this unrelenting decision making, not the mere expenditure of physical labor. To purify this process, the artist requires autonomy. The very presence of the public or the critic in studios and galleries is a threat to rational composition. "An inroad into the laboratory would be locked upon as an intrusion; but before the triumphs of Art, the expounder is at ease" (*GAME* 33). This appeal to the scientist's workplace portrays Ruskin and others of his ilk as interlopers disrupting the scene of artistic production, but Whistler was conflating the scene of production proper (the studio) with the scene of display and consumption (the gallery). The implication is that it is just as crucial to police the public's response to the finished work as it is to keep prying eyes out of the artist's laboratory. Under the logic of professionalism, as the artist becomes more autonomous and accountable, he is increasingly insulated from the public; and Ruskin's presence at the Grosvenor seems just as problematic as that of the woman Henry James overheard, his criticisms of no more import than her wish for novelty.

In fact, one of the nocturnes was entered in court as evidence upside down. Apparently no one noticed except Whistler, and he seemed not to care, not because he thought the nocturnes could be hung any way, but because, to his mind, modern art simply could not be seen in a courtroom. It only becomes visible in a museum and then only to the few who know how to look. But if aesthetic values cannot appear in court, why did Whistler bother to sue Ruskin in the first place and risk becoming a caricature in the popular press as the trial turned into a media event?

Perhaps we can find a clue in Oscar Wilde's humorous review of Whistler's lecture. Wilde heard Whistler argue that "the slightest appearance among a civilized people of any interest in beautiful things is a grave impertinence to all painters." The painter "explained to the public that the only thing they should cultivate was ugliness, and that on their permanent stupidity rested all hope of art in the future." Wilde surmised that Whistler's audience "was extremely gratified at being rid of the awful obligation of admiring anything."[8] They are left blind and happy by the very logic of modern art. Thus Whistler's day in court must be seen in retrospect as an unqualified success for the painter and his supporters. By simultaneously granting him autonomy and refusing to recognize the value of his work, the jurors found a way not to have to worry about hating, loving, or fearing art, while the modern painter found a way of protecting his work from the bourgeois appetite for moralistic narrative by insisting on his own superficiality.

The duplicity of the verdict—art is autonomous and valueless—reflects the doubleness in Whistler's carefully cultivated public persona. He insisted on presenting himself to the jury as both a professional and a dandy, accountable for every step in the composition process yet throwing off paintings with little effort or thought, performing a public service but with no apparent concern for the consequences. If Whistler tried to place art within rationalized production, he did so subversively, by miming its instrumental logic and making a fetish of technique while foreclosing any discussion of use. What makes Whistler's performance at the trial so fascinating is his refusal to dispel the fear that his modern art might be a hoax after all. Like Poe before him, Whistler appeared as both scientist and humbug, his work constantly confusing rationality and unreason. When Whistler undermined the process of consuming pictures by giving a glimpse instead of a gulp, he provided what Adorno calls a determinate negation of the system of industrial production; it is the modernist formula for keeping art both protected and offensive and stands in marked contrast to Ruskin's notion of an art that would itself police and purify relations of production and consumption and to the postmodern effort to forge an antiaesthetic art.

For Henry James, Whistler's nocturnes could only be appreciated as "incidents of furniture or decoration" (*PE* 165); their presence in the Grosvenor exhibit served only to confuse works of art with ordinary commodities like wallpaper. Yet, in his most famous theoretical statement, the novelist seems to have aligned himself with Whistler: "We must grant the artist his subject, his idea, his donnée; our criticism is applied only to what he makes of it."[9] In other words, James would have the critic attend only to questions of execution and treatment, and he wants to expand the reading public's sense of what counts as a literary subject or story. Still, disturbed by Whistler's effort to reduce the authority of the critic and limit the range of his commentary, the novelist goes on to say, "Art lives upon discussion . . . upon the exchange of views and the comparison of standpoints" (*PP* 376). If the critic's work is parasitic on the artist's, the artist is, at least to this extent, parasitic on the critic. James was concerned, I would suggest, with reestablishing the role of criticism as a means of regulating artistic production in the wake of Ruskin's libel. He agreed with Whistler that, while art itself is "one of the necessities of life," criticism is no more than "an agreeable luxury" (*PE* 177). But, as he reflected on the critic's role in the modern marketplace where novels and paintings are mass produced, he came to advocate a paradox: criticism is an essential luxury, secondary but nonetheless requisite. James resolved this paradox by conceiving the critic's office as fundamentally sacrificial. It is his job to understand and experience for others too busy or too distracted to encounter art themselves. The critic is then the artist's exemplary audience and, increasingly, the public consumes only vicariously through him. In this view, the critic cannot be said to judge the work according to a set of universal standards as Ruskin believed he did; instead, the critic masters the practice of consuming art.

Jamesian criticism, therefore, is not the closed conversation among professionals Whistler envisioned. It is, rather, the primary means for recuperating the relation between the artistic work and its world. Yet the reading public must feel more and more tempted to consume vicariously through the critic, consuming the consumption of art as they read only criticism. One way of reading James's late fictions is to see them as essentially fables of the critical office, dramatizing the danger implicit in it. Narrating his tales through the eyes and minds of partially detached observers, the novelist suggested that it is difficult if not impossible to distinguish consuming a story from creating it. Indeed, his late style is as modern as Whistler's because it conflates luxury and essence, production and consumption.

In an effort to escape the paradoxes implicit in the aesthetic ideology of modernism, recent artists have sought to break down the wall between the gallery and the outside world Whistler helped to construct. Believing that the ideals of disinterest and autonomy stand in the way of artistic production and troubled by the unacknowledged affinities between Whistler's rationalized professionalism and contemporary modes of social domination, postmodern artists reject modernist logics of display and evaluation. Yet defenders of postmodernism acknowledge that we cannot quite do without the museum: "If it was true that much art could be seen as art only within the museum, it was also true that much art (often the same) was critical of the museum."[10] Hal Foster has argued that this contradiction is resolved in the postmodernist's "dialectical supercession of modernism."[11] What this means is that each new work comes into being as a direct challenge to the founding distinctions of modernism: these antiaesthetic or antiauratic projects are only original when they call attention to their derivativeness, can only have integrity when they violate the limits of any given medium, and can only be serious by being irreverent. They are, in short, antimodern by virtue of being thoroughly antiprofessional.

The problem, however, is how to distinguish works engaged in a serious rethinking of art as a cultural institution from those that merely exploit the fluidity of forms in our postindustrial, multimedia world. Can we talk about the artistic merit of avowedly antiaesthetic works? The only possible answer is that the best art is art that resists most powerfully the canons of taste and evaluation. Postmodernism, therefore, risks making a fetish of resistance where modernism fetishized technique.

My intent in discussing the Cincinnati trial is to point out that work that could be called postmodern was protected there by an appeal to the modernist ideology of art. Mapplethorpe's images are actually quite easily assimilated into the modernist canon. Self-consciously arty treatments of nontraditional subjects, the photographs are marked by a tension between form and content. As the jury recognized, just because these are black and white images they seem more like art, offering the viewer a distanced, mediated encounter with the objects and events instead of pornography's immediacy. One of the city's disappointed crusaders for decency implicitly acknowledged this as he vowed to continue the fight: "If they come back with those pictures and they're in color or are bigger, our citizens will demand that it go to a grand jury."[12] Under the modernist logic that identifies art with the difficult and the distant, the more simulacral works are the less likely that they will be protected as art.

This may be why the attacks of cultural conservatives have centered on performance art as well as photography; "live" performances seem less mediated and more easily reducible to their "meaning" or "value content" to a public brought up on Whistlerian notions of the art object. The defense of artists who have been denied funds by the NEA four has more often than not turned on questions of free speech and the constitutional right to self-expression. At a time when it is increasingly difficult to distinguish speech from action, performance art can easily be defended as symbolic conduct, like burning a cross or a flag. But this defense is beside the point since it offers no response to the conservative argument that there is no reason for funding this particular speech by calling it "art." The issue becomes particularly cloudy when self-styled "post-porn modernist" Annie Sprinkle puts on a performance at the Kitchen—an NEA-funded New York performance space—that is largely indistinguishable from the one she puts on at a *Screw* magazine party. The Kitchen's director insists that the performances were different simply because one took place "in an art context."[13] As Sprinkle told one critic, the audience at the Kitchen was willing to regard her performance "from lots of different perspectives."[14] This defense actually recuperates the modernist aesthetic, merely relocating "form" in the response of the audience. Champions of postmodernism like to believe that these new forms of art resist outdated legal and aesthetic categories, forcing critics to reconceive what the art object is and can be. But I am suggesting that "art" remains the same disinterested interest; it is merely located more absolutely in the consuming subject. Commenting on the Cincinnati trial, conservative constitutional lawyer Bruce Fein seems to recognize this: "People don't usually walk into museums to have their prurient interests aroused."[15] The question is not what is shown but to whom it is shown and under what conditions. This virtually removes all formal grounds for censorship (anything is art if it is found in an art gallery, and an art gallery is wherever art lovers gather to respond aesthetically to objects). At the same time, this argument suggests an alternative justification for the NEA: what is being funded is not today's masterpiece (with a special relation to the tradition); rather, the government is sponsoring aesthetic responses, giving more people the opportunity to be Jamesian critics and disseminating the critical office that both Whistler and Ruskin wanted to monopolize.

NOTES

1. Cited in Edward De Grazia, *"Girls Lean Back Everywhere": The Law of Obscenity and the Assault on Genius* (New York: Random House, 1992), 655. De Grazia offers a fairly extensive account of the Cincinnati trial and the ensuing attacks on the NEA.

2. "Life Guards of the New Life," *Fors Clavigera* Letter 79 in *The Complete Works of John Ruskin*, ed. E. T. Cook and Alexander Wedderburn (London: George Allen, 1903-12) vol. 29, 146-69 (this passage, 160). Subsequent quotations from Ruskin will be taken from this collection, abbreviated as *CW* followed by volume and page numbers.

3. Arthur Symons, *Studies in the Seven Arts*, in *The Collected Works of Arthur Symons* (London: Martin Secker, 1906, reprinted 1967), vol. 9, 35.

4. Henry James. *The Painter's Eye: Notes and Essays on the Pictorial Arts*, ed. John L. Sweeney (Cambridge, Mass.: R. Hart-Davis, 1956), 161. Subsequent references to this volume will be abbreviated *PE*.

5. Cited in Laurie Adams, *Art on Trial from Whistler to Rothko* (New York: Walker, 1976), 17.

6. Cited by Whistler in *The Gentle Art of Making Enemies* (London: Heinemann, 1892; reprinted New York: Dover, 1967), 15. Subsequent references to this volume will appear parenthetically as *GAME*.

7. Cited in Linda Merrill, *A Pot of Paint: Aesthetics on Trial in Whistler v. Ruskin* (Washington, D.C.: Smithsonian Institution Press, 1992), 138. Merrill offers by far the most complete account of the trial.

8. "Mr. Whistler's 'Ten O'Clock,'" in *The Artist as Critic: Critical Writings of Oscar Wilde*, ed. Richard Ellmann (New York: Random House, 1969; reprinted Chicago: University of Chicago Press, 1982), 14.

9. Henry James, *Partial Portraits* (New York: Macmillan, 1889; reprinted Ann Arbor: University of Michigan Press, 1970), 394. Subsequent references will be abbreviated *PP*.

10. Hal Foster, "Postmodernism: A Preface," in *The Anti-Aesthetic: Essays on Postmodern Culture*, ed. Hal Foster (Port Townsend, Wash.: Bay Press, 1983), 14.

11. Ibid., 14.

12. De Grazia, *Girls Lean Back*, 655-56.

13. Cited in Amy Adler, "Art and Obscenity," *Yale Law Journal* 99: 1359-78, 1370.

14. Ibid.

15. De Grazia, *Girls Lean Back*, 653.

Freud and the Scene of Censorship
Michael G. Levine

In a letter to his friend Wilhelm Fliess announcing the completion of *The Interpretation of Dreams*, Freud compares his own style to that of the dreamer described in his pioneering work:

> The dream material itself is, I believe, unassailable. What I dislike about it is the style, which was quite incapable [*unfähig*] of noble, simple expression and lapsed into facetious [*witzelnde*] circumlocutions straining after metaphors. I know that, but the part of me that knows it and knows how to evaluate it is unfortunately the part that does not produce.
>
> It is certainly true that the dreamer is too witty, but it is neither my fault nor does it contain a reproach. All dreamers are equally insufferably witty, and they need to be because they are under pressure and the direct route is barred to them.[1]

The contrast here is clear enough. While the dreamer is obliged to be overly clever, the writer (who would one day be awarded the Goethe Prize for Literature) simply cannot help himself. While the former uses circumlocutions to get around obstacles, the latter merely "lapses" into them. While the creative, wish-constructing part of the dreamer works in tandem with its censorial counterpart, in the author the hand that evaluates "unfortunately" has nothing to do with the one that produces.

A little over a week later Freud returns to the matter of style in another letter to Fliess:

> Somewhere inside me there is a feeling for form, an appreciation of beauty as a kind of perfection; and the tortuous sentences of my dream

book [*Traumschrift*], with their parading of indirect phrases and squint-
ing at ideas, deeply offended one of my ideals. Nor am I far wrong in
regarding this lack of form [*Formmangel*] as an indication of insufficient
mastery of the material.[2]

Once again the self-deprecating tone and expression of an offended aesthetic sensibility give voice to insecurities—as though Freud
were still wondering at this point just how finished his manuscript
really is. Yet the insistent identification of his own style with that of
the dreamer—even as he excuses the latter while finding fault with
the former—suggests another way of understanding the professed
shortcomings of his text. In "straining after metaphors" to describe
the unconscious activity of dreaming, it is no accident that Freud
makes repeated use of *textual* metaphors throughout *The Interpretation of Dreams*. As has often been observed, he compares dreams
to pictograms, rebuses, and hieroglyphs and describes the dream
content as a kind of "transcript of the dream-thoughts into another
mode of expression" (*S.E.* 4, 277).[3] He even goes so far at one point as
to claim that "the phenomena of censorship and of dream distortion
correspond down to their smallest details" (*S.E.* 4, 143). Thus, while
the tortuous sentences of his dream book remind him of the indirect
modes of expression proper to dreams, a proper understanding of
those dreams in turn requires that they be treated as enigmatic, tran-
scribed, and censored texts. Freud's chiasmatic coupling of text and
dream—of text as dream and dream as text—effectively displaces the
relative value of each of the terms brought together here. While he
complains to Fliess that his dream book is "lacking in form," one
begins to suspect that this alleged deficiency is not merely an indication of "insufficient mastery," as Freud suggests, but instead the
index of a *different kind of relationship* of the psychical and the
textual.

In his pathbreaking essay on "Freud and the Scene of Writing,"
Jacques Derrida begins to outline just such a relationship. If his reading is, as he says, guided by Freud's investment in the metaphor of
nonphonetic writing, his aim is less to determine how Freud uses
such metaphors for didactic ends than to ask how the insistence of
such terms "makes what we believe we know under the name of
writing enigmatic."[4] In other words, the question for him is not
whether

a writing apparatus—for example, the one described in the "Note on the Mystic Writing Pad"—is a *good* metaphor for representing the working of the psyche, but rather what apparatus we must create in order to represent psychical writing. [The question is] not *if* the psyche is indeed a kind of text, but: what is a text, and what must the psyche be if it can be represented by a text? For if there is neither machine nor text without psychical origin, there is no domain of the psyche without text. (199, emphasis added)

Derrida's decision to focus on the metaphor of writing is thus motivated by a desire to reinterpret and displace the traditional status both of metaphor and of writing—the point being that these issues are so bound up with one another that to address the one is always in a sense to talk about the other. Derrida argues that "scriptural images have regularly been used to *illustrate* the relationship between reason and experience, perception and memory" (199) from Plato and Aristotle on. What for him distinguishes "the gesture sketched out by Freud" is the way that metaphor and writing come to inhabit and constitute the very relationships they are usually called upon simply to illustrate.

While Derrida reads the tracing of this gesture in a wide range of texts, the professed aim of his essay is to follow "a strange progression" in Freud's own work from the *Project* of 1895 to the "Note on the Mystic Writing-Pad" (1925). Charting the course of this progression, which along the way follows the "advance of the metaphors of path, trace, breach," Derrida describes how

the structural model of writing, which Freud invokes immediately after the *Project*, will be persistently differentiated and refined in its originality. All the mechanical models will be tested and abandoned, until the discovery of the *Wunderblock*, a writing machine of marvelous complexity into which the whole of the psychical apparatus will be projected. The solution to all the previous difficulties will be presented in the *Wunderblock*, and the "Note," indicative of an admirable tenacity, will answer precisely the questions of the *Project*. (200)

If all roads thus seem to lead to the *Wunderblock*, it is not simply because this text provides the solution to a long-standing problem, but rather because it *restages* in a more complex, dynamic, and rigorous way *an earlier question* already raised in the *Project* concerning the relationship of metaphor, writing, and spacing. Leaving aside the details of Derrida's discussion of Freud's "Note," which I have sought to analyze elsewhere, I would instead like to call attention to the way the question of censorship emerges at this point in his essay.[5]

"Writing," he says, "is unthinkable without repression. The condition for writing is that there be neither a permanent contact nor an absolute break between strata: the vigilance and failure of censorship" (226). While these remarks undoubtedly have a more general import, they refer specifically to Freud's *Wunderblock* and the two hands required to operate it. As Freud says, to appreciate fully the comparison of the writing pad to the functioning of the psychical apparatus, we need to "imagine one hand writing upon the surface ... while another periodically raises its covering sheet from the wax slab" (*S.E.* 19, 232). Derrida reads this scene of two-handed writing described by Freud as gesturing toward a different kind of relationship between writing and repression, one that may no longer be understood simply in terms of the alternating logic of "on the one hand, on the other." To follow the movement of these hands is, in other words, to approach writing and repression as processes that are at once more intimately connected and more internally divided than has hitherto been imagined. It is for this reason that Derrida speaks of both "the vigilance *and* [the] failure of censorship."

Yet why does Derrida find it necessary to wait until the "Note on a Mystic Writing-Pad" to begin to address the question of censorship in Freud? Certainly the most obvious place to broach the issue would be *The Interpretation of Dreams*, in which the notion of a *dream censorship* is assigned a pivotal role in Freud's understanding of the dream as a "(disguised) fulfillment of a (suppressed or repressed) wish."[6] If Derrida only seriously takes up the issue of censorship in his reading of Freud's "Note," this delay is at least in part related to the fact that he does not take the Freudian notion of dream censorship all that seriously. "At the beginning of the *Traumdeutung*," he says, "Freud seems to make only a conventional, didactic reference to it" (226). As to the question of what Freud does with it elsewhere in the text, Derrida does not say.[7] What remains to be explained, then, is how one might move from this "conventional, didactic," and illustrative use of the "metaphor of censorship" to the more complex articulation of writing and repression discussed in the context of Freud's note on the *Wunderblock*.

Although Derrida's essay tends to pass lightly over the topic of dream censorship, "Freud and the Scene of Writing" nevertheless sets the stage for a reading of *The Interpretation of Dreams* and its own staging of another scene of censorship. In order to follow the complication and destabilization of a metaphor that, as Derrida observes, *is* used in a rather conventional way at the beginning of Freud's text, it is necessary to examine not only certain shifts in the use of the particular metaphor of censorship, but also the general displacement of the very status of metaphor in this text. While Freud claims that "the kernel of [his] theory of dreams lies in [his] derivation of dream distortion from the censorship" (*S.E.* 4, 308), a close examination of the strains, breakdowns, and dissimilarities engendered by his comparisons reveals a different mapping of the relationships among textual, psychical, and political spaces and a very different notion of censorship. Not only does this notion clearly *diverge* from the model of press censorship upon which it is initially based, but it also and above all transforms and distorts that model in the process of translating it.

To begin to grasp some of the problems involved in understanding Freud's borrowing of the notion of dream censorship from the area of politics concerned with the deletions, blanks, and disguises of writing, it might be instructive to return to a well-known story recounted in the course of Freud's analysis of the seminal dream of Irma's injection:

> The whole plea—for the dream was nothing else—reminded one vividly of the defense put forward by the man who was charged by one of his neighbors with having given him back a borrowed kettle in a damaged condition. The defendant asserted first, that he had given it back undamaged; secondly, that the kettle had holes in it when he borrowed it; and thirdly, that he had never borrowed a kettle from his neighbor at all. So much the better; if only a single one of these three lines of defense were to be accepted as valid, the man would have to be acquitted. (*S.E.* 4, 119-20)

Before commenting on this story and its connection to censorship, it should be noted that Freud rarely speaks of a dream *censor* (*Traumzensor*) in his work. Indeed, his lecture "The Censorship of Dreams" explicitly warns against picturing this instance "as a severe little manikin or a spirit living in a closet in the brain and there discharging his office" (*S.E.* 15, 140). In fact, if Freud almost exclusively uses the term *dream censorship* (*Traumzensur*), it is clearly in order to exploit its institutional connotations—its various levels of authority and delegated responsibility, and the censoring and policing of one level by another.[8]

Yet, the Freudian notion of censorship would be rather trivial were it modeled simply on an organizational flow chart. What gives the term its dynamism is the fact that in addition—and in opposition—to its bureaucratic aspects, it also involves processes comparable to the activity of *self*-censorship. Needless to say, this latter form of censorship is itself internally conflicted and must be understood as a practice structured by the interplay of competing forces that, on the one hand, attempt to circumvent official sanctions and, on the other, cannot help but internalize them to varying degrees as forms of writer's block. What is thus gathered together and condensed under the rubric of the single covering term of dream censorship is a complex of incompatible pressures and opposing tendencies. Freud thus introduces a term that is not only lacking in conceptual integrity but that might also be brought up on charges of conflict of interest. One imagines a trial proceeding along the lines of the kettle story defense: the order to censor was received and duly executed; the order already had loopholes in it when it arrived; the order was never received in the first place. Obviously, none of these versions alone can account for the paradoxical functioning of censorship as it is elaborated in *The Interpretation of Dreams*. Yet, if one is prepared to consider these competing "pleas" together, it becomes possible to follow the dynamic interaction of the forces driving, structuring, and dislocating this internal border guard.

The Barred Path to Censorship

As Mikkel Borch-Jacobsen notes in *The Freudian Subject*, at the beginning of *The Interpretation of Dreams* it would appear that if an unconscious wish is never clearly represented to consciousness, "no inherent opacity on the part of the wish is to blame. The wish is not clearly represented because access to consciousness is *denied* it by an 'agency' assigned the task of sorting out representations at the entrance to the preconscious-consciousness."[9] Thus, the wish must somehow be concealed and disguised if it is to get around this censorship. As Freud says:

> A similar difficulty confronts the political writer who has disagreeable truths to tell to those in authority. If he presents them undisguised, the authorities will suppress his words—after they have been spoken if his pronouncement was an oral one, but beforehand, if he had intended to make it in print. A writer must be aware of the censorship, and on its account he must soften and distort the expression of his opinion. According to the strength and sensitiveness of the censorship he finds himself compelled either merely to refrain from certain references or he must conceal his objectionable pronouncement beneath some apparently innocent disguise. . . . The stricter the censorship, the more far-reaching will be the disguise and the more ingenious too may be the means employed for putting the reader on the scent of the true meaning [*auf die Spur der eigentlichen Bedeutung*].
>
> The fact that the phenomena of censorship and of dream distortion correspond down to their smallest details justifies us in presuming that they are similarly determined. (*S.E.* 4, 142-43)

In taking over the analogy of political censorship, Freud at least at first takes with it the accompanying hierarchies. Thus, as one might expect, he posits two separate and opposed forces or systems, one of which creatively "constructs the wish," while the other "forcibly brings about a distortion in the expression of [it]." To illustrate the effects of this distortion and its links to press censorship, Freud adds a footnote in 1919 in which he adduces the so-called dream of the "love services." In this dream the effects of the censorship may be discerned in the replacement of reprehensible statements by an incomprehensible mumble. Commenting on this dream in *The Introductory Lectures* (1916-17), Freud remarks:

> You will, I hope, think it plausible to suppose that it was precisely the objectionable nature of these passages that was the motive for their suppression. Where shall we find a parallel to such an event? You need not look far these days. Take up any political newspaper and you will find that here and there the text is absent and in its place nothing except the white paper is to be seen. This, as you know, is the work of the press censorship. In these empty places there was something that displeased the higher censorship authorities and for that reason it was removed—a pity, you feel, since no doubt it was the most interesting thing in the paper—the 'best bit' [*es war 'die beste Stelle'*]. (*S.E.* 15, 138-39)

Freud's mention of "die beste Stelle," an allusion to Heinrich Heine's famous poem *Germany: A Winter's Tale,* marks a shift in focus in Freud's lecture. Whereas he had heretofore dealt only with the more blatant signs of censorship associated with the deletion of sensitive material, he now turns to the subtler ruses employed by the self-censoring author. That a passage from Heine serves to mark this transition is significant for a number of reasons: first, the passage referred to here—possibly the most famous "bit" of Heine's text—is one in which the censor's scissors do to the poet's body what they usually do to texts:

> The shears are clicking in his hand—
> He plunges like a possessed one
> Upon the body—hacks the flesh—
> Alas! that part was the best one.[10]

This allusion is but one indication of the way that Heine serves as a privileged point of reference for Freud in his thinking about censorship.[11] Moreover, in marking the transition in Freud's lecture from the blatant signs of external censorship to the subtler and more prevalent forms of dream distortion analogous to the politics of self-censorship, this passage literally places Heine and his own equivocal relationship to censorship somewhere between the two.

At this point in his lecture Freud describes the self-censoring author as one who "has contented himself with approximations and allusions to what would genuinely have come from his pen." According to Freud, this form of censorship is not only much more subtle and insidious, but it is also the form most often employed in the censorship of dreams. "The censorship," he says, "takes effect much more frequently according to the second method, by producing softenings, approximations and allusions instead of the genuine thing [*an Stelle des Eigentlichen*]" (*S.E.* 15, 139). This comparison of dream distortion to press censorship and the sense of propriety (*des Eigentlichen*) underwriting it is discussed by Borch-Jacobsen:

What these 'analogies' presuppose is obvious: the newspaper is legible before the censor's scissors make holes in it; the writer knows what he wants to say before he starts to play the game of concealment. In other words, dream-thoughts are indeed thoughts, *cogitationes*, and they are perfectly intelligible ones. . . . Nothing sets them apart from conscious representations except the simple fact that repression keeps them inaccessible to consciousness.[12]

Borch-Jacobsen is undoubtedly correct in his assessment of the assumptions underlying one particular stratum of Freud's thinking about censorship. Yet, in restricting his comments to this layer he fails to appreciate the significance of the general shift in Freud's brief lecture and more extensively in *The Interpretation of Dreams* toward the dynamics of self-censorship. For the more dream censorship comes to resemble self-censorship, the harder it is to assign responsibility for the work of distortion and the more difficult it is to say exactly whose interests are being served by it. While Borch-Jacobsen is not wrong in describing censorship as a one-sided "agency" whose function consists in denying representations access to consciousness, Freud's texts *also* seem to suggest that censorship is a kind of double agent with multiple and divided allegiances. If these competing accounts are permitted to coexist in Freud's texts, they are as much an indication of the various thresholds and institutional levels of dream censorship as a sign of the unconscious kettle logic structuring and unsettling this notion.

Freud may thus speak of "the presence of two psychical agencies and a censorship between them" (*S.E.* 4, 235), while elsewhere warning against taking the term "in too 'localizing' a sense" and adding that "it is nothing more than a serviceable term for describing a *dynamic relation*" (*S.E.* 15, 140, emphasis added). If censorship thus tends to resist definition as a stable concept and seems to be difficult to locate simply as a particular psychical frontier, its instability is not only an indication of the very dynamism of the relations in which it is enmeshed but moreover a sign of its close and equivocal connection to the Freudian notion of displacement. As is well known, Freud considered displacement to be the essential portion of the dreamwork. He describes it as "a psychical force ... which on the one hand [*einerseits*] strips elements having a high psychical value of their intensity, and on the other hand [*andrerseits*], by means of overdetermination, creates new values from elements of low psychical value" (*S.E.* 4, 307). Only these newly created values find their way into the dream content.

In contrast to the cruder forms of dream distortion in which the sides, battle lines, and traces of violence are all too clearly defined, displacement represents a two-handed process that redefines both the terms and the field of conflict. Whereas Freud earlier seemed to suggest that the diversions and detours imposed by censorship merely put greater physical distance between dream thoughts and their expression, decreasing their intensity through excisions, approximations, and circumlocutions, it now appears that the distortion of dreams can also involve the creation of new values. Rather than simply toning down and distancing highly charged material, displacement would thus effect a transvaluation of psychical values. Yet, how exactly it does this and on whose behalf it acts remain to be seen.

As to the question of whose interests are served by the mechanism of displacement, Freud's response is surprisingly unequivocal. An obvious consequence of displacement, he argues, is that the dream content no longer resembles the core of the dream thoughts and that the dream gives no more than a distorted version of the dream wish existing in the unconscious:

> But we are already familiar with dream distortion. We traced it back to the censorship which is exercised by one psychical agency in the mind over another. Dream displacement is one of the chief methods by which that distortion is achieved. *Is fecit cui profuit.* We may assume, then, that dream displacement comes about through the influence of the same censorship—that is, the censorship of endopsychic defence [*jener Zensur, der endopsychischen Abwehr*]. (*S.E.* 4, 308)

Thus, it seems that displacement and the distortions it brings about simply serve the interests of an endopsychic defense intent on censoring the expression of unconscious wishes. Yet, this conclusion is immediately called into question by a seemingly innocuous remark in the following paragraph, which closes the chapter on displacement. In the guise of summarizing his argument Freud surreptitiously reposes the problem:

> We can state provisionally a second condition which must be satisfied by those elements of the dream thoughts which make their way into the dream [the first being that they must be overdetermined]: *they must escape the censorship imposed by resistance* [*daß sie der Zensur des Widerstandes entzogen seien*]. (*S.E.* 4, 308, emphasis in original)

Whereas a moment earlier Freud had claimed that displacement takes place under the influence of the endopsychic defense (*Is fecit cui profuit*), it now seems that this mechanism is also one of the means employed by elements of the dream thoughts to *escape* censorship. Is it in order to avoid this apparent contradiction that Freud introduces the terminological modification "the censorship imposed by resistance"?[13] Here it seems that there is one form of censorship, a kind of precensorship, which enables dream thoughts to escape another form of censorship designated by the term "censorship of resistance." Or is it simply the case that, contrary to Freud's initial claims, displacement does not in fact occur in conjunction with or on behalf of the censorship imposed by the second agency on the first, but instead takes place prior to censorship, precisely in order to avoid it? If these questions are left unresolved in *The Interpretation of Dreams*, the space opened by Freud's equivocations, while perhaps indicating an "insufficient mastery of the material," also implicitly suggests a more complex interaction of displacement and censorship, a more layered, multiple staging of the latter, and finally even a dreamlike displacement of the very notion of censorship in Freud's text.

Such a displacement involves not only a rearticulation of psychical space, but also a splitting of the very time frame in which censorship might be assumed to *take place*. For insofar as distortions that are produced in anticipation of censorship are already implicated in its dynamics—precisely to the extent that censorship must be taken into account as a real possibility—it becomes difficult to locate a stage clearly prior to (pre)censorship. Thus, not only will there have been a *censorship effect* before censorship ever actually occurs, but it is precisely this proleptic structure that effectively divides censorship from within and prevents it from ever simply being itself here and now. Similarly, in his *Introductory Lectures on Psychoanalysis* Freud identifies a related difficulty in locating the point where something like a (post)censorship will have ceased to function:

> The resistance to interpretation is only a putting into effect [*Objek-tivierung* literally, making it objective JS] of the dream censorship. It also proves to us that the force of the censorship is not exhausted in bringing about the distortion of dreams and thereafter extinguished, but that the censorship persists as a permanent institution which has as its

aim the maintenance of the distortion [*daß diese Zensur als dauernde Institution mit der Absicht, die Entstellung aufrecht zu halten, fortbesteht*]. (*S.E.* 15, 141)

In short, there seems to be no getting around censorship—at least as a moment simply before or after it—and if there is no ultimate detour around this instance, it is because censorship "itself" will have only taken place as pre- and/or postcensorship. Whereas the splitting of this instance undoubtedly reveals an extension and diffusion of its functioning not heretofore imagined, it also draws attention to censorship's inherent instability and untimeliness. To say that there is no proper time or place for it is above all to claim that censorship will have always taken place too early and/or too late. Indeed, it is precisely because censorship is always somewhat out of place that it can be so easily caught off guard. Yet, the question raised by the Freudian displacement of censorship is not so much why this instance is repeatedly taken unawares but rather what drives it to collaborate in its own undoing in the first place.

The Other Scene

Whereas censorship is initially described as an agent of repression situated at the entrance to the preconscious-consciousness system, Freud's displacement of it forces one to view it instead as a split and double agency with affiliations both to the repressing and to the repressed. The repeated undoing of censorship is thus merely an indication of the double bind that ties it to the mechanisms of the dreamwork in a relationship that can best be described as one of conflictual interdependence. What matters here is not so much *whether* an unconscious representation in fact gains access to a forbidden psychical realm but rather *what kind of link* is forged between the elements that do gain access and those that are kept out. Moreover, if what is in question here is precisely the status of a psychical frontier, one must further ask how such linkages may in effect constitute the very boundaries they cross and transgress.

Freud's description of the process of identification in dreams is particularly useful in helping one to grasp the compromises involved in the formation of these boundaries. In identification only one of the persons linked by a common element succeeds in being represented in the manifest content of the dream, while the second or remaining persons seem to be suppressed in it (*unterdrückt scheinen*). This single covering figure (*deckende Person*), Freud says, appears in all the relations and situations that apply either to him or to the figures that he covers. Freud further suggests that these covering persons not only come forth *into* the manifest content of a dream in the way characters in a play might appear on stage, but they may also come to the fore in it.

In an explicitly theatrical example of identification, Freud says that the scene of the dream (*die Szene des Traums*) is attributed to one of the persons concerned, while the other, usually more important person, appears as an attendant figure without any other function. Insofar as little attention is paid to such figures, they tend to blend into the background and serve merely as backdrops for the action downstage. To put it in more dynamic terms, as one figure comes to the fore as a kind of "front" set up perhaps by those with a need to stay in the background, the other persons linked to it by a common element not only *seem* to be suppressed (*unterdrückt scheinen*), but in effect *are* absent insofar as no attention is paid to them. While the covering person thus takes his place on the scene of the dream as a stand-in for others, the *link* to those other concealed persons may never be discovered. This is precisely what Freud calls the objectification of censorship as resistance.

Because there are no set boundaries delimiting the front or back of the scene of the dream, the difference between an element coming to the fore *in* it and one coming forth *into* it, making it onto the stage at all, is one of quantity rather than quality. In other words, the borders of the scene are defined less by the criterion of actual existence than by that of effective appearance, less by the nature of the representations than by the intensity of their cathectic charge.[14] Only as figures fade, withdraw, or are driven into the background is the backdrop of the scene of the dream temporarily constituted. Whether attention is paid to such figures depends to a large degree upon the power of the actors downstage to monopolize the audience's attention.

Before asking who exactly the audience of a dream is and why the covering figures described by Freud should be worthy of special attention, it may be useful to read his discussion of identification in conjunction with his remarks about reversal added to the section entitled "The Means of Representation" in 1909:

> Reversal, or turning a thing into its opposite, is one of the means of representation most favored by the dreamwork and one which is capable of employment in the most diverse directions. It serves in the first place to give expression to the fulfillment of a wish in reference to some particular element of the dream thoughts. 'If it had only been the other way round!' This is often the best way of expressing the ego's reaction to a disagreeable fragment of memory. Again, reversal is of quite special use as a help to the censorship, for it produces a mass of distortion in the material which is to be represented, and this has a positively paralysing effect, to begin with, on any attempt at understanding the dream. (*S.E.* 4, 327)

Reversal thus involves nothing less than the transformation of a repressed wish into its opposite. The wish is "realized" in the double sense of being fulfilled and of being represented as though it were actually happening. It thereby loses its subjective, subjunctive, and irreal character. As Freud says, "the dream represses [*verdrängt*] the optative and replaces it by a simple present" (*S.E.* 5, 534). As the use of the term *repression* in this passage implies, the process of reversal also involves elements of conflict and compromise. Indeed, it is significant for our purposes that only a particular element (*ein bestimmtes Element*) of the dream thoughts is realized; that is, one particular element is *singled out* from a complex dream thought or from a complex of dream thoughts (the point being that the two are practically one and the same since every dream thought insofar as it is overdetermined is complex).

Before proceeding it is important to stress the shift in the status of the dream thoughts implied by this relationship. Whereas Freud's earlier descriptions of censorship led one to believe that distortions appear in dreams in place of something more genuine and self-identical (*das Eigentliche*), here it would seem that the dream thoughts subjected to distortion will have been less than authentic from the very beginning. Not only are these thoughts overdetermined in the sense of being polyvalent, they are also irreducibly plural because they are internally split by the *mutually contradictory* thoughts and desires that inhabit them. Such contradictions may thus coexist in the "same" thought complex or, what amounts to the same thing, each particular thought may serve as a substitute for another.[15]

Returning to the question of reversal, one recalls that it is from such a complex of dream thoughts that "a particular element" is singled out and allowed to come forth as a "realized" wish. Similarly, in the case of identification a covering figure is said to come forward in(to) the dream, upstaging a complex of related figures that are both represented and repressed by it.[16] In both cases censorship seems to allow one particular element to come forth both as a way of keeping other associated elements in the background and as a means of avoiding a long and costly struggle.[17]

Yet like most halfway solutions, such compromises raise as many questions as they answer. For if a particular element of the dream thoughts comes forth into the dream as a realized wish, is it singled out and drawn forth as a "safety valve" or is it somehow pushed forward as a kind of front? Similarly, if the covering figures in Freud's discussion of identification serve both to represent and to repress a complex of related figures whom they stand in for, who exactly sets them up as "covers" and who is in turn set up by them into believing that they were more than mere fronts to begin with? If censorship itself is not merely deceived by material that gets past it, how exactly *does* it collaborate in its own subversion?

To begin to respond to these questions we return to Freud's discussion of identification where, as it turns out, a certain *I* is said to be responsible for setting up covering figures:

> What the censorship objects to may lie precisely in certain ideas which, in the material of the dream thoughts, are attached to a particular person; *so I proceed to find a second person*, who is connected with the objectionable material, but only with part of it. The contact between the two persons upon this censorable point *now justifies me* in constructing a composite figure characterized by indifferent features derived from both. This figure, arrived at by identification or composition, is then admissable to the dream content without censorship, and thus, by making use of dream condensation, *I have satisfied* the claims of the dream censorship. (*S.E.* 4, 321–22; emphasis added)

Whereas *The Interpretation of Dreams* often alternates between third- and first-person narration, here Freud impersonates the voice of the dreamer described within it. In thus identifying with the *I* of the dreaming subject Freud seems to make a point of conflating the waking ego with that of the dreamer. Yet, while this conflation perhaps invites one to consider the *I* of the latter as a kind of alter ego modeled on the identity of the conscious self, it also leads one to ask how this *I* may in its turn alter the very sense of egoistic self-identity in the guise of simply repeating it:

> It is my experience, and one to which I have found no exception, that every dream deals with the dreamer himself. Dreams are completely egoistic. Whenever my own ego does not appear in the content of the dream, but only some extraneous person, I may safely assume that my own ego lies concealed, by identification, behind this other person; I may fill in my ego [*Ich darf mein Ich ergänzen*]. On other occasions, when my own ego *does* appear in the dream, the situation in which it occurs may teach me that some other person lies concealed, by identification, behind my ego.... Thus, my ego may be represented in a dream several times over, now directly and now through identification with extraneous persons. (*S.E.* 4, 322-23)

Insofar as these remarks merely describe the various ways in which one's ego may be multiply represented in dreams while also serving to represent the identities of others, they never really call into question the identity of the dreaming subject as such. Yet, if such questions do arise in this passage, it is significant that they emerge only through the ambiguity of the German phrase *Ich darf mein Ich ergänzen*. In other words, they emerge not so much in the form of a competing, alternative account of the ego, but rather in and as a moment of linguistic instability—as though the potential alterity of the dreaming *I* were of necessity related to the inherent otherness of linguistic equivocation. Commenting on the "notable ambiguity" of this passage, Samuel Weber explains that the phrase *Ich darf mein Ich ergänzen* "means both to complete my ego and to complete the scene by adding my ego to it, in the place of the non-ego that appears. But it would be more accurate to say, 'I may conceal and distort my ego,' for this is precisely what the subject does in the dream. And yet, precisely that is what 'filling in one's ego' amounts to: creating the illusion of fullness, of completeness, of the ego as a self-identical subjective instance."[18]

Here Weber subtly redefines the relation of the ego to the other in dreams and the play of substitution it involves in terms of an otherness *of* the ego and an incessant movement of supplementation (*Ergänzung*) in which it is caught. Instead of one particular ego filling in for another, an "illusion of fullness" fills in for the ego's "own" lack of identity. I would further suggest that it is precisely this uncompleteable movement of supplementation that defines the ego *as process.* To put it in terms of Freud's description of identification, one might say that the pronoun *I* itself serves as a kind of covering figure that not only "fronts" for other egos but moreover acts as a "cover" for the dreaming subject's own multiple and divided identity.

While the notion of a covering figure initially led us to ask how such figures are set up and who could in fact be deceived by them, a certain reading of the phrase *Ich darf mein Ich ergänzen* suggests that these covers not only create a mirage of self-identity but moreover function as *self-deluding* illusions; that is, they do not merely delude the self but beguile with the very lure of identity. As is well known, the last section of the chapter on the dreamwork devoted to the process of secondary revision deals with just this kind of illusion. Here Freud explains how an audience might be driven to participate in its own deception:

> It is the nature of our waking thought to establish order in material . . . ,
> to set up relations in it and to make it conform to our expectations of an
> intelligible whole. In fact, we go too far in that direction. An adept in
> sleight of hand can trick us by relying upon this intellectual habit of
> ours. In our effort at making an intelligible pattern of the sense impres-
> sions that are offered to us, we often fall into the strangest errors or
> even falsify the truth about the material before us. (*S.E.* 4, 499)

To illustrate his point further, Freud draws on the everyday parapraxis of misreading. "In our reading," he says, "we pass over misprints which destroy the sense, and have the illusion that what we are reading is correct" (*S.E.* 4, 499). In contrast to his earlier description of censorship as a process that either alone or in collaboration with the dreamwork produces "softenings, approximations and allusions instead of the genuine thing" (*an Stelle des Eigentlichen*), here the locus of distortion clearly shifts from the body of the text to the reading and interpretation of it. In other words, it is the reader who now supplies the text with the kind of smooth, homogeneous surface formerly constructed by the writer to outwit the censor and by the censor to cover his own tracks. It is also significant that the reader creates this surface not by actively constructing a facade but simply by overlooking apparent faults and discrepancies in the reading material. Here again the criterion of effective appearance seems to be as important as that of actual existence in determining the extent of textual distortion.

Similarly, in the case of secondary revision, gaps in the structure of dreams are filled both by positively adding extraneous material to it and by simply reading the ego's own expectations of intelligibility into it. While this fourth and final aspect of the dreamwork thus seems to be more closely allied to the interests of waking thought than the processes of condensation, displacement, and considerations of representability, it also focuses more attention than the other three on the capacity of conscious thought to delude itself in its pursuit of coherent meaning.

If censorship in its turn is not always simply taken in by the deceptive appearance of fronts and covering figures but at times colludes in its own undoing, it does so precisely to the extent that it collaborates in the creation and perpetuation of illusions of intelligibility, wholeness, and subjective self-identity. Furthermore, because censorship is *set up* by a need "to establish order in material . . . , to set up relations in it and to make it conform to our expectations of an intelligible whole," this compromising activity must itself be supplemented by further acts of censorship.

While the process of secondary revision thus enables one to understand how censorship may be complicitous in its own subversion, it also raises more fundamental questions about the master whose interests it is supposed to serve. For insofar as *das Eigentliche* is no longer merely what is distorted by censorship but itself the very means of distortion, what does this say about the alleged identity and integrity of the ego whose borders censorship is called upon to defend?

In *The Legend of Freud* Samuel Weber follows an extension of the notion of secondary revision from *The Interpretation of Dreams* where, as he says, "its dissimulating function . . . is restricted to the dream-work" to *Totem and Taboo* in which it is used "to characterize systematic thinking in general."[19] Describing the extended scope of this notion, Weber writes:

> Systematic thought organizes the world in the image of this organization [i.e., the libidinally cathected, narcissistic ego]. The intellectual construct we call a 'system' reveals itself to be narcissistic, in its origin no less than in its structure: *speculative*, in the etymological sense, as a mirror-image of the ego, and 'phobosophic' as well. If it is driven to fill in the 'gaps

and cracks' in the edifice of the universe, the fissures it fears are much closer to home. The 'expectation of an intelligible whole' described by Freud, the expectation of a coherent meaning, appears thus to denote the reaction of an ego seeking to defend its conflict-ridden cohesion against equally endemic centripetal tendencies. The pursuit of meaning; the activity of construction, synthesis, unification; the incapacity to admit anything irreducibly alien, to leave any residue unexplained—all this indicates the struggle of the ego to establish and to maintain an identity that is all the more precarious and vulnerable to the extent that it depends on what it must exclude. In short, speculative, systematic thinking draws its force from the effort of the ego to appropriate an exteriority of which, as Freud will later put it, it is only the 'organized part'.[20]

While the notion of secondary revision will eventually come to be associated both with the animistic attempt to comprehend the external world in terms of unity and totality and with the efforts of the narcissistic ego to fill in the "gaps and cracks" in its own self-image, in *The Interpretation of Dreams* it is linked only to the notion of censorship. Yet, what exactly does it mean at this point to speak of a connection to censorship? As I have tried to demonstrate, the term *censorship* does not so much denote a particular psychical frontier or stable psychoanalytic concept. Instead, it functions more like a covering figure whose single name serves to cloak an entire complex of incompatible pressures and opposing tendencies. At times it is said to be as crude as the state censor who excises passages without covering his tracks; at others it seems simply to tone down reprehensible material or to replace it with circumlocutions; at still other times it is said to distort the dream by filling in extraneous material and by creating a semblance of intelligibility. These competing accounts of censorship indeed seem difficult to reconcile. Moreover, it appears likely that any attempt to overlook the obvious differences between these versions, to privilege one version over another in order to view censorship as a localizable and stable instance modeled either simply on self- or on state censorship would be to distort it in exactly the same way that secondary revision is said to distort dream material.

In order to grasp the overdetermination of censorship it is important to recall that reading a dream for Freud involves not only its interpretation but its necessary *overinterpretation* since "each of the elements of the dream's content turns out to have been 'overdetermined'—to have been represented in the dream thoughts many times over" (*S.E.* 4, 283).[21] Similarly, in attempting to read the notion of dream censorship, one must treat the different accounts of it presented in Freud's text as expressions of an overdetermined wish—or rather as the knotting together of a number of incompatible wishes. If one may thus speak of censorship in terms usually reserved for the unconscious material presumed to be censored by it, the ambivalent wishes of censorship express the efforts of this instance to accommodate the demands placed on it by the combined forces of repression and the unconscious repressed. Pulled in opposite directions, censorship thus finds itself doubly bound to the mechanisms of the dreamwork to which it is in principle opposed and with which it is nevertheless forced to conspire. Caught in and moreover *structured by* this double bind, censorship is fated not only to collaborate in its own undoing but also to call into question the very identity of the ego whose interests it is supposed to serve. Thus, as we have seen, it only defends its superior against the incursions of the repressed by betraying the "cracks and fissures" in the ego's own secondarily revised sense of identity. Such betrayals in turn adumbrate Freud's later extension of the notion of secondary revision, his redefinition of the relationship of the ego to the other, and his return to questions of censorship in his metapsychological papers on repression.

What then is the effect of Freud's borrowing of the term *censorship* from the fields of politics and publishing? Are its political implications carried over in Freud's translation or are they simply neutralized and psychologized away? The intellectual historian Carl Schorske tends toward the latter view when he describes *The Interpretation of Dreams* as "an epoch-making interpretation of human experience in which politics could be reduced to an epiphenomenal manifestation of psychic forces."[22] Commenting specifically on Freud's recourse to the metaphor of censorship, Schorske observes that the "selection of the analogy" bears witness to the way "the political realities of the nineties...had penetrated Freud's psychic life."[23] Yet, as the rest of his essay suggests, these realities find their way into Freud's inner world only to be depoliticized there. Thus,

Schorske adds that the "social model [of censorship] provided an analogy for Freud to show us 'a quite definite view of the "essential nature" of consciousness.'" The analogy to press censorship would thus in effect only illustrate certain *intrapsychic* conflicts to the extent that it essentializes the historical dimension of *political* conflict. Such an approach for Schorske is typical of Freud's more general reduction of "his own political past and present to an epiphenomenal status in relation to the primal conflict between father and son" (203). In short, Freud would avoid the struggles of contemporary political life by devising a more global, primal, and personal *theory* of conflict.

Yet, how coherent is Freud's theory and to what degree is a term as unstable as *dream censorship* assimilated and indeed assimilable to it? Does not the volatility of the metaphor of censorship in Freud's text bear witness first and foremost to a theory *in conflict*, a theory that is distorted and dislocated by its own attempts to theorize conflict? Indeed, it would seem that if there is a politics of censorship articulated in *The Interpretation of Dreams*, it is to be sought less in any secondarily revised theory of psychic conflict than in Freud's own writing praxis. Thus, in contrast to Schorske, who reads the metaphor of censorship merely in terms of its illustrative, didactic value—that is, in terms of what it "shows us"—I have argued that it is more important to ask how and why this analogy breaks down. For it is only by studying these breakdowns that one begins to appreciate the extent to which censorship in Freud itself only "works" as a necessarily dysfunctional and self-subversive operation. Moreover, it is this dysfunctional notion of censorship that in turn gives one a sense of the psychological, textual, and political problems faced by writers caught in the double binds of self-censorship. For while such writers are compelled, on the one hand, to develop strategies of dissimulation in an attempt to circumvent censorship, on the other hand, they cannot help but internalize it as various debilitating forms of writer's block. If there is indeed a politics of (self-)censorship articulated in *The Interpretation of Dreams*, it is perhaps to be read, as Derrida suggests, on the level of a certain gesture—namely, as the text's own dumb show performance of a wringing of the two hands of writing and repression: "the vigilance and failure of censorship."[24]

NOTES

1. *The Complete Letters of Sigmund Freud to Wilhelm Fliess*, trans. and ed. Jeffrey Moussaieff Masson (Cambridge, Mass.: Harvard University Press, 1985), 371. Letter dated September 11, 1899.

2. Ibid., 373-74. Letter dated September 21, 1899.

3. Sigmund Freud, *The Standard Edition of the Complete Psychological Works of Sigmund Freud*, trans. James Strachey (London: Hogarth, 1953). All subsequent references will appear in parentheses in the body of the text as *S.E.*

4. Jacques Derrida, *Writing and Difference*, trans. Alan Bass (Chicago: University of Chicago Press, 1978), 199. All subsequent references to this essay will appear in the body of the text.

5. See my book *Writing through Repression: Literature, Censorship, Psychoanalysis* (Baltimore: Johns Hopkins University Press, 1994), chapter 1, "The Other Hand: Censorship and the Question of Style."

6. On the history of the term *censorship* in Freud's writings, see William J. McGrath, *Freud's Discovery of Psychoanalysis* (Ithaca, N.Y.: Cornell University Press, 1986), 165, 245-46.

7. There is only a passing reference to Freud's comparison of censorship to a kind of *Strahlenbrechung* a refraction or more literally a breaking of the ray (215). Such passages would have to be read in conjunction with Derrida's discussion of pathbreaking elsewhere in the essay; see especially 229.

8. See in this regard Marx's discussion of the levels of censorship in "*Bemerkungen über die neueste preussische Zensurinstruktion*" (1842) in *Marx Engels Werke*, vol. 1 (Berlin: Dietz Verlag, 1956), 3-25.

9. Mikkel Borch-Jacobsen, *The Freudian Subject*, trans. Catherine Porter (Stanford, Calif.: Stanford University Press, 1988), 3.

10.   *Die Schere klirrt in seiner Hand,*
          Es rückt der wilde Geselle
          Dir auf den Leib—Er schneidet ins Fleisch—
          Es war die beste Stelle

What is lost in the English translation of these lines is precisely the economy effected through Heine's use of the term *Stelle*, which refers both to the best part of the body and to the most interesting passage in the text. The incision made by the censor's scissors is thus double—not merely because it inflicts two discrete wounds, but rather because it opens an interspace in which text and body transpierce each other in such a way that violence done to the one will have been experienced as a mutilation of the other.

11. Of particular relevance in this regard is the description Heine himself provides in the preface to the French edition of *Lutezia* of the methods he used in his journalistic writings to slip sensitive material past the censorship. These include such techniques as disguising personal opinions as objectively reported statements of fact; shifting the speaker to have another give voice to one's own views; feigning a tone of indifference; and the use of a parabolic style. While Freud never explicitly refers to the passage in question, his extensive knowledge of Heine's work and personal biography suggest he may well have been familiar with it.

12. Borch-Jacobsen, *Freudian Subject*, 3.

13. See J. Lacan, "La Censure n'est pas la résistance" in *Le Séminaire, Livre II: Le moi dans la théorie de Freud et dans la technique de la psychanalyse* (Paris: Seuil, 1978).

14. This problem is taken up again in the essay "The Unconscious," in which Freud dis-

tinguishes between what he calls the functional hypothesis and the topographical hypothesis: "When a psychical act (let us confine ourselves here to one which is in the nature of a representation [*Vorstellung*]) is transposed from the systems Ucs. into the system Cs. (or Pcs.), are we to suppose that this transposition [*Umsetzung*] involves a fresh record—as it were, a second registration—of the representation in question which may thus be situated as well in a fresh psychical locality, and alongside of which the original unconscious registration continues to exist? Or are we rather to believe that the transposition consists in a change in the state of the representation, a change involving the same material and occurring in the same locality?" (*S.E.* 14, 174).

15. As Freud remarks in the section entitled "The Forgetting of Dreams": "The modifications to which dreams are submitted under the editorship of waking life are ... associatively linked to the material which they replace, and serve to show us the way to that material, which may in its turn be a substitute for something else" (*S.E.* 5, 515).

16. Freud further illustrates these foregrounding effects in the following examples: "In preparing a book for the press, I have some word which is of special importance for understanding the text printed in spaced or heavy type; or in speech I should pronounce the same word loudly and slowly and with special emphasis.... Art historians have drawn our attention to the fact that the earliest historical sculptures obey a similar principle: they express the rank of the persons represented by the size [*Bildgröße*]. A king is represented twice or three times as large as his attendants or as his defeated enemies. A sculpture of Roman date would make use of subtler means for producing the same result. The figure of the Emperor would be placed in the middle, standing erect, and would be modelled with special care, while his enemies would be prostrate at his feet; but he would no longer be a giant among dwarfs. The bows with which inferiors greet their superiors among ourselves today are an echo of the same ancient principle of representation" (*S.E.* 5, 595-96).

17. "It begins to dawn on us that it is more expedient and economical to allow the unconscious wish to take its course, to leave the path to regression open to it so that it can construct a dream, and then to bind the dream and dispose of it with a small expenditure of preconscious work—rather than to continue keeping a tight rein on the unconscious throughout the whole period of sleep. It was indeed to be expected that dreaming, even though it may originally have been a process without a useful purpose, would have procured itself some function in the interplay of mental forces.... Dreaming has taken on the task of bringing back under control of the preconscious the excitation in the Ucs. which has been left free; in so doing it discharges the Ucs. excitation, serves as a safety valve [*Ventil*] and at the same time preserves the sleep of the preconscious in return for a small expenditure of waking activity. Thus, like all the other psychical structures in the series of which it is a member, it constitutes a compromise; it is in the service of both of the two systems, since it fulfills the two wishes insofar as they are compatible with each other" (i.e., the unconscious wish and the preconscious wish to sleep; *S.E.* 5, 578-79).

18. Samuel Weber, *Return to Freud: Jacques Lacan's Dislocation of Psychoanalysis*, trans. Michael G. Levine (Cambridge: Cambridge University Press, 1991), 81.

19. Samuel Weber, *The Legend of Freud* (Minneapolis: University of Minnesota Press, 1982), 12.

20. Ibid., 14.

21. For a discussion of overinterpretation in Freud's text, see Jean-Michel Rey's essay "Freud's Writing on Writing," in Shoshana Felman, ed., *Literature and Psychoanalysis: The*

Question of Reading: Otherwise (Baltimore: Johns Hopkins University Press, 1982), especially 303-11.

22. Carl E. Schorske, *Fin-de-Siècle Vienna: Politics and Culture* (New York: Vintage, 1981), 183.

23. Ibid., 187. For a further discussion of Freud's response to the Austro-Hungarian political situation and in particular to the 1897 crisis surrounding the language ordinances put forward by the government of Count Badeni, see William McGrath, *Freud's Discovery of Psychoanalysis* (Ithaca, N.Y.: Cornell University Press, 1986).

24. I have attempted to develop the lines of this analysis through an examination of Heine's struggles with (self-)censorship in chapter 3 of *Writing through Repression.*

Part III

The New Censorship and Postmodernity

Censoring Canons:
Transitions and Prospects of Literary Institutions in Czechoslovakia
Jiřina Šmejkalová-Strickland

I find myself in a liminal position: between two worlds, two cultures, and two historical periods. I wrote my dissertation in Czechoslovakia before the revolution of 1989 and defended it afterward. There I dealt with Czech literary institutions, with the system of centrally controlled publishing houses and distribution networks, and with the habits and preferences of readers. I then came to the United States to study current Western cultural theories, nurturing the idea that what I would discover here would lead me to ask new questions about my world—a world I thought I already knew, a world that, in the theoretical context I now find myself entering, remains largely unknown. Although the forces behind the institutional structure I examined in my dissertation no longer exist, I am more than ever interested in its transitions and the prospects for the future.[1]

Because of the research I conducted under specific historical conditions, both before and after 1989, I still find it difficult to treat censorship as the oppressive exercise of centralized power by clearly defined "others"—agents of cultural imperialism, consumers within the commercialized media market, or clerks of a special department of the Ministry of Culture in a communist government—who decide on the inclusion or exclusion of certain texts. It is important to remember that prohibited texts do not disappear. My question therefore is how the readers' *access* to the text is constituted and instituted. I want to look at censorship as an institutional practice of selection taking the form of *limits*, whether these limits are manifested at any level of book production, in concentrations of literacy, or in particular reading habits. I understand "censorship" to be a far-reaching phenomenon closely related to the process of canon formation embedded within a web of social institutions.[2] Rather than the direct prohibition of particular texts, an "either/or" activity manipulated by one central agent, my interest is the formation of boundaries and the performance of roles that connect people and texts. I want to look at what they tend to mask and what they lead us to ask.

The institutional structure on which I am focusing was just one part of a complex of social and cultural practices in my country. After 1968, Czechoslovakian literary life became sharply divided into three spheres: state-controlled, officially published literature; "self-print" texts produced within dissident circles; and exile literature published abroad. These three domains were mutually impenetrable. An author who once published in the self-print sphere would have had very little chance of ever seeing his or her book on the shelf of a bookstore. Even the relationship between exile and dissident literature seems to have been quite complicated, since exiled authors moved only in one direction—out of the country. Although their works might return illegally, the authors' role in dissident cultural circles was ambiguous. The limited space of this essay forces me to postpone a detailed investigation of the complicated relations among these domains.

The institutional web of the official sphere to which I devote my attention here served as a tool for protecting and conserving the mutual impenetrability of all three domains. It not only built barriers to the movement of both people and literary works "in" and "out" of its own space, but also made the other, nonofficial spheres invisible.

Furthermore, the sphere of official literature involved the majority of members of the community and actually operated on their everyday cultural life. At least five years before the revolution, it began to show signs of the deterioration that was to become widespread throughout the whole system of the centrally controlled society and economy. Today, the official institutional sphere is the crucial domain of ongoing transitions, since the two other spheres have collapsed into it and are in various ways experiencing the consequences of its past. Both émigré and dissident "men of letters" are entering this structure in order to make their works public and at the same time struggling with rising competition and people's decreasing interest in buying books.

It is probably not surprising that, unlike the widely publicized dissident and émigré spheres, the official system of literary production in Eastern Europe has not been particularly attractive to those participating in Western theoretical debates, and has therefore been largely misunderstood. To the extent that the official sphere has received attention, it has focused on the figure "censoring" the text. By reinforcing the image of the censor as a relatively autonomous agent exercising control from above, such discussions tend to encourage the idea that getting rid of the censor exhausts the problem of censorship.[3]

While I was looking for theoretical stimuli in current American writing on the problems of censorship, on the first page of the first book I accidentally opened in the library I discovered the name of Václav Havel. The "previously censored and imprisoned Czechoslovakian playwright" whose current position "at the head of his own government" was presented as "the most visible symbol" of "the extraordinary changes that have occurred in Eastern Europe, rendering the 'Free World' obsolete as a term of political differentiation."[4]

"I cannot take Havel as the starting point of my essay!" screamed my internal censor. Why? Not because I would disagree with his discovery that "truth lies not only in what is said, but also in who says it, and to whom, why, how and under what circumstances it is expressed,"[5] but because I do not want to participate in canonizing the person whose work I deeply respect by following the ongoing fashion in my country directed now by the principle "no text without quoting Havel." In other words, since the very beginning I have been part of the process both of censoring the canons and at the same time reinforcing them—I did quote Havel anyway. To be fair, one cannot ignore one difference: today I have some hope for this text to be published in a book read by a larger audience no matter whom I quote. That would hardly have been the case in my country before 1989.

There is a dominant premise shared by many recent debates on censorship, and not only in my country. These debates presuppose a world of free expression guaranteed by the development of modern high-tech civilization and "welfare democracy," which previously just happened to be absent from the official culture. To put it differently, the powerful idea now prevails that a change of political system and the importation of computers and copy machines will automatically open up communication through the written word. Looking at "censorship" in terms of instituted access to the text, and acknowledging the larger limitations on the production of books and the spread of literacy, this picture takes on another shape.

It is perhaps well known but nonetheless rarely seriously considered that current book production is concentrated in relatively limited geographical and linguistic regions, and that the celebrated "books revolution" that resulted from the explosive development of new printing technologies in the 1950s represented a revolution of copies rather than of titles. The growth of world book production has come more in spurts than in a continuous linear movement.[6] This global pattern is borne out by statistical evidence in Czechoslovakia as well, although the development of publishing policy under the communist government was controlled by conditions specific to that time and place.

Similarly, it would be hard to establish any positive correlation between literacy and civilization, industrialization, or urbanization. Even Friedrich Engels, who cannot be suspected of distrusting the progressive model of history, noted in *The Condition of the Working Class in England* that it was particularly the development of industry and the spread of child labor in factories that effected the increase of illiteracy.[7] New communication systems, democratization, and extensive growth of educational institutions during the past forty years have contributed to a global decline in illiteracy, but the absolute number of illiterate people has also risen along with the rapid growth in the world's population. But "civilization" need not limit the competence of potential readers in order to obstruct access to texts. In Czechoslovakia, with a population of 15 million people, the centralized compulsory primary education overseen by the communist government almost wiped out illiteracy. At the same time, the book production and distribution on which I am focusing was among the first institutional systems of production to be deprivatized a year after the communists came into power in 1948.

A large number of small publishers were eliminated in the late 1940s and were replaced by a smaller number of big state publishing houses that concentrated on national literature, children's literature, and translated literature, among other genres, while district publishers mostly focused on local literatures. After this administrative reconstruction of the prewar system, the publishing of so called "mass-reading" materials was almost stopped in favor of the publication of officially "valuable" literature. One intention of this strategy applied during the late 1940s and early 1950s was the canonization of certain texts characterized by the Ministry of Culture as part of a "national literary tradition" or as "progressive cultural world traditions."[8]

Between 1937 and 1983 the number of titles published per year rose by 10 percent, while the number of copies almost doubled. A dramatic decline in the number of titles published occurred during the first two years following the communist rise to power in 1948: from 6,640 to 3,797. The proportion of so-called belles lettres (i.e., fiction and poetry for both adults and children) has remained stable: about 13 to 14 percent of titles and 20 percent of copies of the total production of books.[9] The tendency to allow the number of titles to lag behind while continually increasing the size of print runs coincides with two basic directions of state cultural politics after 1948. On the one hand, there was an attempt to democratize access, that is, to increase the number of people able to read a particular text. On the other hand, such a policy, by actually limiting the variety of texts to which a reader could gain access, limited the possibilities for individual selection.

For further discussion, the following scheme of literary institutions as they were constituted in Czechoslovakia before 1989 may be helpful:

State production five-year plan

Paper supply and printing companies	Ministry of Culture Department of Books

Publishing houses

Book distribution (*Kniha*) and wholesale authorities (*Knižní: velkoobchod*) Central warehouse	Authors Unions of writers State prizes and awards "National Artist" title

Bookstores
Libraries
Readers' clubs

Literary journals
Daily newspaper literary journalism

I cannot provide exhaustive analyses of all units of this structure. In order to explain recent transitions, I will briefly describe some of the institutions and their interconnections in the processes of editorial and print run planning, as well as in the production, storage, distribution, and sale of books.

The book production process began with publishing houses that provided the Ministry of Culture with the initial plans for books to be printed. During the late 1970s and 1980s a number of prestigious authors occupied responsible positions within this institutional system. As publishers and editors, they influenced editorial plans and print runs. As book reviewers, they regularly filled pages of two existing journals specifically devoted to literature.

The Books Department at the Ministry of Culture not only revised publication plans in consultation with publishers but also, and most importantly, divided the supply of paper assigned by the Ministry of Industry to the printing companies. The amount of available paper—strictly limited by the five-year state plan of production—dictated the number of books to be produced. Even the authors' royalties, legislatively unified in the 1950s for all types of books, were contracted per page for prose, per verse for poetry. Royalties were only partially dependent on the number of printed (not sold) copies. Indeed, the main idea was to insulate the realm of culture completely from the vagaries of the marketplace, and hence from those of readers as consumers of the book.

Publishers informed bookstores of the titles that passed through the corrected editorial plan by means of a bulletin with brief descriptions of the content of each book. Based on this bulletin, booksellers were supposed to guess the expected interest of their customers one to two years before the book actually appeared on the shelf and to order a certain number of copies from the district distribution authorities (*Kniha*). Most of the bookstores—except those run by publishers themselves—were administratively subordinate to and even controlled by the distribution authorities.[10]

Booksellers had very little chance to determine the character of their stores in anticipation of or response to the interests of their customers. At the same time, the sellers were under certain economic pressures: their wages were partially dependent on the number of books sold, and a penalty was assessed for the inventory of unsold books stored for more than 180 days. The actual sale of books often resembled the sale of bread. Any physical contact with the book was limited. The buyer could not really open the book without asking the salesperson, whose counter was a barrier between the crowd and the bookshelves. "Browsing" was unknown.

New books came out regularly once a week. Every "books Thursday," huge lines formed in front of stores from early in the morning when some attractive title was supposed to appear. One may ask what actually constituted the "attractiveness" of a book. Among the most desired were those that would be characterized in the United States as belonging to the canon dominated by white males. Not only the ambiguous relationship of communist cultural politics to the Western modern tradition but also the connection of the works of Kafka, Sartre, Heidegger, et al. to the reformists of 1968 excluded these works from publication until the mid-1980s. The stamp of "previously forbidden text" was perhaps the best advertising to attract an audience to a book. More than suggesting a high level of cultural maturity of the nation, the crowds surrounding bookstores every Thursday reflected the gradually increasing dysfunction of cultural production. For example, when I was a student of literature at Charles University from 1979 to 1984, some of these books were on lists of required reading. This meant that I was forced either to rob my older friends' libraries or to run around frantically from one used-book store in Prague to another.

Used-book stores occupied a unique position in the system. Unlike regular bookstores, where the price of the books was fixed, these stores could set their prices more freely, and they became important centers for the relatively uncontrolled distribution of books that had been excluded from libraries and were no longer published after 1968. They were also favorite gathering and reading places. The books were on open shelves to be searched, seen, and touched. Nevertheless, both new- and used-book stores had in common an involvement in the shadow market economy, with its corruption, under-the-counter sales, and chains of "mutually supportive friendships."

The central wholesale authority (*Knižní velkoobchod*) collected orders from the local distribution authorities and was responsible for storing books produced by printing companies in the central warehouses (mostly old buildings without basic technical equipment or air-conditioning). This authority distributed books throughout the whole state (about two thousand bookstores). Unlike publishers and booksellers, the wholesaler owned trucks for transporting books from place to place. Distribution of certain titles (approximately fifty per week) had to start at least four weeks before actual selling in order to keep up with the "books Thursdays" system.

Even this brief account shows that the whole system had the effect of reducing the variety of accessible texts, thus unifying, conserving, and protecting canons. In reference to Wittgenstein's linguistic models, Charles Altieri discusses canons as sources of a "grammar for interpreting particular experiences or projecting self-images that have significant resonance in how we make decisions in the present."[11] The aim of promoting shared values was represented in many complex practices. It must be quite shocking for an outsider to visit a number of houses of educated people in my country and to discover more or less the same collection of books in all of their libraries.

In spite of a centrally prepared publishing plan, each of the institutions I have described was relatively autonomous. Strict boundaries between them made the mutual coordination of their activities less and less possible. This allowed the ostensible concentration of power, while encouraging a dispersal of responsibility. The resulting lack of coordination accounted for the increasing inability of particular institutions to react to changes not just inside but also outside the system of book production, for none of its participants was quite certain about the extent of his or her decision-making power, and there was no clearly defined center on which one could rely.

The contradictions between the internal weakness of the official domain of literary production on the one hand and its *performed* stability and consistency on the other were particularly important in generating an atmosphere supportive of books produced outside the official framework and within émigré and dissident circles. Paradoxically, conditions within the official sphere of state-controlled literary production promoted the "attractiveness" of texts and authors who were inaccessible within that domain.

In his essay "The Power of the Powerless," Václav Havel raises the issue of "performance" by telling the story of a greengrocer decorating his window with "politically correct" slogans in which he does not believe. As a player in the game that reproduces the world of appearances, he becomes both a victim and an instrument of the system. Havel develops his notion of performance in order to emphasize the involvement of all members of a given community in the automatism of the system, thus undermining models of "individualized autonomous power" that pit "ruled" against "ruler."[12] To this extent, Havel rejects the models that are quite commonly applied by both Western and émigré analysts of post-1968 Czechoslovakian life. He resists labeling the state of culture in the country as a "Biafra of the spirit" and refuses to accept the role of an "unthinking expert in suffering."[13]

The tropes of stage, scene, and act have always been significant in Havel's writing. As president, he is experiencing "something that might be called stage fright"; he is afraid that "I won't be able to make the proper moves in this very unsettled political scene, to accomplish the tasks I've taken on, to meet expectations that cling to my sojourn in this office."[14] But his personal suspicion of this political project has not led him to question his strong roots in the tradition of Heideggerian phenomenology that has dominated dissident circles in my country. Havel's notion of performance is grounded in the opposition between "living within the truth" and "living within the lie," between resistance and collaboration. The idea of a performance within the world of appearances presumes another world beyond these appearances in which performance would no longer be necessary. Not *all* the world is a stage; there still *is* the naked king. For Havel, one must unmask the game in order to understand the central conflict between the lie and the truth, between appearance and essence, between the stage and real life.

My understanding of the notion of performance is closer to the explicitly anti-ontological concept of "performativeness" developed by Judith Butler in her theory of gender identities. For Butler, there is no essence beyond the "performative" act; it "has no ontological status apart from the various acts which constitute its reality":

> Such acts, gestures, enactments, generally construed, are *performative* in the sense that the essence or identity that they otherwise purport to express are *fabrications* manufactured and sustained through corporeal signs and other discursive means.[15]

The notion of performativeness allows Butler to open up the issue of gender identity as an ongoing process, "a becoming, a constructing that cannot rightfully be said to originate or to end."[16] Unlike

Havel's performance, Butler's performativeness is not a temporary deviation from forthright behavior, but the process that, through repetition, creates the appearance of natural stability. Havel too uses the idea of performance to unmask the constructed appearance of normality as a game. The difference lies in Butler's insistence that this game is not a false surface hiding anything more fundamental. The idea I want to develop is that censorship, like gender identity, emerges from "a set of repeated acts within a highly rigid regulatory frame that congeal over time to produce the appearance of substance, of a natural sort of being."[17]

By acknowledging the importance of repetition in establishing and maintaining communally shared perceptions of the limits of possible performances and by denying their ontological status, Butler's approach captures some important aspects of my understanding of censorship as canon formation. What I would add to her account and Havel's is the position of *audiences* whose reactions each performance must anticipate. To acknowledge a role for the audience, for spectators who are also always potential actors, is to recognize that performances have consequences. Different performances before differently constituted audiences may have vastly different stakes, demand different prices for participation, and promise different awards.[18]

By acting as though existing institutions were fully legitimate entities that functioned to achieve commonly desired goals, individuals performed the roles of "authors," "editors," "sellers." Not only did people perform what they considered to be their own roles, but they also acted in anticipation of the possible reaction of an imagined audience, taking into account the expectations of and constraints on other actors. The publisher might propose a low print run for a certain book in anticipation of paper supply limits; the editor might make an author remove "rebellious" chapters from a novel in anticipation of comments expected from the clerk in the Ministry of Culture; the author might avoid writing certain passages in anticipation of the reaction of individuals throughout the institutional system of publishing who were familiar with guidelines issued by the Ideological Committee of the Communist party. The limits on individual performances were uncertain to the extent that every decision was built upon the anticipation of other performances. This structure of mutual anticipation, rather than direct restrictions, created the environment that controlled access to the text. By assuming a role within a network of performances, individual actors stabilized the institutional system. Daily experiences were made to appear natural and integrated into a larger unity through the performance of consistency. The appearance of consistency was desired and, under certain historical conditions, necessary for the effective maintenance of the identities of both the ruling regime and its opposition.[19]

Nevertheless, the performed consistency of the system has been constantly challenged in many ways by both individuals and texts. To understand how such gestures met the institutional system, it is important to recognize that concepts of "authorship," "public sphere," and "market" acquired meanings and significances quite different from those prevalent in Western cultural and social contexts.[20] The connections between an author's name, historical actions, and written work were unstable. For example, many excluded writers were publishing under someone else's name (not a pseudonym, but a name belonging to an actual person who was willing to take the risk). More than financial exchange, interpersonal bonds and mutual trust were at stake here. Some authors who were forbidden to publish their own work were allowed to support themselves with translations.[21] The works of writers who had been denied access to the biggest publishers in Prague could have been released in small district publishing houses. An author may have been restricted from publishing works for adults but tolerated in writing for children.[22] Authorship was defined in terms of where and how, rather than who. The reformulation of the line between the person, the name, and the text that resulted from the policies instituted within the official sphere of literature actually eroded the boundaries between the official, émigré, and dissident spheres and challenged the controlling intentions of the official state system.

In spite of the dramatic character of the revolution in Czechoslovakia, the transition of the whole institutional system did not start suddenly on November 17, 1989. Disproportions within the web of literary institutions as well as mild economic reforms introduced by the communist government gradually contributed to the breakdown of the performed consistency of the system. Postrevolutionary changes cannot be understood outside of this context of censorship as a process of canon formation instituted within the officially controlled sphere.

Already in 1988, the director of the central wholesale authority publicly discussed the problem of warehouses overfilled with unsold books on the one hand and, on the other, the profound lack of books demanded by the market.[23] Not only the time needed to produce a book (minimally two to three years) but also the strictly fixed assignment of paper, printing colors, book-binding glue, and other products made it almost impossible to coordinate print runs with readers' actual demands. As early as January 1989, the printing and paper production authorities—which controlled one of the crucial elements determining access to the printed text—opened themselves to both local and international market pressures and raised paper prices by 30 percent. This move confused financial obligations among state publishing, production, and distribution companies.

Also in the beginning of 1989, the first small publishers asked for licenses for private enterprise. Voices openly acknowledging the "unnatural" separation of the three spheres of national literature had been heard since late 1988. Some restricted writers were allowed to reenter the official cultural institutions either through public reading or publication of their works. In 1988, books written by poets who were known for their critical attitudes to the ruling political system appeared in surprisingly high print runs of up to ten thousand. Rather than serving as evidence of ideological "tolerance," this breach seems to have been an additional sign of the untenability of the system. Publishers were forced to release books that would be bought and read.

After several weeks of ecstatic postrevolutionary celebration of "freedom of speech," all three spheres of official, émigré, and dissident literature collapsed into the existing publishing and distribution systems. In other words, the émigré and samizdat literati who had for years struggled in opposition to the official literature—and whose existence had actually been conditioned by it—now became part of the common problem. It may not be surprising, therefore, that the resulting changes in literary life have been presented in apocalyptic stories told both by journalists and by people professionally involved in the institutions undergoing transition. Everyone is caught up in the same chaos.

During the early 1990s two kinds of publishing agencies coexisted in Czechoslovakia: the big "old" state companies survived, and "new" private companies, including former dissident samizdat and some émigré publishers who returned to the country, emerged. By August 1991, about 1,200 private publishers had registered in the Czech Republic alone.[24] The new private publishers have tended to employ from one to six people (as many as twenty, under exceptional circumstances) and to produce from four to a hundred books per year in runs ranging from 60 to 150,000 copies. As a result of their limited staff and a great deal of self-victimization, these much smaller publishers significantly decreased the time and expenses required to complete a book. They are now able to produce a profitable book in a press run as low as two thousand copies within a matter of months rather than years.

Intense competition has forced them to introduce various kinds of experimental projects, such as reading clubs, book cafés, and galleries in their bookstores. Their publishing projects have included a wide range of books of general interest, including cookbooks, dictionaries, maps, and postcards. Some of them have based their editorial plans on supposedly attractive texts that were largely inaccessible before 1989. They have released books on religion, mysticism, alchemy, magic, oriental philosophy, politics, and sex. Both local and foreign pornographic literature and journals appeared on the tables of street booksellers as one of the first outcomes of "liberated democratic culture" after 1989. The street sale of books on folding tables also exploded after the revolution, partly as a way of satisfying the immediate hunger for previously unavailable books, partly as a consequence of the breakdown of the central distribution system. Active entrepreneurial members of the "liberated community" were ready to exploit the confused political and economic system, which lacked a strict policy of taxation.

In this new context, most of the state's large publishing houses could not continue their activities without introducing significant changes. During 1990 and 1991 they cut the number of editors and staff by two-thirds and had to limit the number of titles in preparation. A rather ambiguous situation developed in their print run strategies. By the end of 1989, when many institutional barriers seemed to have fallen apart, some publishers produced an enormous number of copies of books (as many as 250,000 to 500,000) anticipating the demand of hungry audiences. Nevertheless, since the book market was already oversupplied, the maximum number of saleable copies was no more than 100,000 by 1991.

The physical process of producing books has become tremendously expensive in a market environment that has simultaneously grown more sensitive to price increases for "nonessential" goods. Print services rose by 200 to 300 percent; the price of one kilogram of paper reached the equivalent of one dollar by 1991. Moreover, the available printing technology is virtually obsolete. Thus, a full 60 percent of the price of the book goes into production costs; 30 percent is the bookseller's share, and about 10 percent goes to the publisher. Of the 10 percent publisher's share, 65 percent must be paid out in taxes. The result has been an immediate doubling or even tripling of book prices. Prices quickly reached the equivalent of two to four dollars for a paperback and fifteen dollars for a hardback with color reproductions printed on high-quality paper. For most of the reader-consumers whose average annual income still lies between $1,000 and $1,500, buying books has become an unbearable addition to the constant inflation of everyday living expenses, which has already led to a decline in the standard of living.

The centralized wholesale and distribution system practically broke down. It got stuck in a circle of obligations that brought it close to total bankruptcy. The central warehouses rapidly became overcrowded with books no one was going to buy: old books published under the former government, postrevolutionary overproduction of previously restricted books, and books collected from the stocks of a large number of liquidated bookstores.[25] One of the reasons for the failure of at least some of these books to meet their buyers was a breakdown in the system of distributing information about new titles. The wholesaler stopped its centralized registration of books in print in 1991.

In order to find an alternative solution to a dysfunctional process, the central wholesale authority signed a contract with the newly formed private distribution company in 1991 to share the management of warehouses and distribution. Some private publishers have been trying to develop their own distribution chains, but high postal rates (books cost as much to mail as to buy) and transportation costs (gasoline prices have risen almost to Western market levels) have made this difficult.

There seem to be two points that people involved in literary life today have in common. First, all of them swim in the river of confusions and difficulties of the production and distribution systems on which they rely and are increasingly dependent on rising material costs. Secondly, they all participate in the production of a common discourse in the horror stories they tell about the realm of culture. These stories are mostly catastrophic, as the following titles of newspaper and journal articles dealing with these problems show: "Goodbye Books," "National Shame," "Could We Afford to Buy a Book Afterwards?," "Why?" The cultural arena has always been an effective space for assigning blame, for solving interpersonal conflicts, and for the construction of the "other" framed in the discourse of a search for sinners. Publishers are accused of an irresponsible overproduction of books, the central wholesaler of collecting books without the coordination of booksellers' orders, and the current Czech government of destroying an important area of national culture by underestimating its critical situation.[26]

The discursive representation of the realm of art and literature developed in the process of canon formation before the revolution has yet to undergo profound change. The postrevolutionary rhetoric retains a strong sense of what should be included and excluded, where the past ends and the future starts, who the "us" and "them" are. Perhaps the most significant feature of recent stories of literary life is the certainty that those who tell them can clearly discriminate "good" from "bad" literature. The security of one's ability to distinguish texts appropriate for entertainment from those with "real" aesthetic value goes unquestioned. Claims like "now I will produce mass reading in order to raise capital for publishing good literature later" do not seem to be shadowed by any form of suspicion.

Here it is difficult to avoid the temptation of reminding ourselves of the clear line Havel has drawn between pure art and "external" contamination. His rhetoric coincides with the postrevolutionary stories in their common assumptions about "good" and "bad," in their unshakable conviction in a shared "grammar for interpreting particular experiences," and thus, in a strong sense, in their faith in the process that produces Altieri's *canons*.[27] Writing in 1985, Havel insisted that "the only thing that matters is the urgency of artistic truth." It was not the overt political content of a work of art that posed a threat to the government, thus provoking the system of censorship, but the aesthetic quality of the censored work. "If anything matters, it is, quite logically, only the degree to which an artist is willing, for external reasons, to compromise the truth."[28] However much Havel's observations and contemplations recognize the ambiguities of cultural and social life, they always lead to one final unquestionable, uncompromisable point.

What all these stories underestimate is, as Jonathan Culler puts it, "the questioning of the centralizing and universalizing project itself, which is necessarily exclusionary and ideological, whatever the intentions of its agents."[29] As dissident and market criteria of value replace the communist government's lists of prohibited texts and authors, they continue to lack sensitivity to their own power and to the forms of marginalization and silencing within them.

One may ask at the end of all this explanation: Where is the *censor*—the angry guy completing lists of "libri prohibiti"? By leaving out the censor I do not want to hide the fact that a list of almost 150 writers and a number of translators whose books were excluded from the libraries and editorial plans was issued in Czechoslovakia after 1968.[30] Consequently, for many years the works of Hemingway, Brecht, Morgenstern, and Lorca were not available because the people who translated them were persona non grata. Nor do I completely agree with the Czech poet Miroslav Holub that "the censor was not a great obstacle" since they were "dull people" and "the less dull ones did not remain censors for long—they got smart by reading and reading, and had to be dismissed."[31] The role of the censor certainly was quite an effective and active part of the cultural scene. At the same time, as I have tried to show, reference to this role cannot exhaust the complex question of censorship in cultural and social practices.

I have to admit that I have censored the figure of the censor in my work twice. First, of necessity, in the course of my research up to 1989, as I prepared to defend my dissertation at an academy of sciences controlled by a communist government. I performed my role as an author by anticipating the reaction of my supervisors. A dissertation on the censor would simply not have been accepted. Second, in the present account I have silenced the censor again as part of an experiment in order to open up the complex of barriers created by a web of literary institutions that have shaped the space between the reader and the written word. I would not want to equate those two gestures. What makes them different are the prices one must pay for entering these two games and the consequences of not entering.

Through this experiment I have hoped to challenge the simplistic model of "censorship" that is derived from its own internal utopian idea that the administrative exclusion of certain texts can generate expected effects on the reception of these texts and can produce desired changes in the "re-education" of a particular community. I have tried to express my suspicion with models of an autonomous censor, a victimized author, and a deprived reader rooted in the seductive "oppression-domination" explanatory dichotomy. Rather, I am interested in institutions and their structures and in the performances that form systems of censorship—not simply as the disapproval of certain texts, but as the institutionally limited access of the reader to the text. Although the censor did have a particular role to play in this system, when the censor and related political and social forces disappear, the other actors still hold on to some of their familiar discourses and performative habits. The vestiges of former institutions, though in their transitional forms, continue to frame them.

I see "censorship" as a part of the process of canon formation; the former both generates and reproduces the latter. To look at the ways in which censorship has been deeply embedded in the institutions of literary production in Czechoslovakia is to introduce questions that complicate both the idea of censorship and the idea of canon. The cultural practices of prohibition never fully succeeded in excluding texts and paradoxically produced a fruitful atmosphere for alternative reception of them in other spheres. Similarly, the breakdown of certain restrictions does not immediately open the unlimited spaces one might desire.

The limited access of readers to certain texts during the past forty years seems to have reinforced a literary canon. Or maybe the issue is not so much one of reinforcing a particular canon, but rather one of bolstering trust in the canon-formation processes, with all of their capacity to generate hierarchies, freeze points of view, and hence to reconstruct further limits. Each of the three spheres of Czechoslovak literature produced its own specific canon. What they had in common was an unshakable belief in canon formation as the way of pursuing cultural life. This unifying tendency seems likely to continue. People have settled into the roles they used to perform and are reluctant to give up the hope of someday unmasking them. However impressive the unmasking of the rules of the game was in 1989, we seem to be having a hard time realizing that the performances may not be over.

NOTES

I would like to thank Helene Moglen and my dear friend Stuart Strickland for their inexhaustible patience in reading with me and working with me through the process of writing in their language. Without their intellectual and personal support this essay could never appear. I am grateful to all of my colleagues at the University of California at Santa Cruz, and particularly to members of the Center for Cultural Studies, before whom I was fortunate to be able to present an early draft. Without the generous support of the American Council of Learned Societies I would never have gotten into "a liminal position."

1. My account is limited in terms of time to the period up to the summer of 1991 and, in terms of space, focused on problems of Czech literary life. Comparison to circumstances specific to Slovakia will be further elaborated in a larger project.

2. I use the notion of "institution" to refer to sets of relatively defined activities organized within certain structural units (e.g., publishing houses) and shared by their participants, including systems of regulative principles that both guarantee and produce their coherence. Such a concept of institution also involves the concrete communication processes mediated inside institutional units and the interactions between them. For a fuller elaboration of the issues of institutions and cultural practices, see Raymond Williams, *Culture* (Glasgow: Fontana, 1981); Jonathan Culler, *Framing the Sign: Criticism and Its Institutions* (Oxford: Basil Blackwell, 1988); Janet Wolff, *The Social Production of Art* (New York: New York University Press, 1984); Pierre Macherey, *A Theory of Literary Production*, trans. Geoffrey Wall (London: Routledge & Kegan Paul, 1978); Linda Kauffman, ed., *Feminism and Institutions: Dialogues on Feminist Theory* (Cambridge: Basil Blackwell, 1989); and Gerald Graff, *Professing Literature: An Institutional History* (Chicago: University of Chicago Press, 1987).

3. For a more nuanced portrait of the figure of the censor, see Robert Darnton, "The Good Old Days," *New York Review of Books* 38, no. 9 (May 16, 1991): 44-48.

4. Annabel Patterson, *Censorship and Interpretation: The Conditions of Writing and Reading in Early Modern England*, with a new introduction (Madison: University of Wisconsin Press, 1984; 1991), 3.

5. Václav Havel, *Letters to Olga*, trans. Paul Wilson (New York: Holt, 1989; Knopf, 1988), 347. The canonization of Havel does not seem to be exclusively the local obsession of writers in my country. For example, the *New York Review of Books* published at least seven articles by or about Havel between January 1990 and September 1991.

6. The literature on book production is extensive. Here I refer to Robert Escarpit, *Trends in Book Worldwide Development 1970-78* (Paris: UNESCO, 1982); Escarpit, *The Book Revolution* (Paris: UNESCO, 1966); *Geshichte des deutschen Buchhandels*, 4 vols. (Leipzig: 1886-1913); R. E. Barker, *Books for All* (Paris: UNESCO, 1956); Robert Estivals, *La statisque bibliographique de la France sous la monarchie au XVIII. siècle* (Paris: Mouton, 1965); *International Book Year Plus Ten: An Analysis of Present Trends and Forecasts for the Future* part 1 (Paris: UNESCO, 1982).

7. Friedrich Engels, *The Condition of the Working Class in England*, trans. and ed. W. O. Henderson and W. H. Chaloner (Stanford, Calif.: Stanford University Press, 1958).

8. For a more detailed discussion of Czechoslovak literature and cultural politics during the period 1945-1989, see, for example: Milan Jungmann, *Cesty a rozcestí* (London: Rozmluvy, 1988); Milan Jungmann, *Průhledy do české prózy* (Prague: Evropský kulturní klub, 1990); and Robert B. Pynsent, *Conceptions of Enemy: Three Essays on Czech and Slovak Literature* (Cambridge: Cambridge Associates, 1988).

9. My inquiry is based on data published in *Statistická ročenka ČSSR* (Prague: SNTL, 1988) and *Historická ročenka ČSSR* (Prague: SNTL-Alfa, 1985), the state central source of statistical information. Not just because the statistical records completed under the communist government were often accused of intentional alteration to suit the leading power but also because of the relative reliability of quantitative data generally, I use these figures simply to outline some of the circumstances rather than to provide evidence for my arguments. The absence of disciplines resembling Anglo-American cultural studies or even a sociology of literature in my theoretical context has resulted in a profound lack of academic monographs dealing with the topics discussed above. Thus, I have drawn in my research on journalists' articles, interviews, ambiguous information derived from oral resources, and, of course, my personal experiences.

10. One effective way of silencing an author and a text was to print a book without reviewing it in journals or even announcing it in bulletins. The whole print run would simply be transferred directly from the printing company to the warehouse without ever being distributed. This happened, for example, to some books written by the Nobel Prize-winning poet Jaroslav Seifert. For a representative story of silencing books within the distribution system (the translation of Joyce's *Ulysses*), see Robert Hardy, "Joyce Meets Kafka—'A Prague Odyssey,'" in *Censorship and Political Communication in Eastern Europe*, ed. George Schöpflin (New York: St. Martin's, 1983), 24-26.

11. Charles Altieri, *Canons and Consequences: Reflections on the Ethical Force of Imaginative Ideals* (Evanston, Ill.: Northwestern University Press, 1990), 17. Altieri's articulation of "canon" allows me to complicate my understanding of censorship as closely related to canon formation. I would argue that, at the same time, the capacity of canon-formation processes to produce normative universals for "readers occupying different cultural positions" should not be overlooked (ibid.). I am interested in not only how canons offer spaces for sharing common points, but also how, as Jonathan Culler puts it in relation to the unifying model of the university as the transmitter of a cultural heritage, the emphasis on shared values and integration can "manifest itself as intolerance of dissidence and difference." Jonathan Culler, *Framing the Sign: Criticism and Its Institutions* (Oxford: Basil Blackwell, 1988), 35.

12. Václav Havel, *The Power of the Powerless: Citizens against the State in Central-East Europe*, ed. John Keane (New York: Sharpe, 1990).

13. Václav Havel, "Six Asides about Culture," in *Living in Truth: Twenty-two Essays Published on the Occasion of the Award of the Erasmus Prize to Václav Havel*, ed. Jan Vladislav (London and Boston: Faber & Faber, 1990), 124, 126. Resisting the impulse to canonize dissident literature, Havel argued in 1984 that "there are no more gifted writers, painters or musicians in Czechoslovakia today than there were at any time in the past.... Even in *samizdat*, there will always be countless bad books or poems for every important book." Although he considers the "parallel" alternative, nonofficial cultural movements to be "the sole bearer of the spiritual continuity of our cultural life," he admits that "it will be in the 'first' [official] culture that the decision will be made about the future climate of our lives." Ibid., 129, 134.

14. " 'Uncertain Strength': An Interview with Václav Havel," trans. Paul Wilson (from the magazine *Mladý svět*), *New York Review of Books* 38, no.14 (August 15, 1991): 6-8.

15. Judith Butler, *Gender Trouble: Feminism and the Subversion of Identity* (London and New York: Routledge, 1990), 136.

16. Ibid., 33.

17. Ibid.

18. It is perhaps the idea of the linear, playful, "stylized repetition of acts" that, by leaving out the perspective of the audience and the actors' anticipation of the consequences of the game constituted by the audience, blocks Butler from a deeper elaboration of the question she explicitly asks: "What interventions into this ritualistic repetition are possible?" Ibid., 140, 146.

19. Yes, there were poets sitting in the prison. A reader could have ended up there as well. Anyone who read a book by Kundera produced after 1968 by an émigré publisher or in samizdat in the streetcar would have a reasonable chance of being followed by an agent of the secret police and later being accused of "disturbing the peace" by distributing "provocative texts." On the other hand, this would probably not have been the case for a reader holding one of Kundera's books that had been officially published before 1968. While his work had been expelled from public libraries and official publishing plans for almost twenty years, his earlier work still could have been found on the shelves of used-book stores. Different performances carried with them different risks.

20. By talking about the meaning that concepts take on through their use in different contexts, I am consciously avoiding the language of "deformation," "destruction," "devastations," etc. that is deployed by most recent commentators on the experiences in the communist and postcommunist world. The more politically powerful these may sound, the less theoretically fruitful they seem to be. This strange amalgam of medical and building metaphors runs the risk of producing immediate prescriptions, presupposing a clear idea of "normality." The point at which normality leaves off and deformation begins is not at all clear at this moment.

21. Let me include one example. Not only the beauty of his verses but also the prestige of his translator, Kamil Bednář, who was forbidden to publish his own work for many years, made Robinson Jeffers one of the most famous American poets in Czechoslovakia.

22. Albatros—a publishing house that focused on literature for young people and children—collected a number of editors, authors, and designers with "suspicious" histories.

23. As a result of difficulties in meeting the state production plan, the printing companies used to move into the central warehouse over 40 percent of the whole year's production during the last quarter of the year. At the same time, booksellers began refusing to order books they were unable to sell (e.g., explicitly pro-regime poetry or fiction) because they had to pay a penalty for unsold books remaining in the store for more than 180 days. The number of books stored in the warehouse increased by 25 percent between 1980 and 1988.

24. As noted earlier, my account breaks off in the middle of 1991. Further economic changes were projected, especially the reprivatization of large companies, including many of the institutions analyzed here.

25. The story of bookstores would require its own essay. There were 374 of them in Prague in 1948. By the end of 1990, there were predictions that only twenty bookstores would be left in Prague as a consequence of the bankruptcy of distribution systems and the privatization and auction of both stores and the buildings in which they were located. Not very many people are interested in buying bookstores at auction because of the enormously high price, which includes the inventory of unsold books. Furthermore, this business is not the easiest way to get rich. The salespeople who formerly worked in the stores as employees of the state might be potential buyers, but since their wages were always well below the national average, lack of capital usually excludes them from the competition.

26. See, for example, Vladimír Pistorius, "Zpráva o knižním kolapsu" (Report on Book

Collapse), *Tvar*, no. 27 (July 4, 1991): 1, 4. *Literární Noviny*, the literary supplement to the former samizdat newspaper *Lidové Noviny*, which by 1991 was one of the most widely read newspapers in the country, regularly published interviews with book publishers in its series "Náklady a nakládaní. 10 otázek pro 2 soukromé nakladatele" (Print Runs and Publishing: Ten Questions for Two Private Publishers), *Literární Noviny*, no. 15 (April 11, 1991): 7; no. 20 (May 16, 1991): 7; and no. 28 (July 11, 1991): 7.

27. Altieri, *Canons and Consequences*, 17.

28. Havel, "Six Asides," 132-33.

29. Culler, *Framing the Sign*, 46.

30. For more details on direct practices of exclusion in journalism and literature, see "The Czechoslovak 'Black List,'" trans. in *Censorship and Political Communication*, ed. Schöpflin, 29-31.

31. From an interview with Miroslav Holub, "Death Has No Adjectives," *Economist*, June 2, 1990, 97-98.

"Degenerate 'Art' ": Public Aesthetics and the Simulation of Censorship in Postliberal Los Angeles and Berlin

Richard Burt

Madonna Meets the Nazis

Just before the release of Madonna's backstage/performance movie *Truth or Dare* in May 1991, the *Los Angeles Times* ran an interview with the superstar that began at the Los Angeles County Museum of Art (LACMA) exhibition entitled "Degenerate Art": The Fate of the Avant-Garde in Nazi Germany.[1] The LACMA exhibition documented and reconstructed the 1937 exhibition of some 625 modernist paintings the Nazis called "degenerate 'art,' " which they auctioned off, burned, or kept in storage after the exhibition. The agenda of the LACMA exhibition, reiterated in the guidebook, catalog, related events guide, and first room of the exhibition, was twofold: to suggest first that the 1937 exhibition was, so to speak, a bad day for art and second that there is a disturbing parallel between the Nazi assault on modern art and the recent controversy over National Endowment for the Arts (NEA) funding of avant-garde artists.[2]

During a seventy-minute tour of the Los Angeles exhibition, curator Stephanie Barron explained to Madonna that the Nazis vilified the paintings as "degenerate trash." Madonna responded, "Degenerate trash, huh? I know what you mean. Just like 'A Current Affair' and 'Hard Copy.' "[3] Toward the end of the interview, Madonna drew a parallel between the exhibition and her own experience with censorship:

Look at this Rev. Donald Wildmon character and all his Moral Majority people. They're obsessed with me—and there's hostility to that obses-

216

sion. They have a hatred for the power and fame and freedom that I have. For them to go around banning records and books and trying to get people arrested, it's a pretty clear statement about their own obsessions. Obviously I've tapped into something in their unconscious that they're very ashamed of. And since they can't deal with it, they tell everyone it's shameful. I was really reminded of that in the "Degenerate Art" exhibit. It's like Hitler—they want to purify your thoughts.[4]

The reporter condescendingly notes that Madonna is an astute if untrained art critic, and indeed it is clear from her remarks that she grasped perfectly the exhibition's twofold agenda. (Of course Madonna characteristically draws the parallel between past and present in terms of her own experience with censorship.)

From a modern point of view, a *Los Angeles Times* interview promoting Madonna's *Truth or Dare* that begins as this one did might seem puzzling, even scandalous. Apart from considerations of the parallel artistic status of the paintings and film clips on display in the exhibition and Madonna's music videos (between, say, Fritz Lang's *Metropolis* and Madonna's rewriting of it in "Express Yourself"), one might note that reception of their works differs markedly: while the works of German avant-garde artists were confiscated and many of the artists emigrated, "censorship" of Madonna's music videos has only affirmed her cultural centrality and made her more successful commercially.[5] When MTV announced that it had "declined" to air "Justify My Love," for example, the video aired that same evening on "Nightline," and Madonna immediately sold the video as a single, a move unprecedented in the video industry. Madonna is, as it were, "like a victim."[6] One might wonder too why the curator of an exhibition funded by the NEA at a publicly funded museum arranged a private after-hours tour for a Hollywood celebrity.

Yet to be scandalized by Madonna's private tour would be to position oneself as the Warren Beatty of cultural studies. From a postmodern perspective, Madonna's presence at the museum is an instance of the implosion of high and low culture that has generally been regarded as both the end of a modernist aesthetic and its displacement and sublimation by a postmodern, multicultural aesthetic based on identity politics, oriented toward performance. Los Angeles has increasingly been regarded as the central, productive site of this aesthetic both by post-Marxists like Jean Baudrillard and Jean-François Lyotard and by neo-Marxists from Theodor Adorno to

Edward Soja to Fredric Jameson and, most recently, Mike Davis.[7] In his provocative book *City of Quartz: Excavating the Future of Los Angeles*, Davis suggests that Los Angeles has become central to Marxist accounts of administered culture because it is now a stand-in for late capitalism in general.[8] Davis argues that Los Angeles has historically offered two takes on capitalism, a utopian or "sunshine" view and a dystopian or "noir" view. His present assessment of what he terms "postliberal" Los Angeles is noir. In his view, a band of émigré critics, filmmakers, and artists who fled Nazi Germany and central Europe in the 1940s (including Adorno, who, while he lived in Los Angeles, wrote *Minima Moralia* and, along with Horkheimer, the famous critique of the culture industry in *The Dialectic of Enlightenment*)[9] developed a critical, expressionist-inflected film noir take on capitalism. According to Davis, their critique has been replaced by a group of mercenary boosters who have furthered a remarkably repressive capitalist development epitomized by Los Angeles. What Davis terms the "university-museum megacomplex," now part of the culture industry itself, is central to the legitimation of this repressive development project.[10]

From a postmodern perspective—what I will henceforth call a noir perspective—that Los Angeles should be the location of an exhibition of avant-garde paintings that documented the reception of those works in a Nazi exhibition and that Madonna's presence at that exhibition should have been covered in the *Los Angeles Times* makes perfect sense: the LACMA exhibition and Madonna's tour of it register the extent to which Los Angeles now represents the total implosion of high and low culture, the triumph of the culture industry and of administered aesthetics.[11] One might even say it is predictable that Los Angeles should be the site of an exhibition on degenerate art when *Art News* featured as its November 1991 lead story "Hollywood Collects," with photos of "collector" Jack Nicholson on the cover and of Madonna on the first page of the story; when *Art in America* featured as its January 1992 lead story "LA: The New Patronage"; when *Art and Auction* featured "LA Story" on its January 1992 cover; when the price of expressionist paintings is going up and when those paintings are collected in Hollywood (works by George Grosz, for example, are owned by Hollywood producer Gerald Kamitaki).[12] Of course Madonna, who has her own personal art adviser (and whose acquisitions have driven up prices),

will show up at the LACMA exhibition.[13] Of course the LACMA curator, whose board includes movie star collectors like Steve Martin
(who shot part of his movie *LA Story* in the museum) would lead
Madonna on a private tour, especially given that private lenders
(Madonna owns coveted works by Frida Kahlo and Tamara de Lempika) are crucial to the success of major museum exhibitions.

While I will adopt a noir perspective to illuminate certain features
of the LACMA "Degenerate Art" exhibition, I have begun this essay
by focusing on Madonna's reception of it in the context of her own
experience with censorship in order both to reinforce the usual
terms by which noir critique is conducted and to complicate them.
On the one hand, a noir critique helps to account in significant ways
for the LACMA exhibition and for the way the exhibition began
with oversized photographs and brief quotations from émigrés from
Nazi Germany who went to Los Angeles more or less directly and
ended with Thomas Mann's 1938 comments on what he took to be a
shift of the center of European culture to America. The museum
installation was designed by Frank Gehry, a regional architect who
has now had global success and who, according to Mike Davis, has
been crucial to the development of the carceral city Davis calls
"Fortress LA."[14] With its economic focus, the noir critique could also
account for the emphasis on museum acquisition and on auctions
(two chapters of the catalog are devoted to the Nazi art auction) and
for the way the market value of the paintings is constructed as an
index of their artistic value. It could also help illuminate the technology of reproduction used in the exhibition itself, the way the
LACMA exhibition was produced as a megaspectacle.

The noir critique is problematic, however, when it comes to
accounting for a central feature of the LACMA exhibition, namely,
censorship. My interest in the LACMA and Nazi exhibitions lies
largely in way they call into question the traditional modern understanding of censorship as pure repression, the Nazis being perhaps
the central trope for the modern censor. What remains open to question within the traditional (one might say "party") line on nazism
and modernism and on Nazi art policy adopted by LACMA is why
the Nazi Degenerate "Art" exhibitions ever took place, and why,
more broadly, the Nazis took such a deep interest in the arts. Why
did the Nazis exhibit instead of burn the art they hated, if in fact
they did burn it? Given that it had a low market value, why did they

auction it off? And why did the Nazis document the Degenerate "Art" exhibitions so extensively that it is possible to reconstruct them now in such detail? To address these questions, we need to redefine censorship and, by extension, revise a traditional understanding of the Nazis' relation both to modernity and to modernism. I will contend that censorship operates not only in repressive terms (as in the confiscation and destruction of art, say), but also as a complex network of productive discursive practices that legitimate and delegitimate the production and reception of the aesthetic in general and of the avant-garde in particular. Acts of seemingly literal repression such as Nazi book burnings (shown on a video in the LACMA exhibition) were always publicly staged, filmed to reach the widest possible audience. The burnings were less about blocking access to particular books than they were about purifying the blood of the *Volk* from corrupting influences. Even at its most destructive, then, censorship is always simulated, always paradoxically staged as a legitimating and delegitimating performance.

In addition to making available a critique of the LACMA reproduction, redefining censorship as a set of strategies staged for the purposes of cultural legitimation and delegitimation enables a larger critique of the present postliberal so-called new world order. The LACMA exhibition staged a "liberal" opposition between modern art and fascism in a neoconservative, postliberal way, putting a "spin" on the Nazi reception of modernism that effectively suppressed the modernist aspects of the Nazi exhibition, itself a performance of censorship, and ignored the left's contradictory reception of modern art, particularly expressionism, in Weimar Germany. The LACMA exhibition provided its American audiences with the illusion that they are safe from censorship, that only a few neofascist Americans favor censorship of the arts.[15] Similarly, in its Berlin installation, the exhibition reinforced the illusion that a newly reunified Germany had consolidated the triumph of parliamentary democracy over fascism in the midst of postliberal developments. Yet redefining censorship as simulation also complicates noir critique insofar as it calls into question recent narratives of Los Angeles (particularly Hollywood and Disneyland) as either the paradisical or the degraded destination of Western culture. Redefining censorship as a simulated performance undermines as well many of the oppositions (between freedom and repression, aestheticizing politics and politicizing aesthetics, simulated and Historical) that have been central to leftist critiques of fascism. I take up these complications in the concluding section of this essay.

Modernist Reactions

I want to begin my critique of the LACMA exhibition by focusing on a central, glaring contradiction in its reproduction of the Nazi exhibition: on the one hand, there is a will to reproduce the original Nazi exhibition; on the other, there is a will not to reproduce it exactly. LACMA studiously departed from the Nazi original in several ways: the floor plan of the installation was different; the paintings were hung differently (figs. 1 and 2); and the "graffiti" was not always translated—in some cases, the German was not even reproduced legibly (fig. 3).[16] These changes served to set up a distinction between the Nazis' defamation of art and LACMA's "dignified" treatment of it.

Fig. 1. Room three of the 1991 LACMA "Degenerate Art" exhibition

Fig. 2. Room three of the 1937 Munich Degenerate "Art" exhibition. Photo courtesy of the Los Angeles County Museum of Art.

Fig. 3. LACMA scale model reproduction of the 1937 Munich exhibition

This contradictory will to reproduce the original and yet not reproduce it registers the curators' fear that an exact reproduction of the Munich exhibition would void a critique of its original politics—that it would be received as the Nazis wanted their exhibition to be received. Although mounting a critique of the Nazi exhibition is an admirable and timely project, LACMA's commitment to a modern definition of censorship paradoxically implicated its reproduction in the disturbing delegitimating features of the Nazi exhibition it wished to criticize. The Nazi exhibition was itself a total work of art used to legitimate censorship of modern art, and the Nazis paradoxically imitated the avant-garde, particularly the dadaists, in doing so; similarly, the LACMA reproduction legitimated modern art by delegitimating would-be censors (in the past and present), as pointed references to the Mapplethorpe case made clear, and imitated the techniques in the 1937 Munich exhibition to do so. Just as the Nazis' attempt to delegitimate modern art was inextricably bound up with avant-garde techniques, so too the LACMA exhibition legitimated the avant-garde and modern art in general by adopting techniques the Nazis used to delegitimate it. Though the LACMA and Nazi exhibitions had opposite aims, they both used the institution of the museum to regulate the reception of the avant-garde through the display of delegitimating tactics. In failing to recognize how the Nazi exhibition was already itself avant-garde, the LACMA exhibition was at once both more avant-garde and more nazified than the Nazi original it claimed to have "partially" reproduced.[17]

A concrete, close examination of the LACMA exhibition makes clear how it replicated many features of the Nazi exhibition it criticized. The guidebooks for both exhibitions, for example, do versions of the same thing: the Nazis put the word *art* in quotation marks, which the LACMA catalog notes as evidence of the Nazi wish to defame avant-garde art, yet the LACMA guidebook uses quotation marks around *degenerate art* in order to "dignify" the art as art (figs. 4 and 5). It thus ironically did to the Nazi exhibition what the Nazis did to the art they exhibited. Moreover, the LACMA guidebook imitates a Nazi aesthetic. On the cover is a colorized version of a black and white photo taken by the Nazis of the 1937 exhibition. The color scheme for the program (and the cover of the catalog) is that of the Nazi brownshirts: khaki brown, red, and black (colors carried through in the guidebook's display of the installation and floor plan).

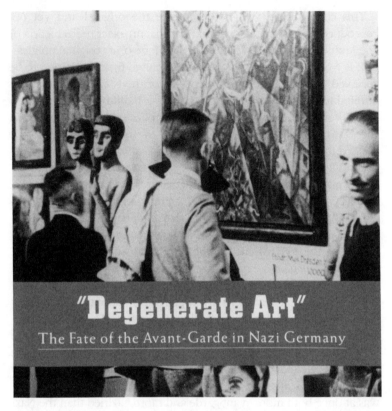

Fig. 4. Guidebook for the LACMA exhibition. Cover designed by Jim Drobka. Photo courtesy of the Los Angeles County Museum of Art.

The LACMA exhibition was itself a Wagnerian *Gesamtkunstwerk*, a total work of art, a multimedia spectacle.[18] It followed the megaspectacle exhibitions of the 1980s in using a unified spectacle to override critical analysis available through attention to the exhibition's otherwise heterogeneous elements.[19] Significantly in this regard, Wagner's *Tannhäuser* overture was the unannounced and uncredited sound track on the videos in the first and third rooms documenting the history of Nazi art policy.[20] (We may give thanks, I suppose, that LACMA didn't use the "Ride of the Valkyries" from *Die Walküre* or the "Rhine Journey" from *Gotterdämmerung*.) The LACMA exhibition adopted a postmodern multimedia apparatus, even if its message was high modernist. There were four continu-

Fig. 5. Guidebook for the Munich exhibition. Photo courtesy of the Los Angeles County Museum of Art.

ously running videos: in the first of three historical rooms (documenting Nazi art policy and exhibitions), a video that documented Hitler's art and his official parades and another that showed clips from films banned by the Nazis; in the second historical room, a

Fig. 6. Room six of the LACMA exhibition. The video in this room was footage of spectators at the Munich exhibition.

video of Nazi book burnings and concentration camps; and in the largest room of the exhibition, footage of people wandering through the 1937 exhibition (fig. 6). In the third historical room, one could listen to music by composers delegitimated in the Degenerate Music exhibition. In his installation, Gehry drew, knowingly or not, on expressionist lighting techniques to create an "oppressive" atmosphere.[21] After walking down a narrow, well-lit hallway with windows on one's right and oversized photographs of émigrés positioned slightly above eye level on one's left, one walked into the dimly lit historical rooms; in the first of them hung a large, intentionally corroded metal sign that said "Degenerate Art" (fig. 7). One then moved into the well-lit rooms where the paintings were on display. And, of course, there were the usual audiotape guides.

As a multimedia, total work of art, the LACMA exhibition clearly reinforced the "didactic walls" in the installation itself and the traffic patterns of the audience.[22] One had to pass through the historical rooms before viewing the art. Near the entry to the first historical room, a metal bar with a "no entry" sign and a guard standing beside

Fig. 7. The first historical room of the LACMA exhibition

it blocked direct entry to the paintings (in the sixth reconstructed room). The LACMA exhibition regulated documentation of itself. Photography of the exhibition was not allowed for "security" reasons. Moreover, the LACMA exhibition never examined the extent to which its documentation of history depended on photography.[23] By these diverse means, audience reception was carefully regulated (one might say guided) so that any criticism of the art effectively aligned the critic with the Nazis. (The LACMA guidebook clearly equates critics with the young man on the cover, who apparently has turned away, scoffing [see fig. 4].) Criticism of the LACMA exhibition and the works in it was, in short, delegitimated in advance. The LACMA exhibition gave its viewers, as a *New York Times* reviewer put it, a tour de force.[24]

Whether this is good or bad art was not open to debate, nor were the criteria for determining good art open for discussion. In closing down debate, LACMA ironically opened up a critique of the educational function on which its NEA funding depends, one that replicated the critique of the Nazi exhibition announced in the second chapter of the LACMA catalog, "An 'Educational' Exhibition."[25] LACMA criticized the Nazis for controlling rather than educating public opinion, yet LACMA's "educational" function may be similarly put in quotation marks. To receive federal funding, public museums must have "permanent facilities open to the public on a regularly scheduled basis and their tax exempt status depends on providing educational experiences to the public."[26] Education is generally defined as "promoting public awareness of art."[27] But in the LACMA exhibition, education depended on excluding debate over what counts as art. This raises two issues: how was LACMA's predetermined "education" (viewers had to agree that they were seeing great art) different from Nazi propaganda, and who needed to come to the LACMA exhibition to be "educated"? LACMA clearly excluded from its public those who are arguably most in need of being educated—namely, the neo-Nazis of Los Angeles, who might have contested its view of the art—and did so, paradoxically, in order to legitimate the exhibition. The neo-Nazis might not have been educated by it; more precisely, to have invited them to see the exhibition would also have been to allow them to contest the judgment of the curators. Even without any direct contestation, a problem remained: for the very means of regulating the reception of museumgoers (to prevent them from sympathizing with Hitler's position) disturbed the differences between them and those who saw the Nazi exhibition, a disturbance felt acutely at the LACMA exhibition in the uncanny moment when one looked at video footage of people in the 1937 exhibition and then looked around at the people in the LACMA exhibition. I, for one, could see no difference between the way the two groups responded to the two exhibitions (fig. 6).

In giving a postliberal "spin" to the Nazi reception of the avant-garde, the LACMA exhibition engaged in a different kind of administrative regulation, one closer to censorship as it has traditionally been understood, which has to do with the historical memory it documented, what LACMA distorted through downplaying, marginalizing, recasting, or omitting.[28] The Nazi interest in the avant-garde was, for example, left unnoted, as was the counterexample of Italian fascism (which embraced the avant-garde). The debates within the left over expressionism in the 1930s were nowhere mentioned, though in defending expressionism against Georg Lukács's charge that it was fascist, Ernst Bloch took as his point of departure the Munich Degenerate "Art" exhibition, and even though Lukács denied in his rejoinder to Bloch that the Nazi exhibition altered the validity of Lukács's original (1934) analysis.[29] Nor were Bloch's reviews of the Munich exhibition mentioned.[30]

The LACMA curators made similarly problematic selections with regard to the content of the art. Given the homophobia often thought to drive right-wing attacks on the NEA (as in the Mapplethorpe controversy) and the NEA's denials of funding to lesbian and gay performance artists, the understated attention to Nazi persecution of gay and lesbian art and of transgressive sexuality in general seems rather odd.[31] Consider the selection from *Mädchen in Uniform* in a thirty-minute video of clips from movies censored by the Nazis. In this scene, schoolgirls looking at a pornographic book are interrupted by a teacher who confiscates the book. One girl then shows another pin-up photos of male movie stars who, the girls exclaim in English, have "sex appeal." The scene has its charm, but it is arguably the most heterosexist moment in the film. Anyone who had not seen the film would never guess that the girls' crushes on a young female teacher are central to the movie's plot, would have no idea that resistance to the repressive headmistress and her hirelings who run an authoritarian girls' school is figured by a militant and powerfully romanticized lesbian opposition (all of the girls have crushes on a young female teacher).[32] Similarly, in the audiotape that accompanied the exhibition and in the catalog, little or no mention was made of images that seem to call out for comment in this regard. Consider, for example, Otto Dix's 1923 portrait of the jeweler Karl Krall (fig. 8). Krall is posed in campy fashion with hands on hips à la Mae West, and his body is exaggerated accordingly. The painting is reproduced in the catalog, but its obviously homoerotic content is not discussed.[33] Moreover, there is no mention of the Bauhaus, even though the Nazis began their assault on modern art by closing it down in 1933.[34] Finally, the LACMA exhibition distorted the Nazi exhibition by reproducing only one of its two parts. LACMA excluded the Nazi art from the House of German Art exhibition held in conjunction with the Degenerate "Art" exhibition (displaying only video reproductions of some Nazi art in the first historical room, thereby reinforcing the taboo on the display of Nazi art).[35]

Apart from showing the ways in which delegitimating tactics were deployed in the LACMA spin on nazism and the avant-garde, I want to call attention to a more fundamental censorship in the

Fig. 8. Otto Dix, *The Jeweller*

LACMA exhibition, one that functioned in terms of a distinction between what was legible and illegible, receivable and unreceivable in the reconstruction of the Nazi exhibition. The forms of selection, suppression, and distortion I have identified in the LACMA exhibition, along with the spectacular technological apparatus, are determined by what is receivable once one has accepted a modern definition of censorship and an unrevised account of nazism. The distinction between what is and is not receivable becomes operative in relation to the account of history and art history adopted by the LACMA curators and by the American public in general (including many academics). In the standard history of art, 1935 marks the triumph of the banal in Nazi art policy.[36] In this account, the Munich Degenerate "Art" exhibition evinced just how aberrant and exceptional the Nazis were; it marked the revenge of the philistines, in the appreciative words of one reviewer of the LACMA exhibition.[37] Thus the title of the exhibition was put in quotation marks to differentiate "dignified" treatment of the art as art from its defamation as "degenerate 'art' "; any similarities between the Nazi exhibition and modern art were regarded as unintended "ambiguities" or "hilarious contradictions."[38]

My analysis of the Nazi exhibition relies on a revised historiography of modern Germany. In suggesting that the LACMA and Nazi exhibitions were equally sophisticated in their simplification of complexity, I follow Hans Syberberg, Jeffrey Herf, Ian Kershaw, Peter Sloterdijk, and Zygmaunt Bauman, all of whom have contested the notion that the Nazis were stupid and demonic philistines at war with modernism.[39] Herf in particular argues that the Nazis engaged in a political tradition of a paradoxically reactionary modernism dating back to the Weimar Republic. If we grant the Nazis' interest in modernism and modern technology, the way they imitated modern art in the Munich Degenerate "Art" exhibition even as they differentiated it from officially approved art becomes quite clear. Rather than drive toward the construction of simple, "pure" binary oppositions and unwittingly produce ambiguities and contradictions, the Nazis delegitimated modern art through a sophisticated process in which the imitation of modern art worked to clarify its difference from Nazi art. The Nazi exhibition may be viewed as an exercise in the kind of fascist simplification of complexity articulated by Sloterdijk:

Fascism and its side currents were after all—viewed philosophically—in large part movements of simplification. But that precisely the town criers of the new simplicity (good-evil, friend-foe, "front," "identity," "bond") for their part had gone through the modern nihilist school of artfulness, bluff, and deception—that was to become clear to the masses too late. The "solution" that sounds so simple, "positiveness," the new stability, the new essentialness and security: They are but structures that, under the surface, are even more complicated than the complicatedness of modern life against which they resist. For they are defensive, reactive formations—composed of modern experiences and denials of the same. Antimodernity is possibly more modern and complex than what it rejects; in any case, it is gloomier, blunter, more brutal, and more cynical.[40]

As a total work of art, the Nazi exhibition was itself already a post-modern performance: its politics were negotiated as the audience moved through it, determining what and why certain kinds of "art" are degenerate. From this perspective, the Nazi exhibition may be regarded as itself avant-garde rather than as the antithesis to avant-garde. One might go so far as to say that the Nazis outstripped the avant-garde in mounting a postmodern performative exhibition. If regulation of the arts made the Nazi state exceptional among totalitarian regimes, this may evince less its aberrant character than its advanced status relative to other cultural administrations.

Several examples might be used as evidence of the Munich exhibition's sophisticated simplification of complexity. Consider the similarity between a poster for the Nazi exhibition and one for a 1923 Bauhaus exhibition (fig. 9) or the obvious imitation of expressionist woodcuts in another Nazi poster (fig. 10). The strongest example of this simplification is the so-called "dada wall," on which both the Nazis and the LACMA curators had a clear fixation (fig. 11); it appears on the cover of the LACMA catalog (and in magazine articles covering the exhibition). In the LACMA account, this wall was a typical example of the Nazis' attempt to defame modern art by surrounding it with "graffiti." This account fails to note, however, that the so-called graffiti are from a 1920 dada exhibition held in Berlin (fig. 12). The phrase "Nehmen Sie DADA ernst, es lohnt sich" (Take dada seriously! It's worth it) was written on a placard in the dada exhibition above Otto Dix's *Kriegskrüppel* (*War Cripples*). The dada exhibition played with the relation between text and image in a

Fig. 9. Nazi Degenerate "Art" exhibition poster indebted to a Bauhaus poster designed by Kandinsky

way that was echoed by the Nazi exhibition as a whole and by the dada wall in particular.[41] The Munich exhibition resembled dada in its very organization as well. The dada exhibition, according to Hanne Bergius, had a disconcerting diversity created not only "by

Fig. 10. Nazi Degenerate "Art" exhibition poster indebted to German expressionist woodcuts

the crowding of the walls, but also by the variety and contrast of the various materials employed."[42] The exhibition was, according to Odo Marquard, a "negative direct *Gesamtkunstwerk*."[43] One might try to differentiate between dada's desire to turn art into politics and the Nazis' attempt to aestheticize politics. Dada seeks to break down bourgeois institutions of art and thus might be seen as the radical antithesis of the Nazis.[44] Yet the cards with the slogans "DADA ist politisch" (dada is political) and "Kultur ist Tod" (culture is dead) might be said to call forth an imitative fascist counterresponse.

LACMA's failure to recognize how the Nazis imitated the avant-garde is remarkable given that the LACMA catalog notes that Otto Dix's *War Cripples* was exhibited in the dada fair. Moreover, the LACMA chapter on the exhibition shows that Dix's painting was in the Nazi guidebook and in room three of the Munich exhibition. The LACMA curators' unwillingness or inability to account for data that called their own interpretation of the Nazi exhibition into question is not so much a question of incompetence or knowing suppression as of their political unconscious, their inability to receive that data. The data just don't make sense to them; in Thomas Kuhn's

Fig. 11. The dada wall of the 1937 Munich exhibition. Photo courtesy of the Los Angeles County Museum of Art.

Fig. 12. 1920 Berlin dada exhibition

terms, the data are anomalous and hence either recognized and discounted or just misrecognized.[45]

You Are Leaving the American Sector

If LACMA's misrecognition of the Nazi exhibition is a symptom of LACMA's spin on nazism and the avant-garde, a symptom of its ideological will to legitimate a simplistic notion of modern art (and by extension all art), it remains to be considered how the simplifications and suppressions of this spin advance a postliberal agenda. Within art world debates, curator Stephanie Barron implicitly aligned the exhibition with a neoconservative account of modernism (advanced by Hilton Kramer and Roger Kimball) against a postmodern account of it (advanced by Hans Haacke, Douglas Crimp, and Rosalind Kraus).[46] Barron's identification of expressionism with the avant-garde rather than dada (ignoring the dadaist critique of expressionism as the death of German art) registers her personal stake as a curator in a positive evaluation of the paintings. (Barron is married to Robert F. Rifkind, a collector of expressionist paintings and founder of the Robert F. Rifkind Center at LACMA, which Barron heads.)[47] Similarly, Christoff Stolzl's interest in bringing the LACMA show to Berlin's German Historical Museum, which he directs, is linked to his interest in putting presently warehoused Nazi "art" in his museum.[48]

These art world curatorial politics intersect with more directly political interests in legitimating postwar Germany's place in the new world order, and it is worth noting that members of Parliament intervened to have the LACMA exhibition shown in Berlin.[49] The move from the Los Angeles *art* museum to the Berlin *historical* museum reinforced a distinction between history and art already built into the exhibition, making it potentially easier to invert the Nazi view of degenerate "art" by putting Nazi "art" in quotation marks and thereby heightening a contrast between an authoritarian Nazi Germany and a postwar denazified liberal Germany. Since the late 1980s there has been an explicit interest in resolving the embarrassment posed to Germany by Nazi art.[50] The LACMA exhibition helped German museum administrators to manage a series of problems brought up in the debate over whether the art should be shown and, if so, where and how. Thus far, no solution has proven acceptable, and Nazi art remains a double embarrassment: no art museum will show it for fear of legitimating it, yet to keep it out of sight makes museums look like censors. The proposals for displaying the art thus far recycle in inverted form the tactics the Nazis are said to have used on modern art and disclose the possibility that German artistic tastes have not been denazified after all. One member of Parliament, Antjie Vollmer, argued that if they were shown, the Nazi paintings would be revealed in "all their triteness and the laughter will help clear away the ghosts of the Nazi period," precisely the aim—ridicule—of the 1937 Munich exhibition.[51] More skeptically, Claudia Siede, another member of Parliament, said that "there is still uncertainty in dealing with official Nazi art because the so-called 'beautiful art' which in those days was intended to reflect the 'healthy taste of the people' is closer to the taste of the broad majority of the public even today than the so-called modern art."[52] Siede suggested that the Nazi art be de-demonized by exhibiting it side by side with works denounced by Hitler. In an effort to educate people, Seide proposed an inversion of the twin 1937 Nazi exhibitions of official and degenerate art.

Though the LACMA catalog omits any mention of this controversy over displaying Nazi art, as Emily Braun notes, the exhibition helped to resolve it by putting the question of Nazi art and Nazi art policy within a historical category.[53] The Nazi "art" can then be shown (rather than censored), but displayed relatively comfortably as historical artifacts, as documents (precisely because it has been politicized) rather than as art; liberal regimes can be set against totalitarian ones (in which politics and art are identified). The Berlin installation implicitly positioned the United States as the instructor of Germans (in line with the United States as an instrument of denazification). The show was, so to speak, "good for Germans," a form of criticism and compliment; as a reviewer maintained, the art displayed was true German art (as opposed to the historical documents of Nazi Germany left by Hitler's "artists"), evidence that there were "resistance heroes" in the Third Reich.[54]

More broadly, the LACMA exhibition's installation in Berlin was an instance of a cultural exchange between Los Angeles and Berlin that is increasingly central to a broader exchange of power between a post-Gulf War United States and a reunified Germany, an exchange already well under way. (Witness the opening of the Museum of Tolerance in Los Angeles, with its reproduction of 1930s Berlin, and the fragments of the Berlin Wall in the Nixon and Reagan presidential libraries in Yorba Linda and Simi Valley, respectively [fig. 13].)[55] The reception of the LACMA exhibition in the (previously West) German press suggested that this cultural exchange between Los Angeles and Berlin aimed, undoubtedly without recognizing that it did so, to reinforce the doctrine of American exceptionalism with regard to imperialism and the doctrine of Nazi exceptionalism with regard to German nationalism. Just as the United States did not dominate Iraq but liberated Kuwait, so the Third Reich marked an aberration in an otherwise democratic German national character. Los Angeles and Berlin now serve as metropolitan centers that enable cultural exchanges that to a degree stabilize differences between self-identical terms: art and nonart; art and history; Germans and Americans; censorship and free expression; simulation and History.

The German press's response to the LACMA exhibition and its relation to the Gulf War depended on simulated censorship and simulated opposition. In an essay on the LACMA exhibition in *Die Zeit*, Petra Von Kipphoff noted that many lenders were worried about sending their paintings to a country engaged in censorship of the arts and involved in a "clean and sober" war.[56] Lenders were apparently satisfied by token opposition to the war: a single radio station in Los Angeles regularly aired an antiwar show. The LACMA reconstruction was reviewed in the German press as superior to the 1987 version in Germany because the "courageous LACMA curator" connected the original exhibition to topical issues in the United States.[57] In Germany, the original Los Angeles venue was regarded as an ironic revenge of sorts: the painters and artists exiled by Hitler were part of an exhibition that showed the history of how they got there.

At the same time, the management of this cultural exchange will only serve to expose, in a noir fashion, the administrative corruption and severely repressive "censorship" on which the staged stability of the new world order depends. It is difficult to manufacture a consensus about liberalism within a postliberal society. In fact, the terms that determine reception—*Nazi, censorship, fascist*, and so on—are extremely volatile; rather than cement a consensus between the LACMA curators and the NEA over the right-wing attacks on the arts, an exhibition on Nazi censorship threatened to explode it. The

Fig. 13. Fragment of the Berlin Wall in the Richard Nixon presidential library. Photo courtesy of the Richard M. Nixon Library and Birthplace.

history of the exhibition's funding was itself troubled. Though the LACMA exhibition paid deliberate homage to the NEA in the foreword to the catalog and in a large display card in the first historical room (both acknowledged NEA funding), the NEA in fact withdrew funding in 1990 during the Helms hearings on the renewal of NEA funding; moreover, the Smithsonian, originally one of three museums scheduled to show the exhibition, withdrew on the grounds that it did not have room. NEA representatives asked that the words *Nazi* and *censorship* be struck from the catalog. The LACMA curators complied and retitled the exhibition 1937: A Crucial Year in Art History. Sometime in 1990 after the hearings, the funding was restored, apparently because the NEA thought it better to risk holding a controversial exhibition than to face almost certain controversy over not funding one, as in the case of the 1989 Witness show at Artists Space. (After withdrawing funding for the exhibition, NEA head John Frohnmayer restored it, but not for the catalog.)[58] The LACMA curators then restored the censored words. (It is difficult to tell this censored or cover-up story with exact dates because one would need to use the Freedom of Information Act to get access to the original applications and NEA responses.)[59]

Similar contradictions obtain in Germany. A socialist perspective on fascism, for example, has been wiped out in formerly East Berlin museums (now closed), and formerly East German universities have faced wholesale firings of professors and researchers.[60] In 1990, masses of East German books ended up in a garbage dump.[61] Even as the socialist version of German history has been censored (the East Berlin Historical Museum was closed in 1990), East German censorship has been put on show.[62] Which East German art will be exhibited, if any, is now the subject of fierce dispute, and the market value of the avant-garde escalates.[63] Furthermore, recent exhibitions of avant-garde artists like Otto Dix and photographers like John Heartfield have already proven controversial on grounds that they depoliticize their work in the name of representing its diversity.[64] The reception of the 1992 Otto Dix exhibition at the Tate Gallery did not square with the aims of the LACMA "Degenerate Art" exhibition. Either Dix was seen unfavorably or the exhibition was an occasion to rethink the relation between Hitler and modernism and claim that Hitler saved modernism by opposing it. The way that the Weimar Republic has served equally well (and with increasing frequency) as an analogy both to present-day Germany and to the United States is perhaps the clearest register of their postliberal contradictions.

What is the status of these contradictions? Can they be turned against the postliberal order as it is presently administered in the United States and Germany? More narrowly, we might ask whether there is an alternative to the LACMA reproduction that could undo a repressive postliberal order. The usual affirmative answer to this question would reverse the tendency to divide art from history and aestheticize politics, and instead show how art is historical and aesthetics are political. A progressive alternative reproduction might advance the agenda of critics from Peter Bürger to Rosalind Krauss, who have distinguished the emancipatory goal of the avant-garde's attack (the avant-garde being identified with dada), namely, the conflation of artistic and everyday praxis from a simulated reconciliation of the ideological split between them, a conflation institutionalized through an oppressive culture industry.[65]

In my view, however, a reproduction of the Nazi exhibition that politicized aesthetics would not be an antidote to the problems I have identified in the LACMA exhibition. To be sure, one could imagine a counterexhibition on degenerate art, one with a countermemory more ample or more radical than the one supplied by LACMA, one that included a greater diversity of viewpoints and staged the conflicts between them, one that highlighted the politics of exhibition and the institution of the museum, one that called into question the auratic status of painting. Two critics suggested that the LACMA exhibition should have included more history or more forms of censored media such as photography. Similarly, the exhibition of Nazi art could have been problematized. The role of the curator could have been foregrounded, particularly her decision to exhibit the paintings as she did, so as to call attention to the politics of the art on show and the politics of museum exhibition.[66] The issue of censorship could have been brought forward so that it became clear that censorship is a performance. The point of the exhibition would have been to raise questions such as: What is art? How is it legitimated? What is the relation between word and image? When are wall texts coercive, when informative? Just what is censorship?

Yet a progressive alternative to LACMA could not transcend the kinds of problems I pointed to in the LACMA exhibition, however much more inclusive and diverse its historical contextualization, however much it foregrounded conflicts within the history of reception or the politics of museum display or the curator's role. For any exhibition would inevitably regulate reception so as to legitimate certain perspectives and delegitimate others. Undoing the repressive effects of the LACMA spin on Nazi art policy, returning the repressed, would itself involve the deployment of similar kinds of delegitimating tactics, similar kinds of simulation, the production of a counterspin. A politicized version would be just as programmatic as an apolitical one: questions about the relation between art and politics would be largely rhetorical, since it would be assumed that art is political. Moreover, it is hard to see how an alternative exhibition would not aestheticize politics in an effort to politicize aesthetics. In showing that historical documentation (both then and now) is political, a progressive reproduction of the Nazi exhibition would presumably highlight even more than LACMA's the way that documentation itself was and is part of an aesthetic performance; similarly, to show that art is political would necessarily involve aestheticizing its display (one would have to call attention to the art of political exhibition).[67]

Similar problems would no doubt have arisen if an alternative exhibition had been shown in Berlin. It would presumably have made clear how denazification has always depended on censorship, as the recent calls to ban German neo-Nazi rock and attempts to ban discussions of topics like euthanasia confirm.[68] Indeed, reunification has unsettled the former landscape of East German literary culture. Younger critics have asked whether writers like Christa Wolf, who claimed to be a victim of the East German regime and its secret police apparatus, the Stasi, was really a collaborator.[69] In displaying how modernism linked destruction to creation, culture to barbarism, a politicized exhibition might also have complicated current attempts to memorialize the Holocaust in Germany. As it was, an exhibition that ran concurrently at the Martin Gropius Bau entitled Patterns of Jewish Life, which included religious items, seemed uncannily like the realization of Hitler's planned museum of Jewish artifacts.[70]

That the problems of censorship in the LACMA reproduction cannot be entirely corrected may be seen if we consider briefly three anticensorship exhibitions. A topical exhibition entitled Scandal,

Outrage, and Censorship: Controversy in Modern Art, held in December 1991 at the Galerie St. Etienne in New York, juxtaposed works by German avant-garde artists from the 1930s (some of them in the Nazi Degenerate "Art" exhibition) with paintings and etchings by contemporary American avant-garde artists like Sue Coe.[71] The force of the juxtaposition, however, was to affirm only the predictable moralistic and ahistorical parallels between Nazi Germany and the Reagan/Bush United States. Another topical anticensorship exhibition, Too Shocking to Show, sponsored by the Brooklyn Museum and Franklin Furnace, ran performances of four artists who were denied funding by the NEA. The title quoted Pat Buchanan's ad, which used footage from Marlon Riggs's documentary on gay black males, Tongues Untied. The same imitative, antagonistic dynamic as in the 1937 and 1991 "Degenerate 'Art'" exhibitions was at work here.[72] Perhaps the clearest illustration of the impossibility of mounting an exhibition opposed to censorship is The Play of the Unmentionable, shown at the Brooklyn Museum in 1990.[73] Organized and curated by the conceptual artist Joseph Kosuth, this exhibition directly addressed the NEA controversy while also departing from the conventions that govern museum exhibitions. The installation gathered censored works from the museum's permanent collection and displayed them in relation to quotations from politicians (including Hitler and Goebbels) and artifacts including Bauhaus furniture (fig. 14). Like the Berlin dadaists, Kosuth mounted a critique of the museum as institution, politicizing the relation between text and image, questioning how a work (and what kind of work) is displayed. At the same time, Kosuth explicitly opposed his political art to that of "unambiguous" work of artists like Hans Haacke. For Kosuth, according to David Freedberg, "the whole of art became the questioning of art. A truly political art, he realized, would not content itself with the message alone; it would— it had to—engage the viewer in a questioning of the nature and process of art itself."[74] Yet Kosuth's political art in fact resembled the 1937 Nazi exhibition in two respects: first, it had a clear agenda (in this case, anticensorship and proplay); second, in advancing this anticensorship agenda, the playful displays of text and artworks was arguably indebted more to the Nazi dada room (fig. 11) than it was to the more purely negative Berlin dada exhibition of 1920 (fig. 12).

Fig. 14. Joseph Kosuth's Play of the Unmentionable exhibition at the Brooklyn Museum. Photo courtesy of the Brooklyn Museum.

Ambiguity and play functioned unambiguously as antidotes to a censorship supposedly opposed to play.

The misrecognition and panic evinced in the LACMA exhibition cannot be "corrected," in short, by an exhibition that would politicize aesthetics, for the very pervasiveness and complexity of censorship contaminate any corrective critique of the LACMA exhibition: if LACMA's deployment of complex, diverse, and pervasive forms of delegitimation called into question the conventional terms of "liberal" accounts of Nazi history (so that *liberal* and *censorship* have to be put in quotation marks), so too does any "left" critique. If censorship is part of a panic discourse, then so too is any criticism of censorship. Every term one would use to historicize the Nazi exhibition (from any given political perspective) must be put in quotation marks as its self-identity, its difference from its opposite, is called into question: "art"; "history"; "education"; "graffiti"; "guidebook"; even "conservation" (as opposed to censorship) and "collection" (as opposed to confiscation).[75] Museum administrators, the NEA, and its critics, whether they are for or against censorship of the arts, participate in a common panic discourse of denunciation in the public sphere: each calls the other "fascist" and "philistine"; each accuses the other of being "hysterical" or "panicked"; each adopts the same moralistic language of "decency," "healthy debate," "virulent attack," "barbarism," "decadence," and so on.[76] The Hitler analogy was applied by the left to Jesse Helms, Pat Buchanan, and Ronald Reagan, while the right applied it to Saddam Hussein.[77]

The current widespread panic and hysteria over censorship arise precisely because censorship cannot be limited to a recognizable state censorship apparatus. Censorship can be "found" everywhere—in the practices of curators, lenders, the NEA, magazine editors, journalists, art historians, historians, cultural critics—and it can be found by everyone—neoconservatives, the religious right, liberals, and the "radical" left. What counts as censorship will always be contested precisely because censorship is simulated; display and visibility cannot in and of themselves be antidotes to repression and invisibility since censorship involves not simply destruction but also displacement, transvaluation, and distortion.[78]

Eurotrash: The Nazis Meet Mickey Mouse

In arguing that censorship cannot be corrected precisely because it is a simulated performance, I want to suggest that the left's interest in politicizing aesthetics and cultural reproduction might be rethought in terms of the politics of the cultural migration of Europe to virtually the furthest point west in the United States, namely, Los Angeles. This means complicating two familiar accounts of Los Angeles, what Mike Davis terms "sunshine" and "noir." In the noir account, Los Angeles typifies the most decadent tendencies of capitalism, fulfilling a post-Nazi threat to European culture. As Mike Davis remarks, "Even as the walls come down in Eastern Europe, they are being erected all over Los Angeles."[79]

Twentieth-century critique of ideology in general is driven by the sense that the aestheticization of politics leads to fascism and war, and that accounts of fascism regularly link nazism and Hollywood; that is, fascism is generally defined as the desire to collapse the difference between the world and art, between the real and a simulated reality. In *Hitler, A Film from Germany*, Hans Jürgen Syberberg takes the collapse of the real and the false to be the Nazis' understanding of art:

> Hitler understood the significance of film. Now we are just as used to regarding his interest in film pejoratively, as if he had only wished to use it for propaganda purposes. We might even wonder whether he did not merely organize the Nuremburg rallies for Leni Riefenstahl, as certain elements might lead us to suppose, and, taking the argument a little further, whether the whole of the Second World War was not indeed constructed as a big budget war film, solely put on so it could be projected as newsreel each evening in his bunker.... The artistic organization of these mass ceremonies, recorded on celluloid, and even the organization of the final collapse, were part of the overall programme of the movement. Hitler saw the war and its newsreel footage as his heroic epic.[80]

As Philippe Lacoue-Labarthe points out, Syberberg has in mind here the production of a "Hollywood aesthetic" in Nazi Germany itself.[81]

Los Angeles has been for these critics the future of nazism, a more advanced form of fascism. The Gulf War, known commonly as the video war for a number of reasons, only appeared to provide further confirmation of this view of fascism. The attention paid by Mike Davis and others to Los Angeles focuses in part on the way Hollywood manufactures the collapse between the real and the simulated in the public sphere of the United States. (Coincidentally, a week after the LACMA exhibition closed, parades celebrating the Gulf War victory were held in Hollywood.) In left critiques of the video war, Hollywood figured centrally. Consider a *Nation* editorial on a commemorative fireworks display just before the Fourth of July, 1991:

> The bizarre aerial ballet was the climax of a fireworks display in honor of the warriors of Desert Storm that had opened with strains of *Thus Spake Zarathustra*—better known to most Americans as the theme from the movie *2001* (and, appropriately, written by Richard Strauss, one of the Nazis' favorite composers). An observer remembered how Ronald Reagan, who fought World War II exclusively in Hollywood, had told Israeli Prime Minister Yitzhak Shamir that he had served as photographer with the troops liberating the Nazi death camps. Now all New York City had moved into Reagan's mind: The distinction between movies and life, fantasy and reality, had blurred and vanished.[82]

The Gulf War and George Bush's new world order for many marked the installation of a *homo Reaganus* unconcerned with the difference between the real and the simulated image. It is indeed only too easy to imagine a commercial that would have followed the logic of the Superbowl celebration that began the patriotic, jingoistic celebration of the Gulf War: the all too appropriately named General Schwarzkopf (in full military regalia, of course) comes out of a battle scene full of burning tanks and responds to a voice-over question, "General, what are you going to do now?" by exclaiming with a broad smile, "I'm going to Disneyland!"

Indeed, Disneyland, even more than Hollywood, has stood for hypersimulation of a specifically American cultural politics. As Baudrillard writes:

> In fact, the cinema here [in the United States] is not where you think it is. It certainly is not to be found in the studios the tourists flock to—Universal, Paramount, etc., those subdivisions of Disneyland. If you believe that the whole of the Western world is hypostasized in America, the whole of America in California, and California in Disneyland, then this is the microcosm of the West.[83]

In his essay "What National Socialism Has Done to the Arts," Adorno presciently anticipates Disneyland's simulation of Europe. He closes by citing a "last danger" to European culture, namely, that it may be "theme-parked":

> I may call it the danger of the transformation of European culture into a kind of National Park, a realm tolerated and even admired, but mainly in terms of its quaintness, its being different from the general standards of technological manipulation of European culture. We have to be equally on our guard against an artificial preservation, its being put on exhibition, its being enjoyed for the sake of its uniqueness rather than for any inherent qualities. What happened to certain artists of the Boulevard Montparnasse, whose colorful appearance made them lovely to look at, but at the same time gave them the stigma of being fools, may happen to European culture as a whole. It may share the fate of European style furniture or of European titles.[84]

From Adorno's perspective, one could argue that the LACMA exhibition resembled less a *Gesamtkunstwerk* than a kitschy ride in Disney's Fantasyland. That is to say, the exhibition followed out a trajectory from Adorno's "National Park of Culture" to what Louis Marin and Umberto Eco have termed the "degenerate utopia" of Disneyland.[85] In this trajectory, Disneyland comes to figure the degeneracy not only of Los Angeles but also of American culture as a whole, degeneracy being defined in part as the replacement of a political party system with apolitical house parties. The struggle over human rights is thereby reduced to struggle over the right to party; historical understanding is reduced to the ahistorical slogan of *Bill and Ted's Excellent Adventure* (set in San Dimas, California)—"Be excellent. Party on!"[86] The disastrously homogenizing effects of Disney on European culture have been noted by a critic who asserted that EuroDisney is a "cultural Chernobyl."[87]

In the "sunshine" left account, Los Angeles and kitsch in general provide an oppositional space, some kind of liberatory potential in an avant-garde postparty politics of the hangover. Mickey Mouse was at the center of the debate between Adorno and Benjamin over popular culture and high culture (in which new technologies of reproduction that make up mass culture are regarded either as liberating or as constraining and homogenizing).[88] (In the first version of his essay "The Work of Art in the Age of Mechanical Reproduction," Walter Benjamin had a section entitled "Mickey Maus." Adorno discussed Mickey Mouse critically in a critique of the sadomasochism of American jazz.)[89] Benjamin celebrated Mickey Mouse along with Charlie Chaplin and dada as examples of the progressive shock effect of avant-garde mechanically reproduced culture, namely, photography and cinema. Adorno saw Benjamin's attempt to defend "kitsch" as undialectical, "out-and-out romanticization."[90]

Benjamin's celebration of Mickey Mouse and Adorno's critique of his celebration were both anticipated by the Nazis, who were of course extremely interested in kitsch, and it is worth pointing out that by the 1920s, German art criticism had connected the topics of kitsch and degeneration.[91] The Nazis' ambivalent attitude toward Disney products mirrors the ambivalence in Benjamin and Adorno. On the one hand, the Nazis were fond of Mickey Mouse, putting him on everything from bomber airplanes to coffee cups.[92] On the other hand, they condemned films like *Fantasia* as a grotesque American "Verkitschung" (kitschification) of high German culture, objecting in particular to the "hot jazz" sequence in the middle of *Fantasia.* Confiscated copies of Disney's animated feature films were nevertheless unofficially shown to Nazi elites (many turned up in Hitler's bunker).[93] A distinction between a neoconservative (supposedly apolitical) auratic art and a progressive, antifascist, mechanically reproduced, kitschy "Kunstpolitik" is hence a non-starter. As Adorno said in a letter to Benjamin, "When you mention Mickey Mouse, things get complicated."[94]

One might want to argue that both the sunshine and the noir left accounts of the migration of European culture to Los Angeles are irrelevant given the present status of Europe. Reduced to "Euro-trash," Europe no longer provides an alternative place from which one could criticize the decadent, degenerate developments of the United States. The classic ideal of the city that has informed critiques of Los Angeles has fallen apart as Europe itself has suffered cultural deterioration. As André Corboz points out in his *Looking for a City in America*, Europe now bears a paradoxical resemblance to what it claims to despise in the United States.[95]

In my view, the problem with the sunshine and noir accounts of Los Angeles is not so much their irrelevance as that Eurotrash— understood not simply in a pejorative sense but dialectically, as a tension between civilization and its destruction, deterioration, and ruination—has always been both the origin and the telos of European culture. Cultural transmission has always meant cultural reproduction, and reproduction in turn has always meant displacement and distortion. Viewed as Eurotrash, Nazi art and art administration look deeply paradoxical, and this paradox is precisely what present "oppositional" stances toward nazism and neonazism fail to address.[96] A revised understanding of nazism might help us to contextualize rather differently what many on the left and right see as a return in the United States and in Germany to the cultural and political crisis of the Weimar Republic. For however barbaric the Nazis were (and I take it that this point is not in dispute in academic circles), the very charge of barbarism typically complicates the ethical drive to remember the Nazi past by inculcating a stupefaction at its horror/banality: nazism was an aberration, the Nazi account of world history was an aberration, the Nazi account of art was an aberration in a world march toward modernism; hence, nazism is exceptional and unworthy of sustained attention. Yet any museum exhibition (or critical analysis) that assumes stable differences between the Nazis and the avant-garde (or, more broadly, modernism), that simply demonizes the Nazis, will paradoxically make that exhibition less historically and aesthetically significant and introduce in turn a comic irony that allows one to laugh the Nazis off. The Nazi case is thus intelligible only as a particularly acute instance of a long battle between censorship and artistic expression.

Rather than see (neo)nazism, fascism, censorship, and Hollywood hypersimulation as something to overcome, with Los Angeles representing either the disastrous eclipse of Western civilization or its displacement and preservation in a more liberal environment, we might see in the Nazis' dialectical relation to modernity a paradigm of the extreme contradictions of Western civilization, in which culture and barbarism have always met, as Walter Benjamin famously pointed out, though not always in the same way or for the same reasons.[97] Instead of being horrified at the cultural destruction of European culture (or the European destruction of other cultures), we might consider regarding the Nazis as a paradoxically reactionary—dare one say it? avant-garde—instance of European culture: for Eurotrash, understood dialectically, has arguably always already been the destination of Western culture.

NOTES

Versions of this essay were delivered at a special session of the 1991 Modern Language Association convention entitled "Policing the Aesthetic: Political Criticism and the Public Sphere" (I chaired the session); at the University of Michigan Department of English; and at the 1992 Rethinking Marxism conference at the University of Massachusetts, Amherst. I would like to thank Nancy Vickers for drawing my attention to the LACMA exhibition and for her brilliant insights into it. I am also indebted to Christine Kravits (aka TinaK), Jeneen Hobby, Jeffrey Wallen, and Jim Wald for helping me with my German and for alerting me to (and in many cases providing me with) resources on modern German history. I would like to thank Christine Kravits for accompanying me to the Berlin installation of the LACMA exhibition. I am indebted to Hussein Ibish for his thoughtful remarks about nazism and its relation to modernism. My thanks as well to Eric Pauls, coordinator of twentieth-century art at the Los Angeles County Museum of Art, for making press material available to me, including the two photographs of the Nazi dada wall, and for allowing me to reproduce the cover of the guidebook (fig. 4, designed by Jim Drobka). My thanks to Dave Smith of Disney Archives for material on Mickey Mouse and the Nazis, to Tim Street-Porter for his photographs of the LACMA installation, to the Brooklyn Museum of Art for the photo of the Joseph Kosuth installation (fig. 14), and to the Richard M. Nixon Library for permission to reproduce the photo of the Berlin Wall (fig. 13). I am particularly indebted to Mary Russo, who helped me frame my discussion of Los Angeles in relation to the debate over Eurocentrism and for the term *Eurotrash*; I am also grateful for a copy of her unpublished essay "Venice, Venice, and L.A.," delivered at the 1992 Rethinking Marxism conference in a panel (which we co-organized) entitled "Displacing Europe: Los Angeles as the End of Western Culture?"

1. The LACMA exhibition opened in Los Angeles (February 17 to May 12, 1991), then traveled to the Art Institute of Chicago (June 22 to September 8), the Smithsonian (Octo-

ber 16 to January 12), and the Akademie der Kunst, Berlin Altes Museum (March 3 to May 31, 1992). A documentary on the exhibition and its tour aired on PBS stations April 11, 1993. For the catalog, see Stephanie Barron et al., eds., *"Degenerate Art": The Fate of the Avant-Garde in Nazi Germany* (Los Angeles: Museum Associates, Los Angeles County Museum of Art, 1991).

2. Stephanie Barron spells out this agenda at the close of her introductory essay to the catalog: "Newspaper articles on public support of the arts and the situation facing the National Endowment for the Arts emphasize an uncomfortable parallel between these issues and those raised by the 1937 exhibition, between the enemies of artistic freedom today and those responsible for organizing the *Entartete Kunst* exhibition" ("1937: Modern Art and Politics in Prewar Germany," in *"Degenerate Art,"* 24).

3. Patrick Goldstein, "It's Not Easy Being Notorious... Unless You're Madonna," *Los Angeles Times*, May 5, 1991, C1.

4. Ibid., C7.

5. I would argue for the sophistication of Madonna's video "Express Yourself" on two grounds: director David Fincher's brilliant editing and his inclusion of Grosz's boxing imagery in the last sequence. See John Willet, *The Weimar Years: A Culture Cut Short* (New York: Abbeville, 1984), 106-7.

6. Consider Madonna's MTV commercials for *Truth or Dare* just after it was released. They focused on the attempted censorship of "Like a Virgin"; in the second version, the word *masturbation* was bleeped out. The second version broadcasts an undecidable definition of censorship: one could read the commercial as a self-conscious joke about censorship (MTV makes fun of failed censors) or as an invitation to take seriously attempts to censor Madonna.

7. Jean Baudrillard, *America*, trans. Chris Turner (London: Verso, 1989); Theodor Adorno, *Minima Moralia: Reflections from Damaged Life* (London: New Left Books, 1971); Harvey Gross, "Adorno in Los Angeles: The Intellectual in Emigration," *Humanities in Society* 2, no. 4 (Fall 1979): 339-52; Fredric Jameson, *Postmodernism: or, the Cultural Logic of Late Capitalism* (Durham, N.C.: Duke University Press, 1991); Edward W. Soja, *Postmodern Geographies: The Reassertion of Space in Critical Social Theory* (London: Verso, 1989); Edward W. Soja, "Inside Exopolis: Scenes from Orange County," in *Variations on a Theme Park: The New American City and the End of Space*, ed. Michael Sorkin (New York: Noonday, 1992), 94-122. See also Jean-François Lyotard, *Pacific Wall*, trans. Bruce Boone (Venice, Calif.: Lapis, 1989), and Jacques Derrida, "Faxitexture," in *Anywhere*, ed. Cynthia C. Davidson (New York: Rizzoli, 1993), 18-33.

8. Mike Davis, *City of Quartz: Excavating the Future of Los Angeles* (London: Verso, 1991), 18. See also Mike Davis, "Hollywood et Los Angeles: un mariage difficile," in *Hollywood 1927-1941: La propagande par les rêves ou le triomphe du modèle américain*, ed. Alain Masson (Paris: Autrements, 1991), 16-30. On the L.A. riots, see Mike Davis, "Burning All Illusions in L.A.," in *Inside the L.A. Riots* (New York: Institute for Alternative Journalism, 1992), 96-100.

9. Max Horkheimer and Theodor Adorno, "The Culture Industry: Enlightenment as Mass Deception," in *The Dialectic of Enlightenment* (New York: Seabury, 1969), 120-67. Even when they were not writing cultural criticism in Los Angeles, the city dominated the imagination of these cultural critics. See Jean-Michel Palmier, *Weimar en exil* vol. 2, *Exil en Amérique* (Paris: Payot, 1988).

10. Davis, *City of Quartz*, 20.

11. The terms of Mike Davis's critique of Los Angeles, *sunshine* and *noir*, echo a long tra-

dition of cultural criticism of Adorno's "pessimistic" account of administered culture, a criticism first made by Adorno himself. See Theodor Adorno, "The Culture Industry Reconsidered," in *The Culture Industry: Selected Essays on Mass Culture*, ed. J. M Bernstein (London and New York: Routledge, 1991), 85-92; Douglas Crimp, *On the Museum's Ruins* (Cambridge, Mass.: MIT Press, 1993); Terry Eagleton, *The Ideology of the Aesthetic* (Oxford: Basil Blackwell, 1990); and Martin Jay, *Adorno* (Cambridge, Mass.: Harvard University Press, 1984).

12. Cathy Curtis, "Hollywood Collects," *Art News* 90, no. 9 (November 1991): 102-7; G. Luther Whitington, "L.A.'s New Look," *Art and Auction* 14, no. 6 (January 1992): 82-85; Eleanor Hartney, "The New Patronage," *Art in America* 80, no. 1 (January 1992): 72-79. The photo of Madonna at a gallery opening is in Curtis, "Hollywood Collects," 103.

13. Michael M. Thomas, "Architectural Digest Visits Madonna," *Architectural Digest*, November 1991, 198-209. It is noteworthy that Kahlo in the 1920s and 1930s was on the left (married to Diego Rivera) while de Lempika was on the right (she painted Italian fascist nobility). Both artists had exhibitions in Paris during the 1920s. Madonna is considering making a movie of Kahlo's life (Goldstein, "It's Not Easy Being Notorious," C7), and she adapts paintings by de Lempika in her video "Open Your Heart," for which she subsequently ran into censorship difficulties with de Lempika's estate. (See Walter Robinson, "Tamara v. Madonna," *Art in America* 80, no. 11 [November 1992]: 37.) One could regard Madonna's interest in these painters as another instance of her implosion of opposites. What unites Madonna and the two artists, apart from gender, however, is their common interest in publicity. On Madonna's art collection, see Susan Kandel, "Madonnarama," *Artspace* 16, no. 6 (December 1992): 42-43. Kandel compares Madonna's artistic practices to those of Cindy Sherman and Jeff Koons. For another favorable assessment that tries to save Madonna for feminism (in this case by linking her to Kahlo), see Janice Bergman-Carton, "Like an Artist," *Art in America* 81, no. 1 (January 1993): 35-39.

14. Mike Davis, *City of Quartz*, 236-40. Davis's assessment of Gehry is confirmed by Gehry's work for Disney. See Mark Swed, "Pacific Overtures," *Connoisseur*, February 1992, 16-19, 92-94.

15. For a similar point, see Steven Kasher, "The Art of Hitler," *October* 59 (1992): 81.

16. As Peter Selz points out, LACMA reproduced the Nazi exhibition in "minute detail," so minute, in fact, that many details are effectively censored (Peter Selz, "Degenerate Art Reconstructed," *Arts Magazine* [September 1991]: 59). The model did not translate the quotations from Hitler and Goebbels, and other wall texts were not even written in German (only a kind of scrawl was visible). Similarly, the "graffiti" under the statues and paintings was so small as to be unreadable. Thus, even if one knew German, one could not have overcome the censorship here, although one could turn to the LACMA catalog, which did reprint the graffiti legibly. (Conversely, the German "Entartete Kunst" rather than "Degenerate Art" was used throughout the LACMA exhibition to mark it as other.) The small scale prevented one from seeing that the paintings were hung in an expressionist manner (by one string rather than the customary two) so that they all look distorted and off-kilter. The minute reproduction of the Munich exhibition seemed designed to reduce it to insignificance. This strategy, undoubtedly unconscious, seemed to be furthered by the reproductions in the LACMA exhibition of the original Munich exhibition on black and white display cards. By contrast, the LACMA display cards of the paintings bought by German museums between the end of the nineteenth century and the Nazis' rise to power reproduce the artworks in color. Furthermore, the heterogeneity of the typography in the Nazi exhibition deflected attention from the monolithic typography in the

LACMA exhibition. The Nazis institutionalized typography pioneered by the Bauhaus because the old German script was too difficult for many Germans to read.

17. The modifier *partially* is used inconsistently by the LACMA curators to describe the reconstruction. In many cases, it is dropped (as in the catalog dust jacket copy).

18. On the Wagnerian *Gesamtkunstwerk* and mass culture, see Annette Michelson, "'Where Is Your Rupture?': Mass Culture and Gesamtkunstwerk," *October* 56 (1991): 43–63.

19. Jonathan Crary, "Spectacle, Attention, and Counter-Memory," *October* 50 (1989): 97-107.

20. In addition to the overture to Wagner's *Tannhauser*, the overture to Wagner's *Rienzi*, which deeply influenced Hitler, also played—also uncredited—on a continuously running video in the first room.

21. LACMA *Degenerate Art Exhibition Guidebook*, 4.

22. The phrase "didactic walls" was used by Eric Pauls, coordinator of twentieth-century art at LACMA, in our telephone conversations.

23. Bertold Hinz, "Degenerate Art," in *Art in the Third Reich*, trans. Robert and Rita Kimber (New York: Pantheon, 1979), 173-86; Benjamin H. D. Buloch, "From Faktura to Factography," in *October: The First Decade, 1976-1986*, ed. Annette Michelson et al. (Cambridge, Mass., and London: MIT Press, 1989), 76-113.

24. Michael Kimmelman, "Examining Works by Artists the Nazis Hounded and Scorned," *New York Times*, February 25, 1991, B1.

25. Christopher Zuschlag, "An 'Educational' Exhibition: The Precursors of *Entartete Kunst* and Its Individual Venues," in Barron, *"Degenerate Art,"* 83-104.

26. Andrea Fraser, "Notes on the Museum's Publicity," *Lusitania: A Journal of Reflection and Oceanography* 1 (Fall 1990): 49. See also Andrea Fraser, "Museum Highlights: A Gallery Talk," *October* 57 (1991): 103-22.

27. Fraser, "Notes on the Museum's Publicity," 53.

28. My notion of censorship operating positively as spin is indebted to Edward S. Herman and Noam Chomsky, *Manufacturing Consent: The Political Economy of the Mass Media* (New York: Pantheon, 1988), xiv-xv. My account of censorship differs only in that I think the alternative to a given spin is another spin, not "the Truth."

29. For the Bloch and Lukács debate, see Ernst Bloch, "Discussing Expressionism," in *Aesthetics and Politics, Debates between Bloch, Lukács, Brecht, Benjamin, Adorno*, ed. Rodney Livingstone (London: Verso, 1977), 16-27; Georg Lukács, "Realism in the Balance," in *Aesthetics and Politics*, 28-59; and Georg Lukács, "Expressionism: Its Significance and Decline," in *Essays on Realism*, ed. Rodney Livingstone and David Fernbach (Cambridge, Mass.: MIT Press, 1980), 76-113. See also Georg Lukács, "The Ideology of Modernism," in *Realism in Our Time: Literature and the Class Struggle*, trans. John and Necke Mander (New York: Harper & Row, 1964).

30. For Bloch's reviews, see "Jugglers' Fair Beneath the Gallows" and "Expressionism, Seen Now," in *The Heritage of Our Times*, trans. Neville and Steven Plaice (Berkeley and Los Angeles: University of California Press, 1991), 75-80, 234-50.

31. Barbara Harrington and Elizabeth Hess, "Editor's Introduction to 'NEA Offensive Plays: A Special Supplement,'" *Drama Review* 35 (Fall 1991): 128-30; David Wojnarowicz, *Witnesses: Against Our Vanishing* (New York: Artists Space, 1989); *David Wojnarowicz: Tongues of Flame*, ed. Barry Blinderman (New York: Art Publishers, 1990). See also Joe Jarrel, "God Is in the Details: Wojnarowicz Is in the Courts," *High Performance* 51 (Fall 1990): 20-21.

32. For a discussion of this film in the context of Weimar culture, see Richard Dyer, *Now You See It: Studies on Lesbian and Gay Film* (New York: Routledge, 1990), 7-47.

33. The LACMA catalog does address the question of homosexuality. See George L. Mosse's essay, "Beauty without Sensuality/The Exhibition *Entartete Kunst*," in Barron, *Degenerate Art*, 25-32. The audiotape mentioned the "homosexual theme" in relation to two paintings by Karl Hofer entitled *Friends* (one is of two lesbians, the other of two gay men).

34. Perhaps LACMA excluded the Bauhaus because it compromised with the Nazis. Mies van der Rohe expelled a socialist director, introduced new student disciplinary measures, and forbade discussion of political topics. See Frank Whitford, *Bauhaus* (London: Thames and Hudson, 1984), 192-96.

35. For recent attempts to question this taboo on displaying Nazi art, see Steven Kasher, "Art of Hitler," and Peter Adam, *Art of the Third Reich* (New York: Abrams, 1992).

36. Hinz, "Degenerate Art"; Jens Malte Fischer, " 'Entartete Kunst,'" *Merkur* 38, no. 33 (April 1984): 46-52; George Bussman, " 'Degenerate Art'—A Look at a Useful Myth," in *German Art in the Twentieth Century: Painting and Sculpture 1905-1985*, ed. Christos M. Joachimides et al. (London: Royal Academy of Arts, 1985), 113-24; Igor Golomstock, *Totalitarian Art* (New York: HarperCollins, 1990), 102-10; Frank Whitford, "The Triumph of the Banal: Art in Nazi Germany," in *Visions and Blueprints: Avant-Garde Culture and Radical Politics in Early Twentieth Century Europe*, ed. Edward Timms and Peter Collier (Manchester: Manchester University Press, 1988), 239-69; Selz, "Degenerate Art Reconstructed," 58-60. For a view with which I am in sympathy, see Fred Dewey, "Fascinating Fascism," *New Statesman and Society* (May 1991): 10, 30-32. For a more modest but nonetheless powerful critique of the limited historical context for relating fascism and modernism, see Emily Braun, "The Return of the Repressed," *Art in America* 79, no. 10 (October 1991): 116-23, 174.

37. Peter Clothier, " 'Degenerate Art' Redux," *Art Space* 34, no. 2 (Summer 1991): 86-87.

38. Robert Darnton, "The Fall of the House of Art: Hitler's Blitzkrieg against Modern Art," *New Republic*, May 6, 1991, 33; Frank Whitford, "The Triumph of the Banal," 248.

39. I have drawn on the following writers: Hans Jürgen Syberberg, *Hitler: A Film from Germany*, trans. Joachim Neugroschel (New York: Farrar, Straus & Giroux, 1982); Jeffrey Herf, *Reactionary Modernism: Technology, Culture, and Politics in Weimar and the Third Reich* (Cambridge: Cambridge University Press, 1984); Ian Kershaw, *The Hitler Myth: Image and Reality in the Third Reich* (Oxford: Clarendon, 1987); Peter Sloterdijk, *Critique of Cynical Reason*, trans. Michael Eldred (Minneapolis: University of Minnesota Press, 1987); and Zygmaunt Bauman, *Modernity and the Holocaust* (Ithaca, N.Y.: Cornell University Press, 1989).

40. Sloterdijk, *Critique of Cynical Reason*.

41. The connection is made in the 1987 Munich catalog. See Peter-Klaus Schuster, "München—das Verhängnis einer Kunststadt," in *Die "Kunststadt" München 1937: Nationalsozialismus und "Entartete Kunst"*, ed. Peter-Klaus Schuster (Munich: Prestel-Verlag, 1987), 30-31. A photo of the dada exhibition appears in virtually every history of Weimar and dada. See, for example, Marc Dachy, *The Dada Movement 1915-1923* (New York: Rizzoli, 1990), 106, where the parallels between the dada and Nazi exhibitions are noted. The parallels are also noted by Peter Adam in his *Art of the Third Reich* (New York: Abrams, 1992), 123.

42. Hanne Bergius, "Berlin, the Dada Metropolis," in *The 1920s: Age of the Metropolis*, ed. Jean Clair (Montreal: Montreal Museum of Fine Arts, 1991), 262-63.

43. Cited by Bergius, ibid., 263.

44. Bürger, *Theory of the Avant-Garde*, 53-57. Partly what is at stake in a reading of the dada wall is a reading of the politics of avant-garde and modernism, particularly the way the avant-garde often embraced fascism. On this point, see Raymond Williams, "The Politics of the Avant-Garde," in *The Politics of Modernism: Against the New Conformists* (London: Verso, 1988), 49-64, and Fredric Jameson, *Fables of Aggression: Wyndham Lewis, the Modernist as Fascist* (Berkeley: University of California Press, 1979).

45. Thomas Kuhn, *The Structure of Scientific Revolutions* (Chicago: University of Chicago Press, 1970).

46. Associated with *New Criterion* and *October*, respectively, the two groups have engaged in a long feud over art and politics. Crimp attacks Kramer at length, for example, in "The Art of Exhibition" (see note 11). See Hilton Kramer, "Hitler and the War against Modernism," *New Criterion* 10, no. 1 (September 1991): 1-3.

47. Bernhard Schulz, "Portraiert: Kalifornischer Kunstverstand," *Der Tagesspiegel*, March 21, 1992, 4.

48. Serge Schmemann, "West Germans Debate Disposition of Nazi Art," *New York Times*, May 23, 1988, C13.

49. Stephen Kinzer, "Nazi Show of 'Bad' Art Reopens in Berlin," *New York Times*, March 5, 1992, C15.

50. In addition to Schmemann, "West Germans Debate," see Titus Arn, "Aus dem Depot ins Museum?" *Frankfurter Allegemeine Zeitung* (January 17, 1991): 18; Klaus Staek, "Nazi Kunst in Museum?" *Die Zeit* (overseas) no. 40-3 (October 1987), 14; Karl-Heinz Jansen, "Sonder-auftrag Linz," *Die Zeit* (overseas) no. 2-9 (January 1987): 11-12.

51. Schmemann, "West Germans Debate."

52. Ibid.

53. Emily Braun, "The Return of the Repressed," 116-23, 174.

54. On the Berlin installation, see Matthew Collings, "Resistance Heroes of Art," *Guardian Weekly*, May 31, 1992, 13; Suzanne Muchnic, " 'Degenerate Art' Attracts Berliners," *Los Angeles Times*, April 2, 1992, F14; Kinzer, "Nazi Show of 'Bad' Art Reopens," C15, C19.

55. The Museum of Tolerance opened February 9, 1993. See "Near Riot's Ashes, a Museum Based on Tolerance," *New York Times*, February 10, 1993. On the fragment of the wall behind the Reagan Library, see Maud Lavin, "Berlin after the Wall," *Art in America* 78, no. 2 (February 1990): 69-73. The fragment that was dedicated at the Nixon Library on August 13, 1992, "matched pound for pound the chunk at the Reagan Library a few miles to the north" (Seth Mydans, "Painting of Heroic Size Shows Nixon to Match," *New York Times* [August 13, 1992]: A16). The paradoxical way that the Museum of Tolerance terminates intolerance was made concrete in a CBS-TV "Good Morning America" interview with Arnold Schwarzenegger at the Museum of Tolerance on February 8, 1993. Bizarrely, Paula Zahn ended the interview by congratulating Schwarzenegger on *Terminator 3*. For a fine critical analysis of this museum, see James E. Young, *The Texture of Memory: Holocaust Memorials and Meaning* (New Haven, Conn.: Yale University Press, 1993), 306-9.

56. Petra Von Kipphoff, "Schöne Rekonstruktion des Schrecklichen," *Die Zeit*, no. 9 (February 22, 1991): 63.

57. For an opposite take on the exhibition (that it was not topical enough) when it appeared in Chicago, see Susan Snodgrass, "Ambiguous Politics," *Dialogue* 14, no. 5 (September/October 1991): 11.

58. On this case, see Stephen C. Dubin, *Arresting Images: Impolitic Art and Uncivil Actions* (New York: Routledge, 1992), 205-17.

59. My account here is based on interviews with William Moritz, who helped construct the historical room devoted to film in the LACMA exhibition, July 26 and 28, 1991.

60. Peter Marcuse, "Purging the Professoriat," *Linguafranca* 2, no. 2 (December 1991): 32-36. See also Marshall Tyler, "New Wall Goes Up in Germany," *Los Angeles Times*, August 20, 1992, A1, A18-19.

61. Katie Hafner, "A Nation of Readers Dumps Its Writers," *New York Times Magazine*, January 10, 1993, 22-26, 46-47.

62. Christian Caryl, "DDR Censorship on Show," *Times Literary Supplement*, May 31, 1991, 14. For the catalog, see Ernest and Herbert Wiesner, *Zensur in der DDR: Geschichte, Praxis, und Aesthetik der Behinderung von Literatur, Ausstellungs Buch* (Berlin: Literaturhaus Berlin, 1991).

63. Ferdinand Protzman, "Is East German Art Really Art?" *International Herald Tribune*, January 5-6 1991, 6; Maud Lavin, "Berlin after the Wall," *Art in America* 78, no. 2 (February 1990): 69-73; Giulia Ajmone Marsan, "Reunited Germany: The Painful Westernizing of the 751 Museums Once Behind the Wall," *Art Newspaper*, no. 13 (December 1991): 5; Michael Z. Wise, "Berlin Struggles to Unite Museum Landscape," *Journal of Art* 4, no. 8 (October 1991): 18; David Galloway, "The New Berlin: 'I Want My Wall Back,'" *Art in America* 79, no. 9 (September 1991): 98-103.

64. "The National Socialists pronounced Otto Dix's work Degenerate Art, but nowadays his paintings are worth millions. Four hundred million marks is the sum for which the latest [1992 Tate Gallery] Dix exhibition is insured" (*Scala: The Magazine from Germany*, no. 4 [August/September 1991] 44). On the Dix exhibition at the Tate, see Nicholas Serota, ed., *Otto Dix, 1891-1969* (London: Tate Gallery, 1992) and Neal Acherson, "The Fuhrer's Freak Show," (London) *Independent, Sunday Review*, February 1992: 12-13. On the Heartfield exhibition, which began in Berlin and ended in Los Angeles, see Susanne Schreiber, "Shooting to Kill: The Camera as Weapon: John Heartfield, Ambassador for Dada to Berlin, and Agit-Prop Artist Extraordinaire," *Art Newspaper*, no. 12 (November 1991): 7, and William Wilson's review of the LACMA installation (which opened October 22, 1993, and closed January 2, 1994), "Heartfield's Powerful Attack on Elitism, Society's Ills," *Los Angeles Times*, October 22, 1993, F17.

65. Peter Bürger, *Theory of the Avante-Garde*; Rosalind Krauss, *The Originality of the Avant-garde and Other Modernist Myths* (Cambridge, Mass.: MIT Press, 1987). See also Christa Bürger, "The Disappearance of Art: The Postmodernism Debate in the U.S.," *Telos*, no. 68 (Summer 1986): 93-106, and Peter and Christa Bürger, *The Institutions of Art* (Lincoln: University of Nebraska Press, 1992).

66. According to William Moritz, LACMA did consider alternative ways of constructing the exhibition. In one proposal, the graffiti would have been written on a glass wall placed two to three feet from the paintings; museumgoers would have been able to look at the paintings in front of the glass and through the glass.

67. I allude here to Douglas Crimp's essay "The Art of Exhibition" in *On the Museum's Ruins*, 236-81. That any counter-Nazi exhibition would in this sense inevitably be implicated in fascist strategies is clear from the problems of reproducing Nazi art. Steven Kasher says that an exhibition of Hitler's art would politicize aesthetics and counter contemporary fascism ("Art of Hitler," 81). But it is not that straightforward. Peter Adam's *Art of the Third Reich*, for example, has been criticized for taking pleasure in the art it criticizes: "What is disturbing about *Art of the Third Reich* is that, like the art it discusses, it too

seems designed to please a popular audience.... There is a curious ambiguity to the book. Though Adam's text includes the necessary critical and political disclaimers, the layout and format pander to a widespread fascination with Nazi memorabilia, attractively displaying the kind of 'forbidden' art that will hopefully sell books." See Brooks Adams, "Art for the Fuhrer," *Art in America* 80, no. 9 (October 1992): 50. The reproduction of Nazi art, in short, is just as complex as the reproduction of modern art.

68. On censorship of neo-Nazi rock music, see Ferdinand Protzman, "Music of Hate Raises the Volume in Germany," *New York Times*, December 2, 1992, A1, A10. On euthanasia, see Peter Singer, "On Being Silenced in Germany," *New York Review of Books* 38, no. 14 (August 15, 1991): 36–42. On neo-Nazis, see "Racism's Back," *Economist*, November 16–22, 1991, 12–13; Frederick Kempe, "Neonazi Menace: Germans Try to Stem Right Wing Attacks on Foreigners," *Wall Street Journal*, December 4, 1991, A1, A13; Thomas Kielinger, "Why the Neonazis Pose a Threat to the New United Germany," *European*, October 11–13, 1991, 10; and Stephen Kinzer, "Klan Seizes on Germany's Wave of Racist Violence," *New York Times*, November 3, 1991, 15.

69. Hafner, "A Nation of Readers," 26. On Wolf's collaboration with the Stasi, see "Die Angsliche Margarete," *Der Spiegel*, no. 4/47 (January 25, 1993): 158–65.

70. For the catalog, see *Jewish Thought and Beliefs: Life and Work within the Cultures of the World* (Berlin: Argon, 1992).

71. On the cover of the invitation to the opening at the Galerie St. Etienne was a Sue Coe graphic of Anita Hill being burned as a witch in front of U.S. senators, ahistorically implying an equivalence between Hill's status as a "victim" and prisoners killed in Nazi concentration camps. My thanks to my colleague James Young for calling my attention to this exhibition.

72. See Maurice Berger, "Too Shocking to Show?" *Art in America* 80, no. 7 (July 1992): 37–41.

73. David Freedberg, *The Play of the Unmentionable: An Installation by Joseph Kosuth at the Brooklyn Museum* (New York: New Press in association with the Brooklyn Museum, 1992). See also Grace Glueck, "At Brooklyn Museum, Artist Surveys the Ojectionable," *New York Times*, December 17, 1990, C11, C14; Roberta Smith, "Unmentionable Art Through the Ages," *New York Times*, November 11, 1990, 39, 43; and Ken Johnson, "Forbidden Sights," *Art in America* 79, no. 1 (January 1991): 106–09.

74. David Freedberg, "Joseph Kosuth and the Play of the Unmentionable," in *Play of the Unmentionable*, 45.

75. For attempts to fuse Baudrillard with Freud through the use of terms like *panic* and *hysteria*, see Arthur Kroker and David Cook, *The Postmodern Scene: Excremental Culture and Hyper-Aesthetics* (New York: St. Martin's, 1986), and Arthur Kroker, ed., *The Panic Encyclopedia* (New York: St. Martin's, 1989). It is tempting, of course, to think that there is a distinction between those who panic and those who do not. Though it is probably impossible to resist making such a distinction in practice, I would argue that it can only be made through a significant degree of self-repression and misrecognition.

76. See Kasher, "Art of Hitler," 82, 84.

77. For an example of the collapse of the distinction between conservation and censorship, one might consider Frank Gehry's display of books burned or approved by the Nazis. According to Gehry, "this installation is all about fragility—and about censorship and conservation" (LACMA guidebook, 2). The viewer could sit on a bench to look at the books but not read the books since they were enclosed in glass cases. The difference between conservation and censorship (in terms of public as opposed to scholarly access)

was called into question. The hyperaestheticism of the display itself (the bookcases and the benches were made of beautiful red wood) attempted to negate this question. One might also note puns on "collecting" that the exhibition unintentionally admitted. The exhibition called into question the notion of collecting oneself in relation to the collection of works one puts on display. Furthermore, it called into question the relation between an art collection and historical recollection.

78. I take up the issues of invisibility, distortion, and displacement at length in my essays "Baroque Down: The Trauma of Censorship in Psychoanalysis and Queer Film Revisions of Shakespeare and Marlowe," forthcoming in *Shakespeare in the New Europe*, ed. Michael Hattaway et al. (Sheffield: University of Sheffield Press), and "(Un)Censoring in Detail: Thomas Middleton, Fetishism, and the Regulation of Dramatic Discourse," forthcoming in *Thomas Middleton and Early Modern Textual Culture: A Companion Volume*, ed. Gary Taylor et al. (Oxford: Oxford University Press, 1994).

79. Davis, *City of Quartz*, 226.

80. Syberberg, *Hitler, A Film from Germany*, 63.

81. Philippe Lacoue-Labarthe, *Heidegger, Art, and Politics*, trans. Chris Turner (Oxford: Basil Blackwell, 1990). See also Paul Virilio, *War and Cinema: The Logistics of Perception*, trans. Patrick Camiller (London: Verso, 1989).

82. "The Video War Comes Home," *Nation*, July 1, 1991, 558. See also Michael Rogin, *Ronald Reagan: The Movie and Other Episodes in Political Demonology* (Berkeley and Los Angeles: University of California Press, 1987).

83. Jean Baudrillard, *America*, 55.

84. Theodor Adorno, "What National Socialism Has Done to the Arts," in *Theodor W. Adorno Gesammelte Schriften* vol. 20: 2, ed. Rolf Tiedemann (Frankfurt am Main: Surkamp Verlag, 1984), 428.

85. Louis Marin, "Disneyland: A Degenerate Utopia," *Glyph*, no. 1 (Baltimore: Johns Hopkins University Press, 1977), 50–66; Umberto Eco, "Travels in Hyperreality," in *Travels in Hyperreality*, trans. William Weaver (New York: Harcourt Brace Jovanovich, 1983), 1–58.

86. Some might want to see Disney censorship as further evidence of this degeneration. See "Disney v. Oppenheim," *Art in America* 80, no. 12 (December 1992): 25; "Cable Networks Censor Toon Characters' Foibles," *Frighten the Horses*, no. 10 (1992): 52; and Gail Lane Cox, "Don't Mess with the Mouse," *National Law Journal*, July 31, 1989, 1–26.

87. Henri Haget, "Qui a peur de Mickey Mouse?" *L'Express*, March 27, 1992, 35.

88. For the primary texts of the debate, see Livingstone, *Aesthetics and Politics*, 100–141.

89. Walter Benjamin, "Das Kunstwerk im Zeitalter seiner technischen Reproduzierbarkeit," in *Walter Benjamin Gesammelte Schriften* vol. 1, no. 2, ed. Rolf Tiedemann and Hermann Schweppenhauser (Frankfurt am Main: Surkampf Verlag, 1974), 431–70 (first version); 471–508 (second version). Benjamin also discusses Mickey Mouse in "Zu Mickey Maus," *Schriften* vol. 6: 44–45; and *Schriften* vol. 2: 3, 962–63. For Adorno's own account of Mickey Mouse in an essay he saw as a reply to Benjamin's, see "Über Jazz," in *Gesammelte Schriften* vol. 17: 105.

90. Adorno, "Letters to Walter Benjamin," in Livingstone, *Aesthetics and Politics*, 122, 123.

91. The images and products are reproduced in *Im Reiche der Mickey Maus: Walt Disney in Deutschland 1927–1945: Eine Dokumentation zur Austellung im Filmmuseum Potsdam* (Berlin: Henschel Verlag, 1991) and Carsten Laqua, *Wie Mickey Unter die Nazis Fiel: Walt Disney und Deutschland* (Hamburg: Rowholt Taschenbuch Verlag, 1991). According to my informant, Rolf Flor, who unsuccessfully attempted to purchase a copy of *Im Reiche* for me in Berlin in May 1993, the book is no longer available because of

"copyright" violations. The editor of the book and curator of the exhibition was in prison at the time. For a provocative take on similarities between the Frankfurt school and the Nazis, see Laurence Rickels, "Mickey Marx," *Luisitiana*, 1992: 205-15; and Laurence Rickels, *The Case of California* (Baltimore: Johns Hopkins University Press, 1991). On Disney war propaganda, see also "Donald in Uniform," *Stern*, June 4, 1992, 204-6.

92. Laqua, *Wie Mickey*, 104-5, 108.

93. Adorno, "Letters to Walter Benjamin," in Livingstone, *Aesthetics and Politics*, 122.

94. See Fritz Karpfen, *Der Kitsch: Eine Studie über die Entartung der Kunst* (Hamburg: Weltbund-Verlag, 1925), Rolf Steinberg, ed., *Nazi-Kitsch* (Darmstadt, 1975), and Udo Pini, *Liebeskult und Liebeskitsch: Erotik im Dritten Reich* (Munich: Klinkhardt und Biermann, 1993). Adorno's writings on kitsch include "Zum *Anbruch*: Expose," *Schriften* 19: 601-02 and "Kitsch," *Schriften* 18: 791-94. *Anbruch*, the journal Adorno edited and in which he published, appeared in the Nazi "Degenerate Music" exhibition.

95. André Corboz, *Looking for a City in America: Down These Streets a Man Must Go*, trans. Denise Bratton (Santa Monica, Calif.: Getty Center for the History of Art and the Humanities, 1992), 58.

96. Christopher Phillips, "Berlin Museum Staffers Organize to Protest Right-Wing Violence," *Art in America* 81, no. 1 (January 1993): 23

97. Benjamin, "Theses on the Philosophy of History," in *Illuminations*, trans. Harry Zohn (New York: Schocken, 1969), 256. As Philippe Lacoue-Labarthe points out in *Heidegger, Art, and Politics*, Walter Benjamin's alternative to the fascist aestheticization of politics, namely, politicizing aesthetics, is itself a totalitarian aesthetic insofar as it conflates politics and asethetics; put more pointedly, Benjamin's assumptions about art and politics are not the opposite but the symmetrical counterpart of Goebbels's. See Lacoue-Labarthe, *Heidegger, Art, and Politics*, 61-70. For an account of the Russian avant-garde and Stalinism that complements my account of nazism, see Boris Groys, *The Total Art of Stalinism: Avant-Garde, Aesthetic Dictatorship, and Beyond*, trans. Charles Rougle (Princeton, N.J.: Princeton University Press, 1992).

The Contrast Hurts: Censoring the Ladies Liberty in Performance

Timothy Murray

> *Then I remembered my constitutional right to the pursuit of happiness,*
> *which says: even if there is no such thing as happiness, I got a right to*
> *pursue it.*
>
> —Lethal Weapon, in *The Lady Dick* by Holly Hughes

Two corollary binary oppositions have dominated artistic responses to debates over National Endowment for the Arts (NEA) funding and creative liberty: freedom versus censorship; individual expression versus governmental prohibition. There is little doubt that such binaries reflect the American habit of relying on the discourse of constitutional liberty to make the case for artistic license. Some of America's most politicized artists have adopted this universalist strategy in response to repressive charges made against them. Many activist art producers have relied on claims of freedom of expression rather than analyzing the attack on the critical imperatives of their work—even when the rhetorical thrust of their art produces a blatantly political or theoretical message. Adoption of this strategy responds primarily to the chilling reality that censorship, not misogyny, homophobia, or racism, is what the sympathetic politicians, journalists, and patrons seem to accept as an identifiable and unacceptable threat to the arts. Nevertheless, it is precisely this equation of liberty and anticensorship that I would like to challenge here by focusing on a few highly publicized attempts to "administer" aesthetics over the past two decades.

Since this essay will dwell more on conceptual tensions than on historical details, permit me to open with some brief introductory remarks on the paradox of censorship guiding my reflections. Even in the wake of governmental attempts to banish formidable feminist and gay projects in the arts, I wish to emphasize the paradox of the structural necessity of censorship in any administration of aesthetics, be it public or personal, political or psychoanalytical. For the economy of choice, whether in practice or theory, always entails the articulation of critical positions themselves governed by epistemological principles of selection and regulation. At issue in the administration of aesthetics, I suggest, is not so much the principle of artistic regulation itself as the aesthetic principles governing regulation, many of which can have exceptionally productive social effects.[1]

Of course censorship's negative psychopolitical effects are what fuel the anticensorial prejudice. Even the most fundamental aspect of censorship, that is, its constitutional role in psychic administration, can easily render the subject paranoid of its ever present pressures and powers. While censorship has been recognized since Freud as a fundamental attribute of productive libidinal communication (permitting preconscious communication between different ideational contents),[2] it is also understood in the same psychoanalytical context to serve as the core representational fabric of both repression and sublimation, of psychic regulation and intellectual productivity. In Freudian terms, censorship is what provides the agency of the superego's regulation of psychic waste "in keeping a watch over the actions and intentions of the ego and judging them."[3] And one would have no difficulty, following Foucault, in relating the modernist psychoanalytical notions of internal, sadomasochistic surveillance to early modern social formations that relied on the same nexus of perfidious observation and judgment to maintain a paranoid economy of social harmony and cultural productivity. Stated succinctly: paranoia of censorship and its effects are constitutional attributes of the human psyche and its cultural manifestations.

Paradoxically, Freud himself fell prey to the same anticensorial prejudice, which he theorized so well, by wishing to remove the receptive analyst from the troubling divisions of censorship. He recommends that the analyst maintain an "open line":

> The doctor must put himself in a position to make use of everything he is told for the purposes of interpretation and of recognizing the concealed unconscious material without substituting a censorship of his own for the selection that the patient has foregone. To put it in a formu-

la: he must turn his own unconscious like a receptive organ towards the transmitting unconscious of the patient. He must adjust himself to the patient as a telephone receiver is adjusted to the transmitting microphone. Just as the receiver converts back into sound-waves the electric oscillations in the telephone line which were set-up by sound waves, so the doctor's unconscious is able, from the derivates of the unconscious which are communicated to him, to reconstruct that unconscious, which has determined the patient's free associations.[4]

Wishing to deny the steadfastness of the interpreter's censorial prejudice, which Lacan has since identified as a function of "counter-transference,"[5] Freud equates the ideal analytical interaction with a transnarcissistic model of unmediated telecommunications. Freud's uncharacteristic trust in the freedom of expression belies, in much the same way as recent condemnations of artistic censorship, acknowledgment of the epistemological frames mediating any technological model of reception. This paradoxical tendency to link free and open reception to the look away from the censorial structures framing all communication is typical of the anticensorial prejudice and its frequent blindness to the hegemonic discourse of liberty containing it. Just such a trust in the freedom and liberty of expression, whether the medium be telecommunications, transnarcissism, or artistic performance, is precisely what blinds the analyst, artist, and critic to the structural censors of power and surveillance on which they have been led all too passively to depend.[6]

Consuming Lady Liberty

If Freud had been writing in the more contemporary environment of postmodernism, he might have turned to a different kind of sensory device for his seductive model of open analytical reception. I am thinking of the temporary sound and light machine designed by Iannis Xenakis for the opening of the Paris Pompidou Center in the mid-seventies. This was a geodesic dome filled with hundreds of lightbulbs and eight (I recall) laser beams bouncing off some forty tiny mirrors, all shifting and pulsating to the computer-controlled beat, to the *gestus*, of Xenakis's synthetic music. Inside this rhythmically blinding amoeba, the human spectators-as-performers became mesmerized by the "electric oscillations" of uncensored, phenomenological overkill, the postmodern victims of Artaudian assault. Much like Freud's infatuation with the open telephone line, Xenakis's interiorized spectacle may be representative of a bygone era in which the self-creating and self-consuming artistic machine was enough to wow its beholders into assuming the revolutionary importance of transnarcissistic engagement.[7] Under the veil of "uncensored" absorption, the novel glaze of laser-computer technology (perhaps like Freud's telephone) mystifies the ideological referents of the performative mechanics of reception, from the restricted use rights of international news satellites to the censorial power relations endorsed by seemingly benign technological celebrations.

These are the referents framing the excessive restaging of an earlier technological artifact from France, one whose lights still point to the stars but in a way more vividly reinscribing technology in the realm of the Symbolic, in the name of the forefathers, in the hands of the protectors of cultural extravagance and its capitalistic simulacra. I refer to the unveiling of the American idol of the 1980s, not the young lady Madonna, but the older one with the face-lift, the Lady Liberty.

For one seemingly endless Fourth of July weekend in 1986, the American media mustered its best forces to transmit the electronic oscillations of the Liberty Weekend Celebration that commemorated the restored statue and the liberty for which it stands. At the time, I was particularly struck by the ease with which the Liberty Weekend Celebration was represented both as immediately visible to the entire world and as a necessarily enviable spectacle of capitalism's ideological freedoms and technological achievements. Attesting to Webster's definition of *technology* as "the totality of the means employed by a people to provide itself with the objects of material culture," corporate America continued to capitalize on the event for weeks after that "very special day" (to recall the *New York Times* headline of July 5). Bloomingdale's, for one, turned pride to capital with "our Liberty Shops for an un-ending variety of souvenirs" and, returning to the media concern of this essay, "our Photo Essay and Video Tapes; documentation of the fabulous 4th. The magic is far from over. New York only." These alluring promises of unending delight appeared in fine print at the bottom of Bloomies's full-page newspaper advertisement on Sunday, July 13 (fig. 1). Framed under the watchful eyes of "Miss Liberty," the ad copy exudes patriotic

Last weekend was for everyone.
No exceptions. No one excluded.
The city, the country, the world was invited,
and all experienced a warm and positive celebration:
a re-affirmation of our values and beliefs.
It was a privilege for us to have contributed
to this historic event. To have been able to bring
4 consecutive days of the most memorable
fireworks in our history to Miss Liberty's Party.
From the opening ceremonies, thru the 4th, over
Liberty State Park, Central Park
and during the closing ceremonies
the skyline never looked more incredible.
Happy Birthday, and here's to the
next 100 years from everyone at
Bloomingdale's and A&S.

CELEBRATION PATRONS OF THE LIBERTY WEEKEND FIREWORKS

A&S bloomingdale's

A&S Search Is On For Spirited Woman '86! Phone 1-800-624-6831 for details. Applications at A&S Misses Better Sportswear Department.
The Celebration At Bloomingdale's Continues: come visit our Liberty Shops for an un-ending variety of souvenirs. Now open on 2 and 6. And, on Wednesday look for
our Photo Essay and Video Tapes; documentation of the fabulous 4th. The magic is far from over. New York only.

Fig. 1. Bloomingdale's advertisement, *New York Times*, July 13, 1986

confidence: "Last weekend was for everyone. No exceptions. No one excluded. The city, the country, the world was invited, and all experienced a warm and positive celebration: a re-affirmation of our values and beliefs. It was a privilege for us to have contributed to this historic event." This remembrance humbly echoed earlier boasts by the ABC television commentators—you know, the progressive ones like Ted Koppel and Barbara Walters—who just could not resist making claims that the celebratory weekend was staged "for the whole world to watch." From coast to coast, continent to continent, proud corporate sponsors from ABC, AT&T, and Chrysler to the upbeat subsidiaries of Procter & Gamble (Joy, Bounce, Ivory, Always, Bounty, Pampers, Sure) pooled their resources in admiration and nostalgia to celebrate liberty, that singular product of American material culture (fig. 2). It took but a metonymic slide for the sponsors of the popular soap operas "Another World," "As the World Turns," "Guiding Light," and "Search for Tomorrow" to shift their endorsement from one televisual "star" to another.[8] Although capitalistic enterprises have been known to join television in making centralizing claims just as brash, the mere possibility that the "whole" world could be imagined to be tuned to the same picture for four days (as it *was* during the Gulf War) suggests the extent to which video technology has widened the potential of the limitless performance of political "freedom" as combined ideology/commodity.[9]

This is the performance of *techné* that Martin Heidegger discussed in the fledgling years of video as something different from the neoclassical concept of theater as a picture mirroring the world, as something fundamentally different from Aristotelian mimesis. "With the word 'picture,'" writes Heidegger,

> we think first of all of a copy of something. Accordingly, the world picture would be a painting, so to speak, of what is as a whole. But 'world picture' means more than this. We mean by it the world itself, the world as such, what is, in its entirety, just as it is normative and binding for us.... Hence world picture, when understood essentially, does not mean a picture of the world but the world conceived and grasped as picture. What is, in its entirety, is now taken in such a way that it first is in being and only is in being to the extent that it is set up by man, who represents and sets forth.[10]

Thus we have the reshaping of Lady Liberty from an oversized artis-

CELEBRATE A "STAR" SPANGLED CENTENNIAL!

Another World
As the World Turns
Guiding Light
Search for Tomorrow

JOIN YOUR FAVORITE SOAP OPERA STARS TOMORROW AT 12 NOON ON PIER 11!

Come to Pier 11, South and Wall Streets, where Procter & Gamble Productions, the producers of ANOTHER WORLD, AS THE WORLD TURNS, GUIDING LIGHT, and SEARCH FOR TOMORROW, together with Soap Opera Festivals, will host an array of spectacular events featuring daytime TV's hottest stars. The action starts at noon and goes non-stop past nightfall! Plus, there'll be special surprises and free gifts from the sponsoring Procter & Gamble brands. Don't miss a minute of the excitement on Pier 11. It'll be the highlight of the Centennial!

SPONSORED BY:
Always, Bounce, Bounty, Cascade, Ivory. Joy, Pampers, Sure, Tide.

Fig. 2. Procter & Gamble advertisement, *New York Times,* July 3, 1986

tic gift that more or less haphazardly found itself poised opposite Ellis Island to a carefully crafted media event apparently giving the entire world no choice but to watch; for Liberty itself has become the "world picture."

Liberty weekend was uncanny in its embodiment of Heidegger's 1955 discussion, which maintains that "the fundamental event of the modern age [is] the conquest of the world as picture. The word 'picture' [*Bild*]," he adds,

> now means the structured image [*Gebild*] that is the creature of man's producing which represents and sets before. In such producing, man contends for the position in which he can be that particular being who gives the measure and draws up the guidelines for everything that is. Because this position secures, organizes, and articulates itself as a world view, the modern relationship to that which is, is one that becomes, in its decisive unfolding, a confrontation of world views.... For the sake of this struggle of world views and in keeping with its meaning, man brings into play his unlimited power for the calculating, planning, and molding of all things.[11]

Heidegger's comments work in retrospect as a particularly accurate summary of the calculated staging of an American political spectacle, yet another instance of man's locking his horns onto the politically feasible vision of the Virgin Mother (the "Lady," "Miss").

The four-day birthday party was calculated to transmit a maternal image of an America politically unified by its commitment to liberty regardless of the deep divisions of race, gender, and class better signified by the statue's corrosion than by the revitalized Lady's debut. While the Campbell Soup Company strategically cut against the grain by advertising that "even in the shadow of her torch—homeless Americans go hungry" (fig. 3), the opening night audience paid $5,000 a person to witness flag-waving testimonials by nostalgic cold war entertainers and their buddy, President Ronald Reagan. The staged event of the statue's unveiling even glorified the form of technology then pushing the confrontation of worldviews to a breaking point. From a command post on Governor's Island, and in front of the same French President Mitterrand who had most recently refused to grant air rights to American bombers headed for Libya, Ronny Ray-gun relit the statue by pushing a button activating the laser beams of his Strategic Defense Initiative. Here the unstable technology of war presented itself as a dependable and efficient agent of political spectacle—and if the former Hollywood cowboy had his way, the theatrical delight of watching his technological wizardry won adherents to the "'star wars" concept of nuclear war as universal video game (indeed, the later "light shows" in the Persian Gulf attest to the popular wonder of this medium).[12]

Very much unlike the overly sensual production of Iannis

At a birthday party, everybody should eat.

For 100 years, the Statue of Liberty has welcomed the poor of other nations to a wealthier life in America.

Yet today, on her nation's birthday – even in the shadow of her torch – homeless Americans go hungry.

To the people who work at Campbell Soup Company, and to working people everywhere, their plight is especially painful. Because for so many of us, both as individuals and as corporations, the American dream *has* come true.

The contrast hurts. And it should.

That's why this year we're donating 350,000 cases – 7000 tons – of food products throughout the nation. And, on this very special weekend, 40 tons of soup to shelters for the homeless in New York City.

Yes, it's only a beginning.

But the company that wants to help more Americans eat right thinks it's important to help every American eat.

Campbell Soup Company

Fig. 3. Campbell Soup Company advertisement, *New York Times*, July 4, 1986

Xenakis, the extravaganza of Liberty Weekend relied on the devices of technology to fortify through mechanical reproduction a sublimated and recognizable image of Liberty, standing forth for the whole world to admire. Even during the more subliminal moments of the celebration, its theatrical producers worked to maintain control of the image and its projection. I was struck, for example, by a moment during the popular culture extravaganza of the final evening when, just for a moment, the agency of the human body became one with the technological picture. Reminiscent of football card stunts, the exuberant crowd filling New Jersey's Giants Stadium held aloft colored flashlights to create a preconceived pattern of patriotic imagery. Far more striking than the pictures themselves was the public's impromptu gasp at its own unrealized, representational potential. The crowd momentarily acknowledged its possession of the power and aura of the entertainer. And yet, before the spectators could usurp the liberty of performance either by replacing flashlight with flashbulb, thus diminishing focus on the image of Liberty, or by deviating from the set agenda by bringing their own oscillating bodies into visual play, the dimmed stadium lights returned almost immediately to full force to illuminate the primary entertainment event. The television cameras followed suit by focusing on a moving platform whose dazzling lights eclipsed the human musicians performing on it.

But always in this careful televisual negotiation between ocular focus and blinding light rests what Jean-François Lyotard calls the acinematic stuff of diversion and libidinal ruin, that which lays waste to the ordered economy of performance. Lyotard bases his analysis on a simple pyrotechnic example of the misspending of energy, a diversion (*détournement*) enjoyed by the child who lights a match:

> He produces, in his own movement, a simulacrum of pleasure in its so-called "death instinct" component. Thus if he is assuredly an artist by producing a simulacrum, he is one most of all because this simulacrum is not an object or worth valued for another object. It is not composed with these other objects, compensated for by them, enclosed in a whole ordered by constitutive laws (in a structured group, for example). On the contrary, it is essential that the entire erotic force invested in the simulacrum be promoted, raised, displayed, and burned in vain. It is thus that Adorno said the only truly great art is the making of fireworks:

pyrotechnics would simulate perfectly the sterile consumption of energies in jouissance.[13]

Just such a marvelous consumption of energies captivated Liberty
Weekend participants on the night of July 4 when New York Harbor
was bombarded by a fireworks display of unprecedented propor-
tions. As a technological event deriving its energy from the wonder
of the simulacrum, it brilliantly defied complete visual recuperation
and forced the television networks to intercut still shots of the forgotten Lady, reminding the home viewer that the pyrotechnic bac-
chanal should be taken to symbolize a return to the principles of Liberty, not merely the coming of *jouissance.* As a vicarious participant
from upstate New York, I absorbed the electric oscillations of the
cameras and mixing machines while wanting to resist their strategic
attempts to fix my gaze on the look of the Lady and, thus, to capture,
transmit, and maintain the world's picture of Liberty.

Tele-Visions

It is on this performative role of the apparatus and its attempts to
stabilize the fluid and changeable referents of performance that we
might focus as the ultimate paradox of Liberty Weekend. The technological process is what beckoned the majority of American spectators, those of us lacking the resources to join Ron and Nancy for
$5,000, to approximate what Lyotard describes as the mediated "con-
sciousness of [our] own identity as well as the approval which [we]
thereby receive from others—since such structures of images and
sequences constitute a communication code among all of them."[14]
The camera as relay device and communication code is laden with a
long history of increasingly complex ideological formations of technological and philosophical structures. As Mimi White argues, the
ocular project of American (*commercial*) television is to "engage in
practices that assert unity and address the spectator-as-ideal-subject
across temporal, spatial, and narrative diversity."[15] White here aligns
the ideological theory of the film apparatus with that of the television camera. Her argument situates television in the abstract relationship of the development of the camera with the colonial history
of Occidental humanism, as outlined by the French film theoreti-

cians Marcelin Pleynet, Jean-Louis Baudry, and Jean-Louis Comolli. In Pleynet's terms:

> The film camera is an ideological instrument in its own right, it express-es bourgeois ideology before expressing anything else.... It produces a directly inherited code of perspective, built on the model of the scientif-ic perspective of the Quattrocento. What needs to be shown is the meticulous way in which the construction of the camera is geared to "rectify" any anomalies in perspective in order to reproduce in all its authority the visual code laid down by renaissant humanism.[16]

It remains true, as stressed by feminist and revisionist film theoreti-cians, that this model is flawed by its blind phallocentrism, which fails to account for historical alternatives to monocularity and for ideological resistances to the notion of the camera as universal agent of the ideology of the visible.[17] But it is just as clear that strategic attempts to administer such a monocular ideology have indeed reared their ugly heads ever since centralized programs of aesthetics were advanced by the early modern absolutists. The administration of such an aesthetic banks on the ideological fiction that, in Comol-li's words, "the human eye is at the center of the system of represen-tation, with that centrality at once excluding any other representa-tive system, assuring the eye's domination over any other organ of the senses and putting the eye in a strictly divine place."[18] As Bloom-ingdale's might say, this system wants to leave room for no excep-tions. "No one excluded."

The philosophical corollary is transcendental subjectivity, which positions the gazing (yes, *male*) Subject as the unifying agent. The ideological mechanism at work here is the rapport between camera and Subject (as well as image and commodity), the maintenance of a dominant ideology of visibility sustaining the idealization of the rep-resenting Subject—the power-laden Subject conceiving and grasping the world as picture. The complex relation of camera and transcen-dental philosophy remains as a prior horizon to contemporary spec-tacle's casting of the camera as a performer of visual knowledge and social advancement. Further reflection on this horizon in terms of its epistemological implications begs for clarification of the relation of the ideology of the visible to the censorial ideology of cognitive agreement. This problematic has been the focus of much of Lyo-tard's recent work, in which he analyzes how the mechanical "objects and the thoughts which originate in scientific knowledge and the capitalist economy convey with them one of the rules which supports their possibility; the rule that there is no reality unless testified by a consensus between partners over a certain knowledge and certain commitments."[19] The ideology of consensus operates according to the principle that we can agree on cognitive boundaries allowing us to recognize what lies inside or outside reality, or similarly vis-à-vis Liberty Weekend, allowing the construction of an American "us," a united notion of Americans reveling in our common liberty. Sustaining the celebration of freedom, then, are the well-established ideologies of consensus and visibility replayed by the media celebration of Liberty's spectacle. "All experienced a warm and positive celebration: a re-affirmation of our values and beliefs."

Suggested by the ease with which the television sponsors of Liberty Weekend proclaimed it a teary-eyed success, not to mention the more recent ready embrace of the discourse of "liberty" by alternative artists faced with the prospects of censorship, the complicated marriage of spectacle, telecommunications, and censorship clearly needs re-vision. Of importance is a clearer articulation of the radical differential of power relations structuring the censorial scenes of the spectacle of consensus, from Freud's electric oscillations to Liberty's positive celebrations. Underlying all regulation of social discourse is the censorial effect of what Lyotard calls the *differend*: "a case of differend between two parties takes place when the 'regulation' of the conflict that opposes them is done in the idiom of one of the parties while the wrong suffered by the other is not signified in that idiom."[20] What remains to be a critical imperative of performance, politics, even psychoanalysis, suggests Lyotard, is the acknowledgment of differends by "finding idioms for them."[21]

Some theoreticians of performance, the most vocal being Richard Schechner and his colleagues in "performance studies," would recommend turning our sights toward more primitive idioms of performance, in which spectacle is primarily a matter of the soul—whose manifestation is made corporeally immediate and fragile by the presence of participatory spectators. The hope here would be that anthropological absorption of non-Western performance would free theater from the death of the absorptive gaze that Schechner thinks has been enhanced by recent theatrical experiments with the proscenium arch (by Robert Wilson and Richard Foreman, say) or by performance art's flirtation with the video technology of representation.[22] I am reluctant, however, to place too much confidence in the possibility of (not to mention the urgent need for) the immediate transcultural germination of performance studies. Being mindful, as a former student of comparative religion, of how the discourse on the primitive is framed by the Occidental epistemologies underlying academic study per se, I am more inclined to recommend facing head-on the censorious, Occidental ideology of the visible.[23]

This might entail further consideration of what I have called elsewhere "the theatricality of the van-guard."[24] Reworking the idealistic notion of the *avant-garde*, I choose to emphasize the paradoxical censorial sense of the term suggested by the *O.E.D.: van*, "the fore or front part of a thing"; *guard*, "to find out or ascertain by watching," "to keep in check, control (thoughts, utterances)." In the context of the technology of performance, attentiveness to the theatricality of the van-guard would concentrate on two differend, although related, zones of material and conceptual phenomena: (1) the hegemonic myth of unmediated reception and the attendant absorptive eye of the controlling world picture and (2) the continual mediations and disruptions of re-presentation and the concomitant demystification of the world picture as an uncensored image of the imaginary relationship of individuals to the psychopolitical conditions of their existence. In the pages that follow, I would like to sketch out a prolegomena to a future analysis of the theatricality of the van-guard, one that acknowledges the fine censorious fibers distinguishing the overlapping constructs of omniscient and deconstructive performance.

We might turn directly to television for a theoretical model of the technological oscillations now dispelling the reality of the camera-subject match. While it is not difficult to note television's drive to control the world picture, it is just as important to acknowledge how the apparatus of television actually disrupts the ocular model from which it descends. In her astute essay "Psychoanalysis, Film, and Television," Sandy Flitterman-Lewis stresses television's swerve away from the cinematic model of identification. In noting that cinema's primary identification is based on the association of the spectator's look with that of the camera, she argues convincingly that television breaks down the voyeuristic structure of primary identification. Television differs from film by catering to a distracted home viewer with a variety of "looks," machineries, and transmissions. The "telespectator" never receives the kinds of sutured transmission conventionalized by Hollywood film, as well as expected of telecommunications by Freud. Instead, "television's fractured viewing situation explodes this coherent entity, offering in the place of the 'transcendental subject' of cinematic viewing, numerous partial identifications, not with characters but with 'views.' "[25] In this sense, then, we can expect the tele-visions of the Liberty Weekend Celebration to have been partial, if not "differend" and incommensurable with the aims of its political and corporate sponsors. While television exchange is not always up-front, I would argue that the theatricality of the van-guard, the performative watching over and judging of the fore and front part of the cultural thing, is inherent in the televisual.

This deconstructive potential to produce competing "censorious" views (what Freud calls communication between different ideational contents) is what the televisual apparatus shares with recent efforts in the field of experimental performance. With the aim of representing Occidental humanism in the context of its colonializing systems of pictorialization, broad collaborative projects in performance and theory have been probing the differential relations of the technological to gender, race, and representation. Exemplary of such efforts are substantial performance pieces by Ntozake Shange, Amiri Baraka, Robbie McCauley, and Ping Chong that situate the interrelated histories of spectacle and camera in relation to the politics of colonialism (I would also include Richard Foreman's departure from formalist aesthetics in *Africanus Instructurs*).[26]

In the mixed arena of text and performance, experiments with the theoretical frames of narrative also result in a better understanding of the role of Occidental technology as a hegemonic device of the world picture. Herbert Blau's performative essays on "theater at the vanishing point" extend his earlier work with the group KRAKEN into written enactments of the terror of theater and its invisibilities.[27] Just as significant is the continual influence of 1970s feminist theoretical experiments with the inconstant look of female identity in psychoanalysis, say *Dora* by Hélène Cixous, *The Singular Life of Albert Nobbs* by Simone Benmussa, and *India Song* by Marguerite Duras.[28] These and similar pieces set the stage for the look's current reinscription in lesbian and gay performance, film, and video, as recently theorized in *How Do I Look? Queer Film and Video* by the activist reading group Bad Object Choices.[29]

On the more specialized front of performance itself, feminist practitioners and theoreticians have embraced the "live act" as a strategy of further distancing female representation from the voyeuristic framings of male subjectivity and vision. Such distancing has been understood to occur on both conceptual and materialist grounds. To Judith Butler, the "acts" of performance force "a revision of the individualistic assumptions underlying the more restricted view of constituting acts within phenomenological discourse. As a given temporal duration within the entire performance, 'acts' are a shared experience and 'collective action.' "[30] Taking a somewhat different view, Holly Hughes attributes this collectivity less to the theoretical conditions framing it than to the diversity of the performers themselves: "performance art is accessible to disenfranchised persons to express themselves—*that's* why it's under attack."[31] Finally, in an essay that dwells on the conceptual interrelation of actress and "act," Jeanie Forte argues that the strong emphasis placed by performers like Hughes, Rachel Rosenthal, Robbie McCauley, and Karen Finley on the female body and its many ethnic and erotic acts affords "the performance artist the possibility for frustrating fetishistic practices and asserting an alternative viewing practice."[32]

Just such a frustration of fetishistic practices may well account for the NEA's 1990 refusal of a peer-review committee's recommendation to fund a piece by lesbian writer and performer Hughes, who is especially well known for her work with the Split Britches Company of the WOW Cafe (which was "defunded" along with pieces on social oppression, sexual politics, AIDS, and homosexuality by Karen Finley, John Fleck, and Tim Miller).[33] The censorship of Hughes's performance piece *The Lady Dick* is especially pertinent to this discussion since it restages many of the feminist differends silenced by the idiom of the Lady Liberty celebration. In this script, the character Garnet McClit, the Lady Dick, stands forth not as the beautified affirmation of phallocentric aesthetics but as the butch possessor of its vulnerable psychosexual authority, "a dick and lady at the same time."[34] If they are understood to speak for the other silenced lady, Liberty, the narratives performed by the butch's many femmes demystify the very conditions of oppressive sexual and social administration symbolized by the Liberty Weekend Celebration. Angel, the true diva, laments that there will be no happy ending for her midwestern mother—"just clean sheets and boredom in a nice neighborhood," while her dad is out "foolin' with cherries" (206). The femme tending a different sort of neighborhood is Con Carne, who sports a colossal imitation of Lady Liberty's spiked tiara. Played by Carmelita Tropicana, she is "the hot stuff with the meat" who owns The Pit, the club where lesbian seduction happily takes place. She stands in for the many women of color earlier forgotten by the American celebration of the European symbol of liberty. As a disenfranchised Latino islander who was dragged unwillingly into the American way by colonialist economic enslavement, she recounts how her survival entailed numerous transformations of identity. Her autobiography spans from the lesbian innocence of her Latin paradise ("The rivers they run with rum. In the trees, the fruit. In the bushes, the girls. Everybody gay! Then one day your people come" [213]) to her current position as a bourgeois, bisexual entrepreneur (" 'bi-sexual?' Is American way, no?" [213]). Only she possesses the tenuous authority to remind her butch Dick of her marginal place in the televisual scene: "Outside Con Carne's bar and grill you are a dirty joke. They see you and they think you runaway from freak show. When there is nothing buena on the TV you are what they watch for laughs" (213). Finally, *The Lady Dick* is a performance piece highly reflective of the irony of American freedom. Lethal Weapon, who makes the performers "feel as though they are being taken hostage," openly mimics the bland principles of liberty adopted in 1990 by the arts coalition the National Campaign for Freedom of Expression: "Then I remembered my constitutional right to the pursuit of happiness, which says: even if there is no such thing as happiness, I got a right to pursue it" (212). Not coincidentally, Lethal Weapon is the character performed by Holly Hughes.

The Contrast Hurts

The political friction of her lines is echoed by Hughes in her interview with Charles M. Wilmoth:

> The anticensorship movement has not made a case for validating controversial work, nor have they stated that these four defundings [of

Hughes, Finley, Miller, and Fleck] are about sexual politics—and homophobia. They made this generalized appeal, talking about freedom of
expression. Another failure was that, in the effort to save the NEA, there
wasn't enough acknowledgment that the NEA was flawed. A white-
wash was done on the NEA that it was this wonderful, perfect institution. But number one, it's way too small. There's not enough money,
even in the best of circumstances, for it to do what it was chartered to
do, which was to fund the cultural diversity of America. The second
thing is that it can't do that because it's riddled with as much bigotry as
the rest of the world. There's what Lynn Schuette of Sushi calls "structural discrimination." Most individuals and organizations that are coming
from disenfranchised communities—because of class, race, geographical
location, or whatever factors make you an outsider, like being a queer
artist—are unlikely to achieve enough visibility and legitimacy in the
eyes of the NEA to get funded in the first place.[35]

An additional factor in the NEA equation is its sponsorship and control not only of live performance but also of its cultural administration—its curatorial preservation, textual documentation, and critical
evaluation. For Hughes and the other three artists who were refused
funding, the representational fallout was enormous. Although the
script of *The Lady Dick* was published by *TDR*, along with scripts
by Fleck and Miller, even *The Lady Dick*'s inclusion in the review's
"Offensive Plays" supplement carried the marks of broader cultural
censorship. Its editors, Barbara Harrington and M. Elizabeth Hess,
note their failure to publish a monograph of the artists' "obscene"
texts, which would have aimed to counter the reduction of media
coverage of these artists to sensational sound bites: "Finley smears
herself with chocolate; Miller wants Helms' porky pig face out of his
asshole; Hughes' mother taught her to masturbate; and Fleck pees
onstage."[36] But their attempts to publish such a book "proved impossible for countless reasons, most of which stemmed from the nature
of the controversy and what exactly it does to people and art, and
people in art."[37] In terms of the mediated conditions of reception,
then, these performative examples of the theatricality of the van-
guard challenge the broader cultural and political program of the
regulation of performance as art—when it is appropriated as a cultural artifact for television broadcast, museum exhibition, academic
analysis, and even department store display, all traditionally aiming
to rigidify the attentive, unmediated gaze, the absorptive eye of the
world picture.[38] At issue is how curators, critics, and teachers might

turn to the exhibition, documentation, and academic re-presentation of performance art for the demystification of the world picture, for the re-vision of performances framed by (un)familiar aesthetic environments and products. This matter, I feel, lies behind my initial reflections on the showing of Lady Liberty and any possible vanguard benefit we might derive from her unveiling. The problems raised by documentation do not revolve merely around matters of inclusion, *what* to document, but also, and more significantly, around questions of method, *how to document*, and, even more importantly, around the veiled issues of ideology, *document to what purpose, to what end, to what audience*. To repeat my introductory assertion, at issue in the administration of aesthetics is not so much the principle of artistic regulation itself as the oscillating aesthetic principles governing regulation.

Even though this volume includes many detailed discussions of the oscillations of literary and cultural governance, I would like to retrace one more protracted clash between live performance and the administration of high culture. This one is from Paris, 1978. I begin with a story told by Derek Jarman about his trip to the Cannes film festival to screen *Jubilee* along with its star, the punker Jordan known in fashion circles for her Lady Liberty-style hairdo (fig. 4):

> Jordan is at the height of her media fame as "punk princess," with her ripped Venus T-Shirt, Bunsen-burner hair and extrovert make-up.... We stop in Paris and I take her to the Louvre to see Caravaggio's "Death of the Virgin." As she walks through the gloom of the great galleries whole parties of soporific tourists switch their attention from the Poussins and Rembrandts and illuminate her with a thousand flashbulbs. All this reaches its climax in a momentous confrontation with the "Mona Lisa." For the first time in her 470 years or so of existence the Mona is utterly upstaged; for a fleeting moment life triumphs over art. Then the walls open, guards rush out and bundle us into a secret lift; and we descend into a basement office where an embarrassed lady expels us from the gallery for "disturbing the aesthetic environment."[39]

This is only part of the story. What Jarman apparently did not realize was that theirs was a performance waiting to happen. For their chance encounter with the Mona Lisa took place soon after the performance artist Jean Dupuy extended his invitation to forty artists to perform individual pieces in the Louvre on a Sunday, the day of free admission to the museum. While news of Jordan's visit to the Lou-

Fig. 4. Jordan with David Bowie at Cannes, 1978. Reprinted from Derek Jarman, *Dancing Ledge*.

vre seems to have eluded Dupuy, the specter of her being illuminated by a thousand flashbulbs may well have contributed to the museum's resistance to his idea of "collective action," which developed into a performance piece of its own. First, the museum agreed to take only fifteen "actions" and only, in Dupuy's words, "on the condition that these performances be held according to the rules imposed on tourists, which means no permission to bring along any objects, no disturbing noise, no action which might hold up the flow of visitors or which might prove morally shocking, etc."[40] The show could go forward only on the condition that it contribute to the smooth administration of the aesthetics of the museum, to the moral conditions of quiet, privatized voyeurism. Second, after an initial agreement to allow a limited number of performers to invade the museum space on a Sunday afternoon, the only day of free admission, the Louvre attempted to coerce Dupuy into scheduling the performance on a Monday (the only day the museum is closed to the public). The result was a compromise, violated by Dupuy, who invited more artists than agreed and who blocked the public passages of the Louvre by inviting the Sunday spectators to sit and witness the subsequent unveiling of hidden contraband that desecrated the museum space. The majority of the performances commented on the ideological and cultural codes of the museum, its art and moral codes. The group Untel wore pants, shirts, and jackets clearly marked with the sign of the limitations imposed on them, "touriste." A more combative comment on the Louvre's contradictory moral codes was made by a topless Jacqueline Dauriac who, standing adjacent to the topless *Gabrielle d'Estrées and Sister*, held the exposed breast of her partner to restage the painting's infamous nipple touch. Further commenting on painting's capitalization on the display of the female nude was Orlan's painting of her own crotch in front of a group of Rubenesque nudes (fig. 5). What is more, these unwelcome "tourists" contributed to the subliminal threat of performance when someone set off three small smoke bombs, interrupting—or rather extending—the scope of artistic *jouissance*. Although this provoked the museum to close the Salle des Etats, the performances continued under tremendous tension only to be extended in the street when the artists were met by waiting police.

This charged example suggests the implications of regulating and documenting performative art according to museum codes of consensual visibility. Regulation here comes perilously close to the aesthetic and moral cleansing of an unpredictable event, and ends finally in a state of police surveillance of legitimate, institutionally sponsored aesthetics. In generating resistance through surveillance, Dupuy's performance event played out what he calls the gallery/museum/grants network: "We are not controlled by the classical structure of artist-gallery-collector-museum. In that structure, when you reach the museum, you are finished—you don't make anything new anymore."[41] Ironically, this is the same negative effect recounted by Hughes as the result of administrative censorship: "It's been impossible for me to write anything creative since this happened."[42] The museum and its defensive economic network clearly stand counter to the creative oscillations of collective performance.

I cite this example, however, only to contrast it with an earlier, historical example of the necessary breakdown of documentation and its traditional inscription in patriarchal forms of power and gaze. Holbein's *The Ambassadors* provides a perfect example of the early aims of documentation. This well-known sixteenth-century portrait presents two ambassadors posing among the produces of their cultural and imperial activities. What is clearly of value here is less the

Fig. 5. Orlan in Jean Dupuy's "Art Performance/One Minute," Musée du Louvre, October 1978. Reprinted from *Collective Consciousness: Art Performances in the Seventies*, ed. Jean Dupuy. Photo by André Morain.

art of portraiture than the desire for wealth and power represented by the portrayal of accumulation and patronage per se. This portrait is made even more fascinating by the curious anamorphic image competing with the ambassadors in the low, frontal plane of the picture. Viewed from the side, this shows itself to be an uncanny representation of a skull. Might this not suggest that any representation of power, accumulation, or wealth inscribes itself in a drive toward death, toward fragmentation, or even toward deconstructive, split vision?[43] This picture provides documentation of a different sort of libidinal enterprise, the fateful performance of the evolving body that performance art reminds us underlies all aesthetics. Such alternative vision of de-composition is reminiscent of the conditions of documentation that too often repress the subliminal energies and texts underlying their own aesthetic regulations.

Performance art, I want to suggest, re-presents a similar double-edge reversal of the van-guard that underlies traditional forms of aesthetic documentation. This is the documentation drive to release rather than repress the subliminal energies of the body, a drive not merely to make present and visible but more essentially to activate through representational absence and Otherness the sights and scenes that performances always face, but never face, through psychic voyeurism. In many ways, performance is haunted by the paradox of the documentation drive: that for it *to be* means for it also *not to be.* What drives both performance and documentation is the irreversibility of the differend, of the incompletions and vanishings of cultural administration.

In acknowledging the tension between the material restrictions of art documentation and the always incomplete subliminality of bodily and psychological performance, I wish to conclude by repeating the critical issue at stake: not the matter of artistic content, *what to document,* but the interrelation of method and ideology, *how to document* and *document to what end.* The consensual end of celebrating the Statue of Liberty points us in one clearly recognizable direction. AT&T's ad in the *New York Times* is clear about its line (fig. 6):

> "Hello, AT&T? Could you give the Statue of Liberty a perm?" What John [Franey, a corrosion scientist] was worried about, as he perched high in the air above New York Harbor, was how he was going to help patch up the Statue of Liberty without it showing. Four hundred square feet of the old lady—including her curls and a nasty spot under her nose— were badly corroded.... When you see Miss Liberty this weekend, we hope you'll admire her curls (and how nice her upper lip looks).

AT&T's aim is to reinscribe the Hollywood aesthetics of the female "look" into the zone of the gaze, thus patching up "the dreadful things that the environment does to materials" without its "showing." The lead taken most recently by performance art, however, has

"Hello, AT&T? Could you give the Statue of Liberty a perm?"

There was John Franey, sitting 300 feet up in the air, looking worried...

John is a corrosion scientist at AT&T who specializes in studying the dreadful things that the environment does to materials used in our communications system. His particular specialty is copper and copper alloys—AT&T uses over 500 million pounds of copper a year in its products.

What John was worried about, as he perched high in the air above New York Harbor, was how he was going to help patch up the Statue of Liberty without it showing.

Four hundred square feet of the old lady—including her curls and a nasty spot under her nose—were badly corroded. How on earth was he going to take brand-new sheets of copper and instantly turn them just the right shade of green so that Miss Liberty wouldn't look like she had the mange? "It takes years for copper to develop that lovely green patina," says John.

The National Park Service had borrowed John—and his knowledge—from AT&T. Every Friday for six months, John clambered up the scaffolding that surrounded the statue, tried another experiment, and scratched his head.

"Then, all of a sudden one day as I was driving to work, I noticed roofers removing the copper roof of the AT&T Bell Laboratories auditorium," says John. "There I was, thinking about how to form this patina...and all along it was under my nose, already formed!"

In due course, a boat with John Franey aboard delivered 15 crates of copper strips—fresh from that AT&T roof and just the right shade of green—to the Statue of Liberty. When you see Miss Liberty this weekend, we hope you'll admire her curls (and how nice her upper lip looks).

We also hope you'll think of John Franey, who wasn't too proud to make-do with what he had. "Some scientist, eh?" says John. "Oh, well, better something that works today than a more elegant solution somewhere down the road."

P.S. Our specialty is providing systems for the movement and management of information. Call us at 1 800 247-1212. Tell us your problem. And we'll put someone on it who, like John Franey, believes in making things work.

AT&T
The right choice.

Fig. 6. AT&T advertisement, *New York Times*, July 3, 1986

been to suggest that the aim of documenting performance art should be the "end" of this notion of giving the Statue of Liberty an aesthetic *perm*anence, one recuperable only by the voyeuristic gaze and commodification of artificats and artistic knowledge. In fact, *The Ambassadors* can be cited again for pre-facing the transformation of the old lady into the attractive young miss, for it suggests that the ultimate strength of performance lies in the play of perspectives sensitizing spectators to the choices framing their own libidinal and ideological re-presentation of aesthetic objects. In moving their bodies to enact the perspectival options of *The Ambassadors*, the viewers transfer art from canvas to spectatorial and performative space, thus realizing the side and split visions of aesthetic oscillation. The end here is not to present a sanitized image of the art of colonialization, but rather to provide memory traces of the differences enacted by visual immigration and its supplementary libidinal and material vanishings. Enacting a corollary side vision of how the Liberty Weekend Celebration might be documented as something other than a universally "warm and positive celebration," I will close by citing against the hopeful grain of Campbell Soup's corporate interests a longer fragment from its ad on the repressed death drive of the American dream:

> At a birthday party, everybody should eat. For 100 years, the Statue of Liberty has welcomed the poor of other nations to a wealthier life in America. Yet today, on her nation's birthday—even in the shadow of her torch—homeless Americans go hungry. To the people who work at Campbell Soup Company, and to working people everywhere, their plight is especially painful. Because for so many of us, both as individuals and as corporations, the American dream *has* come true. The contrast hurts. And it should.

What else need be said to Campbell's, AT&T, ABC, Bloomingdale's— and let's not forget the Hollywood cowboy and his invited guests— but that electric oscillation and media-tion constitute the disfiguring death drive of Liberty's representation? No exceptions? No one excluded? The contrast hurts. And it should.

NOTES

1. This is the perceptive thesis developed by Annette Kuhn in *Cinema, Censorship, and Sexuality 1909-1925* (London and New York: Routledge, 1988).

2. Sigmund Freud, "The Unconscious," *The Standard Edition of the Complete Psycho-*

logical Works of Sigmund Freud (S.E.), 24 vols., ed. and trans. James Strachey (London: Hogarth and the Institute of Psychoanalysis, 1953-74), 16:593.

3. Freud, "Civilization and Its Discontents," *S.E.* 16: 765.

4. Freud, "Recommendations to Physicians Practicing Psycho-Analysis," *S.E.* 12: 359-60.

5. Jacques Lacan, "L'intervention sur le transfert," *Ecrits* (Paris: Seuil, 1969), 215-26.

6. I do not mean to suggest, however, that acknowledgment of cultural power should necessarily mean resisting it at all costs. I strongly differ, for example, with the censorial position adopted by the feminist antipornographer Catharine MacKinnon, who aligns all pornography with the sexuality of male supremacy that fuses "the erotization of dominance and submission with the social construction of male and female," *Feminism Unmodified: Discourses on Life and Law* (Cambridge, Mass.: Harvard University Press, 1987). This view condemns any sociosexual practice or representation that explores the fine fibers inscribing power in pleasure. For a welcome contrast to this position, see, among many others, Linda Williams, *Hard Core: Power, Pleasure, and the "Frenzy of the Visible"* (Berkeley: University of California Press, 1989), as well as Mandy Merck and Beverly Brown in their contributions to the "Pornography Debate" special issue of *Critical Quarterly* (34, no. 2 [Summer 1992]). These writers argue for the potential sociopolitical value of heterogeneous sexual practice, especially in the realms of female and homosexual sexuality. To cite Williams's excellent summary of the positive effects of fantasies of power in pleasure for and by women, they offer "one important way in which groups and individuals whose desires patriarchy has not recognized as legitimate can explore the mysterious conjunction of power and pleasure in intersubjective sexual relations" (217-18). Williams, Merck, and Brown develop positions made earlier by the Feminist Anti-Censorship Task-force (FACT) in its recently republished collection of textual responses to the antipornographers, along with hard-core imagery, *Caught Looking: Feminism, Pornography and Censorship* (East Haven, Conn.: LongRiver, 1992).

7. On the vicissitudes of "the nerve-wracking immediacy" of the performative event, see Herbert Blau, "Repression, Pain, and the Participation Mystique," *The Audience* (Baltimore: Johns Hopkins University Press, 1989), 144-209.

8. Complex analyses of the oscillation between product and soap opera are provided by Robert C. Allen, "*The Guiding Light*: Soap Opera as Economic Product and Cultural Development," in *Television: The Critical View*, ed. Horace Newcomb (New York and Oxford: Oxford University Press, 1987), 141-63; Lynne Joyrich, "All That Television Allows: TV Melodrama, Postmodernism and Consumer Culture," *Camera Obscura* 16 (January 1988), 129-53; Tania Modleski, *Loving with a Vengeance: Mass-Produced Fantasies for Women* (Methuen: New York and London, 1982), 85-109; and Sandy Flitterman-Lewis, "All's Well That Doesn't End—Soap Opera and the Marriage Motif," *Camera Obscura* 16 (January 1988): 119-27.

9. Stephen Heath credits television for refinement of "the supreme commodity-reality" in "Representing Television," in *Logics of Television: Essays in Cultural Criticism*, ed. Patricia Mellencamp (Bloomington: Indiana University Press; London: BFI, 1990), 267-302.

10. Martin Heidegger, "The Age of the World Picture," *The Question Concerning Technology and Other Essays*, trans. William Lovitt (New York: Harper & Row, 1977), 129-30.

11. Ibid., 134. Gregory Ulmer provides a "grammatological" analysis of this text in "The Object of Post-Criticism," in *The Anti-Aesthetic: Essays on Postmodern Culture*, ed. Hal Foster (Port Townsend, Wash.: Bay Press, 1983), 83-110.

12. In *War and Cinema: The Logistics of Perception* (London and New York: Verso),

Paul Virilio dwells on the seductive flow between the technologies of war and light "where technology finally exposes the whole world."

13. Jean-François Lyotard, "Acinema," trans. Paisley N. Livingston, in *Narrative, Apparatus, Ideology: A Film Theory Reader*, ed. Philip Rosen (New York: Columbia University Press, 1986), 349-59.

14. Lyotard, "Answering the Question: What Is Postmodernism?" trans. Régis Durand, in *The Postmodern Condition: A Report on Knowledge* (Minneapolis: University of Minnesota Press, 1984), 74.

15. Mimi White, "Ideological Analysis and Television," in *Channels of Discourse: Television and Contemporary Criticism*, ed. Robert C. Allen (Chapel Hill: University of North Carolina Press, 1987), 191.

16. Marcelin Pleynet with Jean Thibaudeau, "Economique, idéologie, formel," *Cinéthique* 3 (1969): 10, as cited by Jean-Louis Comolli in "Technique and Ideology: Camera, Perspective, Depth of Field," *Film Reader* 2 (1977): 129. For elaborations on film's relation to perspectival theory, see *Apparatus: Cinematographic Apparatus: Selected Writings*, ed. Theresa Hak Kyung Cha (New York: Tanam, 1980); *The Cinematic Apparatus*, ed. Teresa de Lauretis and Stephen Heath (London: Macmillan; New York: St. Martin's, 1980); William C. Wees, "The Cinematic Image: As a Visualization of Sight," *Wide Angle* 4, no. 3: 28-37; and Serge Daney's "Sur Salador," *Cahiers du cinéma* 222 (July 1970): 39.

17. Jacqueline Rose, *Sexuality and the Field of Vision* (London: Verso, 1986), 199-213; Constance Penley, *The Future of an Illusion: Film, Feminism, and Psychoanalysis* (Minneapolis: University of Minnesota Press, 1989), 57-80; Mary Ann Doane, *Femmes Fatales: Feminism, Film Theory, Psychoanalysis* (New York and London: Routledge, 1991), 165-77; Joan Copjec, "The Anxiety of the Influencing Machine," *October* 23 (Winter 1982): 43-59; Teresa de Lauretis, *Technologies of Gender: Essays on Theory, Film, and Fiction* (Bloomington: Indiana University Press, 1987), 1-30; Trinh T. Minh-Ha, *When the Moon Waxes Red: Representation, Gender, and Cultural Politics* (New York and London: Routledge, 1991), 81-105; D. N. Rodowick, *The Crisis of Political Modernism: Criticism and Ideology in Contemporary Film Theory* (Urbana: University of Illinois Press, 1988), 67-110.

18. Jean-Louis Comolli, "Machines of the Visible," in *The Cinematic Apparatus*, ed. de Lauretis and Heath, 126. In *Theatrical Legitimation: Allegories of Genius in Seventeenth-Century England and France* (New York and Oxford: Oxford University Press, 1987), 111-30, I discuss the "simulacrum of optical potency" nurtured by Richelieu's theatrical performances.

19. Lyotard, "Answering the Question," 77.

20. Lyotard, *The Differend: Phrases in Dispute*, trans. Georges Van Den Abbeele (Minneapolis: University of Minnesota Press, 1988), 9.

21. Ibid., 13.

22. Richard Schechner, *The End of Humanism* (New York: Performing Arts Journal Publications, 1982).

23. See Hal Foster, *Recodings: Art, Spectacle, Cultural Politics* (Port Townsend, Wash.: Bay Press, 1985), 181-208; Gayatri Chakravorty Spivak, "Who Claims Alterity?" in *Remaking History*, ed. Barbara Kruger and Phil Mariani (Seattle: Bay Press, 1990), 269-92; and Trinh's discussion of cultural alterity in the context of television, *When the Moon Waxes Red*, 185-99. In the introduction to my book, *Like a Film: Ideological Fantasy on Screen, Camera, and Canvas* (London and New York: Routledge, 1993), I voice a similar caution about the casual dismissal of Occidental epistemology voiced by many American multicultural critics.

24. I introduce this concept in "Theatricality of the Van-Guard: Ideology and Contemporary American Theatre," *Performing Arts Journal* 24 (Fall 1984): 93-99.

25. Sandy Flitterman-Lewis, "Psychoanalysis, Film, and Television," in *Channels of Discourse*, ed. Robert C. Allen, 190.

26. In addition to two excellent catalogs documenting this intersection—*New Performances on Film and Video*, ed. Richard Herskowitz (Ithaca, N.Y.: Herbert F. Johnson Museum of Art, Cornell University, 1985), and *The Decade Show* (New York: Museum of Contemporary Hispanic Art, New Museum of Contemporary Art, Studio Museum in Harlem, 1990)—see Lowery Stokes Sims, "Aspects of Performance in the Work of Black American Artists," in *Feminist Art Criticism: An Anthology*, ed. Ariel Raven, Cassandra L. Langer, and Joanna Frueh (Ann Arbor, Mich.: UMI Research Press, 1988), 207-26; Marilyn Rivchin, "Robbie McCauley: Performance Artist/History Artist," *Q: A Journal of Art*, May 1990, 58-61; and my essays, "Duck and Cover? 'Radioactive, Inactives Portraits' by Nagatani and Tracey," *Q: A Journal of Art* (May 1990), 31-33, and "Facing the Camera's Eye: Black and White Terrain in Women's Drama," in *Reading Black, Reading Feminist: A Critical Anthology*, ed. Henry Louis Gates, Jr. (New York: Meridian, 1990), 155-75.

27. Herbert Blau, *The Audience: To All Appearances: Ideology and Performance* (New York and London: Routledge, 1992); *The Eye of Prey: Subversions of the Postmodern* (Bloomington: Indiana University Press, 1987); *Blooded Thought: Occasions of Theatre* (New York: Performing Arts Journal Publications, 1982); *Take Up the Bodies: Theater at the Vanishing Point* (Urbana: University of Illinois Press, 1982).

28. For feminist theorizations of specular identifications in these texts, see Elin Diamond, "Refusing the Romanticism of Identity: Narrative Interventions in Churchill, Benmussa, Duras," *Theatre Journal* 37, no. 3 (October 1985): 273-86; Sharon Willis, "Hélène Cixous's *Portrait de Dora*: The Unseen and the Un-scene," *Theatre Journal* 37, no. 3 (October 1985): 287-301; and Sue-Ellen Case, "From Split Subject to Split Britches," in *Feminine Focus: The New Women Playwrights*, ed. Enoch Brater (New York and Oxford: Oxford University Press, 1989), 126-46.

29. Bad Object Choices, eds., *How Do I Look? Queer Film and Video* (Seattle: Bay Press, 1991).

30. Judith Butler, "Performative Acts and Gender Constitution: An Essay in Phenomenology and Feminist Theory," in *Performing Feminisms: Feminist Critical Theory and Theatre*, ed. Sue-Ellen Case (Baltimore: Johns Hopkins University Press, 1990), 276.

31. Charles M. Wilmoth, "The Archeology of Muff Diving: An Interview with Holly Hughes," *Drama Review* 35, no. 3 (Fall 1991): 220.

32. Jeanie Forte, "Women's Performance Art: Feminism and Postmodernism," in *Performing Feminisms*, ed. Case, 261.

33. On Holly Hughes and the WOW Cafe, see Alisa Solomon, "The WOW Cafe," in *The Drama Review: Thirty Years of Commentary on the Avant-Garde*, ed. Brooks McNamara and Jill Dolan (Ann Arbor, Mich.: UMI Research Press, 1986), 305-14; Case, "From Split Subject to Split Britches"; Kate Davy, "Reading Past the Heterosexual Imperative: *Dress Suits to Hire*," *Drama Review* 33, no. 1 (1989): 153-70; and Jill Dolan, *The Feminist Spectator as Critic* (Ann Arbor, Mich.: UMI Research Press, 1988).

34. Holly Hughes, *The Lady Dick*, in *Drama Review* 35, no. 3 (Fall 1991): 297. All references are to this source.

35. Wilmoth, "Archeology of Muff Diving," 219-20.

36. Ibid., 206.

37. Barbara Harrington and M. Elizabeth Hess, "Supplement: Editor's Introduction," *Drama Review* 35, no. 3 (Fall 1991): 128.

38. Douglas Crimp, "The Art of Exhibition," *October* 30 (Fall 1984): 49-81, provides a history of the museum as an institution of regulatory practices. Perhaps the greatest practice of artistic regulation, which I do not detail below, is the exclusion of broad classes of artists and their objects from consideration for exhibition. Eloquent discussions of the exclusion of women, women of color, and homosexuals by the museum/gallery nexus of art are provided by Adrian Piper, "The Triple Negation of Colored Women Artists," in *Next Generation: Southern Black Aesthetic* (Winston-Salem, N.C.: Southeastern Center for Contemporary Art, 1990), 15-22; Douglas Crimp and Adam Rolston, *AIDSDEMOGRAPHICS* (Seattle: Bay Press, 1990), 12-25; Trinh, "The Other Censorship," *When the Moon Waxes Red*, 225-35; Mira Schor, "Girls Will Be Girls," *Artforum* 19, no. 1 (September 1990): 121-27; and Maurice Berger, "Are Art Museums Racist?" *Art in America*, September 1990, 68-77. Although Berger's critique of the 1989 New Museum of Contemporary Art exhibit Strange Attractors: Signs of Chaos displays an impatience with the show's promising dialogue with "chaos theory," it opens by singling out the marginality of what I agree to have been the exhibition's most intriguing piece—David Hammons's mixed-media video installation in which a white mannequin head blankly watches a sixties television interview of Malcolm X.

39. Derek Jarman, *Dancing Ledge* (London: Quartet, 1984), 11.

40. Jean Dupuy, ed., *Collective Consciousness: Art Performances in the Seventies* (New York: Performing Arts Journal Publications, 1980), 84.

41. Ibid.

42. Wilmoth, "Archeology of Muff Diving," 220.

43. Lacan, in *The Four Fundamental Concepts of Psychoanalysis*, trans. Alan Sheridan (New York: Norton, 1978), 67-119, theorizes in relation to a reading of *The Ambassadors* how the subject stands split in the scopic field between the competing constructions of the eye and the gaze. In an argument directly related to the electronic oscillations of this essay, Sean Cubitt argues, in *Timeshift: On Video Culture* (London and New York: Routledge, 1991), 180, that "a major function of new video will be to negotiate the mourning which we have never been able to conclude, to create forms in which the relation to death can be expressed, in which we can face the founding loss on which our [Anglo-European] culture and society [are] based." In acknowledgment of the dismissal of European psychophilosophical reflections on death, mourning, and melancholy by American multicultural critics, I turn at different moments in *Like a Film* to AIDS discourse and to Julie Dash's African-American film, *Daughters of the Dust*, for politicized reflections on the cultural value of melancholic incorporation and its confusions. Countering similar rejections by feminists wishing for a subject grounded more firmly in the Symbolic, Jacqueline Rose dwells on the import of the death drive for a theory of female subjectivity in "Where Does the Misery Come From? Psychoanalysis, Feminism, and the Event," in *Feminism and Psychoanalysis*, ed. Richard Feldstein and Judith Roof (Ithaca, N.Y.: Cornell University Press, 1989): 25-39.

Cyborg America: Policing the Social Sublime in *Robocop* and *Robocop 2*
Rob Wilson

"They [Western citizens] can already smell the terror of the year 2000."
—Jean Baudrillard[1]

"Here it [history] seemed the very fabric of things, as if the city [London] were a single growth of stone and brick, uncounted strata of message and meaning, age upon age, generated over the centuries to the dictates of some now-all-but-unreadable DNA of commerce and empire."
—William Gibson[2]

While the culture of postmodernity confounds even its most commodified admirers as a global tangle of haphazard concerns and genuinely heteroglossic directions, figures of cyborgian sublimity ranging from *Robocop* to *The Terminator* and *Lawnmower Man* are proliferating at century's end like sublime masochists from the political unconscious. Such figures of cybernetic power and recuperated local agency serve, I will contend, as technoeuphoric spectacles producing and socializing, if not policing, the aesthetics of the future. Emerging as sublime technobody from out of our postindustrial future, such cybernetic organisms can be said to prefigure softer collusions of human flesh with high technology, organic meat with machinic assemblage, and animal with spirit-ghost-consciousness as governed into one high-tech package of simulated stimulation.[3] The vastness of transnational cyberspace and leftover territories of Rust Belt waste and national nostalgia will need to be policed, and older cultural policies of Irish-Catholic superego on the beat will no longer do.

The sublimity of nature, which presumed an organic identity tied to majestic mountains and Hudson River trees, seems, in this instance, no longer a matter of nostalgia or even image recall. Positioned as American patriots by national icons into identifying with spectacles of the technological aggressor, as I have elsewhere argued, we need not rush to embrace this sublime cyborg: we might question whether this neopopulist version of a technological sublime is not so much a harbinger of partial, hybrid, nondualistic identities as we might wish, but, rather, a version of a transnational cybercowboy searching for new frontiers of inner space and local geography to territorialize, sublimate, and suppress.

If such a sublime cyborg would insinuate the future as post-Fordist subject, his palpably masochistic locations as ecstatic agent of the sublime superstate need to be decoded as the "now-all-but-unreadable DNA" of a fast deindustrializing Detroit, just as his Robocop-like strategy of carceral negotiation and street control remains the tirelessly American one of inflicting regeneration through violence upon the racially heteroglossic wilds and others of the inner city.[4] Police work as enforcer of transhuman technologies and urban regulation if not as unwitting censor of ideological critique comes with the territory of this distinctly postmodern sublime of awesome domination, ecstatic interpellation, and submission to the codes. The urban space this cyborg imbricates with sublime technologies of moral aggression and polices, arms dripping with blood and wonder, will here be interpreted as prefiguring a future environment we citizens are now entering as terrain of post-Fordist subjectivity and transnational spectacle. If this seems an overcoding of the fetish, it is, but the threat of American soft fascism needs to be distanced and critiqued from within the heart of the technocratic beast, as Robocop and Blade Runner belatedly realize in moves to decapitate the corporate state in Rust Belt Detroit as in futuristic Los Angeles.

"Feminist cyborgs" of hybrid profanity and boundary merger, on the one hand, as well as more regressively masculinist cyborgs of quasi-fascist invulnerability, on the other, have emerged and proliferated in films and novels signifying the "cyberpunk" genre.[5] Cyborgs now serve as fetishized objects of future knowledge and cultural constructions of contemporary empowerment/bewilderment, especially in the context of a global robotization in the service of transnational practices and transnational surplus value. Situated within the social dynamics of nationalist *lack* and a transnational reconfiguration of the male subject as transcendental ego immune to the state, this handsome cyborg can be decoded not just as a transitional figure embodying nomadic "identities [that] seem contradictory, partial, and strategic," as Donna Haraway cunningly contends, but as another masculinist fetish replicating, in many respects, the commonsense patriotism of a sublimely interpellated male American subject.

Although potentially enlightened cyborgs capable of Buddha nature and Deleuzian frenzy remain a promissory terrain of any technoeuphoric sublime and can be constructed, in filmic spectacles of subjective domination, to serve hybrid modes of counterrational subjectivity as well as more properly "technofascist celebrations of invulnerability," my own view of present-day cyborgs is closer to one that recognizes how deeply cyberpunk science fiction as a genre "remains stuck in a masculinist frame" glorifying late capitalist power.[6] Such fantasies of technoeuphoric domination, subordinating fleshly self and racial/sexual other to the social necessities and categorical imperatives of the nation-state to discipline, compete, and make war, remain a staple of the masculinist genre of the technological sublime. Such fantasies help to ratify the terms and subject positions of a master narrative quite close to sublimated fascism, racial evacuation, and territorial dispossession, American style.

Our everyday American cyborg in *Robocop 2* may look back with fitful nostalgia upon phallic bedroom scenes with his flesh-and-blood wife, who mourns Patrolman Murphy's transformation into an instrumentality of corporate metal, and with fleeting tenderness upon his efficient female sidekick, Lewis. But this mutilated male negotiates an even more devastated contemporary terrain, that of the postmodern inner city. This smoldering Detroit of trashed buildings, polyglot streets, empty warehouses, and abandoned metal plants is riddled with prostitutes, street punks, disgruntled cops, and even a demonic Little League team trashing electronic stores after a hard day at the plate as well as kids on the block spray painting the hectoring Robocop just for some Nietzschean kicks. If the twelve-year-old gang boss in *Robocop 2* bears a strong resemblance to Alex Murphy's own Little Leaguer son, the war on the inner city continues and the Third World has come home to stay as the de-Oedipalized uncanny of hometown violence that is as American as apple pie.

Old and young in this technologically and nihilistically dismantled Detroit, by now displaced and out of work, have understandably turned in the context of global deregulation to the mind-blasting euphoria of a made-in-America drug named NUKE ("We can make 'Made in America' mean something again," brags one drug lord to the mayor, threatened as he is by corporate arbitrage) and either hang out in euphoric video parlors or labor in designer-drug factories waiting for the end of the world. Robocop polices a world of fluid spaces, broken boundaries, and crossed extremes. Indeed, the normality of the middle-class subject seems, in cyberpunk generally, a lost proposition. In *Mona Lisa Overdrive*, William Gibson's novel on the making of simulacrous subjectivity, for example, two classes of corporate criminals from Tokyo, London, Hollywood, and Malibu battle their parodic "punk" underclass from dingier regions of Cleveland, the Sprawl, and "Dog Solitude," New Jersey, for travel in space and control of data and loa-ridden "cyberspace": the middle class is not even an absent presence or coherent subject within Gibson's narrative leapfrogging of transnational spaces from high to low and back home again, just as the police in any standard or normative sense are impossible to find.[7] But this interiorization and miniaturization of sublime infinitude into cyberspace is controlled, simulated, and designed by forces and figures within the Matrix of a transnational power that elude nomination or control.

Despite techno-Orientalist fantasies of Japanese takeovers or threats of asexual samurai manipulations of this transnational cyberspace that pervade the genre, the desire of cyborg America remains a drive toward installing (through sublime spectacles of transnational power that inform the Asian/Pacific space of a Japanized Los Angeles in *Blade Runner* or *Rising Sun*) a policed state in which the blissfully interpellated subjects of the democratic nation-state, having overcome more properly modernist moments of what William Gibson has called "universal techno-angst," will no longer object to their subjective entry jacked into pleasure zones of cyberspace nor resist being expelled into deindustrialized streets of exurban sprawl.[8] (Recall that in *Robocop*, the nostalgic goal of the crime-fighting robot, ED 209, had been to achieve "urban pacification.") With dizzying speed and tensile globality, high and low classes of console cowboys commingle and collide in brave new regions of corporate cyberspace. First, however, the American citizens of this waste-, class-, and crime-ridden city will have to be mollified into law and order, and the best candidate for the job of producing this social euphoria will have the fewest objections to urban injustice, mass de-skilling, and his/her corporate sublation into the instrumental rea-son of the state. This calls for the invention, second, of a sublime, quasi-Emersonian cyborg at home with not only liberal self-contra-dictions and fears of incompletion (positioned as vanguard ani-mal/machine/human) but also prosthetic limbs, implanted memory, altered circuitry, cosmetic surgery, genetic reconfiguration, designer drugs, and ideological integration into what can now be called transnational corporate hegemony: however contradictory such pol-itics seem in a world of strategic nationalism, this cyborg subject can be better recognized in his postmodern incarnation as *Robocop*, though Arnold Schwarzenegger of *Terminator* tenderness or the Offworld replicants of humanity in *Blade Runner* could surely be nominated for the task of transnational enforcer.[9]

As a master narrative of transnational quest romance (who makes the cyborg of transnational artificial intelligence cyberspace and who does he/she serve?) and the mimetics of social problems afflict-ing the globalizing present as displaced into a dystopic near future, in sum, the postmodern genre of cyberpunk (in which the cyborg now reigns) confronts us not so much with the problem of symbol-izing the tech-ridden future as such but with that of apprehending the no less awful present that besets a reconfigured, transnational-ized, and economically dismantled nation-state. As William Gibson described his transnational project to negotiate cyberspace in *Neuro-mancer*, "It's a way of trying to come to terms with the awe and ter-ror inspired in me by the world in which we live."[10] The distinct pleasures of sublime terror and euphoric release that inform cyber-punk from a novel like *Neuromancer* (1984) to a movie like *Lawn-mower Man* (1992) have much to do with racing through unpoliced regions wherein wilder forms of subjectivity and more lurid config-urations of hypercapitalist criminality reign. This emerging space of cybernetic immensity summons the god-hungry and the profit-dri-ven into configuring new assemblages of machine and flesh, logic and ecstasy. The mishmash architecture and polyglot collision of Asian and Pacific cultural languages and styles that fascinates urban planners in Ridley Scott's *Blade Runner* (1984), for example, regis-ters not so much an alien Los Angeles in the year 2019, which is the film's premise, as it represents a transnational cyberspace of crossed frontiers, chic Orientalism, spectacular commodification, polyglot density, simulacrous humans (like Leeza Gibbons playing Leeza Gibbons in the *Robocop* films, for example), ecological ruin, and atavistic sweatshops of everyday production already taking place in Los Angeles as paradigmatic city of transnational postmodernity in 1984. The special effects of acid rain and corporate overcoding in *Blade Runner* have an uncanny urban familiarity for American citizens; as Norman M. Klein has observed, this "bladerunner look" instantly achieved something rare in the history of cinema and "became a paradigm for the future of cities, for artists across the disciplines."[11]

In visionary artifices mapping global dimensions of cyberspace and crisscrossed paths of god-hungry visionaries and cybernetic criminals high and low, as Pam Rosenthal argues the case for the connection between such simulacrous imagery in cyberpunk as tied to its postindustrial social base, "cyberpunk is interested in [narrating] a world shaped by transnational corporate hegemony, new forms of core-periphery economic relationships, world beat culture, and identity subcultures" as these disparate spaces, classes, and quests for global power collide, fragment, cluster, and interact.[12] So imagined, with pastoral enclaves of the countryside forever bypassed or out of reach, the city has reached a new condition in which the carceral networks of modernity have broken down or, better said, have turned into malignant forces of domination that produce, for further corporate profit, the very elements of criminality they are designed to police.

In Paul Verhoeven's *Robocop* (1987), to zoom back in on this uncanny movie from the decade of transnationalization, the American nuclear family is gathered happily around the game board, as on the Ozzie and Harriet or Donna Reed shows; but they are not reading *War and Peace* nor discussing the Little League, they are worrying about arms strategies and nuclear missile buildups while playing (simulating) post-cold war games of mutual disaster—"Nuke 'Em Before They Nuke You!" affirms the commercial voice-over, as another atom bomb explodes in cyberspace over the family table. Alex Murphy, soon to be reborn against (or with) his will as the cyborgian crime fighter "Robocop," has a son who typically can be found at home before the surrogate father (the television set) watching "T. J. Lazer." This show stars a high-tech detective who serves as role model for son and father (like son like father) alike in the nervous twitch of the gun, which later becomes Robocop's waning stylistic signature for administering frontier justice, John Ford style. This twitch indicates one (phallic) sign that Murphy is still part human. Within conditions of dehumanized postmodernity, however, as the film goes on to show, the Oedipal family is all but phased out and superseded by more mysterious, deregulated, and fluid forms of subjective incorporation in the workplace and urban enclaves as drug gangs proliferate and research teams from Security Concepts and Omni Consumer Products ruthlessly compete to outsmart labor, government, and the criminal mind by raising a law-enforcement cyborg from the body of the slain officer.

Though no cyberpunk of countercultural energy and nomadic flight, early Robocop can be seen to register this complete and visceral technologization of the human subject. Murphy's point of view as law-abiding citizen of the American nation-state moves relentlessly from organic to cybernetic and back again, assembled by capital logic at the interface of the cyb/org. Film viewers, too, are cast into a distinctly postmodern subject position of ecstatic posthumanization: the film apparatus is shifted to gaze at the postindustrial world from the machinic perspective of a crime-gazing cyborg corporately programmed with four "directives": to serve the public trust, to uphold the law, to protect the innocent, and (so deftly interpellated) to obey corporate superiors like Dick Jones within the white-collar hierarchy of Omni Consumer Products. This program in capital-driven dehumanization eventually wobbles: the pathos of Robocop is not so much that of mechanical drive embodied with metallic suaveness by Schwarzenegger in the *Terminator* movies, returning to contemporary Los Angeles from the postnuclear future to kill the mother of a future world leader, but the tenderness of a re-Oedipalized desire and liberal illusion as Alex Murphy suffers paternal nostalgia, gets critical of male superiors, and undergoes "a process of resubjectivation, changing gradually back from incarnated drive to a being of [male] desire."[13] All but technologized into a robotic cop and disenabled to critique the state, like many a neocon postmodernist, this good cyborg dreams of a recuperated humanization with all the individuated debris and self-division of memory, motivation, affection, and sexual desire. But nostalgia for liberal subjectivity offers little comfort within a landscape of technological detritus and predatory capital-logic invading Murphy's body and conscripting the soul into urban service.

Robocop represents a more resonant threat to the social order. As his cyborgian name blandly suggests, "Robocop" is a robber/cop not only confusing robotic technology with an Irish cop's humanity but also confounding the boundary between criminality and decency within a reified capitalist order of speed and power that, at more fundamental levels of profit, links the profit seeking of the cocaine criminal, Boddicker, to the corporate power and knowledge of total privatization, Jones. Because the social process of robotization reduces the amount of labor required in production and saves capital outlay in human investment, Murphy furthermore has become a cyborgian supercop who endangers not only capital-intensive criminals such as Boddicker and Jones but also the flesh-and-blood police, who are thereby threatened (in both *Robocop* and *Robocop 2*) with elimination of their jobs.[14] The abolishment of the police and threat of criminality are co-produced by the state to serve capital in advanced modes of corporate cynicism.

Whatever the costs of such postmodern dehumanization, this sublime cyborg will have the social work of conversion cut out for him in any "New Bad Future" as he technopolices what is portrayed in *Robocop* as a deregulated, de-Oedipalized, and disoriented United States of America dissolving from within. In Irvin Kershner's *Robocop 2* (1990), lurid sublimity reaches a new level of domination and release. Omni Consumer Products continues its predatory raid upon this heartland industrial city of Detroit by forcing working-class cops to go on strike, all but phasing out the jive-talking mayor, and disfiguring the latest cyborg cop with an even more lethal and profit-driven model/clone of urban pacification. The original Robocop cop confronts an even more lethal and state-interpellated clone, Robocop 2, who has no traces of humanist sentiment left to contest. Given two decades of hostile takeovers, financial greenmail, regional dismantlement, global buyouts and molestations of local spaces and national corporations, the *Robocop* fantasy of American disempowerment is uncanny. It makes sense in this later movie that labor would be more disgruntled, youth nihilistic, and management scurrying to generate an even more sublime police force of spatial domination. Crossbred from Detroit modernity and turned into the "Delta City" of the future, the cyborgian crime fighter Robocop emerges from automotive flames to traverse what can be seen as the industrial detritus of a late capitalist American city. As machine/body fusing technology with ruined affects of the sublime, Robocop is deeply imbricated with the discourse of American nation-state ideology. Sublimating violence into technological spectacle, Robocop cruises the streets as a born-again cyborg elected to the time-honored ideological function of regeneration through violence: Robocop's role, as sublime cyborg, is to transmogrify ordinary citizens of this high-tech American frontier into awe-struck "servomechanism[s] of technology."[15] John Ford meets Henry Ford in the body of this crime-fighting robot policing a crime-ridden west. "Delta City: The Future Has a Silver Lining" urges one utopic billboard in Detroit, punning on the metal of Robocop's glistening transhuman body and his ability to embody a technoeuphoric future.

If cold war nuclear dread still subtends the tech-thick culture and feeling structures of postmodern paranoia pervade the narratives of cyberpunk science fiction, it makes sense, too, that both *Robocop* and *Robocop 2* would be set in Detroit, in that most *Fordist* of heavy-production regions, now going down the depressed path of uneven geographical and economic development that entails, as David Harvey contends, a social system capable of "simultaneously producing 'underdevelopment' where it did not previously exist and de-industrializing many advanced capitalist regions (such as the so-called Rust Belt of the United States)."[16] While foreshadowing emerging modes of technological redemption within such phased-out spaces of modernist waste, it makes social sense, too, that Robocop would do much of his cyborgian crime fighting while moving through the salvational spaces of flaming police cars, apocalyptic gas stations, and abandoned heavy-industrial plants now used as movie sets equally in Houston (where much of *Robocop 2* was actually filmed) as in Pittsburgh (now a movie site for films of nostalgic modernity) or Detroit. For Dutch director Paul Verhoeven of *Robocop*, even more influential than living in postmodern Los Angeles was the 1986 explosion of the space shuttle *Challenger*, which Verhoeven allegorically read in ruins as "a metaphor for the American situation," briefly revealing the conjoined interests of big business and control government as well as the misplaced American faith in technological redemption.[17] (In one news brief spliced into Robo-cop's adventures, the "Star Wars" platform misfires, burning down Santa Barbara and killing two former presidents who have retired there, and in *Robocop 2* a nuclear reactor explodes in Brazil, further endangering the rain forests.)

Invoking the problematics of socialized subjectivity circulated under technologies of the postmodern sublime, as these remain tied to narratives of global capital-logic, we can begin to see the themat-ics within which Robocop's battles for social wholeness will take place: social parameters of the technologically dominated subject of the nation-state will include the reoccupation of urban space by sub-lime cyborgs, the phasing out of individual resistance or deindividu-alization into cyborg, and the semiotic control of an out-of-control transnational future through evoking fetishized spectacles of tech-nological redemption. This love of power and domination, and not just intimations of awesome bliss or sensations of freedom, is what the American sublime has been about in all its agonistic intensity and masculinist fury.

As moviegoers stand in line for the next international blockbuster starring sublime cyborgs and their macho-militarized feminist side-kicks, who are quite capable (despite America's debtor-nation eco-nomic woes) of terminating history with sky-blasting effects in post-nuclear redemption, they cannot help but have the feeling, as William Gibson foreshadows in the lurid bric-a-brac sublimity of his short story "The Gernsback Continuum," that "now this is the real thing, the straight goods from the mass unconscious."[18] This running-down, post-Reaganomics America suggests that cool, cynical world space described with euphoria and dread by Jean Baudrillard in *Mondo 2000*. "It is a world rotten with wealth, power, senility, indif-ference, puritanism, and mental hygiene, poverty and waste, techno-logical futility and violence ... and yet I cannot help but feel that it has something about it of the dawning of the universe."[19]

While the enlightenment telos of European history recedes into millennial delusion, tepid heteroglossia, or representational glut, what this "mass unconscious" wants from the New World imaginary is still subject to large-scale manipulation and semiotic recall, of course, as Merv Kihn suggests to the photographer of tacky moder-nity in Gibson's uncanny "Gernsback Continuum." Rejecting the technophilia of Hugo Gernsback and his "American Streamlined

Moderne" future projected from the 1930s, Kihn's insight into this mass mind is based not upon Lacan, Jung, or Alvin Toffler but upon his mass-cult journalistic knowledge of contemporary "Texas ptero-dactyls, redneck UFO contactees, bush-league Loch Ness monsters, and the Top Ten conspiracy theories in the loonier reaches of the American mass mind."[20] What this American "mass unconscious" wants would remain immune to the politicization of the cinematic unconscious undertaken by socialist and feminist scholars of post-modernity as diverse in method, goal, and style as Paul Virilio and Laura Mulvey who decode the spectacles and spaces of global capi-tal-logic and its desire factories of world cinema.[21]

The cyborgian Gibson ascribes a name and space to this insatiable hunger for imagery and taste for technoeuphoric spectacles in works that have helped to open up the future-colonizing genre of postmodern literature and film recognizable as cyberpunk. Though every now and then a clear sky or running river breaks through, as at the close of films like *Blade Runner* and *Total Recall*, works in this genre serve to imagine the global movement toward a degraded bio-future of postapocalyptic angst; included are films such as *Blade Runner*, the *Mad Max* trilogy, *Escape from New York*, *The Run-ning Man*, *The Terminator*, *Terminator 2: Judgment Day*, *Cherry 2000*, *Max Headroom*, *Millennium*, *Brazil*, *Robocop*, *Robocop 2*, and *Hardware*.[22] As Kihn urges upon his friend, disoriented from the technocratic progress of twentieth-century history, we still hunger for the uncanny return of "semiotic ghosts" from the past that can recycle the trash plots, genres, characters, special effects, stylistic signatures, slogans, clichés, motifs, and stars from decades of modernity with the intensity of simulacra blasting history into a Nietzschean apocalypse of signs. This bricolage of mix-and-match pop imagery is a history postmodern Americans can recognize and consume as their own: "It's all in the mix," as Bruce Sterling sloga-nizes the underlying desire of cyberpunk for "crammed" style.[23] These "semiotic ghosts" and technological spectacles move in strange interzones of hyperreality not so much beyond good and evil (as in Martin Scorsese's film *Cape Fear* [1991]) as beyond cold war codings of capitalist/communist ideology (as in Paul Verhoeven's *Total Recall* [1990]).[24]

The long-standing hope of international modernism had been something like this utopic end: Can we humanize technology? Architecture and art would help to usher in, by figuring forth if not serving to incarnate, social spaces and forms of a massive industrial transformation. The life-world question posed by such modern technologies, at least for the Canadian nation situated within the American empire of the technological spectacle, "always contained paradoxical tendencies to freedom and domination simultaneously."[25] This leads, in Arthur Kroker's reading of the technological sublime, to a double-coded attitude mingling euphoria and dread, bliss and panic, as the post-Hiroshima viewer is situated and subjected, poised between wonder and catastrophe before spiraling technologies. It is no wonder, then, that this utopic longing within modernism has flipped over into something like the more properly postmodernist if not postpolitical question, Can we technologize the human? If *Robocop 2* looked with envy upon the deterritorialized fusions of flesh and machine and drugs in the person of Elvis Presley, media cyborgs now proliferate as mimic models like Michael Jackson fusing white bodies with black souls into grand machines with commodity politics.[26] In this long-dreamt-of metallization of the human body, the cyborg will continue to play a crucial role in this futurist—and post-Fordist—transformation of the urban citizen into awe- and dread-filled subject of the technological sublime.

Bruce Sterling summarizes that synthetic amalgam of hacker and rocker, and soft technology with punkish counterculture with computer wizard/nerd that informs the cyberpunk imaginary that emerged in the 1980s and *Robocop* recalls from a Clint Eastwood-like terrain of frontier justice: "For the cyberpunks, by stark contrast [with the techno-angst of the 1960s], technology is visceral. It is not the bottled genie of Big Science boffins; it is pervasive, utterly intimate. Not outside us, but next to us. Under our skin; often, inside our minds."[27] This recalls the postliberal pathos represented by Alex Murphy as he is getting corporately jacked into Omni Consumer Products on the operating table and becomes subject to the designs and interpellations of the postindustrial corporation transforming its workers into robots. The policeman having become a servomechanism of the Delta City police state, we film-gazers can now see the city, its terrors and wonders, from his cybernetic point of view as he treks through the waste of late-industrial modernity, dancing through the death traps of high-tech weaponry, and fending off laundered corporate money and cocaine cowboys alike, killing and making a killing for anomic, asocial kicks.

At the sublime end of *Robocop*, Boddicker is drowned, fittingly enough, in lurid swamps of toxic industrial waste, bidding Robocop a fond transnational farewell: "Sayonara, Robocop." But the only overall cure films like these can offer to the massive social problems they narrate and confront, at the level of the political imaginary, is the time-honored American one of (1) blaming the capitalist subject of the state and (2) sublimating and thereby renewing spectacular doses of regenerative violence. The plots can only move to scapegoat one predatory capitalist after another (like Gordon Gecko in Oliver Stone's *Wall Street* [1987], say) as one lone agent polluting the fundamental goodness of the whole free-market system, as Robocop does when he overcomes liberal interpellation and tosses Mr. Dick Jones out of the Omni Consumer Products window.[28] Of course the cyborg awaits the next "greedy" threat of deregulated subjectivity to the (deregulated) system when, as in *Robocop 2*, another "Jones" clone with the same desire for total profit and social pacification arises in the corporate nexus to take his place.

In Cyborg America, still emerging in full capital-logic splendor at century's end, a brave new world of technological integration and subjective reconfiguration struggles to be born across Asia and the Pacific. Like Robocop in ancient Detroit or console cowboy Case at home in Chiba City's infinite reaches of data-dense Sprawl in *Neuromancer*, we can only watch in terror and wonder "the sun rise on the landscape of childhood, on broken slag and the rusting shells of refineries."[29] The sublime cyborg of American redemption known as Robocop, however close he seems at times to incarnating a walking nihilist of urban euphoria or hip-hop ghetto dread, again bears out Félix Guattari's rueful lesson on cinematic desiring machines and their postmodern assemblages of flesh and machine: "Capitalist eros becomes a passion for the boundary; it becomes a cop."[30] Capitalist eros would here become a sublime Robocop, or a technofacist Arnold whose steel flesh weeps across the postnuclear ruins and wastes of American history, a Lawnmower Man whose phallic redemption takes place in the sublimated violence of corporate cyberspace.

Hence, Murphy's male subjectivity threatened by corporate obsolesence and the mercilessly creative destruction of hypercapitalism wired into his very brain and so-called limbs, Robocop polices the waste-strewn streets of postindustrial Detroit as a soft American spectacle of fascist domination. Flesh has become wired into the neosublime of cybernetic technology as such. Censorship is self-wired, for better or worse, into the American subject, and this liberal masochist learns to love the stomp of boot and the glow of metal lording it over the streets of Compton or the coke-ridden ghettos of Third World Detroit. Guns are us: Uzis stalk our American dreams of urban redemption. The cultural politics and social policies of this traumatic cyborg are, we can moralize belatedly like cyborgian newscasters on CNN or the enchanted Leeza Gibbons, seldom his/her own desires: "I'd buy that for a dollar, hah hah hah, I'd buy that for a dollar, hah hah hah, I'd buy that for a dollar" runs the sublime banality of this American refrain as it goes global and takes transnational possession of Alex Murphy's wholesome soul.[31]

NOTES

1. Jean Baudrillard, "The Year 2000 Has Already Happened," trans. Nai-fei Ding and Kuan-Hsing Chen, in *Body Invaders: Panic Sex in America*, ed. Arthur and Marilouise Kroker (New York: St. Martin's, 1987), 43–44. With postpolitical euphoria, Baudrillard argues for the disappearance of history and/or political ideology into media-driven "simulacra" as well as, contrariwise, "the apparent inverse obsession of historicizing everything" into anecdotes and tropes of revolution and counterrevolution. On such political cynicism, applied to technological spectacles of the war in the Persian Gulf, see the trenchant critique of hypertextuality in Christopher Norris, *Uncritical Theory: Postmodernism, Intellectuals & the Gulf War* (Amherst: University of Massachusetts Press, 1992).

2. William Gibson, *Mona Lisa Overdrive* (New York: Bantam, 1988), 5–6. The city that is being decoded as late-capitalist "text" of commerce and empire is not postindustrial Detroit (which will figure in my own analysis of *Robocop* as *the* post-Fordist space of American-male lack) but postimperial London.

3. On "machinic enslavement," see Brian Massumi, *A User's Guide to Capitalism and Schizophrenia: Deviations from Deleuze and Guattari* (Cambridge, Mass.: MIT Press, 1992), 198 and 192.

4. To map modes of post-Fordist spatiality, I will draw upon the Marxian geography of Edward Soja, *Postmodern Geographies: The Reassertion of Space in Critical Social Theory* (London and New York: Verso, 1982), especially chapters eight and nine on global molestations of Asian/Pacific/Mexican Los Angeles, as well as the work of David Harvey (see notes 11 and 15). See Michael Shapiro, *Reading the Postmodern Polity: Political Theory as Textual Practice* (Minneapolis: University of Minnesota Press, 1992), especially chapter six on "carceral" dimensions of the by now globalized and class-bifurcated Los Angeles, on spatial textualizations and disciplines. On "carceral" space in American cities, see Michael J. Shapiro, *Reading the Postmodern Polity: Political Theory as Textual Practice* (Minneapolis: University of Minnesota Press, 1992), 101.

5. For a *utopic* reading of the cyborg as posthumanist interface or "humanoid hybrid"

of technology with feminist subject, see Donna J. Haraway, "A Cyborg Manifesto: Science, Technology, and Socialist-Feminism in the Late Twentieth Century," in *Simians, Cyborgs, and Women: The Reinvention of Nature* (New York: Routledge, 1991), 149-81; and Donna Haraway, "Interview" and "The Actors Are Cyborg, Nature Is Coyote, and the Geography Is Elsewhere: Postscript to 'Cyborgs at Large,'" in *Technoculture*, ed. Constance Penley and Andrew Ross (Minneapolis: University of Minnesota Press, 1991), 1-26. For an argument closer to my own that warns against embracing the masculinist genres and cyberspace technologies still tied to capital-logic and the nation-state sublime, see Fred Pfeil, "These Disintegrations I'm Looking Forward To," in *Another Tale to Tell: Politics and Narrative in Postmodern Culture* (London and New York: Verso, 1990), 86-93.

6. See Penley and Ross, *Technoculture*, 7.

7. Gibson's opening four chapters in *Mona Lisa Overdrive* shift from representing Kumiko's Tokyo to Slick Henry's "Dog Solitude" factory to Angie Mitchell's Malibu to Mona and Eddie's sleazy Florida. This disjunctive class structure of spatial and social stratification continues until characters overlap and collide in the corporate designs to take over and occupy the dematerialized reaches of transnational cyberspace. Here capital-logic reaches a new level of dematerialized bliss, where Timothy Leary will become the frontier policeman of such synaptic information.

8. Gibson is describing his own *schizoid* attitude toward enchantedly postmodern technologies of sensory extension, as an American subject fluctuating from moments of technoeuphoria to fits of "universal techno-angst" in "Rocket Radio," *Rolling Stone*, June 15, 1989, 84. On "techno-orientalism" as a trait of predatory transnationals like the postmodern Japanese emasculating Americans at their own agonistic technological game, see David Morley and Kevin Robins, "Techno-Orientalism: Futures, Foreigners and Phobias," *New Formations* 16 (Spring 1992): 136-56.

9. For a social-psychological decoding of the way Robocop serves as a "cultural transitional object" for emasculating traumas of industrial modernity and the way that director Paul Verhoeven's *Total Recall*, by contrast, regresses into a scopic fetishizing of Schwarzenegger as cyborgian "phallus," see Fred Glass, "Totally Recalling Arnold: Sex and Violence in the New Bad Future," *Film Quarterly* 44 (1990): 2-13, and "The New Bad Future: Robocop and 1980's Sci-Fi Films," in *Science as Culture* 5 (London: Free Association Books, 1989). Glass exposes the postnuclear fantasy that governs the spectacular closing scenes of *Total Recall* and haunts the terrain of *The Terminator* (11). On the polymorphous Arnold as phallic cyborg, see Jonathan Goldberg, "Recalling Totalities: The Mirrored Stages of Anxiety," *Differences* 4 (Spring 1992): 172-204.

10. William Gibson, as interviewed by Timothy Leary, "High Tech, High Life," *Mondo 2000*, no. 1 (1990): 59.

11. Norman M. Klein, "Building Blade Runner," *Social Text* 28 (1991): 147-52. On the Gulf War as a cyborgian spectacle of transnational technologies tied to patriotic submission and the dying sublimity of the nation-state, see Rob Wilson, "Sublime Patriot," *Polygraph* 5 (1992): 67-77. On technologies of censorship and spectacles of simulated consensus circulating within American postmodernity, see Richard Burt's essay on "degenerate 'art'" in this volume.

12. See the "post-Fordist" issue of *Socialist Review* 21 (January-March 1991), in particular, Pam Rosenthal, "Jacked In: Fordism, Cyberpunk, Marxism," 79-103. I also draw upon the Asian/Pacific geography of *Blade Runner* mapping the space and time of this postindustrial world order into "time-space compression" as discussed in David Harvey, *The Condition of Postmodernity* (Cambridge, Mass.: Basil Blackwell, 1989), chapter 18. On the *Blade*

Runner novel and movie as policing boundaries and cyborgian interfaces of the human and organic with the machine, see Michael J. Shapiro, "'Manning' the Frontiers: The Politics of (Human) Nature in Blade Runner," a paper delivered at the American Political Science Association August 30, 1991.

13. This is the reading of a social desire for domination as embodied within these two male cyborgs as read by Slavoj Žižek, *Looking Awry: An Introduction to Jacques Lacan through Popular Culture* (Cambridge, Mass.: MIT Press, 1991), 22-23. On Ridley Scott's *Blade Runner* prefiguring a related male fantasy of the ideologically subjectivized cyborg, Žižek conjectures that "the hero's android girlfriend 'becomes subject' by (re)inventing her personal history; here, the Lacanian thesis that woman is a 'symptom of man' acquires an unexpected *literal* value" as sexual difference gets acted out as the binary difference human/android (173, n3).

14. By-product of a microelectronic revolution launched by the postwar American government to accelerate its military and space program, the robot/cyborg will increasingly restructure attitudes of labor toward "work" if not everyday space, time, and family; see Andre Gorz, interviewed by John Keane, "What Way Is Left? Social Change in the Postindustrial Era," *Grand Street* 38 (1991): 131-64. The problems and possibilities the cyborg subject represents to romantic models of organic subjectivity and textuality are traced in Gabriele Schwab, "Cyborgs and Cybernetic Intertexts: On Postmodern Phantasms of Body and Mind," in *Intertextuality and Contemporary American Fiction*, ed. Patrick O'Donnell and Robert Con Davis (Baltimore and London: Johns Hopkins University Press, 1989), 191-213.

15. Arthur Kroker, "Panic Cowboy" entry in *Panic Encyclopedia*, ed. Arthur and Marilouise Kroker and David Cook (New York: St. Martin's, 1989), 81. The high-technological version of the "regeneration through violence" narrative that governs plots of cyborg films such as *Robocop* and *Terminator* has origins in the collective conquest of the indigenous frontier for national purposes of sublime unity and liberal consensus, as in John Ford films of Wild West domestication. See Richard Slotkin, *Regeneration through Violence: The Mythology of the American Frontier, 1600-1860* (Middletown, Conn.: Wesleyan University Press, 1973); John G. Cawelti, *The Six-Gun Mystique* (Bowling Green, Ohio: Bowling Green University Press, n.d.); and the brilliant deconstruction of American imperialism as global outreach and racial evacuation across the Pacific in Richard Drinnon, *Facing West: The Metaphysics of Indian-Hating and Empire-Building* (New York: New American Library, 1980).

16. David Harvey, "Flexibility: Threat or Opportunity?" *Socialist Review* 21 (January-March 1991): 72-73.

17. Verhoeven's remark about the *Challenger* explosion is quoted in Chon Noriega, "Robocop," *Magill's Cinema Annual, 1988* (Pasadena, Calif.: Salem, 1988), 303. For an industrially nostalgic (if not modernist) reading of the working-class subject in Verhoeven's *Robocop*, see Julie F. Coddell, "Murphy's Law, Robocop's Body, and Capitalism's Work," *Jump Cut* 34 (1989): 12-19: "Between his [Murphy's] rebirth and his synthetic resurrection Murphy has gained feeling and free will, owning himself as the means of production and gaining self-determination" (18).

18. William Gibson, "The Gernsback Continuum," *Burning Chrome* (New York: Ace, 1986), 29.

19. Jean Baudrillard, "America," epigraph to William Burroughs's "A Thanksgiving Prayer," *Mondo 2000*, no. 3 (1991): 9.

20. Gibson, "Gernsback Continuum," 28. For a reading of ways that "deep cultural

imagery" from the "mass unconscious" in Gibson's story would repudiate the technoeuphoria of modernity pervading American science fiction from the 1930s through the
1970s, see Andrew Ross, "Getting Out of the Gernsback Continuum," *Critical Inquiry* 17
(1991): 411-33. Ross sees more disenchantment with the technological sublime and the
cybernetic future pervading the worlds of Gibson and cyberpunk cinema than I would;
for an analysis of this ongoing American sacralization of high technology within postmodern sublimity, see Rob Wilson, "Technoeuphoria and the Discourse of the American
Sublime," *boundary 2* 19 (Spring 1992): 205-29, "National Identities and Postnational Narratives," special issue edited by Donald Pease; and Rob Wilson, *American Sublime: The
Genealogy of a Poetic Genre* (Madison: University of Wisconsin Press, 1991) on nation-
state formations of the American subject within decentering technologies of the "postmodern" and "nuclear sublime," (19-64 and 197-263).

21. On the sway of American liberal ideology within depoliticizing special effects of cin-
ematic "spectacle" after World War II, see Dana B. Polan, "'Above All Else to Make You
See': Cinema and the Ideology of Spectacle," *Postmodernism and Politics*, ed. Jonathan
Arac (Minneapolis: University of Minnesota Press, 1986), 55-69; and Paul Virilio, *War and
Cinema*, trans. Patrick Camiller (New York and London: Verso, 1989). Polan argues that
Western mass cinema served to render grand and foreshadow the "perceptual logistics"
of (ongoing) militarization and the "technophiliac transfer [demanded] in a society undergoing militarization" since World War I (22-23). Cinematic complicity in fantasizing war,
imagined on an imperial scale and pervading Great Britain, Japan, and the United States,
informs J. G. Ballard's novel *Empire of the Sun* (New York: Pocket Books, 1985). The ways
a militant empire needs to reproduce war- and technology-infatuated subjects is sublimated into childhood awe in Steven Spielberg's 1987 movie *Empire of the Sun*; see Masao
Miyoshi's cross-cultural critique of this depoliticizing American film, "Out of Agreement:
The Emperor and Christmas," in *Off Center: Power and Culture Relations between Japan
and the United States* (Cambridge, Mass.: Harvard University Press, 1991), 177-79.

22. The argument that an "imagery of global degradation" pervades films in the cyberpunk genre was outlined in a talk by Andrew Ross on "The Ecology of Images" given at
the Hawaii International Film Festival, East-West Center, November 30, 1990. This viewpoint informs the green politics and media-driven moralizations in Andrew Ross, *Strange
Weather: Culture, Science and Technology in the Age of Limits* (London and New York:
Verso, 1991).

23. Bruce Sterling, in the preface to *Mirrorshades: The Cyberpunk Anthology* (New
York: Ace, 1986), xiv.

24. Gibson, "Gernsback Continuum," 30: "Kihn's opinion of what I was already thinking
of as my 'sighting' rattled endlessly through my mind in a tight, lopsided orbit. Semiotic
ghosts. Fragments of the Mass Dream, whirling past in the wind of my passage." Within
deeper reaches of cyberspace in *Neuromancer* (New York: Ace, 1984) and *Mona Lisa
Overdrive* (1988), Gibson's characters encounter vast cybernetic forces and pirated codes
within an inner matrix of voodoo possession, mythic angst, and plasticine media stars.
Such postfeminist cyborgs are subject to invisible manipulation and recall by transnational information capitalists, as is, say, Whitney Houston, who must surpress her racial identity to mate with great white hero Kevin Costner, her machinic bodyguard and house pet
in *The Bodyguard* (1992).

25. See Arthur Kroker, *Technology and the Canadian Mind: Innis/McLuhan/Grant*
(New York: St. Martin's, 1985), 16.

26. On the mixing and matching of contemporary races and multicultural styles (as in

Whitney Houston, Madonna, and Michael Jackson) to serve as lucrative commodities in Motown and Hollywood, see Harryette Mullen, "Miscegenated Texts & Media Cyborgs: Technologies of Body and Soul," *Poetics Journal* 9 (1991): 36-43. For this connection of Robocop and Elvis as simulacrous cyborgs, I am indebted to Jonathan Beller, "Desiring the Involuntary: Circulation and the Machinic Assemblage in Deleuze and *Robocop 2*." Reading this bizarre American film as a process of the modern subject and state formation rejecting its own organization as capitalist desire, Beller concludes, in Deleuzian terms, "Simply put, Robocop may be understood, depending on the standpoint, as either the deterritorialization of the flesh and technology, the machinic assemblage of 'the wasp and the orchid,' or the reterritorialization of the flesh and technology by the new State." (It is the latter position I have argued here, against the "deterritorialization" view of any promissory American cyborg.) Beller's essay on *Robocop 2* is forthcoming in Rob Wilson and Wimal Dissanayake, eds., *Global/Local: Cultural Production in the Transnational Imaginary* (Durham, N.C.: Duke University Press).

27. Sterling, preface to *Mirrorshades*, xiii.

28. Although Steven Best admires technological dimensions and postmodern structures of feeling at work in Verhoeven's film, he comes around to a critique of the film's state-recuperated cultural politics similar to the one I outline here: "The key shortcoming of the film is consistent with its [American] liberalism, its inability to locate the real sources of alienation and reification. At no moment does *Robocop* suggest that the numerous serious social issues it raises—from nuclear disaster to monopoly control—are inherent in or fundamentally related to the corporate system it critiques." See Steven Best, "*Robocop*: In the Detritus of High-Technology," *Jump Cut* 34 (1989): 25. Such critiques of these filmic spectacles remain, oddly enough, rare, as if postmodern criticism itself is enchanted by Hollywood cyborgs and exists at the world-weary end of ideology and political struggle.

29. Gibson, *Neuromancer*, 85.

30. Félix Guattari, "Cinematic Desiring-Machines," *Critical Texts* 3 (1985): 3. On pain-as-pleasure syndromes of sublime masochism and a male-gazed fetishism fascinated by domineering spectacles of flesh and machine such as *Robocop* and *Robocop 2*—if not 3, 4, and 5 (not to mention the array of *Robocop* comics and toys the young American male now plays with around the MTV set)—also see Gilles Deleuze, *Masochism: Coldness and Cruelty* (Cambridge, Mass.: MIT Press, 1991), and Hosea Hirata, "Masturbation, the Emperor, and the Language of the Sublime in Oe Kenzaburo," a paper presented at the Association of Asian Studies conference in Los Angeles, March 26, 1993.

31. My understanding of transnationalization as a process that disturbs spaces of local resistance and national consolidations of identity benefits from two works: Masao Miyoshi, "A Borderless World?: From Colonialism to Transnationalism and the Decline of the Nation State," *Critical Inquiry* 19 (1993): 726-51, and Arif Dirlik, *Waking to Global Capitalism*, forthcoming from Wesleyan University Press.

Reading the Rushdie Affair:
"Islam," Cultural Politics, Form
Aamir Mufti

Gayatri Spivak has argued that, in the case of *The Satanic Verses*, "the praxis and politics of life" intercept the aesthetic object to such a degree that a "mere reading" of the novel has become impossible.[1] In this essay, I will examine the novel's "interception by" (and its intervention in) certain political contexts within the post-1979 Islamic world. The essay is not meant to provide an even partial "reading" of the text in traditional critical terms. Instead, it will focus on "the Rushdie affair" as a complex cultural (and political) *event* within the Islamic world, treating it as a constellation that brings together, highlights, and restructures some of the central elements of contemporary Muslim life. It is well known that Muslim South Asia, both "at home" and in diaspora, figured prominently in the crisis from the very beginning. Accordingly, it is the Indian context that provides the nucleus around which my argument will be built.

As has now become generally evident, the novel presents what is arguably the most serious literary challenge in recent years to the legitimacy of certain brands of contemporary "Islamic" politics. Some of the questions it confronts have been almost constantly present in the political discourse of much of the Islamic world for over a century, but have acquired their present form, as well as their current urgency, in the years since the Iranian Revolution of 1979: What kind of accommodation can Islam reach with "modernity" once "traditional" social structures have collapsed under the pressures of global capitalism? What is the place of women in a "modern" Islamic community? How is contemporary politics to be organized in accordance with Islamic tradition—and how is tradition to be interpreted? What place is there within Islam for claims—nationhood, citizenship, democracy, social and economic justice—that are identified with "secularism" and have their roots in the European Enlightenment? What is the role of Islam in the contemporary struggle against the economic, political, and cultural imperialism of the West? What, precisely, in this age of the globalization of economic, political, and cultural forms, does it mean to be a Muslim?

What has given the novel its transgressive force is that instead of merely thematizing these familiar issues, it also forces a changing of the terms of the discussion itself. Its multilayered engagement with the origin myth of Islamic orthodoxy, its "politics of offense" with respect to Islam,[2] have rightly been read as a forceful refusal to accept the cultural authority of the authoritarian political constellations and discourses, usually grouped under the label of "fundamentalism," that have emerged across the Muslim world in the last decade and a half.[3] The term *fundamentalism* is notoriously slippery. The history of its abuse in the Reagan-Bush era, for instance, by the media and "area studies" establishment alike, is well known. Furthermore, as Ervand Abrahamian has shown, the term has little utility as a description of the doctrinal content of even such a paradigmatic movement of "Islamic militancy" as Khomeinism.[4] I therefore use the term, as will shortly become clear, in a very specific sense: as shorthand for the *public* and popular discourses of domestic and international militancy under the sign of "Islam" that have come to take remarkably similar shape across the Islamic world in recent years. The violence of the novel's reception in South Asia—and within the South Asian Muslim diaspora in Britain—is an accurate indicator of the anger generated by its insistence on a sweeping rearrangement and rethinking of the terms of Muslim public culture. It is the audacity of this insistence, enacted by an "insider," and, as it were, "in full view" of the West, whose hostility to the world of Islam is both continuing and well known, that has been consistently glossed by the novel's Muslim detractors as "irreverence," "apostasy," and "blasphemy."

It is my contention here that the "affair" surrounding *The Satanic Verses* forces us to reexamine notions of literary reception current in critical theory today. Conceptions of reception based on an almost Victorian image of the solitary bourgeois reader have allowed progressive commentators to more or less dismiss the novel as produced for (and "consumed" by) Western audiences alone.[5] Working under similar assumptions, Western accounts of the world-wide demonstrations against the book's publication have often expressed amazement at the passion of crowds that have obviously not read the book.[6] A reconceptualization of reception appropriate to the cultural realities of the present global conjuncture, I will argue, must account for forms of mass "consumption" other than "reading" in the narrower sense of that word. Extracts published in the print media, in English and in translation; commentary in print, on the airwaves, and from the pulpit; fantasticated representation in the popular cinema; rumors and hearsay—such are the means by which the novel has achieved circulation in the Islamic world.

I am arguing that this piecemeal and fitful reception at the popular level is not simply accidental, and that in a sense the novel even *requires* it. First of all, the novel's political project vis-à-vis contemporary "Islam"—to intervene in the public political conversation within the Muslim world—required breaking out of the minuscule anglophone audience to which the English-language writer in South Asia is traditionally confined. And secondly, the almost obsessive attention given in Rushdie's novels to the dynamics of mass communication—the fantasylike distortions and fragmentation that events and objects go through in the process of entering the public sphere—the insistence in *The Satanic Verses* on the "impurity" of any situation in the contemporary world, and the novel's self-conscious use of pastiche and nonlinear narrative themselves point toward the filtered reception the novel has received. So the familiar and sinister-sounding charge, leveled by the likes of Roald Dahl and John Le Carré, that Rushdie "knew what he was doing," must be stood on its head: by inserting itself in bits and pieces within the cultural politics of contemporary "Islam," the novel has indeed achieved—if one may speak of "textual," rather than authorial, intention—what was already inscribed in and suggested by its very form.[7]

Furthermore, this "reception by pastiche" forces us to think again about the meaning and function of pastiche within the text itself. Entirely assimilable neither to the national-allegorical function attributed by Jameson to "Third-World literature" nor to the purely stylistic connotations of "the postmodern" as it has been conceptualized in recent critical theory, pastiche—that is, hybridity of form, in this case the juxtaposition and overlapping of realist, "magical real-ist," and "modernist" modes; the parodic rewriting of historical and religious narratives and of metropolitan texts, genres, and motifs; the use of the resources of literary as well as popular culture—takes on in Rushdie's text a deeply political and critical turn.[8] It is precisely this *ambivalence* of form—is the book about "real" events in Islamic history or is it pure fiction and fantasy?—that constitutes the space within which the novel is able to function as critique. Pastiche, in this context, is neither a purely formal question nor merely the tex-tual correlate of a hybrid "external reality." Pastiche and formal ambivalence are here the very conditions that enable the literary text to enter the public sphere as political act.

Given the meticulous attention Rushdie has always directed toward the critical role of the postcolonial artist-intellectual, and toward the function of writing, it is perhaps ironic that his most politically inter-ventionist work to date should have been read by so many progres-sive critics in the West only as an exercise in cosmopolitan irony and detachment, the work, as Brennan puts it, of a "court satirist."[9] No such piety clouds the discussion in India itself, where the novel has been discussed in explicitly political terms by antagonists and supporters alike, raising questions about secularism, class, citizenship, and the nature and role of the state—the most urgent and explosive constellation of issues facing Indian political life today.

The two earlier novels of Rushdie's trilogy, *Midnight's Children* and *Shame*, have most often been read as wide-ranging examina-tions and critiques of the modern nation-space designated by "India" and "Pakistan" respectively.[10] They portrayed an essentially *critical* role for the artist-intellectual vis-à-vis the national project. While alluding in authorial asides to the substantive questions of intellectu-al "authenticity" in the postcolonial world, the earlier novels never-theless approached the question of the intellectual in terms that were primarily negative: they were concerned with the *failure* of the imaginative work of nation building in two postcolonial coun-tries.[11] In *The Satanic Verses*, a far more positive stand is taken in favor of the hybrid perspectives of postcolonial identity, a stand Rushdie had already elaborated at great length in essays and inter-views.[12] Fredric Jameson has argued that the characteristic form of the "third world text" is "the national allegory."[13] Without ignoring the ubiquitous complicities and connections between literature and the national, it must nevertheless be pointed out that this formulation addresses only one moment in the "worldliness" of the texts it takes as its objects, that it is unable to account fully for the *oppositional* thrust of the first two novels of the trilogy, and that it falls far short of understanding the self-consciously supranational concerns of this third book. The role of the intellectual, as it appears in Rushdie's writings, involves, I will argue, going beyond a mere "telling of the experience of the collectivity itself" to a posing of specific challenges directed at historical fictions of community and representation.[14]

Before proceeding to the specific issues raised by the "Islamic" reception of the novel in India, I wish to take a brief detour and discuss the persistent theme of intellectual and critique in Rushdie's writing, and the change and expansion of focus it has undergone over the course of the trilogy. There is, I suggest, progressively greater foregrounding of the author's persona in each subsequent novel, and greater identification of the author himself with the critical thrust of the work. The passage from *Midnight's Children* to *The Satanic Verses* also marks a shift away from what I shall call a politics of constituency, toward what I have already spoken of as a politics of offense.

In *Midnight's Children*, the intellectual appears in the form of the narrator himself. Saleem Sinai, born at the moment of India's emergence from colonial rule, is "mysteriously handcuffed" to the fate of the nation and endowed with mysterious powers of "seeing into the hearts and minds of men."[15] In order to fully grasp the relation of Saleem to the nation itself, we may begin by recalling that it is under the prophecy of Jawaharlal Nehru, framed and hanging on the wall, that the boy Saleem grows up: "You are the newest bearer of that ancient face of India," the prime minister's letter to the infant reads, "which is also eternally young. We shall be watching over your life with the closest attention; it will be, in a sense, the mirror of our own" (122). The shadow of Nehru, the totemic intellectual of Indian nationalism, hangs heavy over Saleem's life, and his attempts to discover and impose a "third principle" (248-49) beyond "the endless duality of masses-and-classes, capital-and-labour, them-and-us" on the other one thousand mysteriously gifted "midnight's children" are deeply informed by the pedagogic and mediating role that the intellectual-politician is meant to play within the narrative of Indian nationalism.[16]

Saleem's disintegrating body and unfulfilled life highlight not so much the failure as the impossibility of the national (liberal-democratic) project of turning colonial subjects into democratic citizens while simultaneously insisting on the directing and guiding role of the anglicized elite. Saleem's anguished search in the Midnight Children's Conference for a "third principle" is thwarted as each child becomes "distracted by his or her own life" and is swayed by the counterarguments of Shiva, "midnight's darkest child," that "the world is not ideas, rich boy; the world is no place for dreamers or their dreams." And the adult Saleem, the artist-intellectual literally narrating the nation's history, is forced to conclude that "if there is a third principle, its name is childhood. But it dies; or rather, it is murdered."

It is the impossibility and fraud of this mediation or "third principle," so brutally revealed by the repression and tyranny of Indira Gandhi's Emergency Rule, that *Midnight's Children* confronts. It records the historical failure of the elite to "represent" the entire nation—in both the semiotic and the delegational senses of the word. This record does have its allegorical moments: Saleem, raised in privilege, is actually the illegitimate son of the departing Englishman Methwold, and he conceals this colonial patrimony from the Midnight Children's Conference, whose leadership he claims on the basis of superior ability and higher principles; Shiva, who is brought up in the street, and whose "birth-right" is denied him by Saleem, becomes his nemesis both within and outside the conference and is ultimately his undoing; Padma, the earthy "dung goddess" at once fascinated by the urbane Saleem and frustrated by his inability to fulfill her desires, becomes his protector and collaborator in the composition of the autobiography that is also a history of the nation. But the allegory remains incomplete in the resistance of the novel to the very idea of the nation as produced within the "grand narrative" of India's liberation and modernization.[17] And to dislodge the authority of this narrative from *within*, to voice its blind spots, absences, and exclusions, becomes the primary task of that special child of midnight, the postcolonial intellectual.

Hence the series of inversions enacted in the novel. If "national time," as Benedict Anderson suggests, is linear, calendrical time, the time of *Midnight's Children* is cyclical, ritual, or, as Rushdie puts it, "pickled" time;[18] if the typical nationalist narrative proceeds from interior to exterior time and space, giving "hypnotic confirmation of the solidarity of a single community, embracing characters, author and readers,"[19] *Midnight's Children*, like the oral tale, "goes in great loops and circles back on itself, repeats earlier things, digresses,"[20] in order precisely to suggest a multiplicity of voices, interests, communities; and if the solitary nationalist hero moves "through a sociological landscape of a fixity that fuses the world inside the novel with the world outside,"[21] Saleem, this ironic and restless consciousness, his body wracked by the "rip tear crunch" of the nation's history, himself puts the veracity of his narrative in doubt and raises questions about the authority of his class—the anglicized middle class—as an interpretive community.

The critical consciousness that emerges in *Midnight's Children*, then, is double-edged: it is directed at both colonial culture and the myth of cultural authenticity and authority that replaced it. Frantz Fanon argued in "On National Culture" that "the native intellectual who wishes to create an authentic work of art" must overcome assimilation in the culture of the colonizers as well as the temptation to articulate the immemorial "truth" of the nation ("we have the right to ask if this truth is in fact a reality"). He must come to inhabit, Fanon wrote, that "zone of occult instability" where the culture of a people is forged.[22] Deeply aware of its colonial and local-elite affiliations, *Midnight's Children* is at one level an account of the struggle to represent that instability.

While I have so far emphasized the negative moments of the novel's attitude toward the nation, it should be pointed out that this attitude is in the end quite ambivalent. Rushdie's frequent assertions to the effect that *Midnight's Children* was motivated by the desire to reclaim "that part of my life that was in danger of being lost" must not be read at the level of autobiographical memory alone.[23] For the account of the failure of the anglicized elite to "dream up" the nation in its own image is accompanied by a lingering nostalgia for the social order envisioned in that dream, an order reflected in the graceful life of Methwold Estate.[24] This nostalgia has played no small part in creating for the novel an enthusiastic constituency within the very same social class whose self-proclaimed place in society it set out to criticize.

In *Shame*, while the critical relationship of the artist to the false certainties of (in this case, Pakistani) national culture is maintained, there is a formal change that has the effect of increasing the stakes and intensifying the critique. The narrator, no longer a Saleem-like "character" in the novel, is repeatedly identified with the author himself. At various junctures, the "story" is interrupted by passages of varying length in which the author inserts himself into the narrative with commentary and with biographical information that even the relatively uninformed reader recognizes as referring to the author himself. And once again the question of critical authority is raised. By what authority, he imagines his Pakistani readers objecting, can the voluntarily exiled writer speak of Third World realities?:

> *Outsider! Trespasser! You have no right to this subject!*... I know: nobody ever arrested me. Nor are they ever likely to. *Poacher! Pirate! We reject your authority. We know you, with your foreign language wrapped around you like a flag: speaking about us in your forked tongue, what can you tell but lies!* (23)[25]

To which the author-narrator at once replies:

> Is history to be considered the property of the participants solely? In what courts are such claims staked, what boundary commissions map out the territories? Can only the dead speak? (23)

This sudden appearance of the author between the reader and the plot of the novel, aside from insisting on the right to critique, *personalizes* the novel's critical intention, adding a confrontational tone that was not present in *Midnight's Children*. It also marks a shift away from the residual nostalgia for the nation that was still present in the earlier novel. The combined effect is a weaker sense of identification with a constituency within the "community" (Pakistan) that is the object of the novel's representation.

In *The Satanic Verses* this personalization is given a new turn, for one of the forms in which the author now "appears" is that of Salman the Persian, a minor character with respect to the novel as a whole, but pivotal in the Jahilia sequences that are at the center of the Islamic controversy.[26] This "identification" of the author with the Prophet Mahound's scribe, responsible for secretly emending and polluting the word of God, is carried out in a number of ways. Aside from the common name Salman—"Persian" in early Islamic culture was simply synonymous with "non-Arab Muslim"—and the common writer's vocation, a number of textual markers facilitate this identification. Salman's account to Baal of his loss of faith and fall from Mahound's grace, for instance, shifts suddenly from the third person to the first, from "Salman complained to Baal," to "*I* began to get a bad smell in my nose" (365).[27] The effect of course is to associate Salman the author with the doubt, apostasy, and treachery of Salman the scribe. It is this insistence on personalizing the novel's intervention, reinforced by the tone and substance of Rushdie's reactions early in the controversy, that placed him outside the pale of discussion and disputation as far as his critics are concerned. It also made it nearly impossible for the novel to be *publicly* identified with in the context of contemporary political and cultural life in the Muslim world. The shift away from a politics of constituency, in other words, is complete.

Each of the two novels that have followed *Midnight's Children* represents, then, an intensification of political engagement at the same time that it marks a shift away from what might be called a politics of constituency: *Shame* in comparison with *Midnight's Children* and *The Satanic Verses* in comparison with *Shame*, seem less and less concerned with addressing actual audiences in South Asia with whom they might be able to declare a commonality of purpose and position. This is not to say that such constituencies do not exist. If anything, the (traditionally conceived) audience for these novels within the Islamic world is larger than most outsiders suspect. I am simply arguing that the novels go beyond these possibilities, in order to enact what I have called a politics of displacement and offense, transgressing universally enforced norms of literary representation and public discussion—from state-enforced censorship in Pakistan to the political and cultural taboos of contemporary "Islamic" culture—with such force and to such an extent that some aspects at least of the official culture are thrown into question. In the transgressive politics of *The Satanic Verses* vis-à-vis "Islam," this process has reached its climax.

It is worth recalling at this juncture that the offending passages are contained mostly within two chapters—"Jahilia" and "Return to Jahilia"—that add up to less than seventy-five pages in this rather large book. There are, broadly speaking, three areas that, in terms of content, constitute the novel's most transgressive moments. The first, suggested by the title itself, is the incident of the verses that were revealed to Mahound in response to the Jahilian grandee's offer of peace if three of the Jahilian goddesses were accepted as minor deities by the new religion; the verses sanctioning this arrangement were renounced by Mahound as the work of Satan once the grandee's wife Hind had withdrawn her husband's offer of peace (123). The second is the incident involving Salman, already discussed above, in which the scribe, beginning to lose faith in the prophet, tests the prophet by altering the verses as they are dictated to him; Mahound fails to notice the emendations when the verses are read back to him for confirmation (367-68). The third concerns the Jahilian whorehouse named The Curtain, or *Hijab*—the Arabic word is now used widely in the Islamic world for the shoulder-length scarf that has come to be equated, in varying cultural contexts, with the required Islamic headdress for women—whose prostitutes take on the names of Mahound's wives (which happen to be the names of the historical Muhammad's wives as well) in order to heighten the excitement and pleasure of their customers (376-92).

While the first two sequences call into question the infallibility of the revelation—in the first case by problematizing the mode of transmission of the word of God, and in the second by suggesting the addition and emendation of passages by a human—the last personalizes the offense by playing irreverently with figures held in deep reverence by believers. It is these three moments that have most often been extracted from the novel for quotation and transmission and have acquired a sort of iconic value in the mass politics in which it has become embroiled.[28] Syed Shahabuddin, the Indian opposition member of Parliament who led the successful campaign for the banning of the book in India, castigated Rushdie's novel on precisely these points, in an open letter than deserves a closer look, and to which I will shortly return:

> The very title of your book is suggestively derogatory. In the eyes of the believer the Koran is the word of God, and you plead innocence of the possible Muslim reaction. You depict the Prophet whose name the practising Muslim recites five times a day, whom he loves, whom he considers the model for mankind, as an imposter and you expect us to applaud you? You have had the nerve to situate the wives of the

Prophet, whom we Muslims regard as the mothers of the community, in a brothel, and you expect the Muslims to praise the power of your imagination?[29]

Similarly, Shabbir Akhtar, the animus behind the Bradford-based campaign for a banning of the book in Britain, characterized the novel as "a calculated attempt to vilify and slander the Prophet of Islam."[30] It portrays Muhammad, he argued, as "an unscrupulous politician.... The book he claims to bring from God is really just a confused catalogue of trivial rules about sexual activity and excretion.... His household is portrayed in pornographic scenes in a brothel incongruously called 'The Veil'—the symbol of female modesty and chastity in the Islamic ethical outlook."[31] And beyond the mere content of the offending passages, Akhtar pointed to the tone, "the idiom and the temper" of the novel, which are "uniformly supercilious and dismissive," and seem "calculated to shock and humiliate Muslim sensibilities."[32]

It is difficult to convey the transgressive force of the offending passages in the contemporary political atmosphere of much of the Islamic world, but especially in Muslim South Asia. The decade after the Iranian Revolution saw the rise to political center stage of political groupings that had previously been of marginal significance at best. The various fundamentalist guerrilla organizations in Afghanistan that fought the Soviets and the Afghan communists,[33] the Hizbollah among the Shi'i of Lebanon and Hamas in the occupied Palestinian territories, the Jama'at-i-Islami in Pakistan under the army's patronage,[34] such figures as Shahabuddin and the Imam Bukhari of Delhi's Jaama Mosque in India,[35] and organizations such as the Bradford Council of Mosques in Britain[36] have been able to command influence and attention far beyond the numerical strength of their followings. (And as recent experience in Algeria has shown, this influence is capable of turning itself into electoral strength, with devastating results.) The centerpiece of this new political culture is of course "Islam," the sign at once of a return to an authentic past and of passage out of the neocolonial structures of domination toward a more empowering future.

The change even from the 1970s has been so marked and so sudden that Eqbal Ahmed has spoken of an ongoing "crisis" of Islamic society:

Thus, as in all religious communities, there is a repository of millennial traditions in Islam that tend to surface most forcefully in times of crisis, collective stress, and anomie. Times have rarely been as bad or as stressful for the Muslim peoples as they are now. Hence, all the contrasting symptoms associated with deep crises of politics and society—rise of religious fundamentalism, radical and revolutionary mobilization, spontaneous uprisings and disoriented quietism—characterise Muslim politics today.[37]

First the traumas of colonial rule and then economic "modernization" under postcolonial regimes have caused, Ahmed argues, "the erosion of economic, social, and political relationships which had been the bases of traditional Muslim order for more than a thousand years."[38] Secular politics of various hues—Kemalist modernization, Nasserite pan-Arabism, Bhutto's *awami* populism—failed, in the decades since decolonization, either to generate sustained political and economic independence from the West or to acquire hegemonic force within civil society, producing an atmosphere, beginning in the 1970s, that has proven favorable to the rise of fundamentalist, neototalitarian movements across the Islamic world.[39]

Very broadly speaking, the public discourse of Islamic fundamentalism has produced two distinct but related critiques of the contemporary state of affairs in Islamic societies. And while the two typically occur as moments of the same argument against the status quo, they need to be separated for the purpose of analysis. We may speak of the first of these as an essentially *cultural* critique, directed at cultural forms and practices that come to be marked within the discourse as "modern," "Western," "foreign"; in short, as un-Islamic. The range of such practices is, of course, enormous, from habits of eating and dressing to the operation of educational and juridical institutions; but the one area of social life where the cultural critique has come to rest with particular force, and with particularly disastrous consequences, is that of gender and sexuality. The fundamentalist obsession with female "chastity"—the segregation of the sexes, the veiling of women, the minimizing (if not elimination) of women's presence in public life—is well known. These concerns find room, as Fatima Mernissi has pointed out, in the radical split within the individual "between what one does, confronted by rapid, totally uncontrolled changes in daily life, and the discourse about an unchangeable religious tradition that one feels psychologically compelled to elaborate in order to keep a minimal sense of identity."[40] Claims about the *literal* truth of the Koran therefore become the means of insisting upon the possibility of an unmediated reconstruction, in modern times, of the original, "righteous" community. And the "chastity" of women, in the overcoded form outlined here, comes to signify the minimal condition for the desired return to a state of cultural purity and authenticity.[41]

The other, directly *political* moment in fundamentalism's critique of society is directed at neocolonial structures of domination and exploitation, and the ("secular") national elites that function as comprador classes within those structures. It is able, for this purpose, to draw upon collective memories and traditions of resistance to colonialism, which are framed very often in terms of a historical struggle between Islam and the Christian West. (The truth value of these political claims is not the *primary* concern here. But it should of course be noted that there *is* a history of conversation and collaboration between fundamentalist groupings and imperialist interests, as witnessed by the CIA's decade-long sponsoring of the Afghan fundamentalist guerrillas and Iran's "contragate" dealings with Israel and the United States.) As I have already noted, these two assertions—claims about cultural and political authenticity, respectively—typically occur in conflated form in fundamentalist argumentation. Hence secular and "modernizing" tendencies in society—from the securing of legal rights for women to demands for the protection and strengthening of democratic rights, including freedom of expression—are represented as signs of Westernization, and hence of neocolonial bondage. Furthermore, the protracted history of struggle and out-and-out conflict between the secular left and the machinery of the postcolonial state is either erased entirely or at best seen as being of minimal importance. In speaking of Rushdie as an apostate from Islam, for instance, Akhtar is able to make the following astonishing equation:

> There are therefore countless Rushdies in the House of Islam. The Shah of Iran and his supporters were, to a man, atheists blindly imitating Western patterns of conduct.[42]

And of course, as is well known, the accusation of *gharbzadegi* or "West contamination" was the broad brush with which the pro-Khomeini, "populist" segment of the Iranian Shi'i clergy painted the whole range of its opponents, including liberals, communists, and Islamic radicals who especially had played a leading role in the movement against the monarchy, as it sought to eliminate them and consolidate its own hold over the course of the revolution within months of the fall of the shah.[43]

Despite this relative discursive stability, fundamentalism has proven notoriously difficult for the secular left to identify and critically engage. Apart from a recurrent failure of will on the part of the left, too often unable to see its position in Muslim society as anything but anomalous, this has resulted from the very nature of fundamentalist discourse itself. With its *universalizing* language of "Islamic" authenticity, fundamentalism has been able to make alliances with, appropriate, and mobilize sectors of society whose religious life and traditions have themselves been the object of vigorous critique in fundamentalist theology. Thus, the contemporary sense of social crisis and the erosion of popular cultural traditions and social practices under the impact of uneven urbanization, industrialization, and consumerization are easily construed as threats to "Islamic" culture and polity, and the desire for the recovery of that disappearing life is displaced onto the fundamentalist slogan for the reconstruction of the original, "righteous" community of seventh-century Islam.

It should be made explicitly clear that in no sense am I portraying fundamentalism as a *return* to premodern social, cultural, and political forms. On the whole it would be accurate to say that fundamentalism in fact critiques and rejects most of these "traditional" forms, seeing them as violations of the principles of the "righteous" community inaugurated by Muhammad and his early followers at Medina. (Khomeini, of course, went so far as to claim that revolutionary Iran had surpassed even the Prophet's society in the implementation of true Islam "in all spheres of life, particularly in the material and the spiritual spheres.")[44] Not to see this is also to miss the crucial point that what fundamentalism represents is precisely a struggle over the cultural artifacts of modernity—nationhood, citizenship, representative government, the forms of anti-imperialist and revolutionary struggle, the terms and institutions of the public sphere—and who gets to *define* them, and in what terms. The first two years of the Iranian Revolution—which saw a protracted struggle between the "populist" mullahs on the one hand, and liberals, Marxists, and the Islamic radical Mojahedin on the other—are an object lesson in this process of gaining control of, and redefining, the institutions of modern public life.[45] It is in this context that "the West" (and the taint of association with it) becomes a site for negative contestation, as both the historical source of these cultural artifacts and the chief impediment to their acquisition and development.

My purpose in outlining the salient features of the public discourse of fundamentalism—and it will be clear that my concern is with its popular constructions of "Islam," and not with fundamentalist theological discourse—is not to suggest the existence of a monolithic religio-political movement around the Islamic world. The aim here is to sketch out the discursive unity that allows similar fundamentalist arguments to be formulated in very different political and cultural contexts. The self-representation of fundamentalism in terms of "Islamic" cultural authenticity and anti-imperialist political purity is such a constant. So is the insistence on a rationalist-literalist reading of the Koran as a basis for the transformation of society. (Hence the opposition of fundamentalism to the enormous range of forms—including saint worship, the disciplines of the Sufis, the numerous traditions of mystical union with the divine around the Islamic world—in which "Islam" has been lived and practiced by the great majority of Muslims over the centuries.)[46] The diversity of actual fundamentalist groups around the world—as indexed by the kinds of alliances (and enemies) they make in particular historical situations, the political strategies they employ, and even the theological systems to which they adhere—is actually quite staggering. More importantly, the range of political contexts in which one or more elements of this discourse of "Islam" have in recent years been mobilized, by fringe groups and state structures alike, is also enormous.

In Pakistan during the 1980s, for instance, "Islamization" became the means of consolidation of the army's hold on power, a process carried out with the active participation of, among others, sections of the land-owning class, the bureaucracy, industrial and commercial bourgeoisies, and the small but influential Jama'at-i-Islami.[47] The term refers in principle to reform of public institutions such as the judicial and financial systems in accordance with the requirements of traditional Islamic law or *shari'a*. However, the full range of its discursive functions reaches far beyond that institutional focus and rests on an identification of the interests of "Islam" with the state, and until his death in 1988, with the person of Zia in particular.

Despite its self-proclaimed role of citadel of South Asian Islam, however, Pakistan was slow to react to the publication of the novel. The first country to ban it, within weeks of its publication in Britain in the early fall of 1988, was Rushdie's native India. There the book fell victim to an ongoing and bloody struggle between Hindu fundamentalist and Muslim groups over a sixteenth-century mosque in Ayodhya in northern India, claimed by the Hindu groups to have been built by the first Mughal emperor, Babar, on the site of the temple marking the birthplace of the Lord God Rama. The Babri Masjid-Rama Janamabhoomi conflict, which had already taken scores of lives, was threatening to explode out of control:[48] the Babri Masjid Coordinating Committee, consisting of notable Muslim politicians and clerics, with Shahabuddin as one of its leading figures, had promised a huge march to Ayodhya to underline Muslim claims to the site. Hindu groups had promised an equal show of force, and widespread bloodshed was expected. The Congress government of Rajiv Gandhi was having discussions with the Muslim leaders, negotiating to have them cancel their proposed march. On October 5 the government announced its ban; on October 12 Shahabuddin announced that the march had been indefinitely postponed. Despite official denials from both sides, it is difficult not to see a connection.[49]

Rushdie at once denounced the decision in somewhat breathless and vituperative terms, suggesting that Rajiv Gandhi had come out "looking not only philistine and antidemocratic but opportunistic" as well.[50] The reply to Rushdie's harangue came from Shahabuddin, in the open letter published in the *Times of India* of October 13, which I quoted from earlier. The thrust of Shahabuddin's critique is that the novel is in fact an act of cultural imperialism—"literary colonialism," he calls it—coming as it does from the West, "which has not yet laid the ghost of the crusades [*sic*] to rest, but given it a new cultural wrapping." It is Rushdie's willingness to "vend his Islam wares in the West," Shahabuddin argues, that "explains why writers like [him] are so wanted and pampered" there. India would stand up against this act of cultural violation, and not cringe in the face of accusations of loss of expressive freedoms from Rushdie's "British champions and advisors."[51]

But despite the fact that it is actually addressed to Rushdie, much of Shahabuddin's response is an engagement with what he identifies as the "Anglicized elite" and "liberal establishment" of the country. He excoriates them for not having thrown off the psychological fetters of colonialism, as witnessed by their undignified and unconcealed pleasure at the fact that "a book by a writer of Indian origin [has been] nominated, sorry, shortlisted for the highest literary award in the *Vilayat* [that is, Britain] by the sahibs themselves." But what is interesting here is that Shahabuddin defines the Muslims of India as distinct from, and in *opposition* to, the national intelligentsia:

> Even more shocking and saddening at the same time is the communication gap between the Muslim community and the so-called intelligentsia. There is no mental rapport, no instantaneous recognition of pain, no spontaneous sharing of anguish. . . . It's unbelievable that what pains one section gives pleasure to the other.[52]

This strange distinction is due in part, of course, to the majority/minority dynamics of the Indian nation-state and the marginal, though "protected," place of the Muslims within it. But it also articulates with the wider discursive formation I have been attempting to describe. For "Muslim" and "Islam" here are semantic spaces that exclude the experience of secular intellectual life, and Shahabuddin's statement is of one with Akhtar's declaration that

> given that the Koran is the book which defines the authentically Muslim outlook, there is no choice in the matter. Anyone who fails to be offended by Rushdie's book *ipso facto* ceases to be a Muslim.[53]

One of the more astonishing features of the Rushdie affair is the fact of its truly international dimensions, encompassing as it does political contexts as diverse as post-Zia Pakistan, the "communal" problem in India, and the politics of Asian immigration in Great Britain. And public responses by Muslims to the publication of this book, written by a writer of Indian origin naturalized and living in Britain, have been registered not only in Britain, India, and Pakistan, but also in places as diverse and as remote from the scene of the infraction as South Africa, (then) Soviet Central Asia, and Indonesia. What this range allows us to see is that it has become possible today to speak of an "Islamic" public sphere, incorporating elements of the public life of a large and diverse set of Muslim communities, ranging from nation-states in the Third World to ethnic minorities across the globe. Increased access to the international media, either directly or filtered through the regional and national media, continuing links between migrants and their parent communities, and increasing cooperation and coordination between agencies of the state and between religio-political groups in different parts of the world have all led to the transmission of information at unprecedented levels and with amazing speed. Public discussion of the place and meaning of Islam in contemporary life has therefore become surprisingly pan-Islamic in scope. What the response to the publication of the novel has also made clear is that this discussion is dominated by the literalist and universalizing discourse of fundamentalism.

It is the stability of this public sphere, in which resistance to neototalitarian movements and discourses is marginalized, deemed anti-Islamic, and often brutally suppressed, that *The Satanic Verses* disturbs. The concept of "public sphere" as defining institution of modern society owes its elaboration, of course, to the work of Jürgen Habermas. Habermas speaks of the "bourgeois public sphere" as the space for "rational-critical debate" within liberal society, in which "access is guaranteed to all citizens,"[54] and which is characterized by a co-incidence of the narrow interests of those who come to be defined as citizens and the "general interest" of society.[55] I use the term in a significantly different sense. My use of it points, first of all, to the processes of selection and *transfiguration* through which something gets to be constituted and disseminated as an object of dispute and discussion within this public sphere. On the one hand, low levels of literacy in the Third World and on the other, a generally high measure of access to electronic media and means of information transmission—radio, television, cinema, audio- and videotape technology, public address systems, fax machines—produce conditions of reception in direct contradiction to the requirements of most genres of (both indigenous and metropolitan) high literary production, a question to which I will shortly return. Secondly, I wish to point precisely to the enforced *exclusions*—in this case women, peasants and workers, dissident activists, artists and intellectuals—on which this public sphere is based.

But of more immediate concern for us at this point are the discursive constraints I have tried to evoke, which regulate discussions of "Islam" and its meaning and place in contemporary society. By questioning the infallible divinity of the Revelation, by refusing to accept the required code of strict reverence when speaking of the Prophet and his close circle of relatives and companions, and, more generally, by secularizing (and hence profaning) the sacred tropology of Islam in insisting upon its appropriation for the purposes of fiction, the novel throws into doubt the discursive edifice within which "Islam" has been publicly produced in recent years.[56] What this destabilization makes at least possible is the expansion of the discussion about Islam in the contemporary world, the insertion of *other* voices into this public sphere, and greater and more coherent resistance to the discourse of fundamentalism within it. It is in this sense that the politics the novel enacts is not one of constituency, but of displacement and offense. Critics who place the novel only or primarily within the metropolitan context ignore this mode of the novel's self-insertion into the politics of contemporary Islam.[57]

It would be dangerous and naive, however, to see the novel as embodying an unambiguously antireligious viewpoint, for that, of course, is precisely the view of its fundamentalist critics. As Sara Suleri has convincingly shown, the Western liberal appropriation of the embattled author as "one of us" does not "acknowledge the strong possibility that Rushdie's latest novel epitomizes the profound cultural fidelity represented by specific acts of religious betrayal."[58] "Rushdie performs," she argues, "a curious act of faith: he chooses disloyalty in order to dramatize his continuing obsession with the metaphors that Islam makes available to a postcolonial sensibility."[59] For the effect of this disloyalty is not to replace belief with the final certitude of disbelief. It is, rather, to posit *doubt* as "the opposite of faith" (*Satanic Verses,* 92), as the inevitable *corollary* of faith, or, as Suleri puts it, as "the very historicity of belief."[60]

The thematics of doubt appear repeatedly in the Jahilia sequences and are most successfully figured as the dissolution or overlapping of subjectivities. Thus, in the process of "listening" for the divine revelation concerning the three pagan goddesses, Mahound finds himself first reversing positions with Gibreel and then becoming indistinguishable from him, so that it is no longer "possible to say which of us is dreaming the other" (110). Furthermore, Rushdie makes it clear that, in insisting upon doubt as a constitutive modality of human experience, what he is opposing is any conception of belief that denies its materiality, placing it outside the realm of human effort and will:

> Angels are easily pacified; turn them into instruments and they'll play your harpy tune. Human beings are tougher nuts, can doubt anything, even the evidence of their eyes. Of behind-their-own eyes. Of what, as they sink heavy-lidded, transpires behind closed peepers . . . angels, they don't have much in the way of a will. To will is to disagree; not to submit; to dissent. (92-93)

"Doubt" therefore becomes in *The Satanic Verses* a sign of resistance to the fundamentalist hijacking of Islam, a means of prying open, even if ever so slightly, the seamless whole regarding which the only *public* choice offered the contemporary Muslim is submission or disbelief. When Rushdie speaks of his sustained respect for the religious mind, this must be taken not just seriously, but as the very basis of his novel's complex engagement with the culture and politics of contemporary Islam.

Since the beginning of the controversy, Rushdie's Islamic critics have argued that the enormous literary machinery within which these relatively short passages occur—their framing as the hallucinations of a man going mad, their only partial and "fantasticated" use of places, events, and persons significant in the narratives of Islam, their relatively minor place within the "plot" of the novel, traditionally conceived—do not in any way modify or condition the *directness* of the attack. Within weeks of the publication of the book in Britain, Shahabuddin warned Rushdie in his open letter that "you cannot take shelter behind the plea that after all it is a single dream sequence in a piece of fiction." And, responding to Rushdie's charge that "some of us have condemned you without a hearing and asked for a banning without reading the book," he replied:

> Yes, I have not read it, nor do I intend to. I do not have to wade through a filthy drain to know what filth is. My first inadvertent step would tell me what I have stepped into. For me, the synopsis, the review, the excerpts, the opinion of those who had read it and your own gloatings were enough.[61]

Such sentiments were in fact voiced repeatedly in the course of the controversy. Akhtar, for instance, wrote of the offending chapters as

"Rushdie's attempt to rewrite chronologically the history of early Islam ... (and to) proffer an alternative biography of Muhammad, his wives and companions."[62] In other words, the militant opposition to the novel has insisted from the start on a realist *and* fragmented reading. An understanding of this insistence therefore requires critical rethinking of the relationship between reception and form.

The question of form in Rushdie's novels can be approached in a number of ways. I will sketch out three related issues that may be subsumed under the rubric of parody and pastiche: the manner in which an important aspect of the novels' critical self-consciousness—their awareness of colonial-metropolitan affiliations—is worked out on the level of form; the correspondence between the novel's form and its pastichelike reception within the "Islamic" public sphere; and the fact that the formal ambivalence of pastiche becomes in *The Satanic Verses* an enabling condition for this political intervention.

In a series of essays on the functions of pastiche in Latin American fiction, Jean Franco has argued that the notion of pastiche "needs the notion of originality as counterpoint" and is therefore a natural corollary of the exhaustion of modernism's "search for originality."[63] For the same reason, pastiche is also a corollary of the decline of the "high" narrative of the (postcolonial) *nation's* cultural originality. For the purpose of this discussion, I suggest the following working definition: pastiche is hybridity or mélange, but it is also imitation and citation. It is not merely the seemingly random juxtaposition of different discourses; it is also a repetition of something that went before. More specifically, it ironically enunciates the signs of the colonizer in order to subvert their meanings. Against Jameson's stricture regarding the sharp contrast between (postmodern) pastiche and (modernist) parody—"pastiche ... is a neutral practice of ... mimicry, without any of parody's ulterior motives"[64]—it is my argument that parody and pastiche constitute in Rushdie's novels two aspects of the same formal intention, marking the texts' hesitation with notions of originality and purity on the one hand, and their self-critical sense of affiliation on the other. Parody thus provides ironic distance as a means of expressing a simultaneous sense of continuity and discontinuity with the (colonial) past, offering "a workable and effective stance toward the [latter] in its paradoxical strategy of repetition as a source of freedom."[65]

Gayatri Spivak has spoken of postcolonial claims to nationhood, democracy, and social and economic justice as "catechreses," the assigning of new and unfamiliar values to the "concept-metaphors" of metropolitan culture.[66] In *The Satanic Verses*, postcolonial culture incorporates such acts of citation, of repetition "with a difference." In the hybrid identities of the postcolonial world, in these shifting, unsettled perspectives, it is repeatedly suggested, may be found a metaphor for the modern world. Rushdie is unapologetic about an ambivalent "insider/outsider" status, a "historically validated eclecticism," as Zeeny puts it to Saladin (52). To borrow, in *The Satanic Verses*, is therefore also to appropriate and renew.

Already in *Midnight's Children*, Rushdie showed an anxious but ironic awareness of the novel's metropolitan affiliations. The opening, like that of Forster's novel of India, centers on a Dr. Aziz. (And the name of another character in the novel, Wee Willie Winkie, recalls the story by Kipling.) But whereas Forster's novel begins with Aziz in a mosque, anxiously protecting its sanctity from imagined desecration by a European—he thinks Mrs. Moore is wearing shoes in the place of worship—Rushdie's Aziz has an experience during the act of praying that leaves "a hole inside him" and takes him away permanently from religious faith. The Midnight Children's Conference is also an allusion, to both the Marylebone Cricket Club and the "Mayapore Chatterjee Club" to which the anglicized Indian Hari Kumar in Paul Scott's *The Jewel in the Crown* is laughingly said to belong.[67] As Timothy Brennan has pointed out, "Rushdie even mimics Scott's method of introducing the novel's defining themes in a painting's iconography."[68] In Scott's case, the painting referred to in the title shows an Indian prince presenting a bejeweled crown to Victoria, the classic tributary exchange between a colonial subject and his foreign ruler; in *Midnight's Children*, Rushdie gives us a picture of the young Raleigh seated at the feet of "an old, gnarled net-mending sailor ... whose right arm, fully extended, stretched out towards a watery horizon"—and in fact *westward* toward the Arabian Sea, visible from the window of Saleem's room, in which the picture is hung (122). This scene of colonial conquest with its inviting gesture, ominously echoed in Mary Pereira's lullaby, "anything you want to be, you can be," becomes for the child Saleem a source of horror and anguish. At the end of his life, in the final, unstoppable passage of the novel, he hears once again that refrain, with the role it promises for the national elite molded in the image of the colonial rulers, and says, "I hear lies being spoken in the night, anything you want to be you kin be, the greatest of all lies" (445).

In the case of *The Satanic Verses*, *pastiche* comes to refer at the most general level to the novel's formal equivocation between genres and styles, between realism, magical realism, the fantastic, the historical novel, reportage, allegory, autobiography. The question here, first of all, is the old Adornian problem, which reemerges with a vengeance in poststructuralist theory, of the appropriateness of form to the object of representation. Pastiche, in this context, is the textual correlate of a hybrid external reality, the presence/reflection within the text of the Third World's "uneasy and unfinished relationship to modernity."[69] But in fact the question of repeating the colonial text acquires in *The Satanic Verses* an even greater significance. As many of its Islamic critics have pointed out, the Jahilia chapters employ motifs, imagery, emphases, and phrasing—ranging from the use of the medieval derogatory "Mahound" to a fascination with the sex life of the Prophet—that have a well-known pedigree in the discourses of Orientalism.[70] And the fact that the protagonist of Rushdie's novel is called Saladin, and Mahound is merely the figment of a demented mind, recalls Dante's preference for the historical Saladin over "Mahometo" in the *Inferno*. In *The Satanic Verses*, Rushdie himself addresses the question of repeating the Orientalist sign:

> His name: a dream name, changed by the vision. Pronounced correctly, it means he-for-whom-thanks-should-be-given, but he won't answer to that here. . . . Here he is neither Mahomet nor MoeHammered; has adopted, instead, the demon-tag the farangis hung around his neck. To turn insults into strengths, whigs, tories, Blacks all chose to wear with pride the names they were given in scorn; likewise, our mountain-climbing, prophet-motivated solitary is to be the medieval baby-frightener, the Devil's synonym: Mahound. (93)

But in fact the repetition here goes beyond the mere inversion of an Orientalist hierarchy. For, by simply *accepting* the colonizer's words, even if with the intention of standing them on their head, that is, by inserting the polluting colonial sign within the space of the authentic and divine, the novel enacts another, *formal* transgression within the discursive field of contemporary "Islam," calling into question the assumption of purity vis-à-vis colonial-metropolitan culture upon which the authentic and divine are based.

Pastiche therefore becomes a means of appropriating and rewriting the colonial text—novel of empire, Orientalist motif, narrative of adventure and conquest—for contemporary purposes, within a global situation that might simultaneously be termed post- and neocolonial. The rewriting of the metropolitan text is itself in other words, a double-edged activity: on the one hand, it extracts from the metropolitan text a new knowledge of (colonized) self and (colonizing) other, precisely by problematizing that radical alterity; on the other, the rewriting uses the metropolitan text to question the authoritative discourses of public culture within the periphery. The scene of colonial conquest and the iconic presence of the novel of empire therefore make possible in *Midnight's Children* a severe critique of the cultural and material privileges of the national(ist) elite; and the Orientalist term of abuse, hurled down this time by an "insider," challenges in *The Satanic Verses* the premises of authoritarian Islamic theocracy. The fitful, fragmented, and "doubt-ridden" narrative of *The Satanic Verses* must therefore be read as the writing of a *supplement*—in Derrida's double sense of an addition as well as a voicing of the silences and suppressions of the original—to the totalizing narratives of contemporary "Islam." It is, to borrow a phrase once again from Jean Franco, an act of "substitution that undermines all essentialisms."[71]

The second sense of *pastiche* I want to address relates to the novel's reception. I have already suggested that the failure of progressive critics to identify with the novel's anti-fundamentalist "Islamic" politics results in part from outmoded notions of reception. There is now a need for a sustained effort to theorize the kinds of conditions of reception I have tried to evoke, under which a text, after a process of fragmentation and selection, becomes consumed within already existing cultural and political discourses, and becomes an object of debate, dispute, and discussion within different but often overlapping public spheres. As Arjun Appadurai has argued, the "globalization of culture is not the same as its homogenization."[72] Much of the confusion caused in the West by the Islamic reaction to the book is due precisely to this failure of perception: the political life of *The Satanic Verses* in the Islamic world cannot be contained within the rubric of "novel." The same text that has been acclaimed

in the West as a major experiment in that genre (and rejected by
many as a failed experiment) is "read" in very different ways in
what I have called the Islamic public sphere.

It might be useful in this context to quickly check the facts of the
early stages of the anti-Rushdie campaign in Britain, as described in a
Sunday Times report of February 9, 1989:

> Aslam Ejaz, of the Islamic Foundation in Madras, [had] already written to
> Faiyazuddin Ahmad, a friend in Leicester, telling him about the impend-
> ing ban in India. A similar campaign, wrote Ejaz, should be mounted in
> Britain, which still remained largely oblivious to the blasphemous
> nature of the book. ... Ahmad, who came to Britain from India five
> years ago, is public relations director of the Islamic Foundation in Leices-
> ter. His actions, as much as anything, were to spark the row in Britain. ...
> He sent out a secretary to buy the novel for £12.95 at a local bookshop.
> The offending passages were photocopied and immediately sent on
> October 3 to the dozen or so leading Islamic organizations in Britain.
> Four days later copies were despatched to the 45 embassies in Britain of
> the member countries of the Organization of Islamic Conference (OIC),
> including Iran.[73]

This process then repeated itself in several directions, leading to petitions asking various British officials to ban the book, the soliciting of
assistance from Muslim governments and the OIC, and greater coordination between the various organizations in Britain itself. In India
extracts from the book were not widely available even after the
actual ban, but the Hindu fundamentalist Bharatiya Janata Party
announced plans for publishing passages in Hindi translation in its
official newspaper. (I have been unable to determine whether these
plans were carried out.) The "dissemination" of the novel in India—
through written and verbal commentary, and general rumor and
hearsay—therefore involved an even greater degree of fragmentation and transformation. And in Pakistan the novel and its purported
offense against Islam have received greatest publicity in the form of
fantasticated representation in the cinema: the popular Punjabi and
Urdu film *International Guerrillas* tells the story of the men of a
Pakistani family who have taken an oath to avenge the blasphe-
mous act by assassinating Rushdie, here portrayed as the scotch-guz-
zling, woman-molesting agent of an international Zionist conspiracy
to destabilize Pakistan. In the final scene of the film, the defeated
brothers (who had appeared in an earlier scene in Batman cos-

tumes), nailed by Rushdie and his allies to wooden crosses, pray to God for intervention. Help descends from the heavens in the form of three copies of the Koran, which then strike Rushdie down with what looks like a laser beam. The only reference to the *content* of the novel anywhere in the film is a suggestion that it calls the Prophet's wives prostitutes.[74]

What is of greatest interest in this "reception" of *The Satanic Verses* in the Islamic world is the text's own provocation of the manner in which it has been consumed. In the conversation with Günter Grass that I have already quoted from, Rushdie himself makes an attempt to relate the two, usually separate, questions of form and reception. I will quote the passage in full:

> In India the thing I've taken most from ... is the oral narration. Because it is a country of still largely illiterate people ... the power and the vitality still remains in the oral story-telling tradition. And what's interesting about these stories is that they command huge audiences, the best story tellers, with literally hundreds of thousands of people. ... It's a very eclectic form, and of course is not at all linear. ... And it seems to be formlessness. ... Now, it occurred to me to ask the opposite question. Let us assume, for the sake of argument, that this is not formlessness but that this is a form which after all is many thousand[s] of years old and has adopted this shape for good reasons. Now, if so, what could those reasons be? It struck me the answer is very simple, which is that the story teller has the problem of holding the audience. ... And suddenly this suggested to me that what we were being told was [that] this very gymnastic form, this very convoluted, complicated form was in fact the reason why people were listening.[75]

While I do not think that Rushdie's account of the relationship of his work to orality should be taken literally, it is nevertheless interesting that he should have formulated the problem in this way during the period when *The Satanic Verses* was in the works. For it allows us to think through the manner in which "readers" in the Islamic world have been "listening" to the novel's transgressions. The novel's pastichelike structure—the situating of different discourses in juxtaposed, textually marked sections, the playful rewriting of well-known and easily recognizable episodes from the narratives of Islam, the enactment of these Islamic transgressions within brief, self-contained passages—corresponds to the selection, extraction, and the immediate, almost totemic identification of textual episodes with bits of Islamic lore that have characterized the novel's reception in the Islamic world. In linking form with reception, I am not, of course, making an argument about authorial intention. What I am suggesting is that there is, in "the Rushdie affair," a co-incidence of the (political) imperative of "holding the audience," textual form, and the dynamics of mass communication in the contemporary postcolonial world.

Finally, the novel's formal ambivalence also has more fundamental implications for its political life in the public sphere of contemporary "Islam." As we have seen, the Islamic opposition has insisted throughout on a reading that takes the offending passages literally, as a recklessly revisionist account of the birth of Islam, a rewriting of narratives held sacred by every practicing Muslim. Rushdie, on the other hand, has insisted that the novel is "fiction" and "fantasy," and cannot be read as "history."[76] It is the fact that the novel equivocates formally between these possibilities that allows it a positive political role in the Islamic world. Rushdie's demand to be read "fantastically" is, in this context, a demand for expressive freedom. The "Islamic" response to this demand is basically the following: "*Despite* the machinery of freedom you have erected, and beyond its ingenuity and splendor, we can see what the novel is *really* about." The opposition and struggle are not between the prerogatives of literature (fiction) and faith. The kind of cultural autonomy sought by *The Satanic Verses* must not be confused with the claims that are made on behalf of "autonomous art."[77] On the contrary, the conflict is about a particular *kind* of writing and its ineradicable *connection* with reality, and the social and cultural goals for which it can be (and has been) mobilized. Rushdie and the fundamentalists understand each other only too well. For what *The Satanic Verses* represents is an attempt to give "freedom"—not some abstract, universal freedom, but rather the concrete freedom to write outside and against the totalizing discourses of contemporary "Islam"—a literary form.

Discussions of Rushdie and *The Satanic Verses* have been conducted, understandably, in explicitly polemical terms, in the somewhat stark language of "for" or "against." It has been an aim of this essay to at least partially disengage itself from this discourse, in order to distinguish more clearly between the cultural politics highlighted by the "affair" and the person of the author himself. The point is to make it possible for us as critics on the left to identify those elements of this cultural politics of the novel's political intervention in the "Islamic" public sphere that we may consider positive and politically useful, despite the obvious problems posed by what Brennan has quite correctly identified as Rushdie's "complicity...with power."[78] (Khomeini's *fatwa* may be read as an attempt to make this complicity unequivocal, a fact Rushdie himself seems not to have understood.) And we should not be deterred from this task by Rushdie's rather clumsy experiments, through the language of "conversion," with the meaning of Muslim "community."

The situation of secular left intellectuals in South Asia and in the wider Islamic world today is characterized by a problematizing of the category of the "popular" in a manner that bears chilling comparison to the predicament of the German left intelligentsia in the 1930s. To recognize the class-marked nature of "secular" political and cultural claims in much of the Third World is one thing; to then fail to distinguish between *official* secularism and *oppositional* ones, and to reduce "secularism" as such to the ideological reflex of the indigenous national bourgeoisie—as in Brennan's declaration that "the banner of 'secularism' has for more than a century been the standard of a Westernized elite"—and leave the matter at that is quite another.[79] Such critiques of "secularism" do not acknowledge the participation (or at least acquiescence) of sections of the local elites (and of metropolitan interests) in the production of "Islam" and the rise of fundamentalist groups and parties in South Asia and across the Muslim world. While clearly needing to rethink its relationship to Islamic traditions and cultures and to engage in new ways with progressive Islamic groups, the secular left cannot and must not pretend to be anything but that—secular. For us as critics located in the West to reject the ideals of "secularism" in the Third World wholesale because these are not *spontaneously* produced within the domain of subaltern political and cultural life would not be so different, after all, from bureaucratic condemnation of reproductive rights and artistic freedom in the United States as the demands of a "cultural elite" alienated from the values of society at large.[80]

The importance of the cultural-political intervention in the public sphere of contemporary "Islam" that *The Satanic Verses* represents is therefore that it highlights the fact that the fight is far from over. The magnitude of the agony and anxiety it generated is in part a reflection of the fact that it made palpable, however fleetingly, the manner in which "Islam" has been *produced* in recent years. The left must not fail to take advantage of the consequences of this intervention, even as it distances itself from Rushdie's visibly growing comfort in the corridors of metropolitan power.

NOTES

An earlier version of this essay appeared in *Social Text* 29. I am grateful to John Archer for suggesting some of the revisions that have been incorporated in the present version. Final responsibility for its content is of course mine.

1. Gayatri Spivak, "Reading *The Satanic Verses*," *Public Culture* 2, no. 1 (Fall 1989): 79.

2. I am grateful to Homi Bhabha for suggesting the use of this term in the context of *The Satanic Verses*.

3. For a discussion of the necessity (and simultaneous difficulty) of balancing the critique of Western Orientalist discourse with one directed at the authoritarian politics of the contemporary Islamic world, see Eqbal Ahmed, "Islam and Politics," in *The Pakistan Experience*, ed. Asghar Khan (Lahore: Vanguard, 1985).

4. Ervand Abrahamian, "Khomeini: Fundamentalist or Populist?" *New Left Review* 186 (March/April 1991).

5. See, especially, Timothy Brennan, *Salman Rushdie and the Third World: Myths of the Nation* (London: St. Martin's, 1989), chapter 6; for a far more nuanced reading of the cultural politics of the Rushdie affair, but one nevertheless limited to the politics of South Asian immigration in Britain, see Talal Asad, "Ethnography, Literature, and Politics: Some Readings and Uses of Salman Rushdie's *The Satanic Verses*," *Cultural Anthropology* 5, no. 6 (August 1990): 239-69.

6. For a collection of Western reactions to the Rushdie affair, see Lisa Appignanesi and Sara Maitland, *The Rushdie File* (Syracuse, N.Y.: Syracuse University Press, 1990), henceforth *File*. It should be said that Rushdie has himself leveled this charge against his opponents. See, for instance, his open letter to Rajiv Gandhi, written in response to the banning in India, reprinted in *File*, 34.

7. See Dahl's February 28, 1989, letter to the London *Times* in *File*, 200. For Le Carré, see "A Book Not Worth the Bloodshed," *Manchester Guardian Weekly*, January 28, 1990, 26-27.

8. See Fredric Jameson, "Third-World Literature in the Era of Multinational Capitalism," *Social Text* 15 (Fall 1986). I am indebted to Jean Franco's discussion of pastiche in "The Nation as Imagined Community," in *The New Historicism*, ed. H. A. Veeser (New York: Routledge, 1989) and "Pastiche in Contemporary Latin American Literature," *Studies in 20th Century Literature* 14, no. 1 (Winter 1990).

9. Brennan, *Salman Rushdie*, 164. See also Asad, "Ethnography," and David Caute, "Prophet Motive," *New Statesman*, February 16, 1990, 18-19.

10. See Timothy Brennan, "India, Nationalism, and Other Failures," *South Atlantic Quarterly* 87, no. 1 (Winter 1988) and Nasser Hussain, "Hyphenated Identity: Nationalistic Discourse, History, and the Anxiety of Criticism in Salman Rushdie's *Shame*," *Qui Parle* 3, no. 2 (Fall 1989).

11. The idea of nation as imagined community is, of course, drawn from Benedict

Anderson's *Imagined Communities: Reflections on the Origin and Spread of Nationalism* (London: Verso, 1983).

12. See, for instance, "Author from Three Countries," *New York Times Review of Books*, November 13, 1983, 3, 22-23.

13. Jameson, "Third-World Literature."

14. Ibid., 85.

15. All page references are to the 1981 Jonathan Cape edition.

16. For the paradigmatic dramatization of this theme of intellectual mediation, see Nehru, "Bharat Mata," in *The Discovery of India* (New Delhi: Oxford University Press, 1989), 60-61. A thorough and brilliant discussion of this theme in Nehruvian thought is to be found in Partha Chatterjee, *Nationalist Thought and the Colonial World: A Derivative Discourse?* (London: Zed, 1986).

17. See Chatterjee, *Nationalist Thought*, 30: "Even as [nationalism] challenged the colonial claim to political domination, it also accepted the very intellectual premises of 'modernity' on which colonial domination was based."

18. Anderson, *Imagined Communities*, 30-33.

19. Ibid., 33.

20. Rushdie, in conversation with Günter Grass, "Writing for a Future," in *Voices: Writers and Politics*, ed. Bill Bourne, Udi Eichler, and David Herman (Nottingham: Spokesman, 1987), 58.

21. Anderson, *Imagined Communities*, 35.

22. Frantz Fanon, "On National Culture," in *The Wretched of the Earth* (New York: Grove, 1979), 225-27.

23. Rushdie, "Writing," 53.

24. For similar contradictory moments in Latin American fiction, see Jean Franco's introduction to the issue "Contemporary Latin American Fin de Siècle," *Studies in 20th Century Literature* 14, no. 1 (Winter 1990): 6.

25. All page references are to the 1983 Knopf edition.

26. The other autobiographical trace in the Jahilia dream sequences is of course the poet Baal. And there are obvious autobiographical moments in Saladin Chamcha as well.

27. Emphasis added. All references are to the 1988 Viking edition.

28. The passages about the exiled Imam, obviously based on Khomeini and the Iranian revolution, have not played any significant role in the public controversy. What role they might have played in the decision to issue the *fatwa*, however, is not known.

29. Syed Shahabuddin, "You Did This with Satanic Forethought, Mr. Rushdie," *Times of India*, October 13, 1988; quoted in *File*, 39.

30. Shabbir Akhtar, *Be Careful with Muhammad! The Salman Rushdie Affair* (London: Bellew, 1989), 1.

31. Ibid., 4.

32. Ibid., 6, 12.

33. See Eqbal Ahmad and Richard Barnet, "Afghanistan," *New Yorker*, April 11, 1988, and Raja Anwar, *The Tragedy of Afghanistan: A First-Hand Account* (London: Verso, 1988).

34. For the Jama'at's activities around the issue of women, see Khawar Mumtaz and Farida Shaheed, *Women of Pakistan: One Step Forward, Two Steps Back?* (Lahore: Vanguard, 1987).

35. See the special issue on "Communalism: Dangerous Dimensions," *India Today*, October 31, 1989.

36. See Akhtar, *Be Careful,* and "The Case for Religious Fundamentalism," *Guardian,* February 27, 1989, in *File,* 227-31.

37. Ahmed, "Islam," 19.

38. Ibid., 27.

39. For a discussion of the consequences of the Gulf War for the fortunes of fundamentalism, see Eqbal Ahmad's introduction to *Beyond the Storm: A Gulf Crisis Reader,* ed. Phyllis Bennis and Michel Moushabek (New York: Olive Branch, 1991).

40. Fatima Mernissi, *Beyond the Veil: Male-Female Dynamics in Modern Muslim Society,* revised edition (Bloomington: Indiana University Press, 1987), ix-x.

41. The literature on "women and Islam" in the modern world is of course enormous, but much of it is guided by ahistorical and excessively textual notions of Islam. For a critique of such tendencies in diverse writings on Muslim women, see Marnia Lazreg, "Feminism and Difference: The Perils of Writing as a Woman on Women in Algeria," *Feminist Issues* 14, no. 1 (Spring 1988): 81-107. For a set of regional studies that carefully and self-consciously avoid the pitfalls of essentialism by focusing on the *state* as the locus for determinations of notions of gender, see Deniz Kandiyoti, ed., *Women, Islam, and the State* (Philadelphia: Temple University Press, 1991). Also see Nayereh Tohidi, "Gender and Islamic Fundamentalism: Feminist Politics in Iran," in *Third World Women and the Politics of Feminism,* ed. Chandra Talpade Mohanty et al. (Bloomington: Indiana University Press, 1991), 251-67.

42. Akhtar, *Be Careful,* 89.

43. See Ervand Abrahamian, *Radical Islam: The Iranian Mojahedin* (London: Taurus, 1989), especially chapter 2.

44. Quoted in Abrahamian, "Khomeini," 103.

45. See Abrahamian, *Radical Islam,* and Michael M. Fischer, *Iran: From Religious Dispute to Revolution* (Cambridge, Mass.: Harvard University Press, 1980), especially chapter 6 and the epilogue.

46. It should be noted that the Shi'i fundamentalism of the Iranian clergy is a partial exception to this, for reasons that lie within Shi'ism's own status as unorthodox opposition to mainstream, Sunni Islam.

47. See Ziaul Haque, "Islamization of Society in Pakistan," in Khan, *Pakistan Experience,* 114-26.

48. Since the writing of these words, the issue achieved international notoriety following the destruction of the mosque by a throng of Hindu fundamentalist "volunteers" on December 6, 1992.

49. For a somewhat more detailed account, see my "In the Realm of the Censors," *Voice Literary Supplement,* March 1989, 13.

50. Rushdie, "Open Letter," *File,* 36.

51. Shahabuddin, "Satanic Forethought," *File,* 37-41.

52. Ibid., 37.

53. Akhtar, "Fundamentalism," *File,* 228.

54. See Jürgen Habermas, "The Public Sphere," *New German Critique,* Fall 1974, 49.

55. Jürgen Habermas, *The Structural Transformation of the Public Sphere: An Inquiry into a Category of Bourgeois Society* (Cambridge, Mass.: MIT Press, 1991), 88.

56. For a brilliant discussion of the complex dynamic of loyalty and betrayal in this act of appropriation, see Sara Suleri, "Contraband Histories: Salman Rushdie and the Embodiment of Blasphemy," *Yale Review* 78, no. 4 (Summer 1989).

57. Such is the case with Brennan's sense that *all* aspects of Rushdie's art and politics are

to be explained by his membership in a group he (Brennan) terms "Third-World cosmopolitans" (*Salman Rushdie*, viii-ix): "those writers Western reviewers seemed to be choosing as the interpreters and authentic public voices of the Third World—writers who, in a sense, allowed a flirtation with change that ensured continuity, a familiar strangeness, a trauma by inches." For a far more nuanced critique of Rushdie's novelistic intervention, see Asad, "Ethnography, Literature, and Politics."

58. Suleri, "Contraband Histories," 605.

59. Ibid., 606-7.

60. Ibid., 617.

61. Shahabuddin, "Satanic Forethought," 39. The Islamic Society of North America also decried the novel as a "blatant assault on Islam and the Prophet," *File*, 174. And Dr. H. Morsi, director of the Islamic Cultural Center of Chicago, declared that there was "no doubt that the book ... slanders the Prophet in particular and the religion of Islam in general," *File*, 177.

62. Akhtar, *Be Careful*, 4.

63. Franco, "Pastiche," 95; also see Fredric Jameson, "The Shining," *Social Text* 4 (Fall 1981): 114.

64. Fredric Jameson, "Postmodernism, or the Cultural Logic of Late Capitalism," *New Left Review*, no. 146: 65.

65. Linda Hutcheon, "Modern Parody and Bakhtin," in *Rethinking Bakhtin: Extensions and Challenges*, ed. Gary Morson and Caryl Emerson (Evanston, Ill.: Northwestern University Press, 1989), 41.

66. Gayatri Spivak, "Poststructuralism, Marginality, Postcoloniality and Value," in *Literary Theory Today*, ed. Peter Collier et al. (Ithaca, N.Y.: Cornell University Press, 1990), 229.

67. Brennan, *Salman Rushdie*, 82.

68. Ibid.

69. Franco, "Nation," 211.

70. See Shahabuddin, "Satanic Forethought," *File*, 39, and Akhtar, "Fundamentalism," *File*, 228.

71. See Jean Franco's discussion of Silviano Santiago's *Em Liberdade* in "Pastiche," 102-4.

72. Arjun Appadurai, "Disjuncture and Difference in the Global Cultural Economy," *Public Culture* 2, no. 2 (Spring 1990): 16.

73. See *File*, 44-46.

74. Steve Coll, "Salman Rushdie, Blueprint for a Bad Guy," *Washington Post*, June 25, 1990.

75. Rushdie, "Writing," 58-59.

76. Rushdie put it thus in his open letter to Rajiv Gandhi: "The section of the book in question (and let's remember that the book isn't actually about Islam, but about migration, metamorphosis, divided selves, love, death, London and Bombay) deals with a prophet who is not called Muhammad living in a highly fantasticated city—made of sand, it dissolves when water falls upon it—in which he is surrounded by fictional followers, one of whom happens to bear my own first name. Moreover, this entire sequence happens in a dream, the fictional dream of a fictional character, an Indian movie star, and one who is losing his mind, at that. *How much further from history could one get?*" (*File*, 35-36, emphasis added.) See also the interview with *India Today*, September 15, 1988, *File*, 32. However, Rushdie has also suggested that the book itself "metamorphoses all the time" (*File*, 7).

77. In criticizing what appeared to be Rushdie's "embrace" of Islam in late 1990, Sara

Suleri suggested that he is a "naive reader" of his own novels ("Whither Rushdie?" *Transition* 51: 212). A reading of Rushdie's post-*fatwa* pronouncements on the place of art and literature in society will confirm this verdict. See, for instance, his "Is Nothing Sacred?" in *Imaginary Homelands: Essays and Criticism 1981-1991* (London: Granta, Viking, 1991), 415-29. For a completely different account, written in 1984, see "Outside the Whale," in *Imaginary Homelands*, 87-101.

78. Brennan, "Rushdie, Islam, and Postcolonial Criticism," *Social Text* 31/32 (1992): 275.

79. Brennan, *Salman Rushdie*, 144.

80. Andrew Rosenthal, "Quayle Attacks a 'Cultural Elite,' Saying It Mocks Nation's Values," *New York Times*, June 10, 1992, 1.

Conclusion
Political Correctness:
The Revenge of the Liberals
Jeffrey Wallen

Universities are in the news again. Perhaps more than at any time since the Vietnam War, what is occurring on college campuses is a topic for local and national news coverage. Conflict, as was the case twenty years ago, is the central focus. The conflicts now, however, are not between the students and the federal government, or, for the most part, between the students and the university administration. Nor is a matter of national public policy—such as whether or not the United States should be engaged in fighting a war on the other side of the globe—at the heart of current controversies. Oddly, questions of seemingly "internal" interest to the universities—what is being taught, what students can and cannot say, who is being hired and fired—have recently garnered a great deal of "external," national attention, especially in the print media. The current controversies, as opposed to those of twenty years ago, are not very televisual: they do not *look* like serious or threatening confrontations.

The various arguments at different universities are most frequently grouped under the rubric of "political correctness," although the terms *diversity* and *multiculturalism* are also frequently invoked. Is the high level of interest, rhetoric, and passion a sign of the health of the universities, a sign that diverse viewpoints are generating a lively debate about important issues, or is it rather a sign that conflict is actually being suppressed, and that only those who espouse the "correct" positions are being allowed to speak? And is the media giving voice to those who are not being listened to on campus, or does all the press coverage work instead to rebuke and constrain anyone who dares to step outside the boundaries of the cultural main-stream?

Derek Bok, as outgoing president of Harvard, chided the American Society of Newspaper Editors for giving too much attention to political correctness, and added, " 'Whatever silly things may be said or done, there is more debate today ... on campus than at any time in my memory.' " Alan Dershowitz, however, disagreed:

> Ignore what Derek Bok told you this morning. We are producing a generation of students who do believe in political correctness. . . . This is the most serious issue that faces universities today. We are tolerating and teaching intolerance and hypocrisy.[1]

How do we decide whether a conflict is "healthy"[2] or not? Or whether it produces a "genuine" debate, or leads instead to the suppression of debate? Derek Bok himself seems unsure. In the next day's paper, it was reported that in his annual report he "focused on 'serious challenges to the academic mission of American universities' " such as " 'the use of academia for political ends,' " which "jeopardize[s] the 'basic values that allow universities to flourish and to command our loyalty and respect.' " The newspaper also noted that Bok "strongly criticized the 'threat of orthodoxy' from within the university," and that "he cited as an example students and faculty who have frequently expressed opinions against war, discrimination and oppression and have sometimes prompted 'deliberate attempts to harass professors, censor students, or disrupt speeches by visitors believed to hold unacceptable views.' " Also, "Bok was critical of attempts by pressure groups inside and outside the campus to 'embroil the university in political conflicts that divide, distract and ultimately weaken the institution.' "[3] It is not at all surprising that Derek Bok would speak of "lively discussions" and "debate" to one audience, and describe the same phenomena as a *threat* to the well-being of the institution to another; we expect a university president to speak out of both sides of his mouth. His remarks highlight, however, the central importance of debate, politics, and conflict for thinking about the "academic mission of American universities," and the "basic values that allow universities to flourish."[4]

At issue in all of these stories is what sort of community the university should be and which forms of conflict should be encouraged or tolerated, and which discouraged or suppressed. The conflict over political correctness is itself about the nature and purposes of conflict. Does the university have the mission of creating a more supportive, comfortable, and "enabling" environment than exists in the society at large? Should limits be set on speech that might cause harm or discomfort to others, or should all forms of speech by students and professors be allowed? In controversies over these and other issues, the people on each side predictably accuse others of stifling debate, while maintaining that they in turn are promoting a genuine dialogue.

It is never easy to make such distinctions, even though they are central to the "academic mission" and the "basic values" of the university. Conflict, by its very nature, always has the potential for suppressing conflict. In almost any conflict there is an attempt to change—and end—the conflict by overcoming one's opponent. Even the extreme point—killing one's antagonist—can be viewed, in a larger (or another) context, as promoting or enabling rather than as suppressing conflict. The customary means for distinguishing between conflict and the suppression of conflict—both within the university, and more generally in liberal democracy—is by differentiating between "persuasion" and "force." In the university, a conflict is typically deemed "healthy" or "lively" if persuasion is considered essential to the different modes of expression. At the other end of the spectrum, the direct intervention of state force, such as the police or National Guard, is a sign that the autonomy and the entire "mission" of the university are in jeopardy.

In any particular case, however, it is difficult to uphold a clear distinction between persuasion and force, and between conflict and the suppression of conflict. Persuasion always seems to be contaminated by force. One reason for this is that a major tactic of persuasion is to *delegitimate* one's opponent. Thus we are rarely simply presented with two (or more) equally legitimate but opposing voices, among which we are to decide which is the most "persuasive." Stanley Fish, to take an example from the political correctness controversy, asserted that "the National Association of Scholars is widely known to be racist, sexist, and homophobic."[5] The implication here is that one need not even listen to these people; they discriminate, and have thus forfeited the right to participate in legitimate discussion (and they should therefore be kept off hiring and promotion committees). A condition of full participation in institutional life is assumed here to be an *openness* to persuasion—not having decided in advance that blacks, women, and gays, for example, are unfit for employment—yet Fish himself seeks to prevent certain people from being heard (at least in the arenas of hiring and promotion committees). At what point does persuasion (the argument for or against a set of views) become coercion (the use of force to prevent certain views from being expressed)?

Controversies about political correctness are all about who has the right to speak. Thirty-five years ago, it was commonly accepted that anyone who was fundamentally seeking to subvert the educational system should be expelled from the university. In its 1956 statement about "vigilance against subversion of the educational process," the American Association of University Professors (AAUP) declared:

> The academic community has a duty to defend society and itself from subversion of the educational process by dishonest tactics, including political conspiracies to deceive students and lead them unwittingly into acceptance of dogmas or false causes. Any member of the academic profession who has given reasonable evidence that he uses such tactics ... should be expelled from his position if his guilt is established by a rational procedure. Instances of the use of such tactics in the past by secret Communist groups in a few institutions seem to have occurred, and vigilance against the danger of their occurrence in the future is clearly required.[6]

Now, by contrast, when even the president of Duke University will state that a "university is, after all, meant to be a subversive institution,"[7] the imperative may almost seem to be in the opposite direction—expel those who are not subversive enough. Paradoxically, a failure to "subvert" (to challenge the canon, to fight against "institutional" forms of discrimination and oppression, to dismantle elitism, privilege, and hierarchy) can itself now be viewed as a "subversion of the educational process." In any case, "vigilance against subversion of the educational process" is still firmly at work. The "educational process" is sometimes loftily defined as giving free play to the powers of persuasion, but the ever-present threat of expulsion is used to protect the university from the persuasive power of those who might disrupt the academic "community" (in 1956, from those who engage in "political conspiracies," "dishonesty," and "deception"; today, from those with supposedly unreformed "discriminatory" attitudes). And a most effective means of persuasion is to characterize one's opponent as occupying this illegitimate territory, outside the norms of the community.

Force and persuasion are always intermingling. Institutional structures regulate conflict and determine the framework within which persuasion can operate. On the one hand, these structures create the space for debate, and principles such as academic freedom protect speakers from certain forms of recrimination and retribution. Yet these institutional structures also enforce differences of authority and power, differences that undermine any belief in the unfettered reliance on persuasion in the university. The persuasive capacity of any academic discourse always also depends on the identity and position of the speaker.[8] This becomes particularly apparent when a grade, a grant, a job, or a promotion is at stake. The greater "persuasive" power of those in positions of authority does not stem solely from their greater learning, experience, or eloquence; the threat of force—such as the loss of employment or advancement—thoroughly penetrates the academic realm of persuasion.

On a more far-reaching and profound level, the entire Foucauldian project offers a strident critique of the opposition between persuasion and force; Foucault's analysis of the interpenetration of power and knowledge renders untenable any attempt to cleanly separate the two. Moreover, the recent critique of the institution (which has become especially important in literary studies) emphasizes that interpretation is never free of its institutional context, and that this context is one of contending and conflicting forces—forces that necessarily exclude, marginalize, and repress. The many different critiques of the institution all give the lie to any notion of the university as a protected but fundamentally open and free field of persuasion.

Even if we could find a means for distinguishing between persuasion and force, or at least delimit a space—such as the seminar room—in which everything would be done to maximize persuasion and dialogue, and reduce force and coercion, it is not at all obvious that this would allow us either to better fulfill the "academic mission" of the university (the pursuit and the transmission of knowledge) or to bring into the open and address the conflicts that permeate the university. A different possibility—different from the notion that genuine discussion and debate are threatened by force and intimidation—but one with much more disturbing consequences for the university, is that the entire arena of discussion and debate—the realm of persuasion—is itself now a sideshow, an "empty formality," that has little to do with knowledge, and that functions even to mask and displace conflict. What if the notions of openness and discussion, and of the importance of debate, now only serve to reduce conflicting opinions into chatter, into an empty contest of words?[9] The emphasis on debate and persuasion stems from a belief in liberalism. Richard Rorty offers a contemporary philosophy of liberalism when he asserts that *truth* is "whatever the outcome of undistorted communication happens to be, whatever view wins in a free and open encounter."[10] But if the possibilities of "undistorted communication" and "free and open encounters" are discredited, and if a willingness to be persuaded and a belief in the persuadability of others is rejected, then the basic foundations of liberalism are under attack, and the entire project of education through "healthy" conflict and open debate needs to be reexamined.

It may seem that I have made an enormous leap—moving from the latest journalist controversy to a concern for the foundations of liberalism—and that the discussion of political correctness has so far led only to a further muddying of distinctions rather than to a means for separating genuine intellectual conflict from the usual pressures to conform to current attitudes. Moreover, such a move from an incident of media interest and outrage to a hysterical concern for the very foundations of liberal democracy is an all too common gesture of commentators from the far right (and is not surprisingly a prominent motif in articles on political correctness). Right-wing cover boy Dinesh D'Souza argues that our universities are now engaged in a process of "illiberal education." He claims that an "academic revolution," based on the "politics of race and sex" coupled with the latest (French) fashions in literary theory, has undermined the liberal values at the core of a traditional university education.[11] I do not want to espouse the conservative agenda of preserving and consolidating power through an appeal to "traditional standards," yet I will argue that a consideration of press coverage offers a good place for beginning to theorize conflict in the university, and that the controversy over political correctness brings out some of the paradoxes at the heart of many recent theories of institutions and interpretation.

Whenever an academic debate makes it into the mainstream press, it is no longer merely "academic." The reporting of such conflicts signals that something other than a "mere" difference of intellectual opinion is at stake, and the act of reporting also transforms the debate. Even when an article attempts primarily to inform readers of the intellectual content of the opposing positions (and this is rarely the case)[12] so as to allow the public to participate in a well-informed discussion of the issue, the transgression of the institutional boundary already alters the context and thus the nature of the conflict. "Going public" with an "internal" academic dispute, either by alerting the press or by writing an article on one's own, brings new pressures to bear and requires different modes of persuasion. Appealing to another audience implies that the norms and values of a particular department or campus, or of the academic community, are out of step with those of the broader public.

The media, as another major social institution, functions to demarcate the borders of the university. These borders are very porous and often seem unclear, especially in the humanities, where so many boundaries are in question. The efforts to erode distinctions between popular and intellectual, and between different forms of writing, and the increasing study of the media within the university, might seem to be indications that the old tensions between journalism and "belles lettres" are dissolving. Yet the constant bemoaning of the demise of the "public intellectual" provides grounds for the opposite conclusion, and almost the entire spectrum of academic writing attempts to set itself off from the "journalistic"—that which need only be read once, and at only one point in time. The continuing force of these boundaries becomes especially apparent when professors who theorize about misprision, distortion, and uncertainty complain vehemently about having their own views distorted and falsified by the press (an academic discourse presents difficult problems of translation into the public sphere of the mass media).

Any attempt to understand conflict within the university requires an awareness of and attending to institutional boundaries. Theoreticians of the "institution" (and especially of the English department) such as Gerald Graff and Stanley Fish pay too little attention to the interaction *between* institutions in their attempts to explain conflict "within" the institution. The press and the law offer two other arenas for playing out academic conflicts, and I would argue that these institutions have a significant influence even on disputes that do not end up in the hands of lawyers and journalists. And this influence occurs as much, for example, in the *differentiation* between academic and legal forms of arguments as through the legal underpinnings of the university. I will return later to the role of the press in the controversy about political correctness, but here I only want to emphasize that the linking of media accounts to theoretical inquiry is an important rather than a superficial or hysterical aspect of an effort to understand academic conflict.

For many thinkers today, conflict is inseparable from rather than peripheral to the notion of knowledge, and essential to the entire academic enterprise. If conflicts were viewed as temporary disagreements soon superseded by consensus once a new truth is established, or as unfortunate upheavals of differences that have no bearing on the "academic mission" of the university (and that ought to be settled or mediated by those in power), then the question of how conflict is regulated, and the whole issue of political correctness, would not be important. "Political" differences might still temporarily interfere with the process of education, but they would have no real effect on the *content* of education. But now more than ever, and especially in literary studies, there are few adherents to the notion of conflict as mere bumps on the road of knowledge. One might even say that literary theory is a theory of conflict. This conclusion does not depend on whether one agrees with Harold Bloom that literature itself is inherently agonistic—whether the *object* of theory is or is not conflictual, ambivalent, or undecidable. Rather, literary theory is a theory of conflict because it is not grounded in an object at all—not grounded in a text, a reader, a canon, or even an institution. Literary theory attempts to respond to conflict (conflicting meanings within texts, conflicting interpretations of texts); emphasize conflict (always insisting on difference); and expose conflict (revealing the mechanisms by which conflict is habitually suppressed, resisted, and ignored). All of these tasks follow from the abandonment of a "ground" for theory, and especially of the grounding of interpretation in truth.

One of the most important aspects of twentieth-century thought is the critique of *truth*. This critique has taken many forms, and its results are phrased in many different ways: the idea that truth is made rather than found; a rejection of the notion of "truth conceived in terms of the *adequatio intellectus et rei*," and thus a rejection of the priority and separability of thought from its object; or the conclusion that "truths" are only contingent, local, and temporary, rather than "absolute, universal, and timeless."[13] Here I only want to emphasize that this critique dislodges any *absolute* ground for resolving conflicting interpretations, since it renders problematic any autonomous, preexisting, and unchanging object to which one can appeal as the basis of interpretation. Interpretation, rather than being a somewhat steady progress toward a more "adequate" representation, becomes instead a continual contest between newer and older forms of understanding.

There are two major consequences of this critique of truth that I wish to explore. The first is the elevation of "persuasion" to a central position for interpretation. If there is no autonomous ground for truth, independent of language, then persuasion is a mechanism not only for resolving differences, but also for establishing "truth." This elevation of persuasion goes against a long tradition of discrediting persuasion and rhetoric as forms of expression that *interfere* with the search for truth. Yet as I have already begun to suggest, concurrent with the dismantling of the opposition between persuasion and truth (or the qualities traditionally deemed necessary for reaching truth, such as principle, disinterestedness, neutrality, objectivity, etc.), there has also been a challenge to that which defines and delimits persuasion at the other end—to the separation of persuasion and force. Thus the notion of persuasion itself is very much in question, now that it has a greater interpretative load to carry.

The second consequence is the turn to the "institution" in the effort to explore further the processes of interpretation. Without an absolute and autonomous ground, interpretation necessarily depends also on its context. There are many ways to define this context—such as the range of ideas within and against which any interpretation proceeds, or the particular constellation of social, cultural, and historical forces—but the "institution" provides a particularly powerful conception for examining the way that not only ideas or discourses but also actual people and their quotidian practices are organized and employed. Moreover, the university—the institution that pursues and disseminates "knowledge" (and the place where "we" work)—affords a special opportunity for studying the "extrinsic conditions" and

forces of interpretation.[14] Thus, in recent years there has been a burgeoning interest in the "institution," especially in literary studies. The
thrust of much of this critique is to emphasize that the institution (in
a shift similar to the insistence on the centrality of conflict and persuasion) is not a mere vehicle for the knowledge that it transmits.[15]
But this attention to the institution is not without effect; it also
changes the very context that it studies (and of course the desire for
change motivates much of the attention to the institution). The critique of the institution itself thereby gains great importance, for it
can affect the very structures and content of knowledge.

Both of these tendencies (the foregrounding of persuasion and the
turn to the institution) aim to *legitimate* conflict. The insistence that
truth is only an effect of persuasion requires an open conflict of
ideas; if disagreement were always to be minimized in the name of
harmony or obedience to authority, there would be no opportunity
to persuade others of the "validity" of a new interpretation. An
emphasis on persuasion highlights the function of conflict within the
university. Moreover, the critique of the institution brings to light the
ways in which conflict is habitually suppressed or ignored, since the
intention of such a critique is to examine the *contingency* of knowledge and its dependence on institutional structures. The attention to
suppressed conflict always suggests other possibilities, that things
might have occurred, might occur, otherwise. Yet the effect of these
discussions of conflict is not simply to achieve a greater openness or
to ensure the participation of those who have previously been
excluded; at stake in such critiques is the inescapability of conflict,
rather than the possibility of transcending it. Both of these critical
tendencies have therefore not only altered the regulation of conflict
within the university, but also prepared the ground for excluding
others in turn—for excluding, for example, those who do *not* speak
from a previously repressed position, and who therefore might be in
the way of desired institutional change. The epithet "political correctness" is a response to this new legitimation of exclusion (appearing
ironically, but necessarily, in a vocabulary of "inclusion"). It is especially the connections between the legitimation of conflict and of
exclusion that I wish to consider.

At the end of her preface to *Reader-Response Criticism*, Jane Tompkins states: "When discourse is responsible for reality and not merely

a reflection of it, then whose discourse prevails makes all the difference."[16] For Tompkins the result of the conflict—"whose discourse prevails"—is of utmost importance. After all, the prevailing discourse determines not only knowledge and truth, but also "reality" itself. But if this is the case, if the stakes are so high, why allow a free and open conflict? Why let one's opponents speak at all, if they might sway others to the "wrong" conclusion (a conclusion different from one's own)? The notion that "discourse is *responsible* for reality" makes little sense without the "free and open encounter" that Rorty urges. Soviet genetics under Stalin and Lysenko provides a striking example of the attempt to subordinate "reality" to the "prevailing discourse." Yet the traditional mechanisms and rationale for promoting a "free and open encounter" are precisely what are under attack here. Tompkins's conclusion that "language is the ultimate form of power" and all the ensuing corollaries, such as "all discourse is 'interested'" and "free choice is not a meaningful issue," arise directly from a critique of liberalism and its key pillar, the freedom of the individual. The insistence that persuasion is the means for determining truth and reality requires the protection of the liberal political and institutional structures whose philosophical foundations it seeks to undermine.

Contemporary critics of liberalism argue that the traditional oppositions between disinterestedness and interest, neutrality and partisanship, objective discourse and persuasion or rhetoric, and universality and contextuality are all invalid, since it can always be shown that there is no transcendental position beyond institutions and beyond language—God is dead, or at least homeless. A typical next step, and one that Tompkins takes, is to then argue that the "divorce between literature and politics" (or more broadly, aesthetics and politics) has been overcome, since the aesthetic model of "disinterestedness" (located in Matthew Arnold more often than in Kant) has been replaced by the political model of the clash between competing interests. But the invocation of "politics" does not at all provide a new model for understanding aesthetic judgment, comprehending differences of opinion, or choosing between competing interpretations; it only forces us to confront which political model we will use to regulate conflict. The liberal political model depends on the possibility of people *not* being fully bound or determined by (class, partisan, personal) interests. It is worth quoting at length Carl Schmitt,[17] one of the most incisive thinkers on the crisis of liberalism, in order to help clarify what is at issue in the critique of liberalism:

> All specifically parliamentary arrangements and norms receive their meaning first through discussion and openness. This is especially true of the fundamental principle that is still recognized constitutionally, although practically hardly believed in today, that the representative is independent of his constituents and party; it applies to the provisions concerning freedom of speech and immunity of representatives, the openness of parliamentary proceedings, and so forth. These arrangements would be unintelligible if the principle of public discussion were no longer believed in. It is not as if one could ascribe other principles retrospectively and at will to an institution, and if its hitherto existing foundations collapse, just insert any sort of substitutive arguments....
>
> Discussion means an exchange of opinion that is governed by the purpose of persuading one's opponent through argument of the truth or justice of something, or allowing oneself to be persuading of something as true or just. Gentz—in this matter still instructed by the liberal Burke—puts it well: The characteristic of all representative constitutions (he meant modern parliament in contrast to corporative representation or the estates) is that laws arise *out of a conflict of opinions (not a struggle of interests).* To discussion belong shared convictions as premises, the willingness to be persuaded, independence of party ties, freedom from selfish interests. Most people today would regard such disinterestedness as scarcely possible. (emphasis added)[18]

In regard to Schmitt's observations about discussion, one can emphasize that the ability to rise above "selfish interests" is *not* identical with the Kantian aesthetic notion of "disinterestedness" ("the faculty of estimating an object or a mode of representation by means of a delight or an aversion *apart from any interest*"),[19] and that the "deconstruction" of all of the oppositions revolving around disinterest and interest need not result in their collapse: one need not be absolutely "neutral" or "objective" and certainly not disinterested, for example, to be open to persuasion, and to be willing to put aside one's "interests." (The key question is how one defines "interests"; the most insightful critiques are the ones that reveal the ambivalence of this term, rather than reduce it to a specific point in the matrix of race, class, and gender.)

Yet the power of Schmitt's critique lies not in its fairly conventional definitions of discussion, but in its prodding us to question and justify anew liberal institutions, or whatever institutional frameworks sanction persuasion, and even more profoundly, to question the meaningfulness of the entire operation of "persuasion" itself. The thrust of much recent criticism is to discredit not only the philosophical foundations of liberal thought, but the political and institutional structures of liberalism as well—to show, for example, that "justice" is not blind, but reflects the "interests" of those who have the power to administer it. Yet if the principles and the institutions of liberalism are discredited, what is to protect the expression of opinion? If institutions merely reflect interests, why shouldn't those in power do everything possible to eliminate any threats to their interests (such as the freedom of speech of those with competing interests)?

Many of the rights and liberties for resisting institutional power (and in the university, many of the protections of freedom of inquiry, of holding dissenting opinions, etc.) are fundamentally grounded in what Schmitt calls "the principle of public discussion." But if discussion is merely a reflection of a "struggle of interests," and if the participants in this struggle do not share a "willingness to be persuaded" and a measure of freedom from "interests," who is to be persuaded? Dialogue and discussion become pointless, an empty show. The discussions of the parliamentary body become increasingly irrelevant when nothing is to be changed by the procession of speeches (a feeling that applies to the U.S. political arena today, as well as to Weimar), and similar questions about the meaningfulness of discussion in academia also need to be asked. Much of what passes for debate in the university is tiresome and unilluminating precisely because of the sheer unwillingness to open oneself to persuasion, or to consider antagonistic ideas seriously rather than to dismiss them as the distorted products of false ideologies.

There appear to be several ways out of this paradox of seeking to maintain the protections of liberal institutions even while discrediting the fairness of these institutions and critiquing the freedom of the liberal subject. Richard Rorty, who wishes to defend liberal institutions while challenging their philosophical foundations, argues that the founding discourse of an enterprise can, indeed always will be, separated from its historical development. He attacks the authors of *The Dialectic of the Enlightenment* for drawing the conclusion "that liberalism was now intellectually bankrupt, bereft of philosophical foundations, and that liberal society was morally bankrupt, bereft of social glue." Rorty continues:

> Horkheimer and Adorno assumed that the terms in which those who began a historical development described their enterprise remain the terms which describe it correctly, and then inferred that the dissolution of that terminology deprives the results of that development of the right to, or the possibility of, continued existence. This is almost never the case.[20]

Thus the "continued existence" of the institutional protections of freedom of speech, or academic freedom, need not depend at all on a continued belief in the freedom of the individual or the freedom of thought. This is a very complex and interesting issue, but the main point I want to make here is that the relation of the new "terminology" to the historically developed form of the "enterprise" is crucial. The dissolution of the founding terminology need not lead to the collapse of modern institutions, but neither will they necessarily continue to stand, simply out of historical momentum. A new justification of the institutional structures and protections needs to be articulated if the liberal "enterprise" is to continue.

In academia, the adoption of a new terminology has certainly affected the institution. The earlier vocabulary of academic inquiry—disinterestedness, objectivity, and the pursuit of truth (and this was *by no means* a fixed or stable vocabulary during the last hundred years)—did not function simply to suppress, mask, or distort conflict, but rather *to regulate it.* This terminology works to give weight to certain arguments, and to rule out others. The discrediting of these mechanisms for regulating conflict does not finally produce an emergence and unmasking of "genuine" conflict, in which all the previously hidden issues and agendas are now openly addressed (this idea parallels the Reaganesque fantasy of deregulation, in which free markets and genuine competitiveness unhindered by regulation will lead to a new golden [gilded?] age). A "free and open encounter" cannot be achieved simply by breaking down all the apparent barriers to freedom and openness. Such a possibility also requires *protection* from the forces that would restrict such an encounter. Only in a space in which nothing is at stake—in which conflict is purely a game whose results do not matter—would such protections be unnecessary.

In my own case, for example, some people felt that since they taught at an alternative institution (Hampshire College), founded as a "progressive" challenge to traditional colleges, they had the right if not the duty to protect the mission of the college by eliminating anyone whom they viewed as a threat to the school's identity. Thus some professors felt no qualms about putting in writing, as reasons for denying me reappointment, opinions that clearly mixed ideological and personal concerns with issues of supposed "professional competence." Thus, one professor wrote:

> On the basis of his course work and his response to a question raised during his reappointment meeting, I seriously question his understanding of the Third World Expectation except on the most superficial, perfunctory basis. His is a conventional attitude of privelege [sic], inappropriate in a faculty member at a time when Hampshire is moving in such a different direction.

And another faculty member wrote:

> Jeff feels to me encapsulated and a little distant. I had hoped for someone more dynamic, and less prone to polarizing issues in our school meetings in ways that suggest to me no [sic] an independent thinking about the issues.[21]

In order to preserve the "independent thinking" of the alternative institution, anyone with differing ideas must be rooted out. One can compellingly accuse anyone with whom one disagrees of "professional incompetence" (failing to understand the Third World Expectation, or as another colleague put it, failing to offer "any Third World challenge to the canon or to the theoretical priorities in his teaching") for *failing to reflect* certain interests, once it is determined that these "interests" are themselves constitutive of knowledge. Thus an "attitude of conventional privelege [sic]" would disbar someone from being a capable teacher and scholar, since such a person would still be blinded by the ideology of the dominant class, and unable to understand or assimilate any new forms of knowledge.

I was surprised to find that the language of contemporary criticism made it more difficult to defend myself, and to invoke academic freedom as a basic principle and right. My training had always been toward calling into question notions such as the autonomy of the individual and academic freedom, and to point out all the ways in which this principle fails to operate successfully in existing institutions. Academic freedom is traditionally defended by invoking the scholar's disinterested pursuit of truth. The primary AAUP document on academic freedom contains the following claims:

> Institutions of higher education are conducted for the common good and not to further the interest of either the individual teacher or the institution as a whole. The common good depends upon the free search for truth and its free exposition. … Freedom in research is fundamental to the advancement of truth.[22]

It is easy to challenge these assumptions and to argue that all inquiry is interested and political, and, further, that the personal, too, is political. All reasons for insulating academic decisions from "personal" and "political" considerations can thereby be challenged, and academic freedom can be shown to be only a myth or an ideological construct. The net effect, however, is not a lessening of the institutional and professional barriers that inhibit open discussion. Rather than everyone having a greater voice, once the "artificial" constraints of academic freedom are dismantled and political criteria can be clearly raised, everyone instead becomes more vulnerable to administrative discipline. In the university, where who gets hired, tenured, and promoted "makes all the difference," weakening the notion of academic freedom only cedes greater authority to those who have the power to demand conformity. When it becomes acceptable to fire people for having unacceptable political opinions, allegiance to the institution becomes the decisive factor, and the threat of institutional disfavor and discipline further constricts the sphere of persuasion in which political conflicts might be aired.

If the critique of liberal thought is to yield a realm of persuasion that is not more widely controlled by administrative power, a new vocabulary is required to legitimate institutional structures that aim to insulate persuasion from coercion, even as the notions of persuasion and coercion are being radically redefined. Of course it is not only a question of a new terminology—there are certainly many ways to reform these structures so that they function better. Simply hoping to "undermine" or "subvert" them, however, since American institutions are all "racist, sexist, and homophobic," will not produce a more "free and open" institutional environment.

Yet even if the elevation of persuasion is accompanied by an effort to protect the arena of discussion from many forms of coercion, there can be no persuasion without persuadability, a "willingness to be persuaded." Again, it is easy to challenge this notion of "willingness," just as one challenges the possibility of "disinterestedness." But what is the point of discussion if there is a firm unwillingness to be persuaded? Often employed in the aftermath of the critique of oppositions such as disinterest—interest and neutral-partisan is a new set of oppositions that offers only a "struggle of interests" rather than a "conflict of opinions": domination-subordination, for example, or oppressor-victim. The exposure of "interests" functioning under the guise of disinterestedness and neutrality does not necessarily stabilize these interests; quite the contrary, it can reveal how difficult it is to know precisely which "interests" are at stake. The insistence, however, that everyone speaks from a *position* of either domination or subordination, and also that one's discourse should validate one's position—that the purpose of speaking is to define (and hence to some extent to enforce) the boundaries of domination and subordination—casts a "willingness to be persuaded" as betrayal. To give up one's position (as subordinate) would only be to reinforce the structures of oppression. The "conflict of opinions" here is not dialogue or debate, since the determination to reinforce positions forecloses any possibility of exchanging opinions.[23]

Political correctness proceeds from the claim that only certain positions have the right to be heard. Voices speaking from the wrong position—conventional privilege, tradition, Eurocentrism—are to be attacked and silenced on both moral and intellectual grounds. Morally, these positions are said to enforce structures of oppression, and intellectually, they are deemed ignorant, unaware of or blind to their own ideological assumptions. The extreme of political correctness—preventing certain people from speaking and certain opinions from being expressed—is to some extent a logical conclusion to the proposition that "whose discourse prevails makes all the difference." Yet political correctness is only a symptom of a much broader crisis of liberalism, and even without the excessive stance of stifling debate, there still remains the question of the purpose of academic conflict. Without *someone* to be persuaded, and without some communication and interchange between opposing positions, the spectacle of academic conflict is beside the point—only a diversion from more overtly political battles between competing interests that take place elsewhere.

The possibility of being persuaded through discussion is called into question by the critique of freedom of thought,[24] and even more by the insistence that the position from which one speaks "makes all the difference"—that the identity, more than the ideas of the speaker, is what matters. If the speakers do not share certain premises, but are divided into victims and oppressors, there can be persuasion only within these groups, not across their borders. These obstacles to "persuadability" can be partially overcome by invoking the students, and through the notion of "community." The students, starting from ignorance of or noninterest in academic conflicts, can be persuaded (educated). They can provide a significance to these discussions by learning enough to participate in them. Gerald Graff therefore states that we need to "organize and teach the conflict" in order to make it "a productive part of the curriculum."[25] Graff hopes that the students will no longer be "outsiders" to the "academic community."[26]

Graff focuses on a key problem: how to make academic conflict more meaningful and more productive. The notion of community again allows the university to be portrayed as a realm of persuasion, by conjuring a space—if not of "shared convictions as premises" (Schmitt), at least of a shared language (Graff) or shared institutional standards or norms (Fish)—*within which* persuasion is said to operate. If conflict is addressed within the institution, then the apparently unbridgeable chasm between different positions can still be deemed part of the same community. Yet within the university, the notion of community is now used more to enforce than to bridge differences, and in describing the relation to nonacademic communities, the term is frequently employed to challenge any possibility of achieving a common ground for persuasion across cultural and institutional boundaries.

The academic community sets itself off from other communities precisely by claiming a greater openness to persuasion. But since the basic persuadability of the human subject has been renounced, this claim can only be supported by locating a greater denial of persuadability elsewhere, such as in the "public sphere," and especially in the media. A critique of the media—the space in which the central debates of the "public sphere" ought to be played out—is required in order to define a realm of manipulation of discourse and blindness to ideology, in contrast to the awareness if not freedom of the academic community. The dissolution of "the notion of free choice" is offset by the contrast with a realm that is less free and that is deluded by rather than sensitized to ideology.[27] The academic community thus maintains its moral purity and autonomy only by imposing its separation from all others who toil in a realm of delusion—even while thereby pointing to its own "engagement" with the nonacademic world. The price of maintaining a remnant of "persuadability" within the university is to deny it methodologically to others.

It then becomes easy to characterize the media attention to political correctness as a right-wing backlash, since it is the "right" that most strenuously denies the ideological thrust of its academic discourse. This perspective also justifies abdicating a role in the media debates about political correctness; after all, one's ideas will only be distorted and manipulated by the media, and in the media one can only defend a "position," rather than exchange opinions. Moreover, this greater self-awareness that sets apart the academic community requires a constant critique of the "naive" liberal beliefs in freedom, equality, and truth—the liberals, as usual, are the most easily ridiculed for deludedly hoping to forge a common ground. It is therefore no wonder that Mark Starr of *Newsweek* described the media interest in political correctness as "the revenge of the liberals."[28]

NOTES

I would like to thank Samuel Weber, Joseph Riddel, and the participants at the Critical Studies Group at UCLA for their responses to an earlier version of this essay. I would also like to acknowledge the helpful comments of W. J. T. Mitchell, Richard Burt, Stanley Fish, and Gerald Graff.

1. Thomas Palmer, "At Harvard, Dissent on the State of Dissent," *Boston Globe*, April 11, 1991, 29, 32.

2. Catharine Stimpson, for example, in an appearance on the "McLaughlin Report" filmed in January 1991, argued that the "political" controversies on college campuses are signs of a "healthy debate." The notion of a "healthy" conflict could be very productively questioned in the wake of Nietzsche, and of German history.

3. Alexander Reid, "Bok Report Cites Threats to Colleges," *Boston Globe*, April 12, 1991.

4. My own interest in these debates is not entirely "academic." For nineteen months (November 1989 to May 1991) I was involved in a battle with Hampshire College, where I am an assistant professor of comparative literature, over my reappointment. A few people originally objected to my reappointment on grounds that could easily be described now as the determination that I was not "politically correct." I was accused of, among

other things, not properly teaching or understanding the "Third World Expectation," and of not even being able to "think independently," since I didn't always come to the same conclusions (about the criteria for making hiring decisions) as some of my colleagues. After a labyrinthine appeal process, I finally was reappointed. During this time, my case, and that of another colleague (Norman Holland), received a great deal of local and national media coverage. For some examples, see Appendices A and B.

5. This statement has been widely quoted, such as in a *Wall Street Journal* piece of November 13, 1990, and a *Newsweek* story of December 24, 1990. There is apparently some disagreement about exactly what Fish wrote, in which memo, but in the "McLaughlin Report" show on political correctness, he reiterated the assertion that NAS members are known to be "racist, sexist, and homophobic."

6. *Academic Freedom and Tenure: A Handbook of the American Association of University Professors*, ed. Louis Joughin (Madison: University of Wisconsin Press, 1967), 48.

7. H. Keith H. Brodie and Leslie Banner, "Opening Remarks," *South Atlantic Quarterly* 89, no. 1 (1990): 4. The word *subversion* is one of the most frequently used terms today in literary criticism. It often serves only as a more charged synonym to *challenge*, but the idea that education, reading, and the university should be subversive is well worth pondering, and should also be considered in regard to the function of "subversion" in the historical tradition of Socrates to the present, the tradition that is one of the most common targets of subversion.

8. In an essay on academic freedom, law professor J. Peter Byrne offers an unconvincing account of "academic speech": "The speaker cannot persuade her colleagues by her social standing, physical strength or the raw vehemence of her argument; she must persuade on the basis of reason and evidence (concepts vouchsafed, if only contingently, by her discipline)" ("Academic Freedom: A 'Special Concern of the First Amendment,'" *Yale Law Journal* 99 [1989]: 258). Such a disembodied notion of academic speech ignores the institutional context it purports to describe. Stanley Fish is one of the more persistent advocates of an opposing view of academic speech. See, in particular, "No Bias, No Merit: The Case against Blind Submission," in *Doing What Comes Naturally* (Durham, N.C.: Duke University Press, 1989), 163-79.

9. I am borrowing the vocabulary of "openness" and "discussion," and the claim that discussion has now become an "empty formality," from Carl Schmitt's critique of liberalism, and especially of "parliamentarism," the institutional mode of political liberalism. I will be discussing Schmitt more directly later in the essay. I am referring especially to the preface to the second edition of *The Crisis of Parliamentary Democracy* (*Die geistesgeschichtliche Lage des heutigen Parlamentarismus*), trans. Ellen Kennedy (Cambridge, Mass.: MIT Press, 1985).

10. Richard Rorty, *Contingency, Irony, Solidarity* (Cambridge: Cambridge University Press, 1989), 67. As Rorty points out, the notion of a "free and open encounter" is employed by Milton (in *Areopagitica*): "And now the time in special is, by privilege to write and speak what may help to the further discussing of matters in agitation. The temple of Janus, with his two controversial faces, might now not unsignificantly be set open. And though all the winds of doctrine were let loose to play upon the earth, so truth be in the field, we do injuriously by licensing and prohibiting to misdoubt her strength. Let her and falsehood grapple; who ever knew truth put to the worse in a free and open encounter? Her confuting is the best and surest suppressing" (*The Portable Milton*, ed. Douglas Bush [New York: Viking, 1949], 199). Rorty, however, differentiates his argument from Milton's: "It is central to the idea of a liberal society that, in respect to words as

opposed to deeds, persuasion as opposed to force, anything goes. This openmindedness should not be fostered because, as Scripture teaches, Truth is great and will prevail, nor because, as Milton suggests, Truth will always win in a free and open encounter. It should be fostered for its own sake. *A liberal society is one which is content to call "true" whatever the upshot of such encounters turns out to be*" (52, emphasis in the original).

11. Dinesh D'Souza, American Enterprise Institute fellow and former editor of the *Dartmouth Review*, is the author of *Illiberal Education: The Politics of Race and Sex on Campus* (New York: Free Press, 1991).

12. On television in particular, people usually attempt to defend positions rather than to explore or understand a problem; in one sense of the term, they rarely act "academic." One can always easily undermine this opposition between exploring and defending positions, yet professors often talk quite differently on television than they do in the classroom or the lecture hall.

13. I have borrowed these definitions, almost at random, from Richard Rorty, Samuel Weber, and Renato Rosaldo. For Rorty, see page 3 of *Contingency, Irony, and Solidarity*, although the entire book, and especially the first section on contingency, is a response to this critique of truth. For Weber, see the introduction to *Institution and Interpretation* (Minneapolis: University of Minnesota Press, 1987), ix. For Rosaldo, see *Culture and Truth* (Boston: Beacon, 1989), 21.

14. I am citing the phrase "extrinsic conditions" from Derrida, both to point to the work of one of the most important thinkers about the institution (see in particular his recent collection, *Du droit à la philosophie*), and also to indicate some of the directions of this critique. Samuel Weber, in *Institution and Interpretation* (19), states that in "Le parergon" Derrida argues that deconstruction "would have to occupy itself increasingly with the institutional conditions of its own practice": "with what is generally, and wrongly, considered as philosophy's external habitat, as the extrinsic conditions of its exercise—that is, the historical forms of its pedagogy, the social, economic, or political structures of this pedagogical institution. It is by touching solid structures, "material" institutions, and not merely discourses or significant representations, that deconstruction distinguishes itself from analysis or 'criticism' " (from *La vérité en peinture* [Paris: Flammarion, 1978], 23-24; this passage translated by Samuel Weber).

15. It is this difficulty of stabilizing the relation of the university to its contents that people such as Allan Bloom find most troubling today: "The institutions were much more ambiguous than I could have expected.... The university ... is after all only a vehicle for contents in principle separable from it.... Without it [the university], all these wonderful results of the theoretical life collapse back into the primal slime from which they cannot re-emerge" (Allan Bloom, *The Closing of the American Mind* [New York: Simon & Schuster, 1987], 245).

16. Jane Tompkins, "An Introduction to Reader-Response Criticism," in *Reader-Response Criticism*, ed. Jane Tompkins (Baltimore: Johns Hopkins University Press, 1980), xxv. I have selected Tompkins here not for the originality of the thought today (these ideas have become widely espoused in the decade following the publication of the piece), but for its very representativeness. A document that offers perhaps the most "representative" view of some recent trends in the humanities is *Speaking for the Humanities*, co-written by George Levine, Peter Brooks, Jonathan Culler, Marjorie Garber, E. Ann Kaplan, and Catharine Stimpson (New York: ACLS, 1989).

17. The emphasis on politics authorizes, if not requires, thinking about political systems and models rather than limiting the "institutional" model to the university. I hope else-

where to provide a fuller discussion of the relation of Schmitt, and of political theory, to these debates about the "politicization" of the university. Also, Schmitt's writings on the crisis of liberalism, and parliamentarism, is very *historical*; Schmitt points out that the parliamentary emphasis on "openness" and "discussion" arose in *reaction* to earlier political systems, and for him, the crisis arises out of the contradictions between twentieth-century "mass democracy" and parliamentary liberalism. I also hope later to provide a more historical discussion of the role of "openness" and "discussion" in the university, and of the political parallels and differences. Finally, invoking Schmitt always has its risks. After the collapse of the Weimar Republic, Schmitt became a leading Nazi ideologue. Nevertheless, I think he still offers one of the most incisive critiques of liberalism, and his own career illustrates some of the potential dangers of this critique.

18. Carl Schmitt, "Preface to the Second Edition (1926): On the Contradiction between Parliamentarism and Democracy," *Crisis of Parliamentary Democracy*, 3, 5.

19. Immanuel Kant, *The Critique of Judgement*, trans. James Creed Meredith (Oxford: Oxford University Press, 1952), 50.

20. Rorty, *Irony, Contingency, and Solidarity*, 56. Richard Thoma makes a similar point in his response to Carl Schmitt: "The worth and vitality of a political institution in no way depends on the quality and pervasiveness of the ideologies advanced for its justification" ("On the Ideology of Parliamentarism," in *Crisis of Parliamentary Democracy*, 80).

21. These comments are direct transcriptions from the ballots of those who voted against my reappointment. I received transcriptions of these comments from the administration after a nine-month battle, when an appeals committee finally ruled that I was entitled to them.

22. "1940 Statement of Principles on Academic Freedom and Tenure," *Academic Freedom and Tenure*, 34.

23. A rigidly employed opposition between subordination and domination is only one of many ways in which the possibility of persuadability is challenged; it would take an entire paper just to begin to analyze the tension between the elevation of persuasion on the one hand and the decline of an openness to persuasion on the other.

24. Tompkins, for example, states that since "what we choose is determined by our beliefs, which we have not chosen, the notion of free choice dissolves" (xxv). Or in the words of the American Council of Learned Societies (ACLS) manifesto, "All stances in scholarly research, as in the choice of values, imply a prior commitment to some basic belief system" (11). The course of academic arguments will be *determined* finally by the coincidence or clash of "basic belief systems" rather than by *choosing* between different ideas.

25. Gerald Graff, "Other Voices, Other Rooms: Organizing and Teaching the Conflict," *New Literary History* 21 (1990): 827. I think that Graff is motivated as much by the feeling that the important conflicts are always taking place *somewhere else* as by a desire to improve undergraduate education (graduate students are already well aware of ideological conflicts). A fuller critique of Graff, which I will not offer here, would emphasize: (1) His prescription of "teaching the conflict" requires a consensus that could only be achieved by cordoning off some of the most divisive issues at the root of these conflicts, specifically issues of power; even to agree about what precisely the "conflict" consists of is already to contain and delimit it. (2) In this article, Graff offers the example of the "real" encounter between an OMP (old male professor) and a YFP (young female professor). Teaching the conflict necessarily involves such role playing and reduction to types. But if

the conflict is primarily between generations and genders, should it really be the focus of our teaching, and is literary studies really the place to teach it?

26. Graff, "Other Voices," 837.

27. See again, for example, the ACLS document *Speaking for the Humanities*, 11.

28. He made this comment at a student-sponsored forum on political correctness at Dartmouth College on April 15, 1991.

Appendix A

Fracas at Frisbee U.

Hampshire College was supposed to be a haven for free-thinking, but two professors claim that, even there, some kinds of dissent are more equal than others.

by John Brodie

Nestled among the Berkshire Hills, Hampshire College was founded in 1970 to offer students an alternative to standard modes of academic inquiry. Variously known as "Frisbee U." or "Hamster," it was supposed to be the kind of place where ideas reigned supreme and academic freedom was a given. "Academic freedom in its teaching aspects is fundamental for the protection of the rights of the teacher," proclaims the current Hampshire Faculty Handbook.

Unfortunately, the right of academic freedom seems little more than rhetoric at Hampshire today, as two professors, both brought to the college in 1987 after exhaustive national searches, discovered when they challenged the status quo. Last January, Assistant Professor Jeffrey Wallen and Assistant Professor Norman Holland learned they had been denied reappointment. Since then, even their dean has threatened to resign in support, as facts have surfaced suggesting the professors were victims of an intellectual purge.

Though Hampshire president Gregory Prince says the fight "is in no way ideological," the two professors say they have spent much of the past year struggling against the forces of monolithic thinking at Hampshire. Wallen will make one last stab to win reappointment at a final review on October 8; Holland will attempt to do likewise

Village Voice, October 9, 1990

Reprinted by permission of the author and the *Village Voice* later in the term. In his case—he is Hispanic—the Massachusetts Commission Against Discrimination is monitoring the situation.

The unpleasantness would be easy to dismiss if the battle lines were traditional ideological ones, and the situation would be less fraught with irony if Hampshire were a traditional university. This, however, isn't an ordinary fight between the disciples of Allan Bloom and would-be tenured radicals. "Hampshire is not easy to interpret according to conventional ideological categories," says Wallen. "Norman and I are *not* being attacked by a 'radical left, Marxist-feminist' or whatever group of faculty. Our strongest supporter, Mary Russo, is someone whose work could be easily described with [those] adjectives. I prefer to think of this battle as the attempted revenge of the mediocre against the intelligent."

Or, as Russo, a professor of literature and critical theory, sums it up, "I fear that these are merely local and cronyistic disputes over power at our tiny institution." If the forces against them succeed, Hampshire will have become a gleaming oxymoron: a progressive institution that has enshrined institutional conservatism.

Holland's problems may have started even before he got to Hampshire. According to the complaint he's filed, he'd been hired only after what another faculty member called "a long, vexed search filled with rancor and unprofessionalism."

Jeffrey Wallen, on the other hand, may have talked himself into trouble. First he questioned the way a search for a professor had been conducted. Then, in the fall of 1988, a permanent position opened up in the film and photography department. Under Hampshire's affirmative action rules, any such openings *must* go to minority visiting professors, if they've been hired after a national search and meet the job description. By those rules the spot should automatically have gone to Carrie Mae Weems, an African-American photographer who was on a visiting contract with the school. However, two longtime faculty members asked for a search. At an all-school meeting Wallen spoke strongly in Weems's favor. The school eventually voted 20 to 3 for her, but Wallen's stance may have earned him the enmity of the older professors.

The Hampshire faculty is not broken into traditional departments but into four interdisciplinary schools: Communications and Cognitive Science; Natural Science; Social Science; and Humanities and

Arts. Both Wallen, a professor of comparative literature, and Holland, who taught Hispanic literature, fell into the last.

At Hampshire, sometimes competitive groups have formed across school lines. Sadly, perhaps the most polarized cliques are the teachers of Third World Studies and those of Cultural Studies. (Holland and Wallen belong to the latter.) They should have a lot in common: As Prince says, "Between Cultural Studies and Third World Studies there is nothing inevitably in conflict." Both disciplines challenge the traditional canon of literature. Cultural Studies deems both high and low forms of art equally worthy of study. Third World Studies concentrates on the works of exploited nations. Every Hampshire student is required to take a course that focuses on the Third World during his or her time at the college, thus fulfilling the college's "Third World Expectation."

At Hampshire, Third World Studies professors tend to approach texts in sociological terms, while Cultural Studies professors take a more literary approach. On the Third World view, a book like Gabriel García Márquez's *One Hundred Years of Solitude* is fundamentally about the forces of colonialism raping a small South American village. For Cultural Studies professors, it's also about magic realism as a narrative technique, and the influence of William Faulkner on Márquez. Which is what Norman Holland taught in his classes, and what some Third World Studies people labeled "confusing" and "Eurocentric."

Hampshire has no tenure. Full professors receive 10-year contracts, and at the end of 10 years they must undergo a review by their peers. Assistant professors new to the college work on three-year contracts. Halfway through their first hitch, they are reviewed and notified if there are serious problems with their performance (neither Wallen nor Holland received any midcontract warning). At the beginning of the third year, members of the candidate's school vote on whether to reappoint. In most cases, the school vote goes right to the college president, who passes the candidate on to the trustees for a rubber stamp.

Within their school Wallen and Holland received favorable votes (20 to seven and 23 to four, respectively) for reappointment, but instead of giving them a pro forma nod, Prince sent the candidates before the College Committee on Faculty Reappointments and Promotions. Prince says his decision was based upon the number of negative votes each had received, as well as the comments he'd read in their files. As a new president, he thought he could "benefit from CCFRAP's advice."

That body voted four to three and five to two against reappointment. Wallen says two CCFRAP members were allied with the Third World Studies position—he was asked during the meeting whether he had difficulty teaching Third World writers (he answered "No")—and he points out that on such a committee, two vocal members may sway their more uncommitted colleagues. Prince says CCFRAP's decision was based on "appropriate criteria," specifically "the promise of the professors' scholarship, community service, and teaching."

Lynne Hanley, a CCFRAP member, acknowledges the animosity between Cultural and Third World Studies: "Hampshire is a very political school, there are always different struggles among different groups here." But, she continues, "it's my deepest belief that the concerns about these people had to do with their teaching ability. There's no room here for someone who can only reach a few students and who is not caring"—meaning, in her view, Wallen.

Wallen is probably an easy target—a white male who grew up near Beverly Hills and whose academic pedigree is Stanford, Columbia, and Johns Hopkins. But the charges against Norman Holland are reminiscent of *Catch-22*. A bilingual Panamanian-American who graduated from Dartmouth and Johns Hopkins and taught literature at Columbia for a decade, Holland is basically being accused of "not being Hispanic enough" because he threw in his lot with Cultural Studies. Or, as one of his senior colleagues in the field of Latin-American studies, Carollee Bengelsdorf, put it in a letter to his reappointment file, Holland "had chosen effectively not to participate in virtually every aspect of the Third World Studies program."

Bengelsdorf seems to be taking a narrow view of Holland's achievements. He has been an active member of the Five College Latin-American Studies group and he has also advised local high schools about developing Latin-American literature programs. He has added a number of new courses about Latin America to the Hampshire curriculum, and he also brought two renowned scholars of Third World studies to speak at the school. Holland is also an officer at the Hampshire College Day Care Center.

Bengelsdorf denies any ideological motives and maintains, "All I'm concerned with is the quality of his teaching." She adds that students told her Holland's classes were "indecipherable" and "incoherent" and that she worked with at least two students interested in Latin-American literature who refused to work with Holland. A number of minority faculty members say Bengelsdorf's opinion of Holland is wrong—albeit a legitimate concern for her to raise—and they see her statement, that Holland's error was his "strong and heavy commitment . . . to Cultural Studies" as racist and reductive, for it implies that there is a right and wrong way to be a Hispanic and a professor.

Holland claims that some Third World Studies professors believe that to be a minority and not teach in strictly Marxist terms is to be a traitor. Although not a minority herself, Bengelsdorf had taught closely with Roberto Marquez, Holland's predecessor, whose views were closer to her own. Holland's colleagues insist that since he did not teach like Marquez, Bengelsdorf and her allies found him "Eurocentric." It seems that Norman Holland wasn't hired just to teach literature to Hampshire's predominantly white students, but to teach them what a Hispanic was, and in the latter area some people found him lacking. But, says Carrie Mae Weems, "minority faculty members are not the Third World Expectation nor are they token symbols."

Holland says the most galling episode came late last January, when Prince called him into his office to discuss Holland's future. Holland says Prince began by confiding that he too had once been in a bilingual situation and was sympathetic. Then Prince asked Holland to explain his understanding of the modifiers *rapidly* and *only* in two sentences he'd written: "Cuba was rapidly becoming a bourgeois state . . . " and "Only Argentina and Cuba have a continuous literary history." Before the meeting Prince had called an Amherst faculty member, Doris Sommer, a professor of Spanish and Women's and Gender Studies and quizzed her about the meaning of those words. According to Sommer, Prince's questions seemed to be both substantive and about Holland's command of English. This incident, says Holland, caused him "humiliation and professional embarrassment."

Holland, stunned, didn't respond to Prince's baiting, but he now feels this patronizing incident is grounds for a harassment suit. (Prince refused to comment on the specifics of the meeting and would say only that "I don't try to be patronizing, but I cannot deny his feelings.") Wallen lacks such recourse and, if his hearing goes against him next week, he'll soon be just another humanities prof looking for a job. The real losers, though, will be Hampshire's students, for they shall be taught the lesson that some forms of dissent are more equal than others. A nagging question lingers then for those in the Pioneer Valley: If Hampshire College's mission is, in the words of its fourth president, "educating for social justice," why does an intellectual climate akin to apartheid exist wherein minority professors, and those who teach about minorities, dwell in rigidly defined academic homelands and are forbidden to challenge boundaries erected by their colleagues?

Appendix B

Review & Outlook:

PC at Hampshire College

If we had to make year-end awards for Political Correctness, Hampshire College in Amherst, Mass., would surely rank among the finalists. This is no small distinction given the number of eminent colleges and universities now devoted to the political re-education of their students. Hampshire College merits particular notice because of the extraordinary efforts being made there by the administration and some faculty to block the reappointment of two professors whose teachings deviate from the new politicized agenda.

Assistant professor of Hispanic literature Norman Holland, a Panamanian-American, is accused of being "Eurocentric" for having dared include European literature in his courses. "They want Third World people to be frozen in time," Professor Holland says of the colleagues who blame him for not being Hispanic *enough*. "They want me to be either Cesar Chavez or Juan Valdez."

Jeffrey Wallen, assistant professor of comparative literature, was charged with failure to mount a "Third World challenge" to "the canon"—the Politically Correct, derogatory term now used to describe the classic works of Western culture. Professor Wallen was originally attracted to Hampshire College as an experimental institution where, so he had heard, progressive educational values prevailed and academic and intellectual freedom were considered

Wall Street Journal, January 4, 1991
Reprinted with permission of the *Wall Street Journal* © 1991
Dow Jones & Company, Inc. All rights reserved.

sacred. The faculty handbook said so, after all. Today he sees Hampshire as a place where resistance to the political winds—in his case a refusal to teach European literature as a catalog of colonialism and oppression—comes at a high price.

The written comments of those colleagues objecting to his appointment sum matters up nicely. (At Hampshire the decision to reappoint is made largely via ballots from a committee representing the candidate's particular school.) One colleague who charged Professor Wallen with having voiced "disrespectful" attitudes and opinions somehow managed to see in this a sign that the professor lacked "independence of mind." Another ballot similarly rich in doublespeak said that the candidate was given to "polarizing issues in our school meetings," which, this voter concluded, suggested "no independent thinking about the issues." Moreover, the objection continued, Professor Wallen had "a conventional attitude of privelege." Neither correct spelling nor logic, apparently, is among the skills required of faculty members in our new Politically Correct age.

The most startling aspect of this reappointment flap, however, is the way in which Hampshire College's new president, Gregory S. Prince, inserted himself into the dispute. Despite the handful of ballots objecting to them, both professors were recommended for reappointment by large majorities of the voting committees—Professor Holland by a vote of 23 to 4 and Professor Wallen by a vote of 20 to 7. Under such circumstances the normal procedure at Hampshire has been for the president to approve reappointment as a matter of course, but Mr. Prince took the remarkable position that the critical comments of the nay voters were of such significance that he felt impelled to seek higher advice.

The president referred the cases to a college committee on faculty appointments, which, Professor Wallen notes, included some of his most vocal political antagonists, advocates of the Third World Studies agenda. When this small committee voted against both reappointments, Professor Wallen took his appeal to the college panel on academic freedom. He was not alone by now in holding that his academic freedom and that of Norman Holland had been infringed on. The college's academic-freedom panel unanimously agreed and offered Professor Wallen a new contract.

Even this did not end matters. A month later the president of Hampshire College decided to appeal the academic-freedom panel's decision and referred the case to yet another academic body. The administration of the college is now apparently willing to leave no stone unturned in the effort to assert its political values and purge those who don't conform. Professor Norman Holland's case is an instructive example of how dissident minority scholars are treated on the academic liberal plantation.

To their credit, large numbers of Hampshire College students have protested the treatment of these two faculty members, as has the student newspaper. They seem to believe that what happened to Professors Holland and Wallen tarnishes Hampshire's claim to be an institution where the principles of academic freedom are revered. In this they are correct—not Politically Correct perhaps, but correct nonetheless.

Contributors

Richard Burt is an associate professor of English at the University of Massachusetts, Amherst. He is the author of *Licensed by Authority: Ben Jonson and the Discourses of Censorship* (1993) and coeditor of *Enclosure Acts: Sexuality, Property, and Culture in Early Modern England* (1994). His articles on Shakespeare, Renaissance drama, and visuality and censorship have appeared in *Criticism, ELH, Theatre Journal,* and several anthologies. He is at work on a book entitled *Getting off the Subject: Iconoclasm, Sexuality, and Celebrity.*

Stuart Culver is an assistant professor of English at the University of Utah. He is the author of several articles on *The Wizard of Oz* and on Henry James's career.

Donald K. Hedrick directs the Program in Cultural Studies and is professor of English at Kansas State University. He has been a fellow at the Society for the Humanities at Cornell, O'Connor Professor of Literature at Colgate University, and a visiting professor at Amherst College. He has published in the areas of Shakespeare, architectural theory, modern poetry, and language and cultural theory in *New Literary History, ELH, Word & Image, Shakespeare Quarterly,* and elsewhere. He is currently engaged in a project of antimethodological Shakespeare studies.

Christian Jouhaud is a research worker at Centre National de la Recherche Scientifique, Centre de Recherches Historiques, Ecole des Hautes Etudes en Sciences Sociales in Paris. He is the author of

Mazarinades: la Fronde des Mots (1985) and *La main de Richelieu ou le pouvoir cardinal* (1991). He is a coauthor of *The Culture of Print*, edited by Roger Chartier (1989), *Histoire de la France* volume 3 edited by André Burguière and Jacques Revel (1990), and *Atlas des littératures* (1990). He is the author of numerous articles, many of them appearing in *Annales (ESC), Nouvelle Revue de Psychanalyse, Yale French Studies, Quaderni Storici*, and *XVIIe Siècle*.

Michael G. Levine is an associate professor of comparative literature at Yale University.

Aamir Rashid Mufti is a Pakistani doctoral candidate in the department of English and comparative literature at Columbia University.

Timothy Murray is professor of English at Cornell University. He is the author of *Like a Film: Ideological Fantasy on Screen, Camera, and Canvas* (1993), *Theatrical Legitimation: Allegories of Genius in XVIIth-Century England and France* (1987), and a former editor of *Theatre Journal*. His contribution will be included in his forthcoming book, *Performance Reading: Theatre in a Multi-Cultural Age*.

David Norbrook is a fellow and tutor in English at Magdalen College, Oxford, and lecturer in English in the University of Oxford. His publications include *Poetry and Politics in the English Renaissance* (1984), *The Penguin Book of Renaissance Verse* (with H. R. Woudhuysen, 1992), and articles on seventeenth-century poetry and drama. He is currently working on a study of republicanism and literary culture in the mid-seventeenth century.

Dennis Porter is Germaine Brée Professor of French Studies at the University of Massachusetts, Amherst. He is the author of *The Pursuit of Crime: Art and Ideology in Detective Fiction* (1981) and *Haunted Journeys: Desire and Transgression in European Travel Writing* (1991) and has published a translation of Jacques Lacan's *Ethics of Psychoanalysis* (1992). His forthcoming book is entitled *Rousseau's Legacy: Emergence and Eclipse of the Writer in France*.

Jiřina Šmejkalová-Strickland is a lecturer in the sociology department of the School of Social Sciences at Charles University in Prague, where she teaches cultural theory and gender studies, and a member of the advisory board of the Prague Gender Studies Centre. In addition to her work on literary institutions, she has written and

Index

Compiled by Robin Jackson

spoken extensively on the cultural obstacles to feminism and gender thinking in Eastern Europe and is currently at work on a history of women's participation in cultural politics in fin-de-siècle Prague.

Brook Thomas directs the Humanities Core Course at the University of California, Irvine. He has taught at the University of Hawaii, Manoa, the University of Massachusetts, Amherst, the University of Constance, and the Free University of Berlin. His books include *"Ulysses": A Book of Many Happy Returns, Cross-Examinations of Law and Literature: Cooper, Hawthorne, Stowe, and Melville,* and *The New Historicism and other Old-Fashioned Topics.*

Jeffrey Wallen is an assistant professor of comparative literature at Hampshire College in Amherst, Massachusetts. He has published essays on French and British nineteenth-century writers such as Flaubert, Villiers de L'Isle-Adam, Pater, and Wilde, and he is currently at work on a study of literary portraiture in nineteenth-century British writing. He has also written and lectured on academic freedom, political correctness, the popularization of literary criticism, and the relations between the academy and the public. He is working on a book about the breakdown of "dialogue" as a useful model (despite the claims of so many that "dialogue" is in fact what they seek) for describing our contemporary forms of criticism.

Rob Wilson is professor of English at the University of Hawaii in Honolulu. A member of the *boundary 2* and *Bamboo Ridge* collectives and a frequent contributor to *East-West Film Journal,* he is the author of two books: *Waking in Seoul,* a collection of poetry and prose anecdotes about the American presence in South Korea (1988) and *American Sublime: The Genealogy of a Poetic Genre,* a study of the American poetics of national power (1991).